Counting Working-Age
People with Disabilities

Counting Working-Age People with Disabilities

What Current Data Tell Us and Options for Improvement

Andrew J. Houtenville
David C. Stapleton
Robert R. Weathers II
Richard V. Burkhauser
Editors

2009

W.E. Upjohn Institute for Employment Research
Kalamazoo, Michigan

Library of Congress Cataloging-in-Publication Data

Counting working-age people with disabilities : what current data tell us and options for improvement / Andrew J. Houtenville . . . [et al.], editors.
    p. cm.
Includes bibliographical references and index.
ISBN-13: 978-0-88099-346-3 (pbk : alk. paper)
ISBN-10: 0-88099-346-4 (pbk : alk. paper)
ISBN-13: 978-0-88099-347-0 (hardcover : alk. paper)
ISBN-10: 0-88099-347-2 (hardcover : alk. paper)
    1. People with disabilities—Employment—United States—Statistics. 2. People with disabilities—United States—Social conditions—Statistics. I. Houtenville, Andrew J.

HD7256.U5C68 2009
331.5'90973—dc22

                    2008052064

© 2009
W.E. Upjohn Institute for Employment Research
300 S. Westnedge Avenue
Kalamazoo, Michigan 49007-4686

The facts presented in this study and the observations and viewpoints expressed are the sole responsibility of the authors. They do not necessarily represent positions of the W.E. Upjohn Institute for Employment Research.

Cover design by Alcorn Publication Design.
Index prepared by Nancy Humphreys.
Printed in the United States of America.
Printed on recycled paper.

Contents

Preface   vii

1   **Purpose, Overview, and Key Conclusions**   1
David C. Stapleton, Andrew J. Houtenville, Robert R. Weathers II,
and Richard V. Burkhauser

2   **The Disability Data Landscape**   27
Robert R. Weathers II

3   **Disability Prevalence and Demographics**   69
Andrew J. Houtenville, Elizabeth Potamites, William A. Erickson,
and S. Antonio Ruiz-Quintanilla

4   **Employment**   101
Robert R. Weathers II and David C. Wittenburg

5   **Household Income**   145
Richard V. Burkhauser, Ludmila Rovba, and
Robert R. Weathers II

6   **Poverty**   193
Richard V. Burkhauser, Andrew J. Houtenville, and
Ludmila Rovba

7   **Health and Functional Status**   227
Gerry E. Hendershot, Benjamin H. Harris, and
David C. Stapleton

8   **Survey Data Collection Methods**   265
Janice Ballou and Jason Markesich

9   **Program Participants**   299
David C. Stapleton, David C. Wittenburg, and Craig Thornton

10   **The Group Quarters Population**   353
Peiyun She and David C. Stapleton

11 Options for Improving Disability Data Collection   381
    David C. Stapleton, Gina A. Livermore, and Peiyun She

The Authors   419

Index   421

About the Institute   447

Preface

For decades, disability policymakers, administrators, researchers, advocates, and people with disabilities themselves have been frustrated with the lack of quality, comprehensible data and statistics about people with disabilities. This frustration has been heightened by the increased aspirations of people with significant impairments to utilize medical, technological, and economic advances that allow them to live fulfilling lives, and by the corresponding increase in the need for policy and programmatic reforms to support those aspirations. The Department of Education's National Institute for Disability and Rehabilitation Research (NIDRR) addressed this information void when it announced in 2003 its priority for a Rehabilitation, Research, and Training Center (RRTC) on disability demographic and statistics: "Lack of standard definitions, terminology, coding, classification, and measurement of disability and functioning often limits generalization of research findings. Extending use of research findings or population trends to inform policy or clinical interventions is limited due to the difficulty of extrapolating knowledge about disabilities that is gathered from a disparate range of data sources, classification and coding systems, and measures of disability."[1]

NIDRR awarded the RRTC grant (no. H133B031111) to Cornell University and its collaborators, Mathematica Policy Research, Inc., the Urban Institute, the American Association of People with Disabilities (AAPD), the Center for an Accessible Society, and InfoUse under the leadership of Andrew Houtenville, David Stapleton, Richard Burkhauser, and Susanne Bruyere. The new center was dubbed StatsRRTC.

In October 2006, StatsRRTC sponsored a two-day conference in Washington, DC, to present findings from its research and hear from others engaged in related research. (Material from the conference can be found at http://www.ilr.cornell.edu/edi/p-srrtc-2006conference.cfm.) The strong interest in disability statistics—what many might think is a dry topic—was evidenced by the enthusiasm of the approximately 200 attendees, about twice the number expected.

Buoyed by the response to the conference, we decided to produce this book. The book draws on conference material but develops and updates that material in important respects. As demonstrated at the conference and in many of the book's chapters, current data—despite its limitations—contain extensive, valuable information about people with disabilities. And it is heartening that significant steps are being undertaken to improve the data. The American Community Survey (ACS) has allowed us to produce annual statistics at the state level on the status of people with disabilities living in the household population since 2004. The ACS added the group quarters population in 2006.

In 2008, the ACS and the Current Population Survey (CPS) adopted a common set of disability questions, which soon will be introduced in the National Health Interview Survey and perhaps other federal surveys. The demonstrable success of earlier efforts to use administrative data for research purposes has led to increased investment in building longitudinal research files and in matching administrative records across agencies and with survey records. Although much more could still be done, these developments and others are quickly leading to better statistics on people with disabilities.

Many people were involved with the development of this book. Foremost among them is NIDRR's project officer for StatsRRTC, David Keer, who tirelessly supported our efforts to conduct the research, organize the conference, and go beyond the assembly of a conference volume to the development of a more cohesive and comprehensive book. We also extend our appreciation to StatsRRTC's external panel of experts for their support and advice over the years: Barbara Altman, David B. Gray, Richard Horne, Allan Hunt, Gwyn Jones, Thilo Kroll, Corinne Kirchner, Douglas Kruse, Anne O'Hara, Beverlee Stafford, and Sharon Stern.

We are greatly indebted to the authors of the individual chapters for their intellectual contributions, ability to meet deadlines, and patience while we transformed conference papers into a more coherent book: William Erickson and Antonio Ruiz-Quintanilla from Cornell University; Janice Ballou, Gina Livermore, Jason Markesich, Elizabeth Potamites, Craig Thornton, and David Wittenburg from Mathematica Policy Research; independent consultants Gerry Hendershot and Peiyun She; Benjamin Harris from the Brookings Institution; and Ludmila Rovba of Analysis Group, Inc. Houtenville, Livermore, She, Harris, Rovba, and Stapleton completed much of the work on their chapters while employed by Cornell.

We also would like to thank the conference attendees, with special thanks to those who participated on the conference panels. Many of the panelists became chapter authors and have already been mentioned above, and much of the information from their presentations has found its way into the book. Gail Whiteneck provided insightful comments about a difficult topic, measurement of the environment, among other things. Stephen Bell and Pamela Loprest offered equally useful comments on measures of the economic status of people with disabilities. Sue Stoddard led perhaps the most anticipated session at the conference on new developments in the identification of people with disabilities in federal surveys. During that session Sharon Stern discussed how the Census Bureau was planning to improve the ACS questions; Terence McMenamin did the same with respect to the Bureau of Labor Statistics and its plans to improve the CPS disability questions; Barbara Altman presented the disability questions the Washington City Group developed for the World

Health Organization; and Louis Verbrugge provided both historical and international perspectives on the progress made in survey measurement of disability over the last two decades. Anne Ciemnecki, Dawn Hall Apgar, and Alice Gardenhire Crooks presented on methodological issues in the collection of data from people with disabilities, and Paul Beatty provided his perspective on the importance of survey methods research in a domain where much of the information sought is both subjective and sensitive to the environment. Henry Ireys, David Dean, and Paul O'Leary each illustrated the research value of administrative data with examples from, respectively, Medicaid data linked to Social Security Disability Insurance (SSDI) and Supplemental Security Income (SSI) program data, longitudinal data on vocational rehabilitation agency clients that were enhanced through matches to data from other state programs, and SSDI and SSI administrative data and a new nationally representative survey of beneficiaries of these two programs. Finally, Brenda Spillman provided extensive information on measuring the size and characteristics of the older residential care population. In addition, our keynote speakers, Steven Tingus, former director of NIDRR, Christine Griffin, commissioner of the Equal Employment Opportunity Commission, and Andrew Imparato, president and CEO of AAPD, provided unique insights into the need for high-quality disability statistics. The conference would not have been possible without the tireless logistical support of Anne Sieverding of Cornell University.

As part of the summation at the conclusion of the conference, we presented a top-10 list of options for improvement in disability data collection and opened the floor for comment. The response was quite lively and helpful to the chapter authors. Additional comments were sent to us after the conference. Many of these comments are reflected in the book, especially in Chapter 11.

We also owe a debt to copyeditors Laura Bernstein and Robert Wathen, who masterfully improved the clarity and uniformity of the book's chapters. Finally, we thank Kevin Hollenbeck and Richard Wyrwa of the W.E. Upjohn Institute for Employment Research for agreeing to publish the book and for shepherding the manuscript through the publication process.

Ultimately, we take responsibility for the views expressed in the introduction of this volume, and the authors take responsibility for their individual chapters. The book's contents do not necessarily represent the policy of the Department of Education or the Social Security Administration, and one should not assume endorsement by the Federal Government (Edgar, 75.620 (b)).

Note

1. Federal Register. 2003. 68(90): 25004.

1
Purpose, Overview, and Key Conclusions

David C. Stapleton
Mathematica Policy Research, Inc.

Andrew J. Houtenville
New Editions Consulting, Inc.

Robert R. Weathers II
Social Security Administration

Richard V. Burkhauser
Cornell University

"When you cannot measure, your knowledge is meager and unsatisfactory."
—Lord Kelvin[1]

"If you are not counted, you don't count."
—Cyndi Jones, Center for an Accessible Society

Efforts to provide statistics on the number and status of working-age people with disabilities have a history of being fragmented and sporadic. As a group, they are often overlooked in mainstream discussions of the latest statistics on employment, income, poverty, and other measures of the status of the population. In contrast, government agencies routinely compile and report such statistics for groups defined by sex, age, race, ethnicity, and marital status. Indeed, one of the most frequently cited statistical reports on the socioeconomic status of the U.S. population—the U.S. Census Bureau's *Annual Report on Income,*

Poverty, and Health Insurance Coverage in the United States—does not mention this group.

The overarching objective of this book is to support and facilitate efforts to improve statistics and data on working-age people with disabilities. Many of the limitations with statistics and data on this population are well-known. There have been significant efforts to address the limitations, and some progress has been made. That progress, however, has often been at the whim of external forces, such as the extent of support for improvements to federal data collection, advances in information technologies, concerns about privacy protection, and government expenditure priorities, rather than for the purpose of systematically capturing the size and socioeconomic characteristics of this population. As a result, statistics and data for working-age people with disabilities are not on par with those for other "at-risk" working-age populations— groups that are more likely than others to experience adverse socioeconomic outcomes, such as some racial and ethnic minorities, children, unmarried parents, and the elderly. This book provides a systematic review of what current statistics and data on working-age people with disabilities can and cannot tell us, and how they can be improved to better inform policymakers, advocates, administrators, analysts, service providers, and others.

This book will inform two broad audiences. The first consists of those interested in what current data can tell us about the prevalence of disabilities among working-age people and their socioeconomic status, but who are dissatisfied with the limited, and often confusing, statistics cited in the mainstream press. For this audience, the book also offers the best available statistics on levels and trends in their employment, income, poverty, and health and functional status.

The second audience is a more specialized group of professionals (academics, advocates, government policymakers, service providers, etc.) who require reliable information to support evidence-based public policy and administrative decisions. For them, we go beyond "facts" to 1) examine how robust these facts are across data sets, 2) consider the strengths and limitations of current data as a whole, 3) describe current efforts to improve the data, and 4) offer options to advance this process.

In the next two sections of this chapter, we discuss the importance of having reliable data on working-age people with disabilities and the substantial limitations with the currently available data. We then summarize the major components of federal efforts to collect data for this population, both through surveys and administrative data systems. Each of these substantially independent efforts costs millions annually. Although they have not been well-coordinated, they still constitute an informal and substantial "national disability data system" (NDDS). A major conclusion of this book is that better coordination of these independent components could result in an NDDS that would be significantly greater than the current sum of its independent parts. We argue that this can be achieved by the use of a subset of common disability questions on existing survey data sets; expansion and improvements to the matching of agency administrative records to survey data sets, as well as matching of administrative records across agencies; and provision of easier access of the matched data to the broader research community, without compromising individual privacy. We further argue that efforts to improve the quality and usefulness of existing data collection are a more cost-effective method of advancing our knowledge about the working-age population with disabilities than adding yet another new and expensive survey.

We conclude the chapter with a summary of the content of the remaining chapters. These chapters provide the best current statistics on the size and socioeconomic characteristics of the working-age household population with disabilities, discuss the strengths and limitations of the current statistics, and offer alternatives to improving these statistics through greater coordination.

THE VALUE OF RELIABLE STATISTICS AND DATA FOR THE WORKING-AGE POPULATION WITH DISABILITIES

Government statistics and data on population characteristics are used by public policymakers, advocates, the private sector, and individuals for a wide variety of reasons. The primary rationale for government efforts to collect data and publish statistics is that they are the foundation of evidence-based public policy, providing critical information to support the management and improvement of public programs, as well as the formulation, analysis, and evaluation of new programs and policies.

Numerous federal agencies serve the needs of working-age people with disabilities, and they all need information about their program participants, as well as those potentially eligible for their services, to effectively administer and improve their programs. The Social Security Administration (SSA), the Department of Health and Human Services (HHS), the Department of Education (ED), and the Department of Veterans Affairs (DVA) are the most prominent in terms of the number of working-age people with disabilities served and program expenditures. These agencies, as well as the congressional committees that oversee them, need to know the size, geographic distribution, demographic characteristics, and status of the populations their programs are designed serve. They need to know if their "target populations" are obtaining the benefits and services for which they are eligible and the extent to which their needs with respect to health care, family economic status, and participation in major life activities are being met.

Although the primary purpose of data collection and production of statistics is often to meet agency needs, there is an extremely important "public good" aspect of data and statistics. Once created, statistics can be used by others at little or no additional cost. Hence, similar to other such investments in basic science, at their optimal level of investment, their marginal value to society as a whole is greater than the marginal value to those who produce them. Without government support of the initial collection of these data, too little investment in the data collection necessary for both basic and program research would be made. Further, from a social perspective, optimal investment in data collection and the production of statistics on this population ought to exceed the level that can be justified by the narrow interests of the agencies themselves.

Beyond this, the additional value of data and statistics comes from the identification of significant social problems, the formulation and analysis of new policies to address them, and ultimately, the evaluation of the extent to which major policy changes adequately address the identified problems. Such analyses are conducted by researchers and analysts at government agencies, think tanks, universities, and advocacy organizations.

The first step in solving a social problem is to identify its nature. For example, a leading problem for people with disabilities is the increased risk of economic insecurity—loss of household income, increased risk of poverty, reduced employment, and increased need for medical services. The second step is to determine the dimensions of the problem both in terms of the number of people affected (e.g., the incidence and prevalence of disability among working-age people) and the size of the increased risk on each individual (e.g., the average magnitude and distribution of increased economic risks related both to the onset and duration of a disability). To achieve these two steps, it is critical to have reliable data both on the general population and the target population. From a cross-sectional data perspective, how different are the risks of economic insecurity of those with and without disabilities at a moment of time? From a longitudinal data perspective, how much do these risks change at the onset of a disability, and thereafter, as the individual ages and other events occur?

Such investments in data are even more important in considering public policy responses once a social problem is well-defined. Data are necessary to answer the following questions with respect to any proposed policy. Who will the policy benefit and by how much? Who will the policy harm and by how much? What behavior will the policy change and by how much? For example, an increase in Social Security Disability Insurance (SSDI) benefits or a relaxation of its eligibility rules is likely to reduce the loss in income associated with the onset of a disability. It is also likely, however, to cause an increase in the costs of the program. Further, it could discourage some workers who experience the onset of a disability from returning to work, even further increasing the costs of the program and reducing their employment. Each of these questions can be partially answered using currently available data and statistics, but improvements in disability data and statistics could substantially improve our ability to reliably answer such questions.

Although it is important to have data that support projections of the potential consequences of policy changes, it is more important to have data that support assessments of whether changes have or do not have specific outcomes. Even if the implemented policy is functioning well, program administrators need information about changes in the size and characteristics of a target population, including changes in population outcomes, to develop program management plans and budgets.

It is primarily for these reasons that the government routinely produces statistics for population groups such as racial and ethnic minorities, children, unmarried parents, and the elderly. For each of these at-risk groups, there is a clear population concept, a broadly accepted means for identification of members of the population, and well-established outcomes of policy interest. These groups are at risk of adverse socioeconomic outcomes, and it is critical to keep track of their outcomes in substantial detail. Researchers, program administrators, and policymakers collect data on these populations to improve and manage the programs and policies that are designed to reduce risk and provide support to those who experience adverse outcomes.

THE LIMITATIONS TO CURRENTLY AVAILABLE DISABILITY DATA AND STATISTICS

In contrast to the copious statistics produced for the at-risk populations discussed above, the government produces very few statistics on the working-age population with disabilities.[2] This is astonishing, given the size of the working-age population with disabilities and the magnitude of public resources devoted to its support. Based on the 2006 American Community Survey (ACS), almost 13 out of 100 persons aged 25–61[3] in the noninstitutional population have a disability of some sort—an estimated 22.4 million people (Rehabilitation Research and Training Center on Disability Demographics and Statistics 2007). The limited production of disability data may stem from the lack of an agreed-upon operational definition, or set of operational definitions, of disability, as well as the limited amount of longitudinal and state-level data on the population, among other reasons. More than 2 million working-age people with disabilities are not included in this figure because they live in institutions; these individuals constitute more than half of the working-age institutional population.[4]

Operational Disability Definitions

People with disabilities clearly constitute a large, at-risk population, and one that is of considerable interest to policymakers and the general public. Why, then, does the government not publish statistics on this population in many of its major statistical publications? The most immediate reason is that no statistical agency has developed an "official" operational definition of working-age people with disabilities, and considerable controversy still exists in the research community over the appropriate questions to ask to determine this. The absence of an official operational definition for this population is in sharp contrast to the existence of such definitions for other at-risk groups—even groups whose definitions are controversial, such as racial and ethnic minorities.

As a result, the statistics used by researchers to capture this population and its socioeconomic outcomes have been subject to considerable controversy. For example, doubts were initially raised about the accuracy of reports of a long-term decline in the employment rate of people with disabilities (Hale 2001; National Council on Disability 2002). The reports ran counter to expectations about improvements in employment opportunities after the passage of the Americans with Disabilities Act (ADA); indeed, articles published in top economics journals attributed the employment decline to the passage and implementation of the ADA (Acemoglu and Angrist 2001; DeLeire 2000). The reports also seemed to contradict the experiences of well-educated people with disabilities, whose professional opportunities were expanding because of the growing importance of information technology in the workplace.

These statistics were questioned largely on the grounds of how "disability" was identified in surveys. Questions currently used vary across surveys, and they are conceptually unclear and inconsistent. Many people with significant physical or mental impairments might fail to respond positively to some questions, but the same questions might elicit positive responses from people with minor or short-term impairments. Further, answers to some questions, such as those about "work limitations," might be sensitive to the economic environment. How can we be sure, then, that the trends observed in the statistics are not an artifact of how we identify people with disabilities?

These issues and others made it relatively easy to be skeptical of the evidence on the decline in employment. Yet trends in the employment rate from multiple surveys, using multiple definitions of disability and looking across comparable points in the business cycle, were all in the same direction, and they were also consistent with the growth in the percentage of the working-age population that receives federal disability benefits, even after adjusting for changes in the age distribution of the working-age population (Burkhauser et al. 2001; Stapleton and Burkhauser 2003). With time, the existence of a decline in the employment rate among people with disabilities became more widely accepted, but the limitations of federal disability data clearly slowed the process of recognition.

Longitudinal Data

Because the experiences of people with disabilities, and disability itself, are dynamic, longitudinal data on people with disabilities is very valuable but also very limited. This data limitation is an important reason why it has been difficult to determine the causes of the decline in the employment rate. For instance, evidence that the ADA was the cause of the decline relied heavily on trends in cross-sectional (i.e., one period) data from the Current Population Survey (CPS). Acemoglu and Angrist (2001) looked at the number of weeks worked by people who self-reported a work limitation relative to those who did not and observed that this ratio started to fall at the national level as the ADA was implemented. But the CPS measure of the disability population from a single interview does not differentiate between short- and long-term limitations. More recent analysis, using a subset of households interviewed twice for the CPS (12 months apart), compared the weeks worked of those who report a work limitation in both surveys relative to those who do not, and it showed that the employment decline for people with longer term work limitations started well before the passage of the ADA (Houtenville and Burkhauser 2004). These findings do not invalidate the use of existing data to evaluate public policy outcomes, but they do suggest that researchers must be more sensitive to data limitations when making causal inferences. Better use of limited existing longitudinal data would have shown the sensitivity of the research findings to alternative ways of capturing working-age people with disabilities. Longer term longitudinal data would also have been very useful.

Limited State-Level Data and Statistics

In the past, very few disability statistics have been produced at the state level. Yet state-level statistics are critical because the population of working-age people with disabilities is not distributed across states in proportion to the entire working-age population and because important environmental factors vary considerably from state to state as well as influence the status of people with disabilities. These factors include the economic and policy environments, as well as the physical and cultural environments.

The importance of state policy deserves emphasis. All of the major public disability programs are federally financed, in whole or in large part, so there is a strong tendency to think of disability policy as a national, rather than state, issue. In fact, however, state and local governments play important roles in the implementation of these programs. State-administered vocational rehabilitation programs help people with disabilities enter and stay in the workforce. States also run Disability Determination Services that make the initial decision of whether applicants for SSDI or Supplemental Security Income (SSI) are eligible. A number of states also provide state supplements to federal benefits. State welfare agencies have a strong financial interest in helping low-income parents with disabilities transfer from Temporary Assistance to Needy Families to federal disability benefits. State governments also control Medicaid programs within limits set by the federal government, including eligibility determination, fee schedules, coverage for optional services, and eligibility for optional populations of workers with disabilities (under the Medicaid Buy-in). Many other services are delivered by, or under the supervision of, state agencies, even when the federal government provides support. Further, one of the most important disability programs for working-age people, workers compensation, is state run and receives no federal support or oversight.

State leaders and the electorate need to be informed about how working-age people with disabilities in their state are faring, both absolutely and relative to comparable people in neighboring states and the rest of the country. National data cannot identify the specific needs of a state's population with disabilities, how federal funding to meet those needs is commensurate with that of other states, or the extent to which efforts to address the needs of the working-age population with disabilities within a state are successful.

Decennial Census data have long been the primary source for state-level disability statistics, and until 2000, even the long form of the Census had just three disability questions. Since then, the implementation of the ACS has supported the production of annual disability statistics at the state level, although the continuous improvements made to the survey in its first six years have limited cross-year comparability.

The consequences of inadequate state data can also be illustrated by the difficulties encountered in understanding the decline in employment of people with disabilities. The possible causes of the decline likely varied across states. As a specific example, any negative effect of the ADA would be greatest in states that did not have their own disability rights laws before the ADA, and least in the states with the strongest such laws—including reasonable accommodation provisions for employers as well as anti-discrimination provisions. In the 1990s, however, it was not possible to reliably track employment of people with disabilities at the state level except in a few very large states (with large samples in national surveys) or over very long periods (e.g., by examination of moving averages that dampen the effects of annual sampling errors), so differences in trends across states were not readily apparent. In light of a later study (Jolls and Prescott 2005), it seems likely that reliable state statistics would have also challenged Acemoglu and Angrist's (2001) finding that the ADA was the principal cause of the decline in the relative employment of working-age people with disabilities in the early 1990s. Jolls and Prescott demonstrated that the ADA had short-term negative impacts on employment in states that had no disability rights laws before the ADA or had laws with anti-discrimination provisions only, and that longer term declines in employment for people with disabilities were unrelated to pre-ADA laws. This research took longer to complete than the research of Acemoglu and Angrist (2001), which relied on national data, because the researchers had to painstakingly collect data on state disability rights legislation and use it to group states into meaningful categories. Only then could they produce employment statistics for the groups.

Over the last two decades, considerable effort has been invested in improving policies for working-age people with disabilities. Many of these have been instigated by federal legislation, especially the ADA, the Rehabilitation Act, the Individuals with Disabilities Education Act, the Workforce Investment Act, and the Ticket to Work and Work Incentives Improvement Act. The impact of these efforts is very dependent on the actions of state and local governments, as well as other aspects of the state and local environments. These initiatives make it all the more important to produce statistics at the state level.

Other Limitations

The above discussion illustrates just three of the current limitations of disability data for working-age people with disabilities. The growing interest in disability policy and research has exposed many other limitations of disability data as well. As discussed extensively in later chapters, these include the following:

- Some data collection methodologies lead to the exclusion of people with disabilities from surveys, either intentionally (e.g., because they do not live in the household population) or unintentionally (e.g., because interviewers are not adequately trained to interview them). Some federal surveys fail to identify respondents with disabilities in any fashion. People with intellectual or psychiatric disorders are perhaps the most likely to be overlooked.

- Sample sizes in many national surveys are too small to produce statistics for subgroups of people with disabilities. Limitations on state-level statistics are just one example. The availability of statistics on people with specific impairments or conditions is also limited. Yet one of the tenets of disability policy is that people with disabilities are an extremely heterogeneous group. Without information on the heterogeneity of people with disabilities, it is difficult to identify people who are least well served by current policies, those who would benefit the most by a new policy, and those who might be harmed by the same new policy.

- Information on certain topics that are very salient to disability is collected very infrequently or is nonexistent. Examples include the accessibility of the environment, employer accommodations, use of employment and personal services, time use, allocation of expenditures, community participation, living arrangements, and the characteristics of disability onset and progression.

- Program data collected from survey respondents is highly unreliable. Many respondents either fail to report they participate in a program or confuse the program they participate in with a similar program. Information about the services and benefits they receive is also very limited and of low reliability.

- Administrative data for public programs that serve people with disabilities contain a wealth of longitudinal information about the many people with disabilities who participate in such programs, but the quality of the data is limited by its administrative uses. Substantial effort is required to build and document useful research files, and the privacy of the data must be carefully protected. These obstacles can often be overcome, but it is costly and can delay analysis by years.

- There are currently no national or state efforts to collect information on the physical and social barriers that restrict the participation of people with disabilities in work and other major activities.

THE NATIONAL DISABILITY DATA SYSTEM (NDDS)

Given the number of working-age people with disabilities and the magnitude of federal and state assistance provided, investments in the collection of data and production of statistics on this population should be a national priority. Extensive data are collected by numerous federal surveys, and data are captured in the administrative records of the agencies responsible for programs that target people with disabilities. To a large extent, the limitations of these statistics are not the result of low investment in data collection; instead, they are the result of not taking full advantage of the existing efforts.

We use the term "national disability data system" to encompass all federal efforts to collect information about people with disabilities. There is, of course, no formal system. Nonetheless, we find it helpful to think about this large effort as a system because it leads to recognition of significant, and often lower cost, options for substantially improving the system.

The key components of the informal NDDS are the major national household surveys, smaller national household surveys that focus on specific issues, a multitude of surveys of specific subpopulations, surveys of nonhousehold populations, and program administrative data. Livermore and She (2007) provide a more detailed description of these components, and individual components are featured in various ways later in this book.

Major National Household Surveys

Major national household surveys include the ACS, the CPS, the National Health Interview Survey (NHIS), and the Survey of Income and Program Participation (SIPP). These surveys are all integral parts of the federal statistical system. Data from each are deemed critical to monitoring some aspect of the U.S. population and provide basic information needed to administer federal programs. All provide some information about people with disabilities, including information about their demographic characteristics, health and functioning, employment, and economic well-being. All except the ACS (from 2006 forward) exclude people living in institutions, and inclusion of those living in noninstitutional group quarters varies (see She and Stapleton 2009).

Other National Household Surveys

There are a number of other federally sponsored national surveys designed to regularly provide more detailed information on specific aspects of population health, well-being, activities, and expenditures than what is available in the larger surveys identified above. These topical surveys generally have smaller sample sizes than the major surveys, and in some cases, the samples are derived from one of the major surveys. With the exception of those that are focused specifically on health issues, these surveys tend to include few measures of disability. The following are important examples: American Housing Survey, American Time Use Survey, Behavioral Risk Factor Surveillance System, Consumer Expenditure Survey, Medical Expenditure Panel Survey, National Health and Nutrition Examination Survey, Panel Study of Income Dynamics, and Survey of Consumer Finances.

Surveys of Subpopulations

A number of surveys have focused specifically on youth and young adults in the general population, including the National Longitudinal Survey of Adolescent Health and the National Longitudinal Survey of Youth. The Health and Retirement Study provides extensive longitudinal data on the working-age population as it reaches the normal age of retirement, and the National Beneficiary Survey, the Medicare Current Beneficiary Survey (MCBS), and the Longitudinal Study of the Vocational Rehabilitation Services Program collect information on people with disabilities who are participants in major government programs. One federal survey, the 1994–1995 Disability Supplement to the NHIS, collected unusually extensive information about working-age people with disabilities. Many of these surveys contain extensive disability-related information and/or focus specifically on subpopulations with disabilities. With the exception of the annual MCBS, these surveys are conducted very infrequently or have been conducted only once.

Surveys of Nonhousehold Populations

Most national surveys include only the household population and intentionally exclude those living in institutions and other types of group quarters. A few federal surveys of nonhousehold populations have collected information on residents of institutions (including nursing homes, jails, and prisons) and on homeless individuals. The Nursing Home Minimum Data Set (MDS) and the National Nursing Home Survey collect information on nursing home residents. Three periodic surveys by the Department of Justice collect information on the incarcerated population: Survey of Inmates of Local Jails, Survey of Inmates of State Correctional Facilities, and Survey of Inmates of Federal Correctional

Facilities. The only nationwide survey data available for the homeless population is the National Survey of Homeless Assistance Providers and Clients, which collected health and disability-related data on the users of homeless assistance programs. The Decennial Census collects limited data on people in all residential settings, and the annual ACS began to include people living in almost all residential settings in 2006.

Program Administrative Data

Program administrative data are an important source of information about people with disabilities and, especially, statistics on their participation in those programs. There are more than 20 federal agencies and nearly 200 programs that provide assistance to people with disabilities, sometimes in the context of programs that serve a broader target population. Administrative data from these programs can provide extensive information about the income, public benefits, and health care and other service utilization of people with disabilities. Although limited by the fact that they only include people with disabilities who are enrolled in or have applied to a program, the number of working-age people actually participating in programs is about half as large as the ACS estimate of the number of people with disabilities in the household population (see Stapleton, Wittenburg, and Thornton 2009).

SUMMARY OF WHAT IS CURRENTLY KNOWN

The first step in any empirical study of people with disabilities is to define the term "disability." In Chapter 2, "The Disability Data Landscape," Robert Weathers identifies the definitions of disability used in this book, describes the major national surveys, reviews the questions available in these surveys, and places them within a conceptual model of disability. He also compares the prevalence estimates derived from these various definitions and data sources, to highlight both their similarities and differences. The conceptual framework and prevalence estimates in this chapter provide a foundation for the rest of the book.

Chapters 3 through 7 present recent statistics from the major surveys for working-age people with and without disabilities in the household population. The focus on the household population reflects the fact that the vast majority of the information we have on the prevalence and socioeconomic characteristics of working-age people with disabilities comes from social-science-based data sets that track the health, employment, and the economic well-being of the general U.S. population living in households. Some of these statistics are for households, rather than individuals, as the economic well-being of people, including those with disabilities, must be considered in the context of their households, since ultimately income and the risk of poverty is shared among all household members. Each chapter presents the most recent available statistics, assesses their strengths and limitations, compares statistics from multiple sources, and provides some historical statistics. As will be discussed later, however, none of these surveys captured the working-age population that lives in institutions and other group quarters until 2006, when the Census Bureau expanded the ACS sample.

In Chapter 3, "Disability Prevalence and Demographics," Andrew Houtenville, Elizabeth Potamites, William Erickson, and Antonio Ruiz-Quintanilla examine trends in disability prevalence and also consider variation in prevalence across states and demographic subpopulations. A great deal is known about trends in the prevalence of disability among those aged 65 and older, but much less is known for working-age people. The authors examine variation in prevalence across demographic groups, present trends in prevalence estimates, and also provide state prevalence statistics.

In Chapter 4, "Employment," Robert Weathers and David Wittenburg use data from the major nationally representative surveys to examine the employment of people with disabilities, including long-term trends and state-level estimates. As discussed earlier, prior work has shown a long-term decline in employment among persons with disabilities, especially when measured relative to the employment of those without disabilities. This chapter provides clear definitions of the employment rate, labor-force participation, and the unemployment rate. It describes why some numbers often cited in the popular press, notably the 70 percent unemployment rate for persons with a disability, are not comparable to the unemployment rate for the population that is produced regularly by the Bureau of Labor Statistics. The authors update previously published estimates of employment rates (Burkhauser, Houtenville, and Wittenburg 2003; Maag and Wittenburg 2003) through 2006 and expand this literature with statistics from the ACS. They also identify and discuss both consistencies and inconsistencies in the estimates from various sources of data.

In Chapter 5, "Household Income," Richard Burkhauser, Ludmila Rovba, and Robert Weathers examine the household incomes of working-age people with disabilities. The analysis includes examination of trends in income and its composition, the effects of adjustments for household size on income trends, and the sensitivity of income trends to the business cycle. Sources of income include an individual's labor earnings, self-employment income, interest income, Social Security income, SSI benefits, and other miscellaneous personal income sources, plus income from other household members. The authors examine the decline in labor earnings across comparable years in the business cycle over a 16-year span (1989, 2000, and 2004) and the extent to which this decline is replaced by growth in income from public programs and other sources.

In Chapter 6, "Poverty," Richard Burkhauser, Andrew Houtenville, and Ludmila Rovba present and discuss statistics on the poverty rate for people with disabilities, using the official federal definition of house-hold poverty. The Census Bureau provides official poverty rates for most economically disadvantaged populations in the United States, but it does not do so for working-age people with disabilities. The authors also provide background on the measurement of poverty and present statistics from the ACS, CPS, and SIPP. They also analyze trends in the poverty rate from 1981 to 2005, based on the CPS. In contrast to other disadvantaged populations whose economic well-being improved sub-stantially during the 1990s, the poverty rate of working-age people with disabilities increased both absolutely and relative to the rate for working-age people without disabilities over the business cycles of both the 1980s and 1990s.

In Chapter 7, "Health and Functional Status," Gerry Hendershot, Benjamin Harris, and David Stapleton discuss the challenges of collect-ing data on the health and functional status of the population and the history of federal efforts to do so. They present health and functional status statistics for people with and without disabilities from the 2006 NHIS and compare them to those from four years earlier.

SUMMARY OF LIMITATIONS AND OPTIONS FOR IMPROVEMENT

The remaining chapters of the book focus on the limitations of current data and options for improvement.

In Chapter 8, "Survey Data Collection Methods," Janice Ballou and Jason Markesich examine alternative methods for collecting survey data, how these methods affect the inclusion of people with disabilities in survey samples, and whether and how sampled subjects respond. The authors identify the many ways in which survey methodology can lead to the exclusion of individuals with disabilities and inconsistencies in disability statistics derived from different surveys—even if the questions used to identify subjects with disabilities are identical. They point to the need for methodological changes and standards to improve the inclusion of people with disabilities as well as the quality of disability statistics in the areas of sample frame definitions, sampling methods, questionnaire design (structure, question design), and data collection (interview training and interview methods/technology).

In Chapter 9, "Program Participants," David Stapleton, David Wittenburg, and Craig Thornton describe the available data and statistics on working-age people with disabilities who participate in major federal programs. Survey data generally capture program participation poorly because subjects sometimes fail to report participation, or they are confused about which programs they participate in. Further, some program participants are excluded from participation in major surveys, partly because a relatively large share lives outside the household population, but also because of data-collection methodologies. The authors summarize the availability of participation information in major federal surveys and also describe the availability of administrative data and statistics from the federal agencies that are responsible for program administration and oversight. They present state-level program participation statistics for major federal and federal/state income support, health insurance, and employment service programs in 2005, and they compare them to ACS estimates of the size of the state household population with disabilities. The authors conclude with a description and discussion of important efforts to improve data on program participants, including the matching of administrative data with survey data and administrative data across agencies.

In Chapter 10, "The Group Quarters Population," Peiyun She and David Stapleton review the availability of data on people with disabilities who live in institutions and other group quarters. Household surveys exclude most such individuals. Disproportionately large numbers of people with disabilities live in group quarters. This includes disproportionately large numbers in the largest institutional group, the incarcerated population, as well as people in nursing homes, psychiatric hospitals, institutions for adults with cognitive disabilities, and others. There has been a large increase in the share of the working-age population living in jails and prisons and a more modest decline in the shares living in nursing homes and other group quarters. These trends potentially have a substantial effect on the prevalence of disability in the household population, as well as on statistics for people with disabilities in the household population. Available data on this population are inadequate for fully understanding the implications of these trends.

In Chapter 11, "Options for Improving Disability Data Collection," David Stapleton, Gina Livermore, and Peiyun She provide a synthesis of the major limitations of the NDDS based on earlier chapters in the book as well as interviews conducted with producers and consumers of disability statistics. They then present and discuss high-priority options for improving disability data and statistics for the working-age population. Because most of these improvements stem from recognition of the existence of the informal NDDS, they would be relatively inexpensive because they involve relatively small changes to existing data collection efforts and/or improved data usage. The authors also recognize, however, that periodic supplements of existing surveys or additional surveys of specific groups of people with disabilities are needed to address some of the system's most significant limitations.

CONCLUSIONS

This book provides a systematic review of what current statistics and data on working-age people with disabilities can tell us, what they cannot tell us, and how they can be improved to better tell us what we need and want to know.

What We Know

An extensive and valuable disability data collection effort exists in the United States, but to our knowledge, it has never been previously recognized as a "system," as we do in this book. Researchers, analysts, administrators, and others can glean extensive information about working-age people with disabilities from the data sources that comprise the NDDS. This point is illustrated in Chapters 2 through 7, which tell us what we currently know about the prevalence, employment, income, poverty status, health, and functional status of working-age people with disabilities who live in the household population. Chapter 9 provides a sketch of what we currently know about the program participation of working-age people with disabilities, and Chapter 10 provides a very limited set of information on what we currently know about the population that is not captured in most national household surveys and the substantial numbers of working-age people with disabilities who live in institutions or other group quarters.

What We Don't Know

Historically, several important limitations of the NDDS have undermined its ability to inform public policy. The delayed recognition of the decline in employment of this population, the premature attribution of the decline to the ADA, and the widespread failure of scholars and policymakers to recognize the growing gap between the average income and risk of poverty of working-age people with and without disabilities over the last three decades are examples of the consequences of these limitations.

We also do not know the extent to which increases in incarceration represent increases in incarceration for people with disabilities. Nor do we know the extent to which these increases and more modest declines in the proportion of working-age people with disabilities living in nursing homes and other types of group quarters have affected the trends for people with disabilities living in the household population, and we have almost no information on trends for all people with disabilities (i.e., including all those living in group quarters).

Finally, while we know that the ratio of working-age participants in federal disability programs to estimates of the number of people with disabilities in the household population exhibits enormous variation across states, we do not have detailed state statistics that would help us understand the causes of this variation.

What Needs to Be Improved to Better Tell Us What We Want to Know

Significant progress is being made toward addressing some of these limitations, and it is important to sustain the efforts that are responsible for that progress. In Chapter 2, Weathers points out that the inclusion of several disability questions in the 2000 Census long form, and the subsequent implementation of the annual ACS using the same questions, have for the first time made it feasible to produce a wide variety of state-level statistics on the prevalence and status of working-age people with disabilities in the household population on an annual basis. Although changes in the methodology of the ACS during its start-up years have limited the usefulness of ACS disability statistics for trend analysis, these changes are also gradually improving the quality of the statistics themselves. Included among these improvements is the expansion of the ACS sample frame to include most of the nonhousehold population in 2006.

The expansion of, and recent improvements to, efforts that match data from major surveys to administrative records, described by Stapleton, Wittenburg, and Thornton in Chapter 9, are also a very welcome development. These efforts are improving our knowledge about the program participation status of people with disabilities, as well as about their characteristics and health, functional, and economic status.

Records from the SIPP have been matched to SSA records for a number of years and have been a source of important information about program participants. The longitudinal nature of the SIPP and the extensive information about income and program participation in this survey make these matches especially valuable for understanding the dynamics of disability and program participation (e.g., exits from employment and entry into the SSA programs) and for studying participation in multiple programs. The Census Bureau has been developing plans to replace the SIPP with a different system for collection of income and program participation data. A new system would be most welcome by disability researchers, analysts, and users of disability statistics if it addressed some of the limitations of the SIPP, but only if it preserved the scope of information that SIPP offers for people with disabilities. We also applaud the efforts of the National Center for Health Statistics, in collaboration with the SSA and Centers for Medicare & Medicaid, to match data from the NHIS and several other surveys to SSA and Medicare records. Among other things, these data offer the opportunity to learn much about health conditions, health care, functional limitations, and insurance status of people with disabilities who apply for benefits from SSA. This includes those denied as well as those awarded benefits, before, during, and after SSA's lengthy disability determination process. The exploratory efforts by the Census Bureau and SSA to match records from the ACS to the SSA records are tantalizing. The latter match would make it feasible to produce many new state-level statistics about participants in the SSA disability programs.

The efforts of several agencies to develop analytical files from administrative records and to match administrative records across agencies are also contributing to an expansion in our knowledge about program participants (especially those who participate in multiple programs) and to our ability to rigorously evaluate policy initiatives. Because administrative records are longitudinal, these efforts have also expanded our capacity to produce statistics on the dynamics of disability and program participation. Additional efforts in this area could be extremely valuable, including efforts to make existing data more available to responsible researchers under safeguards that protect individual rights to privacy.

In Chapter 11, Stapleton, Livermore, and She describe a number of relatively low-cost options for further improving the NDDS—options that primarily would improve existing data collection efforts and/or our ability to make use of data that are already being collected. Chief among these is establishment of a common set of disability questions to be used in all federal surveys. Significant progress is already being made on this option. The 2008 ACS includes an improved set of disability questions, and the 2008 CPS adopted this same set of questions. These questions are also slated for inclusion in the NHIS. Inclusion of this same set of questions in the SIPP would mean that statistics about people with disabilities from these major surveys would be for the same disability population, at least conceptually; the population represented would vary from survey to survey only because of differences in other aspects of data collection methods and the survey context.

This conceptual population will not be exactly the *right* population for most specific research and policy purposes because the number of disability questions is necessarily limited. However, the production of statistics from all four surveys about the same conceptual population would greatly advance the dialogue about people with disabilities and disability policy. A next step would be to add the same question set to additional federal surveys—ideally all of them. Also, as we proceed to adopt these questions, it is critical to maintain some of the questions used in the past (e.g., the CPS work limitation question) in at least some surveys for purposes of historical continuity; otherwise we will have no basis to compare disability statistics for those identified by the new questions to historical statistics for those identified by existing questions.

Other relatively low-cost options for improvement include development and standardization of survey methods that will increase the inclusion of people with disabilities in federal surveys, as well as minor changes in questions, probes, or response options that will yield relevant disability information (e.g., reasons for not working, accessibility of transportation, etc.). It would be worthwhile to carefully review the data collection methodology and questionnaires of all major federal surveys to identify easy ways to increase the inclusion of respondents with disabilities and increase disability-relevant content.

As elaborated in Chapter 11, some limitations in the NDDS can only be addressed through initiatives that are relatively expensive because they require additional data collection. Nonetheless, several such initiatives might be well worth the expense. Such initiatives include disability topic supplements of existing surveys, and implementation or expansion of periodic surveys on special populations, such as program participants, residents of noninstitutional group quarters, and homeless people.

Although we think periodic national surveys focused solely on the population of people with disabilities, like the 1994–1995 supplement to the NHIS, have considerable value, they are very difficult to design and expensive to conduct. It seems to us that many of the benefits of periodic national disability surveys could be obtained through less expensive improvements to the NDDS. Such improvements would not likely eliminate the need for periodic national surveys, but they might substantially reduce the need, make such surveys easier to design, and be less expensive to conduct.

Notes

1. As etched on the facade of the University of Chicago's Social Science Building when it was built in 1927.
2. For example, the Census Bureau ignores the population with disabilities in its annual report on "Income, Poverty, and Health Insurance Coverage in the United States," and the Bureau of Labor Statistics has yet to produce an official employment rate for this population. The Census Bureau first added disability statistics, based on the ACS, to the annual American FactFinder in 2004. See http://www .factfinder.census.gov.
3. Throughout the book, we define the working-age population as persons aged 25– 61 unless otherwise indicated. The working-age population is often defined as persons aged 18–64 in published statistics. We use a narrower definition because of the large number of persons aged 18–24 whose primary activity is education and the large number of persons aged 62–64 who are retired.
4. Based on the 2000 Census, there were 2.2 million persons with disabilities aged 18–64 living in institutional group quarters in 2000, representing 54 percent of all persons in that age group who were living in institutions (She and Stapleton 2009). The 2006 ACS statistics cited above include the substantial number of working-age people with disabilities who are residents of noninstitutional group quarters; ACS statistics for earlier years that are cited in this book exclude those living in noninstitutional group quarters, however, because they were not included in the ACS sample frame in those years.

References

Acemoglu, Daron, and Joshua Angrist. 2001. "Consequences of Employment Protection? The Case of the Americans with Disabilities Act." *Journal of Political Economy* 109(5): 915–957.

Burkhauser, Richard V., Mary C. Daly, Andrew J. Houtenville, and Nigar Nargis. 2001. "Self-Reported Work Limitation Data: What They Can and Cannot Tell Us." *Demography* 39(3): 541–555.

Burkhauser, Richard V., Andrew Houtenville, and David C. Wittenburg. 2003. "A User's Guide to Current Statistics on the Employment of People with Disabilities." In *The Decline in Employment of People with Disabilities: A Policy Puzzle,* David C. Stapleton and Richard V. Burkhauser, eds. Kalamazoo, MI: W.E. Upjohn Institute for Employment Research, pp. 23–86.

DeLeire, Thomas. 2000. "The Wage and Employment Effects of the Americans with Disabilities Act." *Journal of Human Resources* 35(4): 693–715.

Hale, Thomas W. 2001. "The Lack of a Disability Measure in Today's Current Population Survey." *Monthly Labor Review* 124(6): 38–40.

Houtenville, Andrew J., and Richard V. Burkhauser. 2004. "Did the Employment of Those with Disabilities Fall in the 1990s and Was the ADA Responsible? A Replication and Robustness Check of Acemoglu and Angrist (2001)—Research Brief." Ithaca, NY: Cornell University, Research and Rehabilitation Training Center for Economic Research on Employment Policy for People with Disabilities.

Jolls, Christine, and J. J. Prescott. 2005. "Disaggregating Employment Protection: The Case of Disability Discrimination." Harvard Public Law Working Paper no. 106. Cambridge, MA: Harvard Law School.

Livermore, Gina A., and Peiyun She. 2007. "Limitations of the National Disability Data System." Ithaca, NY: Cornell University, Rehabilitation Research and Training Center on Disability Demographics and Statistics.

Maag, Elaine, and David Wittenburg. 2003. "Real Trends or Measurement Problems? Disability and Employment Trends in the Survey of Income and Program Participation." Washington, DC: The Urban Institute.

National Council on Disability. 2002. "National Disability Policy: A Progress Report (December 2000–December 2001)." Washington, DC: National Council on Disability. http://www.ncd.gov/newsroom/publications/2002/pdf/progressreport_07-26-02.pdf (accessed June 16, 2008).

Rehabilitation Research and Training Center on Disability Demographics and Statistics. 2007. *2006 Disability Status Report.* Ithaca, NY: Cornell University, Rehabilitation Research and Training Center on Disability Demographics and Statistics.

She, Peiyun, and David C. Stapleton. 2009. "The Group Quarters Population." In *Counting Working-Age People with Disabilities: What Current Data Tell Us and Options for Improvement*, Andrew J. Houtenville, David C. Stapleton, Robert R. Weathers II, and Richard V. Burkhauser, eds. Kalamazoo, MI: W.E. Upjohn Institute for Employment Research, pp. 353–380.

Stapleton, David C., and Richard V. Burkhauser, eds. 2003. *The Decline in Employment of People with Disabilities: A Policy Puzzle.* Kalamazoo, MI: W.E. Upjohn Institute for Employment Research.

Stapleton, David C., David C. Wittenburg, and Craig Thornton. 2009. "Program Participants." In *Counting Working-Age People with Disabilities: What Current Data Tell Us and Options for Improvement*, Andrew J. Houtenville, David C. Stapleton, Robert R. Weathers II, and Richard V. Burkhauser, eds. Kalamazoo, MI: W.E. Upjohn Institute for Employment Research, pp. 299–352.

2

The Disability Data Landscape

Robert R. Weathers II
Social Security Administration

According to the Survey of Income and Program Participation (SIPP), there were 26.6 million working-age Americans (aged 25–61) with disabilities in 2002. In contrast, there are only 17.1 million working-age Americans with disabilities according to the 2003 American Community Survey (ACS).[1] Why these and other major federal-government-funded data sources yield such vastly different values for even the most fundamental of statistics on the working-age population with disabilities is the focus of this chapter. More importantly, it will delineate the strengths and limitations of currently available data sets in capturing levels and trends for this population.

This chapter will concentrate on the five major, nationally representative data sets used in the United States (and in this book) to capture the size of the working-age population with disabilities as well as their socioeconomic characteristics (e.g., demographics, employment, income, poverty, and health and functioning status). Four of the data sets are run by the U.S. Census Bureau: the ACS, Current Population Survey Annual Social and Economic Supplement (CPS-ASEC), 2000 Decennial Census, and SIPP. The fifth, run by the National Center for Health Statistics (NCHS), is the National Health Interview Survey (NHIS).

A taxonomy is developed that classifies disability questions found in these five data sets into concepts based on the International Classification of Functioning, Disability and Health (ICF) (World Health Organization 2001). This disability taxonomy places each survey question into one of six classifications—sensory impairment, physical impairment, mental impairment, activity of daily living (ADL) limitation, instrumental activity of daily living (IADL) limitation, and work limitation. Each classification flows from one of the three basic ICF concepts—*impairment, activity limitation,* and *participation restriction.*

The taxonomy is used to document the differences in the disability questions included in these surveys to capture each classification, as well as the ability for each survey to capture all of the classifications and thus the total population with a disability. This chapter also describes how the data sources differ in other important ways, including the degree to which they capture the population living in group quarters (GQ), defined as persons living in nursing homes, prisons, college dormitories, juvenile institutions, and emergency and transitional shelters. These differences can lead to dramatic disparities across the data sets in the prevalence of disability they find among working-age people and in the socioeconomic characteristics—employment rates, income levels, poverty rates, etc.—of the working-age population with disabilities discussed in later chapters of this book.

This chapter concludes with considerations of which data sets are best for answering various public policy questions and the value of the next generation of data sets that have just been or are in the process of being developed to better answer these questions.

DEFINITION OF DISABILITY

Unlike age and sex, which are readily identifiable individual attributes, disability is a complex interaction between a person's health condition and the social and physical environment. Hence, it has been defined in a variety of ways. The Interagency Committee on Disability Research (ICDR) documents 67 acts or programs that define disability. Of these, 35 have self-contained definitions of disability, 26 use definitions from other statutes, and 6 are in more than one statute (CESSI 2007). To compare estimates from the five national data sets used in this volume, we first developed consistent conceptual definitions and factors of disability.

The two most common conceptual models of disability used in the United States are the ICF developed by the World Health Organization (2006) and the disability model developed by Saad Nagi (1965, 1976). Both definitions explicitly recognize disability as a dynamic process involving the interaction of a person's health condition and personal characteristics, as well as the physical and social environment. Changes in any of these factors can impact a person's ability to function and participate in everyday activities. Jette and Badley (2000) provide a detailed description and comparison of these models. In this volume, we adopt ICF concepts to create operational definitions of disability. The concepts used are *impairment, activity limitation,* and *participation restriction* (World Health Organization 2001). A prerequisite for each of these concepts is the presence of a health condition encompassing diseases, injuries, health disorders, and other health-related conditions. Examples of health conditions are listed in the *International Statistical Classification of Diseases and Related Health Problems, 10th Revision* (World Health Organization 2006).

An *impairment* is defined as a significant deviation or loss in body function or structure. For example, loss of a limb or vision may be classified as an impairment. We identify three types of impairments: 1) sensory, which includes difficulty hearing or seeing; 2) physical, which includes difficulty moving, climbing, reaching, and performing other physical functions; and 3) mental, which includes difficulty learning, remembering, concentrating, or performing other mental functions.

An *activity limitation* is defined as a difficulty that an individual may have in executing activities. For example, a person who experiences difficulty dressing, bathing, or performing other ADLs related to a health condition may be classified as having an activity limitation. We identify activity limitations based upon ADL questions.

A *participation restriction* is defined as an inability to engage in societal activities. For example, a working-age person with a severe health condition may have difficulty participating in employment as a result of the physical (e.g., lack of reasonable employer accommodations) or social (e.g., discrimination) environment. In some surveys, participation restrictions are identified by questions that ask whether the person has a long-lasting health condition that limits his or her ability to work or whether a health condition affects his or her ability to go outside the home to go shopping, to church, or to a doctor's office. We identify participation restrictions using IADL and work limitation questions.

A *disability,* then, is the presence of a health-based impairment, an activity limitation, and/or a participation restriction. This concept is similar to the definition used in the Americans with Disabilities Act of 1990 (ADA). The ADA defines a disability as "a physical or mental impairment that substantially limits one or more of the major life activities, a record of such an impairment, or being regarded as having such an impairment."

Although these concepts may seem to follow a progression—that is, an impairment leading to an activity limitation leading to a participation restriction—this need not be so. A person may have a participation restriction that is the direct result of the social environment without having an activity limitation or impairment.[2] For example, someone diagnosed as HIV positive with no impairment or activity limitation may be unlawfully refused employment on the basis of their health condition. Similarly, a person with a history of mental illness, but no current loss in capacity or activity limitation, may also be unlawfully refused employment based on past history. Figure 2.1 summarizes these ICF concepts, showing how they can overlap or occur singularly. The ICF universe is the health of the population, and the shaded area represents the population with disabilities.

Translating questions in currently available surveys into these ICF concepts of disability is not always a straightforward task, and there are no well-defined rules for doing so. For example, some survey questions may be interpreted as both an activity limitation and a participation restriction. The approach I used in these cases is to make consistent judgments. In doing so, I attempt to provide an ICF-based framework for comparing disability populations across surveys.

OVERVIEW OF NATIONALLY REPRESENTATIVE DATA SOURCES

Each of the five nationally representative surveys used in this volume to describe characteristics of the population of persons with a disability was designed for a different purpose, and each uses various methods, survey instruments, and sample designs to identify this population. As described below, these differences can have an important influence on the information that is collected on the population with disabilities. Ballou and Markesich (2009) and Mathiowetz (2000) both

Figure 2.1 Simplified Conceptual Model of Disability Using ICF Concepts

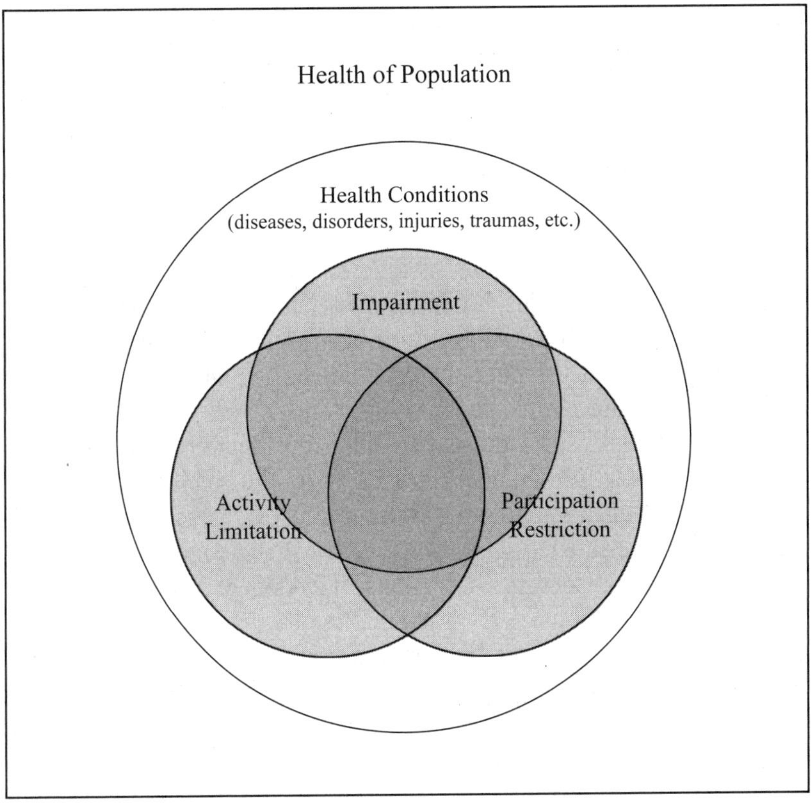

provide a good review of the general methodological issues as well as those specific to the population with disabilities.

American Community Survey (ACS)

The ACS is a relatively new continuous data collection effort by the U.S. Census Bureau designed to produce annual estimates at the national, state, and local levels on the characteristics of the U.S. population. Its purpose is to replace the Decennial Census long form, and it represents an improvement by providing data users with annual information on demographic, housing, social, and economic statistics that can be compared across states, communities, and population groups. One of the main objectives of the ACS is to provide federal, state, and local governments with an information base for the administration and evaluation of government programs.

The population sampled for the ACS has changed substantially during the transition from the testing phase to full implementation. The testing phase began in 2000 and continued through 2004, and it is based on a national sample of addresses with an overall sampling rate of 0.7 percent annually (i.e., approximately 800,000 addresses per year).[3] From 2000 to 2004, the ACS is representative of the U.S. population living in households, but it excluded persons living in GQ such as nursing homes, prisons, college dormitories, juvenile institutions, and emergency and transitional shelters. Full implementation of the ACS national household sample began in 2005 and included the collection of data on an annual basis from a nationally representative sample of approximately three million addresses. In 2006, the ACS added a sample of 2.5 percent of the population living in GQ and a sample of 36,000 addresses in Puerto Rico (U.S. Census Bureau 2003).

The ACS includes three sections: 1) resident characteristics, 2) housing characteristics, and 3) person-level characteristics. The resident section provides basic information on people living in the household, including name, sex, age, and relationship to the person who either owns or rents the house, apartment unit, or mobile home. The housing component contains information on the residence, including the type of building, costs of residing in the building, home equity, and other housing characteristics. The person-level section contains information on each person living in the household, including demographic characteristics, educational attainment, disability status, fertility status, living situation, employment status and conditions, and income.

There are six disability questions in the person-level section of the ACS. The questions were designed by a federal interagency workgroup for the 2000 Decennial Census (Adler et al. 1999). The first three questions identify household members aged 5 and older who have a long-lasting health condition associated with disability, including severe sensory impairment (hearing or vision), physical impairment (substantial limits on activities such as walking, climbing stairs, reaching, lifting, or carrying), or mental impairment (difficulty learning, remembering, or concentrating). The fourth question identifies household members aged 5 and older who have a health condition for at least six months that affects the performance of ADLs (dressing, bathing, or getting around inside the home). The final two questions identify household members aged 15 and older who have a health condition lasting at least six months that affects participation in usual life activities (e.g., going outside the home alone to visit a doctor's office or go shopping and working at a job or business). The Census Bureau identifies a person with a disability based upon a "yes" response to at least one of the six disability questions.

Many features of the ACS will be useful to disability policymakers, service providers, and the disability advocacy community. First, the ACS contains a unique combination of data on disability, demographic characteristics, economic well-being, and employment. Second, the sample size and design of the ACS allow users to examine a variety of annual disability statistics at the national, state, Metropolitan Statistical Area (MSA), and county level. Third, because after 2006 the data will be collected in a consistent manner over time, users will be able to estimate trends in various disability statistics at a level of geographic detail (e.g., the county level) that is not possible in any other national survey. Users will be able to track changes to the disability population so that localized issues can be identified, services can be more effectively targeted to the population, publicly and privately funded disability programs can be more effectively administered, and new programs can be evaluated.

Although the ACS can provide information on a wide variety of topics, there are some limitations. First, the ACS does not detail the prevalence of specific health conditions (e.g., cancer, paralysis, HIV/AIDS, etc.) or distinguish between levels of severity. Second, the ACS definition of disability does not explicitly include important societal and environmental factors such as discrimination and lack of reasonable accommodations. Finally, prior to 2006, the ACS data did not include the population living in GQ.

Current Population Survey Annual Social and Economic Supplement (CPS-ASEC)

The CPS-ASEC is typically collected in March of each year as part of the monthly CPS data collection effort used to describe labor force characteristics of the U.S. population. In addition to providing the usual monthly labor force and demographic data, the CPS-ASEC collects data on work experience, including weeks worked and hours per week worked, as well as reasons for not working full time; total income and income components; noncash benefits, including food stamps, school lunch programs, employer-provided group health insurance and pension plans, private health insurance, Medicaid, Medicare, TriCare (formerly CHAMPUS) or military health care, and energy assistance; and migration. Data on employment and income are for the preceding calendar year, and demographic data are for the time of the survey. The CPS-ASEC is conducted by the U.S. Census Bureau for the U.S. Bureau of Labor Statistics.

The CPS-ASEC sample is drawn from the civilian, noninstitutional U.S. population living in housing units as well as members of the armed forces living in civilian housing units on a military base or in a household not on a military base. Beginning in 2002, the CPS expanded its sample to study the State Children's Health Insurance Program. In March 2007, the CPS completed interviews from members of about 57,000 households containing approximately 112,000 persons aged 15 or older.[4] Prior to 2001, the CPS collected data from a smaller sample of households from the same population.[5]

The CPS-ASEC survey instrument contains one work-limitation question, which has been included since March 1980, and provides a consistently defined annual measure of the population with a work limitation: "(Do you/Does anyone in this household) have a health problem or disability which prevents (you/them) from working or which limits the kind or amount of work (you/they) can do?" The data from this question has been used by researchers and policymakers to measure demographic, employment, income, and poverty trends among the population of persons with a disability.

The question is located in the income section of the CPS survey instrument and was designed to be a prompt for the receipt of disability income from sources other than Social Security Disability Insurance (SSDI) or Supplemental Security Income (SSI). The CPS-ASEC reinterviews part of the sample one year later, and this feature allows users to construct a two-period measure based upon reports of a work limitation in two consecutive March CPS interviews.

Some researchers and policymakers have criticized the use of this question to identify the population with disabilities because it was not designed or tested to measure such a population, and they have also argued that it is too narrow in scope. For instance, those who are limited in the amount of paid work that they can perform, or are prevented from performing, may not capture a population of people with disabilities that is relevant for broader disability policies such as the ADA (see Hale 2001). Although the question may not be useful for estimating the number of persons with a disability using a broader definition, Burkhauser et al. (2002) demonstrated that the trends in both the disability prevalence and employment rate using this measure are not statistically different from data sources that do use a broader definition. Burkhauser et al. (2002) have therefore concluded that the question is useful for studying longer term trends for the population.

The major strength of the CPS-ASEC is that it is the only nationally representative data source that can be used to construct a consistent set of annual estimates of those with a work limitation. It is also the primary source of data on employment, income, and poverty of the U.S. population. Therefore, it provides users with reliable information on important socioeconomic indicators for persons with a disability.

The CPS-ASEC, however, is limited in that its sole means of capturing the population with a disability is the one work-limitation question. And, as will be seen in subsequent chapters, this work-limited population is quite different in size and characteristics from the broader population with a disability that is captured in the ACS and other data sets that include additional disability classifications. However, the trends of the work-limited population closely track shorter term disability trends using the broader disability definitions found in the NHIS and provide plausible evidence that it is a valid measure of trends (Burkhauser et al. 2002). It also excludes those living in institutions, and the sample size in years prior to 2001 is not large enough to adequately measure the annual characteristics of persons with a disability in many states. The

CPS may be used to construct state-level estimates of the work-limited population from 2001 onward.[6]

2000 Decennial Census Long Form

Every 10 years the Census Bureau conducts a census to count the number of people in the United States, including those living in GQ. The data are used for a variety of official purposes, including the allocation of seats in the House of Representatives among the states. But Decennial Census data also provide a snapshot of the social and economic characteristics of the nation.

The Decennial Census includes a short form that collects basic demographic data from five of six households and a long form that adds social and economic data from every sixth household. Data are also collected from GQ, a population that is rarely included in surveys (see She and Stapleton 2009).

The 2000 Decennial Census long form is similar to the ACS. It includes the exact same six questions used in the ACS to identify the population with a disability.[7] The disability questions were newly designed for the 2000 Decennial Census, so it is not possible to compare those results with those from earlier Decennial Census years.

The main advantage of the 2000 Decennial Census long form survey is that it has the largest and most comprehensive sample among the national data sources for studying the population with a disability. Sample sizes are sufficient to produce small area estimates, including those at the state, MSA, congressional district, and even tribal territory levels. It also provides the most complete set of data on the population living in GQ. The addition of the GQ population in the 2006 ACS will provide a new and updated source for this population.

The 2000 Decennial Census long form has many of the same limitations as the ACS. The survey does not allow one to identify the prevalence of specific health conditions (e.g., cancer, paralysis, HIV/AIDS, etc.) and does not directly address external factors that may contribute to a disability, such as discrimination and lack of reasonable accommodations. The Census Bureau discovered problems with two of the questions in the Decennial Census long form. The Decennial Census IADL and work-limitation questions may have been administered in a way that creates an overestimate of the population with these two disabilities as well as the overall population with disabilities.[8]

National Health Interview Survey (NHIS)

The NHIS is the primary data source on the health of the civilian, noninstitutionalized population of the United States. The survey was initiated as part of the National Health Survey Act of 1956 (Public Law 652–84th Congress), "to produce statistics on disease, injury, impairment, disability, and related topics on a uniform basis for the Nation." In general, the NHIS exists to monitor the health of the U.S. noninstitutional population and to display these characteristics by socioeconomic and demographic characteristics. NHIS data are used within government agencies and the academic research community to monitor developments in the prevalence of illness, disability, and other health-related conditions. Researchers rely on the NHIS to measure trends in the U.S. health care environment, including changes in access and utilization. The NHIS is also used to measure the efficacy of federal health programs, and the NCHS cooperates with other federal agencies to meet their needs for health data.

The target universe of the NHIS is all dwelling units that contain members of the civilian noninstitutionalized U.S. population. The NHIS sample does not include those residing in institutions (including those in prisons and long-term care facilities), members of the active duty armed forces, or U.S. nationals living abroad. In 2002, the NHIS sample consisted of more than 36,000 households that yielded a total of approximately 93,000 persons interviewed. For the sample adult component (explained below), 31,044 adults from the 93,000 persons were interviewed.

The NHIS consists of two basic components: a core section that remains unchanged across years and sets of supplemental questions that change annually. The core consists of three general sections: the family core section, which collects demographic and health information on every member of the household; the sample adult section, which randomly selects an adult and collects additional health-related information for that person; and a sample child section, which collects additional health-related information for the randomly selected child. In

2002, there were nine supplemental topics included: 1) alternative and complementary medicine; 2) vision; 3) hearing; 4) asthma; 5) arthritis; 6) child mental health; 7) disability and secondary conditions—assistive technologies and environmental barriers; 8) environmental health—lead paint; and 9) child and adult immunizations.

Data on disability within the NHIS are derived from questions in both the person-level file of the family core and the sample adult file. Within the family core file, the questions used to identify disability are from the "health status and limitation of activity section," which contains survey questions on work, ADL and IADL limitations, difficulty walking without special equipment, and trouble with cognition. Within the sample adult survey, the NHIS asks respondents questions about sensory, physical, and mental health impairments. The specific questions used to identify each of these, and the definition of disability, are described in the next section of this chapter.

There are several strengths of the NHIS relative to other national surveys. The NHIS contains the largest amount of health-related data of all the major surveys, including particularly unique and extensive data on health insurance, health care access and utilization, health status, and health-related conditions and behaviors. The NHIS also contains a broad set of data on disability-related topics, including activity limitations, measures of psychological distress, and limitations in sensory and work ability. Moreover, the NHIS questionnaire asks those who indicated a limitation to a functional activity the source or condition of their limitation. Additional strengths of the NHIS include its continuous administration during the past five decades, which allows for the comparison of some health trends, and the specialized information contained in the supplemental survey section.

However, there are several limitations to the data contained in the NHIS. One significant drawback is the omission of several segments of the population, including the institutionalized and homeless populations, nationals living abroad, and members of the armed forces (although families of active duty military members are included). Second, the NHIS has much less comprehensive socioeconomic information than some of the other major surveys, such as the CPS and SIPP. Although the survey contains a section on income and assets, the NHIS has experienced a high rate of nonresponse for these types of questions.

Moreover, income data are only reported at the family level, making analysis of personal income impossible. Third, due to confidentiality concerns, the NHIS sample does not allow for state-level estimates. This is a significant drawback when analyzing the impact of area-specific public programs or analyzing state-level changes in the health status of the population with disabilities.

Finally, the NHIS core questionnaire items are redesigned every 10 to 15 years, the latest in 1982 and 1997. The redesign has an important impact on the use of the NHIS to track long-term trends. It can be used to track annual trends between 1982 and 1996, for instance, and between 1997 and 2006 but, because of the substantial differences in the questionnaires across these two periods, as well as other changes in the design and administration of the NHIS, it may not be used to track trends across the two periods. Thus, the survey is unable to track the long-term trends from 1980 to the present, whereas the CPS is able to measure such trends using the work-limitation definition. Because many of the important social indicators are sensitive to the business cycle, as shown in Houtenville et al. (2009); Weathers and Wittenburg (2009); and Burkhauser, Rovba, and Weathers (2009), and because the peak and trough years of the business cycle span the two different NHIS time periods, the survey is limited in its ability to describe important changes in social indicators over time. See National Center for Health Statistics (2003) for further details on the NHIS redesign and Hendershot, Harris, and Stapleton (2009) for a more detailed discussion of the strengths and weaknesses of the most recent NHIS data and the relationship between disability and health that it captured.

Survey of Income and Program Participation (SIPP)

The primary purpose of the SIPP, which is administered by the U.S. Census Bureau, is to collect information on the income and program participation of a nationally representative sample of households and individuals living in the United States. The SIPP has been conducted 13 times since it was first implemented in 1984, and each survey is referred to as a "panel" because it includes multiple interviews of sample members conducted every four months over a period of at least 32 months. The 2001 SIPP panel is used in this volume, and it includes nine waves of interviews occurring at four-month intervals.[9]

The SIPP sample is designed to be representative of the civilian noninstitutionalized population living in the United States. This includes the population 1) living in households; 2) living in some types of GQ, such as dormitories, rooming houses, and religious group dwellings; and 3) foreign visitors and their families who work or attend school in this country.[10] Persons who were at least 15 years of age at the time of the interview were eligible to be in the survey. The population excludes 1) institutionalized persons, such as correctional facility inmates and nursing home residents, 2) crew members of merchant vessels, 3) armed forces personnel living in military barracks, and 4) U.S. citizens residing abroad. Members from approximately 35,000 households completed 2001 SIPP wave 1 interviews. The sample sizes for subsequent waves are lower.[11]

Each SIPP interview includes core and topical module questionnaires. The core questions, which address demographic, program participation, and employment information over the previous four-month period, are repeated in each wave of interviews. Topical modules cover a broad range of subjects that vary by interview wave within each panel. The modules also vary by panel and include questions on personal history, child care, assets, program eligibility, child support, disability, school enrollment, taxes, and annual income. In some cases, the topical modules within a panel are repeated in subsequent interviews.

The SIPP includes one question about the presence of a work limitation during the core interview and more detailed questions about health, functional limitation status, and medical history in two topical modules. The question about the presence of a work limitation in the core interview is as follows: "Does [insert name] have a physical, mental, or other health condition which limits the kind or amount of work [insert name] can do?" There is an extensive set of more detailed disability questions in the two topical modules that have been used to identify broader concepts of disability (Steinmetz 2004). The next section describes how these questions are used in this volume to establish different conceptual definitions of disability.

The SIPP has several advantages for disability research. First, it contains a large set of questions on health and disability status that researchers can use to construct a variety of disability measures. Second, it contains a longitudinal component because sample members are reinterviewed every four months for between two to four years, depending on the SIPP panel. Thus, users can examine changes at the individual level among persons with a disability in terms of their health, employment, income, and program participation (e.g., how health is related to employment and economic well-being over time). A third advantage is that data users can obtain special permission to link individual-level Social Security Administration (SSA) administrative data on program participation and earnings to SIPP sample members. As described in more detail in Stapleton, Wittenburg, and Thornton (2009), the ability to link the SIPP to SSA administrative records is important for researchers interested in examining longer term trends in earnings and program dynamics among people with disabilities.

Despite these advantages, the SIPP is also limited in the extent to which it can support other types of disability analyses. The most notable drawback has to do with cross-panel and within-panel comparisons based on the work-limitation question. Because the SIPP is essentially a longitudinal panel, its usefulness in producing trend estimates is limited, particularly relative to cross-sectional surveys such as the CPS and the NHIS. In addition, prevalence rates of work limitations across interview waves change because of the placement of the question (Maag and Wittenburg 2003). Finally, attrition bias is significant, especially from wave 1 to wave 2, and must therefore be accounted for in any SIPP-based analysis.

TRANSLATING SURVEY DISABILITY QUESTIONS INTO CONCEPTS

The heterogeneity among these five data sets in the questions they use to capture the working-age population with disabilities suggests that there will be substantial differences among them in the data they capture. To demonstrate these differences, this section classifies these disability questions into the disability taxonomy flowing from the ICF. This disability taxonomy places each survey question into one of six operational concepts—sensory, physical, or mental impairments and ADL, IADL, and work limitations—each of which flows from the three

previously discussed basic ICF concepts, impairment, activity limitation, and participation restriction.

Because the questions used in these data sets were developed before
the ICF came into being, many are not directly related to the specific
ICF-defined impairments, activity limitations, or participation restrictions concepts. For example, the ACS asks whether a person is blind
or deaf without relating it to the ability to perform specific activities or
participation restrictions, which may allow the concept to be interpreted
as impairment, activity limitation, or participation restriction.

Even within each of these specific disability classifications, there
are substantial differences in the questions used to identify a disability.
These differences include the length of time of the limitation or impairment—some survey questions include qualifiers such as a "long lasting
condition" or a condition "lasting six months or longer," whereas others
do not; how a survey question captures the level of difficulty carrying
out a task or activity—some surveys ask whether a person has difficulty
performing an activity, whereas others ask whether the person needs
assistance from another person to do an activity; and the relationship
between a health impairment and the performance of an activity—some
questions define hearing impairment as a health condition that results
in long-lasting deafness, whereas others define hearing impairment as
difficulty in hearing what is said in normal conversation even with a
hearing aid. Each of these differences changes the definition of disability and may result in variation in estimates of the population across
surveys.

In this section, we present the specific questions used to identify
each disability classification in the five survey instruments and show
the differences in both the population and prevalence rates for each concept across the data sources.[12] Table 2.1 reports the population size and
prevalence rate for each disability concept based on data from the five
data sets.

Sensory Impairments

Sensory impairments include difficulty hearing or seeing. The specific questions used to identify these concepts in each survey are shown
in Table 2.2. The ACS and 2000 Decennial Census include one survey

Table 2.1 Population Size and Prevalence Rate by Survey and Disability Type (Adults Aged 25–61)

Survey year and source	Any disability	Sensory impairment	Physical impairment	Mental impairment	ADL	IADL	Work limitation
Population (in thousands)							
2003 ACS	17,146	3,944	10,819	5,746	2,925	4,227	9,854
2003 CPS-ASEC	11,155	—	—	—	—	—	11,155
2000 Decennial Census	14,005	3,346	9,447	5,218	2,627	—	—
2002 NHIS	23,192	2,730	14,546	4,628	1,351	3,169	13,726
2002 SIPP	26,620	6,490	18,790	4,394	3,363	4,931	14,420
Prevalence rate (%)							
2003 ACS	11.9	2.7	7.5	4.0	2.0	2.9	6.9
2003 CPS-ASEC	7.8	—	—	—	—	—	7.8
2000 Decennial Census	5.5	2.6	6.8	3.8	1.9	—	—
2002 NHIS	16.7	2.0	10.5	3.3	1.0	2.3	9.9
2002 SIPP	18.7	4.6	13.2	3.1	2.4	3.5	10.1

SOURCE: Weathers (2005, ACS), Burkhauser and Houtenville (2006, CPS), Erickson and Houtenville (2005, Decennial Census), Harris, Hendershot, and Stapleton (2005, NHIS), and Wittenburg and Nelson (2006, SIPP).

**Table 2.2 Survey Questions Used by National Surveys to Identify
Sensory Limitations**

Data source	Question
ACS	Does this person have any of the following long lasting conditions: blindness, deafness, or a severe vision or hearing impairment?
CPS-ASEC	None
Decennial Census 2000	Does this person have any of the following long lasting conditions: blindness, deafness, or a severe vision or hearing impairment?
NHIS	Which statement best describes your hearing without a hearing aid: good, a little trouble, a lot of trouble, deaf
	Do you have any trouble seeing, even when wearing glasses or contact lenses? (If yes) Are you blind or unable to see at all?
SIPP	Do you have any difficulties seeing the words and letters in ordinary newspaper print even when wearing glasses or contact lenses if you usually wear them? (Note: "person is blind" response is included in addition to yes/ no response.) Are you able to see the words and letters in ordinary newspaper print at all?
	Do you have difficulty hearing what is said in a normal conversation with another person even when wearing your hearing aid? (Note: "person is deaf" response is included in addition to yes/no response.) Are you able to hear what is said in normal conversation at all?
	Do you have difficulty having your speech understood (Note to interviewer: do not enter yes if they simply can't speak English)? In general, are people able to understand your speech at all?

SOURCE: Actual survey questionnaires as reported in Weathers (2005, ACS),
Burkhauser and Houtenville (2006, CPS), Erickson and Houtenville (2005, Decennial
Census), Harris, Hendershot, and Stapleton (2005, NHIS), and Wittenburg and Nelson
(2006, SIPP).

question that captures long-lasting conditions resulting in hearing or visual impairments, including deafness and blindness. The NHIS includes two questions, one that asks about the level of difficulty hearing without a hearing aid and prompts the respondent to provide one of four answers ranging from "good" hearing to being deaf. The other asks whether the respondent has difficulty seeing even when wearing glasses and/or contact lenses and allows the respondent to provide a "yes" or "no" answer. Finally, the SIPP includes several questions that ask whether the hearing or vision problem results in difficulty with the performance of specific activities and a follow-up question that asks whether the problem prevents the respondent from performing the activity.

Estimates of the size of the working-age population with a sensory impairment and the corresponding prevalence rate differ substantially across the surveys (Table 2.1). The differences may reflect differences in the survey design or differences in the question wording. The NHIS data has the lowest population estimate (2.7 million people) and prevalence rate (2.0 percent), whereas the SIPP has the largest population estimate (6.5 million) and prevalence rate (4.6 percent). Estimates from the ACS data (population, 3.9 million; prevalence rate, 2.7 percent) are similar to those from the 2000 Decennial Census.

Physical Impairments

Physical impairments include difficulty carrying out physical functions or activities, and they may cut across ICF impairment and activity concepts. For example, the NHIS survey instrument asks whether the person can, without the use of special equipment, perform a series of different physical activities. Because some respondents may be able to perform these activities with the use of special equipment, it is unclear as to whether the person has an impairment that, with the use of special equipment, does not result in an activity limitation. Table 2.3 shows the questions used to identify physical impairments in each of the national surveys.

The surveys also differ in both the number and content of the questions used to identify physical impairments. For example, the ACS and Decennial Census both include one question that identifies whether the person has a long-lasting health condition that limits one or more basic

Table 2.3 Survey Questions Used by National Surveys to Identify Physical Limitations

Data source	Question
ACS	Does this person have any of the following long lasting conditions: b. A condition that substantially limits one or more basic physical activities such as walking, climbing stairs, reaching, lifting, or carrying?
CPS-ASEC	None
Decennial Census 2000	Does this person have any of the following long lasting conditions: b. A condition that substantially limits one or more basic physical activities such as walking, climbing stairs, reaching, lifting, or carrying?
NHIS	By yourself, and without the use of special equipment, how difficult is it for you to… a. Walk a quarter of a mile—about 3 city blocks? b. Walk up 10 steps without resting? c. Stand or be on your feet for about 2 hours? d. Sit for about 2 hours? e. Stoop, bend, or kneel? f. Reach over your head? By yourself, and without the use of special equipment, how difficult is it for you to…. a. Use your fingers to grasp or handle small objects? b. Lift or carry something as heavy as 10 pounds such as a bag full of groceries? c. Push or pull large objects like a living room chair? Respondent is classified as having a physical disability if respondent answers "can't do at all" or "very difficult" to any question.

Table 2.3 (continued)

Data source	Question
SIPP	Do you have any difficulty lifting and carrying something as heavy as 10 pounds—such as a bag of groceries?
	Are you able to lift and carry a 10 pound bag of groceries at all?
	Do you have any difficulty pushing or pulling large objects such as a living room chair?
	Are you able to push or pull such large objects at all?
	Do you have any difficulty...?
	a. Standing or being on your feet for one hour?
	b. Sitting for one hour?
	c. Stooping, crouching, or kneeling?
	d. Reaching over your head?
	Do you have difficulty using your hands and fingers to do things such as picking up a glass or grasping a pencil?
	Are you able to use your hands and fingers to grasp and handle at all?
	Do you have any difficulty walking up a flight of 10 stairs?
	Are you able to walk up a flight of 10 stairs at all?
	Do you have any difficulty walking a quarter of a mile—about 3 city blocks?
	Are you able to walk a quarter of a mile at all?
	Do you have any difficulty using an ordinary telephone?
	Are you able to use an ordinary telephone at all?

SOURCE: Actual survey questionnaires as reported in Weathers (2005, ACS), Burkhauser and Houtenville (2006, CPS), Erickson and Houtenville (2005, Decennial Census), Harris, Hendershot, and Stapleton (2005, NHIS), and Wittenburg and Nelson (2006, SIPP).

physical activities such as walking, climbing stairs, reaching, lifting, or carrying. The NHIS includes nine separate questions that identify the amount of difficulty with these activities, as well as with other physical activities such as sitting or standing for about two hours, using fingers to grasp or handle small objects, lifting or carrying up to 10 pounds (e.g., a bag full of groceries), and pushing or pulling large objects (e.g., a living room chair). A key difference with the NHIS is that it allows the respondent to use a response scale ranging from "not at all difficult" to "can't do at all," whereas the ACS and Decennial Census use a "yes/no" response. Finally, the SIPP questions are similar to those in the NHIS, but the SIPP uses a different method to identify the degree of difficulty. The SIPP questionnaire first asks whether the person has difficulty performing a specific physical activity and then asks whether he or she is able to perform that activity at all.

The estimates of the working-age population with a physical impairment are higher among data sources that use a larger number of questions to capture a broader range of physical impairments. The SIPP data contain the most questions, and the estimates show 18.8 million working-age Americans with a physical impairment and a prevalence rate of 13.2 percent. The NHIS contains fewer physical impairment questions than the SIPP but more than the ACS and Decennial Census. NHIS estimates show 14.5 million working-age Americans with a physical impairment and a prevalence rate of 10.5 percent. Estimates based on the ACS data show 10.8 million working-age persons with physical impairment and a prevalence rate of 7.5 percent. Estimates from the 2000 Decennial Census are somewhat lower than those from the ACS.

Mental Impairments

Mental impairments include health conditions that affect a person's ability to perform basic mental activities. The questions used to identify these impairments are shown in Table 2.4. As with the sensory and physical impairment questions, these may capture both impairments and activity limitations, and they do so to varying degrees across the different survey instruments.

Table 2.4 Survey Questions Used by National Surveys to Identify Mental Limitations

Data source	Question
ACS	Because of a physical, mental, or emotional condition lasting 6 months or more, does this person have any difficulty in doing any of the following activities: a. Learning, remembering, or concentrating?
CPS ASEC	None
Decennial Census 2000	Because of a physical, mental, or emotional condition lasting 6 months or more, does this person have any difficulty in doing any of the following activities: a. Learning, remembering, or concentrating?
NHIS	During the PAST 30 DAYS how often did you feel... a. So sad nothing could cheer you up? b. Nervous? c. Restless or fidgety? d. Hopeless? e. That everything was an effort? f. Worthless? Responses were assigned the following point value: (0) None of the time/Don't know/refused (1) A little of the time (2) Some of the time (3) Most of the time (4) All of the time. Individuals with a combined score of 13 or greater were classified, under the Kessler Index, as having a mental disability.
SIPP	Do you have... a. A learning disability such as dyslexia? b. Mental retardation? c. A developmental disability such as autism or cerebral palsy? d. Alzheimer's disease or any other serious problem with confusion or forgetfulness? e. Any other mental or emotional condition?

SOURCE: Actual survey questionnaires as reported in Weathers (2005, ACS), Burkhauser and Houtenville (2006, CPS), Erickson and Houtenville (2005, Decennial Census), Harris, Hendershot, and Stapleton (2005, NHIS), and Wittenburg and Nelson (2006, SIPP).

The differences in the methods used to measure mental impairments are substantial across the national data sources, perhaps reflecting the challenges related to identifying what constitutes a mental disability and how to measure it in survey data. For example, in some cases, the SIPP uses a health-condition-based definition that asks whether the person has conditions such as autism or cerebral palsy, Alzheimer's disease, or other health conditions that are usually related to a person's capability to perform mental activities. The ACS and Decennial Census question focuses on how a person's health condition affects his or her ability to perform activities such as learning, remembering, and concentrating.

The measure used for the NHIS is the Kessler Index (Kessler et al. 2002, 2003), which is based on the person's assessment of how often, over the course of the past 30 days, he or she felt: a) so sad nothing could cheer him up, b) nervous, c) restless or fidgety, d) hopeless, e) that everything was an effort, or f) worthless. The response to each item was assigned a point value ranging from 0 to 4.[13] The Kessler Index identifies those with an aggregated score of 13 or greater as having a mental disability.

The SIPP mental impairment measure is based almost solely on a health condition measure. A person is considered to have a mental impairment if they have a learning disability (e.g., dyslexia), mental retardation, a developmental disability (e.g., autism or cerebral palsy), Alzheimer's disease or any other serious problem with confusion or forgetfulness, or any other mental or emotional condition.

The estimates of the working-age population with a mental impairment and the corresponding prevalence rate are largest in the ACS, with 5.7 million working-age people and a prevalence rate of 4.0 percent. Estimates from the Decennial Census are slightly lower than those in the ACS. The NHIS and SIPP estimates are very similar to each other—data from the NHIS show 4.6 million people with a mental impairment and a prevalence rate of 3.3 percent, and the SIPP estimates are 4.4 million people and a 3.1 percent prevalence rate.

Activities of Daily Living Limitations

ADL questions are used to identify whether survey respondents have a health condition that makes it difficult to perform normal everyday activities such as dressing, eating, bathing, using the toilet, getting in and out of a bed or chair, or getting around inside the home. These questions were originally used to construct an index measuring the physical functioning of the elderly and chronically ill patients, but they are now being used for the broader population in national surveys (Mathiowetz 2000).

The differences across the questions in each of the data sets reflect 1) the number of questions used to identify the presence of an ADL limitation, 2) the number of ADL limitations mentioned in the question or set of questions, 3) the type and duration of the health condition, and 4) the severity of the limitation (any difficulty, need help from others). Table 2.5 shows the questions used in each of the data sets. The ACS and Decennial Census use one question that focuses on only three activities, specifies a physical, mental, or emotional condition lasting at least six months, and asks whether the person has any difficulty with the activity. The NHIS also includes one question, but it includes four activities, specifies a physical, mental, or emotional condition without a duration qualifier, and asks whether the person needs the help of other persons with personal care needs. Finally, the SIPP uses six questions, includes six activities, specifies a physical or mental health condition without a duration qualifier, and asks whether the person has difficulty with any of the activities.

The implied severity of the activity limitation within the questions appears to be related to the population and prevalence estimates. The NHIS, which may be limited to relatively severe limitations because the question defines an ADL limitation as needing the help of other persons, produces the lowest working-age population estimate (1.3 million) and prevalence rate (1.0 percent). The SIPP, which defines an ADL limitation as difficulty with any one of the six activities, has the largest population estimate (3.3 million) and prevalence rate (2.4 percent).

Instrumental Activities of Daily Living Limitations

IADL questions ask about the level of difficulty performing tasks such as preparing meals, doing housework, managing finances, using a telephone, and shopping. Jette and Badley (2000) describe some of the conceptual issues about using IADL questions to measure disability.

Table 2.5   Survey Questions Used by National Surveys to Identify Limitations in Activities of Daily Living (ADLs)

Data source	Question
ACS	Because of a physical, mental, or emotional condition lasting 6 months or more, does this person have any difficulty in doing any of the following activities: b. Dressing, bathing, or getting around inside the home?
CPS-ASEC	None
Decennial Census 2000	Because of a physical, mental, or emotional condition lasting 6 months or more, does this person have any difficulty in doing any of the following activities: b. Dressing, bathing, or getting around inside the home?
NHIS	Because of a physical, mental, or emotional problem do you need the help of other persons with personal care needs, such as eating, bathing, dressing, or getting around inside the home?
SIPP	Because of a physical or mental health condition, do you have difficulty doing any of the following by yourself? (Note to interviewer: this excludes the effects of temporary conditions—if an aid is used, ask whether the person has difficulty when using the aid) a. Getting around INSIDE the home? c. Getting in and out of bed or a chair? d. Taking a bath or shower? e. Dressing? g. Eating? h. Using or getting to the toilet?

SOURCE: Actual survey questionnaires as reported in Weathers (2005, ACS), Burkhauser and Houtenville (2006, CPS), Erickson and Houtenville (2005, Decennial Census), Harris, Hendershot, and Stapleton (2005, NHIS), and Wittenburg and Nelson (2006, SIPP).

As with the ADLs, the differences across the questions in each of the data sets are the 1) number of questions used to identify the presence of an IADL limitation, 2) number of IADL limitations mentioned in the question or set of questions, 3) type and duration of the health condition, and 4) severity of the limitation (any difficulty, need help from others, etc.). Table 2.6 shows the questions used in each of the data sets. The ACS and Decennial Census use one question, focus on only one activity (going outside the home for shopping or a visit to the doctor's office), specify a physical, mental, or emotional condition lasting at least six months, and ask whether the person has any difficulty with the activity. The NHIS also includes one question, but it includes four activities, specifies a physical, mental, or emotional condition without a duration qualifier, and asks whether the person needs the help of other persons with his/her everyday routine. Finally, the SIPP uses six questions, includes four activities, specifies a physical or mental health condition without a duration qualifier, and asks whether the person has difficulty with any of the activities.

Similar to the differences for the ADL estimates, the differences across the national surveys in the working-age population with an IADL limitation and prevalence estimates appear to be linked to differences in the question content. The NHIS uses the most severe definition (needs the help of other persons) and has the lowest population estimate (3.1 million) and prevalence rate (2.3 percent) among the national data sources. The SIPP uses the least severe definition and has the highest population estimate (4.9 million) and prevalence rate (3.5 percent). The ACS estimate falls between the two, with a population estimate of 3.1 million and a prevalence rate of 2.9 percent.

Work Limitations

Work-limitation questions focus on the presence of a health condition that either limits or prevents a person from performing paid work. Although most researchers agree that there are substantial limitations to using this question to measure the size and characteristics of the population of persons with a disability, it is useful for examining trends (Burkhauser et al. 2002), studying the population eligible for Social Security disability benefits (Dwyer et al. 2003), or examining the

Table 2.6   Survey Questions Used by National Surveys to Identify Limitations in Instrumental Activities of Daily Living (IADLs)

Data source	Question
ACS	Because of a physical, mental, or emotional condition lasting 6 months or more, does this person have any difficulty in doing any of the following activities: a. Going outside the home alone to shop or visit a doctor's office?
CPS-ASEC	None
Decennial Census 2000	Because of a physical, mental, or emotional condition lasting 6 months or more, does this person have any difficulty in doing any of the following activities: a. Going outside the home alone to shop or visit a doctor's office?
NHIS	Because of a physical, mental, or emotional problem do you need the help of other persons in handling routine needs, such as everyday household chores, doing unnecessary business, shopping, or getting around for other purposes?

SIPP	Because of a physical or mental health condition, do you have difficulty doing any of the following by yourself?
	(Note to interviewer: this excludes the effects of temporary conditions—if an aid is used, ask whether the person has difficulty when using the aid)
	  b. Going OUTSIDE the home, for example, to shop or visit a doctor's office?
	  i. Keeping track of money or bills?
	  k. Doing light housework such as washing dishes or sweeping a floor?
	  l. Taking the right amount of prescribed medicine at the right time?

SOURCE: Actual survey questionnaires as reported in Weathers (2005, ACS), Burkhauser and Houtenville (2006, CPS), Erickson and Houtenville (2005, Decennial Census), Harris, Hendershot, and Stapleton (2005, NHIS), and Wittenburg and Nelson (2006, SIPP).

population targeted for vocational rehabilitation services (Adler et al. 1999). The limitations associated with these questions are thoroughly covered in Wunderlich, Rice, and Amado (2002), and the influence of the different ways that the work-limitation question is asked in surveys is described in Banks et al. (2005). Table 2.7 shows the wording of the question for each of the national surveys.

The differences in the work-limitation question in each of the national surveys are related to the definition of the health condition and severity of the work limitation. The ACS defines a health condition as a physical, mental, or emotional condition lasting six months or more and the severity as any difficulty working at a job or business.[14] The CPS-ASEC defines a health condition as a health problem or disability and severity as prevention of or limits on the kind or amount of work the person can do. The NHIS defines a health condition as a physical, mental, or emotional problem and severity as "keeping" a person from working at a job or business. Finally, the SIPP also defines a health condition as a physical, mental, or health condition and severity as limiting the kind and amount of work the person can do.[15]

The estimates of the size and prevalence of the working-age population with a work-limiting health condition range from a low of 9.8 million people and a 6.9 percent prevalence rate in the ACS to a high of 14.4 million people and a 10.1 percent prevalence rate in the SIPP (Table 2.1). The CPS-ASEC estimates are closer to those of the ACS, whereas the NHIS estimates are similar to those of the SIPP.

Disability

Disability is defined as the presence of at least one of the six disability classifications identified above. This definition is similar to the one that the U.S. Census Bureau uses within the ACS and posts on its American FactFinder Web site. It is important to note that the definition was not created to measure the population covered by the ADA nor has it been shown to be a valid measure of the ADA definition.

The national surveys differ in measuring this concept in three important ways. 1) The surveys measure each of the six disability classifications differently. 2) The CPS-ASEC and the 2000 Decennial Census do not capture all the disability concepts. The CPS-ASEC captures only

Table 2.7 Survey Questions Used by National Surveys to Identify Work Limitations

Data source	Question
ACS	Because of a physical, mental, or emotional condition lasting 6 months or more, does this person have any difficulty in doing any of the following activities:
	b. Working at a job or business?
CPS-ASEC	Do you have a health problem or disability which prevents you from working or which limits the kind or amount of work you can do?
	Does anyone in this household have a health problem or disability which prevents them from working or which limits the kind or amount of work they can do? If yes to . . . , who is that? Anyone else?
Decennial Census 2000	Because of a physical, mental, or emotional condition lasting 6 months or more, does this person have any difficulty in doing any of the following activities:
	b. Working at a job or business?
NHIS	Does a physical, mental, or emotional problem NOW keep you from working at a job or business?
	Does a physical, mental, or emotional problem NOW keep any of these family members from working at a job or business? (interviewer is instructed to read each adult family member's name)
	Are you limited in the kind OR amount of work you can do because of a physical, mental, or emotional problem?
	Are any of these family members limited in the kind OR amount of work they can do because of a physical, mental, or emotional problem? (interviewer is instructed to read each adult family member's name)
SIPP	Do you have a physical, mental or health condition that limits the kind and amount of work you can do?

SOURCE: Actual survey questionnaires as reported in Weathers (2005, ACS), Burkhauser and Houtenville (2006, CPS), Erickson and Houtenville (2005, Decennial Census), Harris, Hendershot, and Stapleton (2005, NHIS), and Wittenburg and Nelson (2006, SIPP).

the work-limitation concept, and the 2000 Decennial Census work-limitation measure is not used here because of potential problems that have been identified with that question. 3) The five surveys capture different overall populations (e.g., some include noninstitutional GQs and others do not) that are likely to disproportionately include working-age people with disabilities (see She and Stapleton 2009).

These differences contribute to substantial variation in the estimates of the size of the population of persons with a disability and the prevalence rate, as shown in the first column of Table 2.1. The surveys that use a larger number of questions tend to find a larger population with disabilities. The population estimate based upon the CPS data, which uses only one work-limitation question, is the lowest among the data sources, with a population estimate of a little more than 11 million working-age people with disabilities and a prevalence rate of 7.8 percent. Estimates using the ACS data are somewhat larger, with 17.1 million working-age people with a disability and a prevalence rate of 11.9 percent. The NHIS and the SIPP, which use a larger number of questions and both cover some portion of the population living in GQs, have the largest estimates of the working-age population with a disability and the prevalence rate. Estimates based upon the NHIS find 23.1 million working-age people with a disability and a prevalence rate of 16.7 percent, and estimates using the SIPP data show 26.6 million working-age people with a disability and a prevalence rate of 18.7 percent.

STRENGTHS AND LIMITATIONS OF THE DATA SOURCES

Each of the data sets discussed above has its strengths and limitations. The data set that is most appropriate to use to answer a research or policy question ultimately depends on the question itself. In many cases, no perfect data source exists to answer the question, so the researcher must weigh the strengths and limitations of each existing data set. This chapter considers the relative strengths of the five data sets discussed above in answering four generic questions. Later chapters will do likewise with respect to measuring employment (Weathers and Wittenburg 2009), income (Burkhauser, Rovba, and Weathers 2009), poverty (Burkhauser, Houtenville, and Rovba 2009), and health (Hendershot, Harris, and Stapleton 2009) of the working-age population with disabilities.

Capturing Alternative Populations with Disabilities

The number of questions used to identify individuals with a disability, along with the wording of these questions, varies substantially across the national surveys. The NHIS and SIPP provide data users with the largest set of questions to capture alternatively defined populations with disabilities. One advantage of these data sources is that they can be used to capture clearly defined disability subgroups. Houtenville (2003) provides a good example of the strength of the NHIS in his examination of the employment and economic well-being of those with severe vision impairments.[16]

The ACS and the 2000 Decennial Census long form provide users with six questions that may be used to identify a broad population of persons with disabilities, but both of these sources also provide limited opportunities to capture specific subgroups with disabilities. It is not possible to use these data to identify a subpopulation that has vision impairments because the question does not allow users to separate those with vision impairments from those with severe hearing impairments. Similar problems exist for examining specific types of ADL limitations, IADL limitations, physical impairments, and mental impairments.

The CPS questionnaire contains only a work-limitation measure of disability. Although this definition is suitable for some purposes, it is not suitable for others. For instance, whereas the CPS can provide information on trends in the employment of working-age people with disabilities, it will clearly understate the level of employment in the broader population with disabilities, as will be seen in Weathers and Wittenburg (2009). Thus, data users must exercise caution when using the CPS to examine the broader population of persons with a disability.

Capturing State- and Local-Level Disability Populations

The 2000 Decennial Census and the ACS allow data users to construct estimates at a variety of different geographic levels, including counties, cities and towns, ZIP codes, census tracts, and tribal territories. The Census Bureau recommends using the ACS rather than the CPS to construct state-level estimates. However, in some circumstances, the CPS-ASEC may be the only source that contains state-level data on a particular topic, such as health insurance coverage.

The 2000 Decennial Census and the ACS allow data users to construct small-area estimates. They may also be used to construct estimates at a variety of different geographic levels, including counties, cities and towns, ZIP codes, census tracts, tribal territories, and other levels. The 2006 ACS data are available for geographic areas with a population of 65,000 or more, including 783 counties, 436 congressional districts, 621 metropolitan and micropolitan statistical areas, and all 50 states and the District of Columbia. Beginning in 2008, the ACS data will be available for all areas with a population of 20,000 or more, and beginning in 2010, it will cover even smaller geographic areas. Small-area estimates provide policymakers and service providers with the data necessary to identify how local services can be more effectively targeted to persons with a disability and how publicly and privately funded disability programs can be more effectively administered.

Capturing Long-Term Time Trends

The CPS and NHIS may be used to estimate various types of time trends. The NHIS is limited to some extent by the major redesign of the survey that occurred in 1997. Despite its limitations, it has proved extremely useful to verify that the trends in the employment rate of persons with disabilities found in the CPS-ASEC are not an artifact of the definition of disability used (Burkhauser et al. 2002).

The CPS allows data users to examine annual time trends for the population both with and without a work limitation since 1980. These data have been used to examine long-term trends in the population with a work limitation, including their employment rate, poverty rate, and other measures of economic well-being. The data have also been used to examine how the characteristics of those with a work limitation have changed over time and how these changes may be related to the declining employment rate among persons with a disability (Houtenville and Daly 2003). In doing so, the CPS provides information that policymakers can use to understand the underlying structure of long-term trends in employment and economic well-being and the ways that public policy may be used to improve the lives of people with disabilities.

Capturing Movements of Individuals over Time

The SIPP, and to a limited extent the CPS, reinterview sample members, which allows data users to examine how a person's circumstances change over time. The CPS-ASEC reinterviews some participants about one year later. Researchers have used reinterview data to identify those who have longer term disabilities, which are referred to as two-period work limitations and defined as a report of a work limitation in both the first interview and the reinterview. For example, Houtenville and Burkhauser (2004) used the CPS-ASEC to show that the decline in employment appeared to occur soon after SSA rule changes were implemented that made it somewhat easier to qualify for disability benefits.

The SIPP reinterviews sample members up to nine times during the course of a SIPP panel. This allows data users to examine changes over an almost three-year period. Researchers have used the longitudinal component to study those with longer term disabilities, which are defined as a report of a disabling condition in consecutive interviews (Wittenburg and Nelson 2006). The data have also been used to examine changes in employment (Stapleton, Wittenburg, and Maag 2005), income (Bound, Burkhauser, and Nichols 2003), and program participation (Stapleton, Wittenburg, and Maag 2005).

SUMMARY AND EMERGING DEVELOPMENTS TO THE DISABILITY DATA LANDSCAPE

The concept of disability remains contentious, as does the appropriate method of operationally capturing the size and socioeconomic characteristics of those with disabilities in random samples of the population. As a result, dramatic differences can be found in even the most basic statistics on the working-age population with disabilities coming from current data sets sponsored by the federal government. Using a taxonomy that places disability questions found in the five major nationally representative data sets used in the United States into one of six classifications based on ICF concepts of disability, substantial differences were documented. There are differences in the questions used across the data sets to capture each classification, as well as differences in the ability of these data sets to capture all of the classifications. Hence, there are also dramatic differences in the estimates of the total population with a disability. These differences in survey design are responsible for the variations across the data sets discussed in later chapters in both the prevalence of disability found among working-age people and the socioeconomic characteristics of the working-age population with disabilities.

This taxonomy was also used to examine the various strengths and limitations of the current national data sources to answer key disability questions. Although it was shown that at least one of the existing data sources could be used to measure each of these questions, no single existing data set is ideal for answering them all. Indeed, there are substantial gaps in the five surveys that limit the types of analyses that can be performed.

Fortunately, the disability data landscape is rapidly evolving and new data sources provide opportunities to fill these gaps. The Centers for Disease Control (CDC), for example, has recently included two new questions in the Behavioral Risk Factor Surveillance System (BRFSS) to identify the population with disabilities. The BRFSS, which is the world's largest ongoing telephone health survey system, provides an extremely useful new source of data for tracking the health and health behaviors of the population with a disability at the state level (Centers for Disease Control 2006).

The Bureau of Labor Statistics plans to include a new set of questions in the CPS to measure the employment of persons with a disability (McMenamin et al. 2005). This expanded set of disability questions will allow the Census Bureau to provide better statistics on the employment rate, poverty rate, and economic well-being of individuals with a disability.

Finally, the Census Bureau is considering changes to the disability questions within the ACS (Stern 2006). The downside of using new questions in the ACS is that it will delay the date when the ACS may be used to measure trends in both the employment rate and economic well-being for persons with disabilities. However, if these questions are scientifically shown to be an improvement over the ones currently used, then the ACS will provide a more accurate picture of persons with disabilities.

Notes

1. These and other statistics on the working-age population with disabilities can be found in Table 2.1. The differences reported here are similar to ones reported for the entire adult population with disabilities by the Census Bureau using the SIPP (Steinmetz 2004) and the ACS (U.S. Census Bureau n.d.).
2. As will be seen in later chapters, this distinction is one reason that some people may report a work limitation without reporting an impairment.
3. The purpose of the national sample was to compare the national population estimates from the ACS to those from the Decennial Census long form.
4. It also contained demographic data on 31,000 children aged 0–14 years old and 450 Armed Forces members living with civilians either on or off base within these households.
5. For details on the history of the CPS-ASEC sample design, see U.S. Census Bureau (2002).
6. It may also be used to create state-level estimates for many states before 2001.
7. See Adler et al. (1999) for a description of the process used to determine the disability questions that were included in the 2000 Decennial Census.
8. Analysis of the Decennial Census 2000 data by Stern (2003) suggests that the work-limitation measure may be subject to substantial nonsampling error due to respondent and/or enumerator error relating to the enumeration process. In a recent Census Bureau report using Decennial Census 2000 data to examine the population with disabilities, the work limitation question was excluded from the definition of disability due to the potential nonsampling error (Wang 2005).
9. The 2004 SIPP is in the process of being released by the U.S. Census Bureau.
10. People staying in homes, schools, hospitals, or wards for the physically handicapped, mentally retarded, or mentally ill or in drug/alcohol recovery facilities are classified as living in "institutions" and not GQ. For more information on the Census Bureau classification rules, see U.S. Census Bureau (2000).
11. For more information on the sample design of the 2001 SIPP, see U.S. Census Bureau (2005).
12. The Census 2000 questions and estimates are similar to the ACS. The only exception is with the work-limitation question, where the Census 2000 may be subject to substantial measurement error.
13. Specifically, for each item (a) through (f), the survey respondent has an option of five responses. The responses and point values are as follows: "None of the time/ Don't know/Refused" was assigned 0 points, "a little of the time" 1 point, "some of the time" 2 points, "most of the time" 3 points, and "all of the time" 4 points.

14. The 2000 Decennial Census included a work-limitation question, but we do not use it in this volume because of potential problems with the administration of the question identified by the U. S. Census Bureau (Stern 2003).
15. See Wittenburg and Nelson (2006) for a good description of the issues with the work-limitation question in the SIPP.
16. Houtenville (2003) used the 1982–1996 NHIS for his analysis. The 1997–2007 NHIS only asks about specific health conditions for those who report a limitation, and therefore it is not possible to use his methodology to update his analysis. Chapter 7 describes the potential limitations of the NHIS for this purpose in greater detail.

References

Adler, Michele C., Robert F. Clark, Theresa J. DeMaio, Louisa F. Miller, and Arlene F. Saluter. 1999. "Collecting Information on Disability in the 2000 Census: An Example of Interagency Cooperation." *Social Security Bulletin* 62(4): 21–30.

Ballou, Janice, and Jason Markesich. 2009. "Survey Data Collection Methods." In *Counting Working-Age People with Disabilities: What Current Data Tell Us and Options for Improvement*, Andrew J. Houtenville, David C. Stapleton, Robert R. Weathers II, and Richard V. Burkhauser, eds. Kalamazoo, MI: W.E. Upjohn Institute for Employment Research, pp. 265–298.

Banks, James, Arie Kapteyn, James P. Smith, and Arthur van Soest. 2005. "Work Disability Is a Pain in the *****, Especially in England, The Netherlands, and the United States." NBER Working Paper no. 11558. Cambridge, MA: National Bureau of Economic Research.

Bound, John, Richard V. Burkhauser, and Austin Nichols. 2003. "Tracking the Household Income of SSDI and SSI Applicants." In *Research in Labor Economics*, Vol. 22, Soloman W. Polachek, ed. Amsterdam, London, and New York: Elsevier Science, JAI, pp. 113–158.

Burkhauser, Richard V., Mary C. Daly, Andrew J. Houtenville, and Nigar Nargis. 2002. "Self- Reported Work Limitation Data: What They Can and Cannot Tell Us." *Demography* 39(3): 541–555.

Burkhauser, Richard V., and Andrew J. Houtenville. 2006. "A Guide to Disability Statistics from the Current Population Survey—Annual Social and Economic Supplement (March CPS)." Ithaca, NY: Cornell University, Rehabilitation Research and Training Center on Disability Demographics and Statistics.

Burkhauser, Richard V., Andrew J. Houtenville, and Ludmila Rovba. 2009. "Poverty." In *Counting Working-Age People with Disabilities: What Current Data Tell Us and Options for Improvement*, Andrew J. Houtenville,

David C. Stapleton, Robert R. Weathers II, and Richard V. Burkhauser, eds. Kalamazoo, MI: W.E. Upjohn Institute for Employment Research, pp. 193–226.

Burkhauser, Richard V., Ludmila Rovba, and Robert R. Weathers II. 2009. "Household Income." In *Counting Working-Age People with Disabilities: What Current Data Tell Us and Options for Improvement*, Andrew J. Houtenville, David C. Stapleton, Robert R. Weathers II, and Richard V. Burkhauser, eds. Kalamazoo, MI: W.E. Upjohn Institute for Employment Research, pp. 145–192.

Centers for Disease Control and Prevention. 2006. *Disability and Health State Chartbook, 2006: Profiles for Adults with Disabilities*. Atlanta, GA: Centers for Disease Control and Prevention.

CESSI. 2007. "Federal Statutory Definitions of Disability." Prepared for the Interagency Committee on Disability Statistics, 2003. McLean, VA: Cherry Engineering Support Solutions, Inc. http://www.icdr.us/documents/definitions.htm#intro (accessed November 21, 2007).

Dwyer, Debra, Jianting Hu, Denton R. Vaughan, and Bernard Wixon. 2003. "Counting the Disabled: Using Survey Self-Reports to Estimate Medical Eligibility for Social Security's Disability Programs." *Journal of Economic and Social Measurement* 28(3): 109–142.

Erickson, William A., and Andrew J. Houtenville. 2005. "A Guide to Disability Statistics from the 2000 Decennial Census." Ithaca, NY: Cornell University, Rehabilitation Research and Training Center on Disability Demographics and Statistics.

Hale, Thomas W. 2001. "The Lack of a Disability Measure in Today's Current Population Survey." *Monthly Labor Review* 124(6): 38–40.

Harris, Benjamin H., Gerry Hendershot, and David C. Stapleton. 2005. "A Guide to Disability Statistics from the National Health Interview Survey." Ithaca, NY: Cornell University, Rehabilitation Research and Training Center on Disability Demographics and Statistics.

Hendershot, Gerry E., Benjamin H. Harris, and David C. Stapleton. 2009. "Health and Functional Status." In *Counting Working-Age People with Disabilities: What Current Data Tell Us and Options for Improvement*, Andrew J. Houtenville, David C. Stapleton, Robert R. Weathers II, and Richard V. Burkhauser, eds. Kalamazoo, MI: W.E. Upjohn Institute for Employment Research, pp. 227–264.

Houtenville, Andrew J. 2003. "A Comparison of the Economic Status of Working-Age Persons with Visual Impairments and Those of Other Groups." *Journal of Visual Impairment and Blindness* 97(3): 133–148.

Houtenville, Andrew J., and Richard V. Burkhauser. 2004. "Did the Employment of People with Disabilities Decline in the 1990s, and Was the ADA

Responsible? A Replication and Robustness Check of Acemoglu and Angrist (2001)—Research Brief." Ithaca, NY: Cornell University, Rehabilitation Research and Training Center for Economic Research on Employment Policy for Persons with Disabilities.

Houtenville, Andrew J., and Mary C. Daly. 2003. "Employment Declines among People with Disabilities: Population Movements, Isolated Experience, or Broad Policy Concern?" In *The Decline in Employment of People with Disabilities: A Policy Puzzle*, David C. Stapleton and Richard V. Burkhauser, eds. Kalamazoo, MI: W.E. Upjohn Institute for Employment Research, pp. 87–123.

Houtenville, Andrew J., Elizabeth Potamites, William A. Erickson, and S. Antonio Ruiz-Quintanilla. 2009. "Disability Prevalence and Demographics." In *Counting Working-Age People with Disabilities: What Current Data Tell Us and Options for Improvement*, Andrew J. Houtenville, David C. Stapleton, Robert R. Weathers II, and Richard V. Burkhauser, eds. Kalamazoo, MI: W.E. Upjohn Institute for Employment Research, pp. 69–99.

Jette, Alan M., and Elizabeth Badley. 2000. "Conceptual Issues in the Measurement of Work Disability." In *Survey of Measurement of Work Disability: Summary of a Workshop,* Nancy Mathiowetz and Gooloo Wunderlich, eds. Washington, DC: National Academies Press, pp. 4–27.

Kessler, Ronald C., Gavin Andrews, Lisa J. Colpe, Eva Hiripi, Daniel K. Mroczek, Sharon-Lise T. Normand, Ellen E. Walters, and Alan M. Zaslavsky. 2002. "Short Screening Scales to Monitor Population Prevalences and Trends in Non-Specific Psychological Distress." *Psychological Medicine* 32(6): 959-976.

Kessler, Ronald C., Peggy R. Barker, Lisa J. Colpe, Joan F. Epstein, Joseph C. Gfroerer, Eva Hiripi, Mary J. Howes, Sharon-Lise T. Normand, Ronald W. Manderscheid, Ellen E. Walters, and Alan M. Zaslavsky. 2003. "Screening for Serious Mental Illness in the General Population." *Archives of General Psychiatry* 60(2): 184–189.

Maag, Elaine, and David Wittenburg. 2003. "Real Trends or Measurement Problems? Disability and Employment Trends from the Survey of Income and Program Participation." Report submitted to the U.S. Department of Education, National Institute on Disability and Rehabilitation Research. Ithaca, NY: Cornell University, Rehabilitation Research and Training Center for Economic Research on Employment Policy for People with Disabilities.

Mathiowetz, Nancy. 2000. "Methodological Issues in the Measurement of Work Disability." In *Survey of Measurement of Work Disability: Summary of a Workshop*, Nancy Mathiowetz and Gooloo Wunderlich, eds. Washington, DC: National Academies Press, pp. 28–52.

McMenamin, Terence M., Douglas L. Kruse, Tom Hale, and Haejin Kim. 2005. "Designing Questions to Identify People with Disabilities in Labor Force Surveys: A History of the Work of BLS to Measure the Employment Level of Adults with Disabilities." Unpublished technical report. Washington, DC: U.S. Bureau of Labor Statistics. http://www.bls.gov/osmr/pdf/st050190.pdf (accessed September 17, 2008).

Nagi, Saad. 1965. "Some Conceptual Issues in Disability and Rehabilitation." In *Sociology and Rehabilitation,* Martin B. Sussman, ed. Washington, DC: American Sociological Association, pp. 100–113.

———. 1976. "An Epidemiology of Disability Among Adults in the United States." *Milbank Memorial Fund Quarterly: Health and Society* 54(4): 439–467.

National Center for Health Statistics. 2003. "Data File Documentation, National Health Interview Survey, 2002." Hyattsville, MD: National Center for Health Statistics, Centers for Disease Control and Prevention.

She, Peiyun, and David C. Stapleton. 2009. "The Group Quarters Population." In *Counting Working-Age People with Disabilities: What Current Data Tell Us and Options for Improvement*, Andrew J. Houtenville, David C. Stapleton, Robert R. Weathers II, and Richard V. Burkhauser, eds. Kalamazoo, MI: W.E. Upjohn Institute for Employment Research, pp. 351–376.

Stapleton, David C., David Wittenburg, and Elaine Maag. 2005. "A Difficult Cycle: The Effect of Labor Market Changes on the Employment and Program Participation of People with Disabilities." Ithaca, NY: Cornell University, Rehabilitation Research and Training Center for Economic Research on Employment Policy for Persons with Disabilities. http://digitalcommons.ilr.cornell.edu/editcollect/172/ (accessed September 23, 2008).

Stapleton, David C., David C. Wittenburg, and Craig Thornton. 2009. "Program Participants." In *Counting Working-Age People with Disabilities: What Current Data Tell Us and Options for Improvement*, Andrew J. Houtenville, David C. Stapleton, Robert R. Weathers II, and Richard V. Burkhauser, eds. Kalamazoo, MI: W.E. Upjohn Institute for Employment Research, pp. 299–352.

Steinmetz, Erika. 2004. "Americans with Disabilities: 2002." Current Population Reports, P70-107. Washington, DC: U.S. Census Bureau.

Stern, Sharon. 2003. "Counting People with Disabilities." *Proceedings from 2003 Joint Statistical Meetings* (May): 4064–4071. http://www.census.gov/acs/www/Downloads/ACS/finalstern.pdf (accessed June 6, 2008).

———. 2006. "Census Bureau Efforts to Revise Disability-Related Questions in the American Community Survey." Presented at the 2006 StatsRRTC State-of-the-Science conference, "The Future of Disability Statistics: What We Know and Need to Know," held in Washington, DC, October 5–6.

http://www.ilr.cornell.edu/edi/p-srrtc-2006conference.cfm (accessed June 17, 2008).

U.S. Census Bureau. 2000. "Plans and Rules for Taking the Census: Residence Rules." Washington, DC: U.S. Census Bureau. http://www.census.gov/population/www/censusdata/resid_rules.html (accessed November 10, 2008).

———. 2002. "Current Population Survey: Design and Methodology." Technical Paper 63RV. Washington, DC: U.S. Census Bureau. http://www.census.gov/prod/2002pubs/tp63rv.pdf (accessed June 17, 2008).

———. 2003. "American Community Survey Operations Plan." Washington, DC: U.S. Census Bureau. http://www.census.gov/acs/www/downloads/opsplanfinal.pdf (accessed June 17, 2008).

———. 2005. "Source and Accuracy Statement for the 2001 Panel Wave 1–Wave 9 Public Use Files." Washington, DC: U.S. Census Bureau. http://www.census.gov/sipp/sourceac/S&A-2_SIPP2001_w1tow9_20050214.pdf (accessed September 12, 2008).

———. n.d. "American FactFinder." Washington, DC: U.S. Census Bureau. http://factfinder.census.gov/home/saff/main.html?_lang=en (accessed October 17, 2008).

Wang, Qi. 2005. *Disability and American Families: 2000.* CENSR-23. Washington, DC: U.S. Government Printing Office.

Weathers, Robert R. II. 2005. "A Guide to Disability Statistics from the American Community Survey." Ithaca, NY: Cornell University, Rehabilitation Research and Training Center on Disability Demographics and Statistics.

Weathers, Robert R. II, and David C. Wittenburg. 2009. "Employment." In *Counting Working-Age People with Disabilities: What Current Data Tell Us and Options for Improvement,* Andrew J. Houtenville, David C. Stapleton, Robert R. Weathers II, and Richard V. Burkhauser, eds. Kalamazoo, MI: W.E. Upjohn Institute for Employment Research, pp. 101–144.

Wittenburg, David C., and Sandi Nelson. 2006. "A Guide to Disability Statistics from the Survey of Income and Program Participation." Ithaca, NY: Cornell University, Rehabilitation Research and Training Center on Disability Demographics and Statistics.

World Health Organization. 2001. *International Classification of Disability, Health and Functioning.* Geneva: World Health Organization.

———. 2006. *International Statistical Classification of Diseases and Related Health Problems.* 10th rev. Version for 2006. Geneva: World Health Organization.

Wunderlich, Gooloo S., Dorothy P. Rice, and Nicole L. Amado, eds. 2002. *The Dynamics of Disability: Measuring and Monitoring Disability for Social Programs.* Washington, DC: National Academies Press.

3
Disability Prevalence and Demographics

Andrew J. Houtenville
New Editions Consulting, Inc.

Elizabeth Potamites
Mathematica Policy Research, Inc.

William A. Erickson
Cornell University

S. Antonio Ruiz-Quintanilla
Disability and Business Technical Assistance Center

The estimates of the prevalence of disability from various major national surveys have a wide range, depending on which definition of disability is used (Weathers 2009). In this chapter, we focus on trends and demographic patterns in the prevalence of disability among the working-age population and how they vary with the definition used. As much of the research on disability trends has focused on those aged 65 and older, we begin with a brief summary of that literature, then consider the more sparse literature on the working-age population. We then use data from the American Community Survey (ACS), the Current Population Survey (CPS), and the National Health Interview Survey (NHIS) on the working-age household population to examine the following: how disability prevalence rates vary by state of residence, age, ethnicity, education, and sex; evidence on long-term trends in disability prevalence and the extent to which measured trends are sensitive to the definition of disability; how the aging of the baby boom generation (those born between 1946 and 1964) has affected long-term trends; and how long-term trends vary by demographic group.

These statistics have important policy implications for at least four reasons. First, the variation in prevalence across demographic groups will affect the targeting of resources to people with disabilities. For instance, variation in prevalence across states is one factor influencing the distribution of federal funding of programs such as Social Security Disability Insurance (SSDI), Supplemental Security Income, vocational rehabilitation, and Medicare and Medicaid, all of which provide benefits to the working-age population with disabilities. The resources at stake are considerable—public expenditures in federal and federal-state programs for working-age people with disabilities totaled an estimated $276 billion in 2002 (Goodman and Stapleton 2007).

Second, changes in the prevalence of disability in the working-age population influence the productivity of this population, as well as public expenditures and revenues. The employment rate for working-age people with disabilities is much lower than it is for those without disabilities (see Weathers and Wittenburg 2009), so other things held constant, increases in prevalence will lead to reductions in the overall employment rate and lower tax revenues. Federal expenditures to support working-age people with disabilities nearly doubled as a share of all federal outlays from 1984 to 2002 (Goodman and Stapleton 2007). It would be useful to know the extent to which changes in prevalence contributed to that growth.

Third, predictable changes in the demographic composition of the working-age population produce predictable changes in disability prevalence and its effects on public programs. Most notably, the aging of the workforce is having a positive effect on entry of workers into SSDI and Medicare. Increases in prevalence caused by aging are likely to have different implications for public policy than increases attributable to other factors.

Fourth, compositional changes also affect different measures of the well-being of people with disabilities, such as household income (see Burkhauser, Rovba, and Weathers 2009) and poverty rates (see Burkhauser, Houtenville, and Rovba 2009). The distinction between changes in these measures reflecting compositional shifts in the age distribution of workers and those that reflect changes within demographic subgroups have different policy implications. For instance, increases within age groups might signal a need for policy change, whereas increases that reflect compositional changes might suggest reallocation of resources across groups, but no fundamental policy change. How best to react to a change in the prevalence of disability depends on the underlying causes of the change.

BACKGROUND

The *2006 Disability Status Report* (Rehabilitation Research and Training Center on Disability Demographics and Statistics 2007) demonstrates wide variation in prevalence of disability by age, sex, race, ethnicity, and state, using 2006 ACS data. In the next section, we present similar ACS statistics and provide statistics on trends in prevalence from the NHIS and the March Annual Social and Economic Supplement of the CPS (March CPS). We first briefly summarize the extensive literature on prevalence trends among those aged 65 and older and consider the extent to which the lessons learned from this group are applicable to the working-age population. We then turn to the less extensive literature on the working-age population.

One might expect that factors such as medical advances which reduce the risk of death at a given age would also decrease the risk of having a severe disability.[1] For example, Cutler, Landrum, and Stewart (2006) found that improved medical care for cardiovascular disease reduced both disability and death between 1984 and 1999. However, this does not mean that the size of the disabled population is necessarily decreasing. Any decline in the risk of having a severe disability could be more than offset by an increase in the number of people who continue to survive another year with their severe disability.

This is not a trivial statistical point but one with major consequences for the allocation of resources in our society. In the extreme, if the entire improvement in longevity late in life is a function of surviving longer with a severe disability, then this has much greater implications for future social benefits and costs and for the allocation of resources than does the opposite; that is, that the improvement in longevity is a function of being free of severe disabilities.

Freedman, Martin, and Schoeni (2002) provide a systematic review of 12 major studies on trends in the prevalence of disability in elderly populations. They found a general consensus with regard to trends in the prevalence of limitations on instrumental activities of daily living (IADLs) that are *not* accompanied by limitations on activities of daily living (ADLs), or what they called "IADLs-only."[2] Using NHIS data, Crimmins, Saito, and Reynolds (1997) found a decline of 0.7 percentage points (from 14.5 percent to 13.8 percent) in the prevalence of IADLs-only among the population 70 years and older from 1982 to 1993. Using the same data, Schoeni, Freedman, and Wallace (2001) found a further decline in the prevalence of IADLs-only to 10.9 percent in 1996. Using data from the National Long Term Care Survey (NLTCS), Manton and Gu (2001) also found a decline in the age-adjusted IADL-only prevalence among the population 65 years and older, from 6.2 percent in 1984 to 3.2 percent in 1999.

In contrast, studies that focused on ADL limitations have shown mixed results (e.g., Freedman, Martin, and Schoeni 2002). Notably, using the NHIS data, Crimmins, Saito, and Reynolds (1997) and Schoeni, Freedman, and Wallace (2001) found neither an increase nor a decrease in the prevalence of ADL limitations during the 1980s and the early–mid 1990s among people aged 70 and older. Manton and Gu (2001), however, found a decline in the prevalence of ADL limitations between 1982 and 1999, based on the NLTCS data.

A 12-person technical working group, funded by the National Institute on Aging, was convened to reconcile the results from numerous studies and to consider the impact of the wording of questions, survey design, and analytical approach. Although the results were still somewhat unclear, the panel concluded that a per-year decline of about 1.0 percent to 2.5 percent in the prevalence of disability occurred in the mid–late 1990s among the elderly when disability was measured as having difficulty with daily activities and needing help with daily activities (Freedman et al. 2004).

The generally accepted conclusion that there has been a decline in disability among the elderly does not extend to the working-age population. Much less attention has been paid to trends in disability of the latter population, and even less is known with certainty. Using the NHIS data and defining disability as the presence of an ADL and/or IADL limitation, Lakdawalla, Bhattacharya, and Goldman (2004) found an 18 percent rise in disability rates between 1984 and 1996 among noninstitutionalized persons aged 18–69.[3] This increase differed greatly across sub-age groups, and the estimates were strikingly high for those in their prime working years, ages 30–49 (Table 3.1). In contrast, when using the NHIS data for the period following the 1997 NHIS revision, they found no statistically significant changes from 1997 through 2000.

Lakdawalla, Bhattacharya, and Goldman (2004) suggested that two general phenomena may have caused the rise in disability prevalence between 1984 and 1996: 1) changes in the underlying health of the population and/or 2) changes in the reporting of disabilities. They offer obesity as one example of a possible cause that could reflect underlying health changes. Changes in reporting are potentially linked to expansion in the eligibility criteria for SSDI initiated by the Social Security Amendments of 1984, especially for those with psychiatric impairments, followed by changes to the SSA's eligibility criteria for mental disorders in 1985 as well as a later series of court decisions to expand eligibility (Autor and Duggan 2003; Rupp and Stapleton 1995). These changes increased the incentive to report a disability. As a consequence of SSA's indexing methodology, the dollar value of SSDI benefits relative to wages for low-skilled workers increased, which might also have increased the incentives for reporting work limitations (Autor and Duggan 2003; Lakdawalla, Bhattacharya, and Goldman 2004).

Based on the NHIS data, the Institute of Medicine (Institute of Medicine 2007) provided a descriptive look at disability trends from 1984 to 2004 for persons aged 18–44 and 45–64. The findings confirm

Table 3.1 Estimated Increase in Disability Prevalence by Age, 1984–1996

Age group	Increase from 1984 to 1996 (%)
18–29	18
30–39	52
40–49	46
50–59	20
60–69	0

SOURCE: Lakdawalla, Bhattacharya, and Goldman (2004).

and extend the results from Lakdawalla, Bhattacharya, and Goldman (2004)—IADL-only trends were estimated to be flat into the mid 2000s. The report also described trends using part of the NHIS work-limitation question. From 1984 to 1996, the percentage of those unable to work rose slightly for persons aged 18–44 but declined for the 45–64 group. From 1997 to 2004, the percentage of those unable to work declined slightly for both groups.

All of the above work casts doubt on our ability to generalize from results about disability prevalence among the elderly to the working-age population, and highlights the importance of studying the latter group in their own right.

PREVALENCE STATISTICS FOR STATES AND DEMOGRAPHIC GROUPS

In this section we extend the work of Crimmins, Reynolds, and Saito (1999), Lakdawalla, Bhattacharya, and Goldman (2004), and the Institute of Medicine (2007) report by 1) examining variation in disability rates across location and demographic characteristics, 2) expanding the time frame to 2007, and 3) comparing results across data sources and disability definitions.

State Statistics

Tremendous variation in disability rates exists across the states. In 2006, the percentage of the working-age household population that reported having any disability ranged from a low of 9.1 percent in New Jersey to a high of 21.4 percent in West Virginia (Table 3.2 and Figure 3.1). Minnesota and South Dakota are the only other states to have disability rates below 10 percent, and southern states generally have higher disability rates. Eight of the 10 states with the highest prevalence rates (15 percent or higher) are in the South, and the top five states are all in the South (Alabama, Arkansas, Mississippi, Kentucky, and West Virginia). Different measures of disability display a similar pattern. The percentage of people reporting a work limitation ranges from 5.1 per-

Figure 3.1 Prevalence of Any Disability in the Working-Age Population (Aged 25–61) by State, 2006

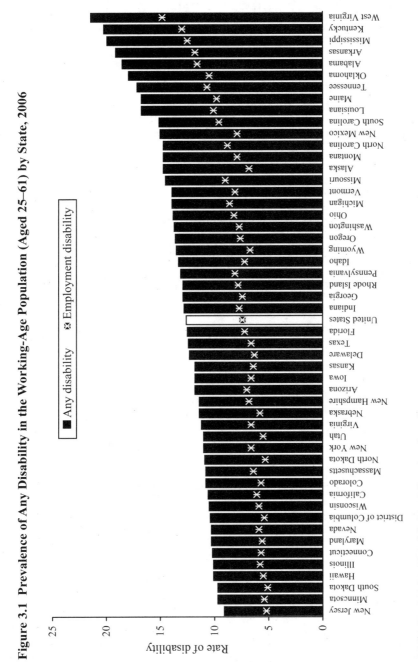

■ Any disability   ✤ Employment disability

SOURCE: 2006 ACS Public Use Microdata Sample

Table 3.2 Disability Prevalence (%) in the Working-Age Household Population by State, 2006

State	Any disability	Sensory disability	Physical disability	Mental disability	Self-care disability	Go-outside-home disability	Employment disability
U.S.	12.6	2.9	7.8	4.5	2.2	3.2	7.4
Alabama	18.5	4.3	12.2	7.0	3.5	5.0	11.6
Alaska	14.7	3.6	8.9	5.1	1.7	2.8	6.8
Arizona	11.8	2.7	7.4	4.3	2.0	3.0	7.0
Arkansas	19.1	4.7	12.8	7.1	3.6	5.1	11.8
California	10.6	2.2	6.3	3.8	1.9	2.7	6.1
Colorado	10.8	2.8	6.4	4.0	1.8	2.5	5.7
Connecticut	10.2	2.1	6.2	3.7	1.6	2.5	5.7
Delaware	12.3	2.3	8.1	4.2	2.5	2.8	6.3
District of Columbia	10.4	2.2	5.7	3.9	1.5	2.3	5.4
Florida	12.5	3.0	8.0	4.3	2.3	3.2	7.2
Georgia	12.9	3.2	7.9	4.5	2.2	3.3	7.4
Hawaii	10.1	2.2	6.3	3.4	1.3	2.4	5.5
Idaho	13.3	3.6	7.9	5.5	2.0	2.8	7.2
Illinois	10.1	2.2	6.1	3.4	1.9	2.7	5.8
Indiana	12.8	2.9	8.0	4.6	2.2	3.3	7.7
Iowa	11.8	2.6	7.2	4.4	1.7	2.4	6.6

Kansas	11.8	2.7	7.5	4.2	1.9	2.5	6.4
Kentucky	20.2	4.9	13.3	7.8	3.7	5.2	13.0
Louisiana	16.7	4.2	10.6	6.1	3.1	4.2	10.1
Maine	16.7	3.5	9.8	6.8	2.5	3.3	9.8
Maryland	10.3	1.9	6.3	3.5	1.7	2.7	5.6
Massachusetts	10.8	2.2	6.2	3.9	1.7	2.6	6.4
Michigan	13.9	3.0	8.6	5.4	2.8	3.8	8.6
Minnesota	9.7	2.3	5.4	3.5	1.4	2.1	5.4
Mississippi	19.9	5.2	12.8	7.7	4.2	5.5	12.5
Missouri	14.5	3.4	9.5	5.6	2.7	4.0	9.0
Montana	14.7	4.6	8.9	5.2	1.9	3.3	7.9
Nebraska	11.4	2.6	6.8	3.8	1.4	2.0	5.8
Nevada	10.3	2.1	6.8	3.0	1.8	2.8	5.9
New Hampshire	11.4	2.7	6.2	4.6	2.0	3.1	6.8
New Jersey	9.1	2.0	5.6	3.1	1.8	2.6	5.2
New Mexico	15.0	4.0	9.3	5.9	2.6	3.4	7.9
New York	11.0	2.2	6.8	3.6	1.9	2.8	6.6
North Carolina	14.7	3.2	9.5	5.1	2.6	3.6	8.8
North Dakota	10.9	2.3	6.7	4.1	1.1	1.9	5.3

(continued)

Table 3.2 (continued)

State	Any disability	Sensory disability	Physical disability	Mental disability	Self-care disability	Go-outside-home disability	Employment disability
Ohio	13.8	3.0	8.5	5.1	2.5	3.6	8.2
Oklahoma	17.9	4.8	11.6	6.3	3.2	4.1	10.5
Oregon	13.6	3.1	8.4	4.9	2.2	3.0	7.6
Pennsylvania	13.1	2.7	8.2	4.6	2.4	3.5	8.1
Rhode Island	12.9	2.5	7.3	4.6	2.0	2.8	7.8
South Carolina	15.1	3.4	10.0	5.3	3.0	4.3	9.6
South Dakota	9.7	2.6	6.4	3.2	1.5	2.1	5.1
Tennessee	17.1	4.3	11.1	6.7	3.0	4.6	10.7
Texas	12.4	3.2	7.8	4.3	2.3	3.1	6.6
Utah	11.0	2.7	6.0	3.9	1.6	2.4	5.5
Vermont	13.9	3.1	8.6	5.5	1.4	3.1	8.1
Virginia	11.2	2.4	7.2	3.8	1.9	2.7	6.6
Washington	13.7	3.3	8.2	5.3	2.2	3.2	7.7
West Virginia	21.4	5.3	15.3	8.3	4.0	6.0	14.8
Wisconsin	10.5	2.3	6.5	4.1	1.9	2.4	5.9
Wyoming	13.5	4.4	7.8	4.6	2.6	3.2	6.7

SOURCE: Tabulations by the authors of the 2006 household ACS sample for persons aged 25–61.

cent in South Dakota to 14.8 percent in West Virginia, and the same five southern states report the highest work limitation rates.[4] Maine and Missouri are the only two nonsouthern states in this top ten. The map in Figure 3.2 shows a band of high disability prevalence rates that sweeps across Appalachia into the South, extending west to Oklahoma and New Mexico.

Statistics for Demographic Groups

Table 3.3 shows 2006 disability rates for the working-age population by sex, age, race/ethnicity, and education.[5] As would be expected, prevalence increases rapidly with age: 55–61-year-olds have rates that are more than triple those for 25–34-year-olds within all disability categories except mental (where it is still more than double). Differences in prevalence rates by race/ethnicity are very high—only 6 percent of

Figure 3.2 Prevalence of Disability in the Working-Age Household Population (Aged 25–61), 2006

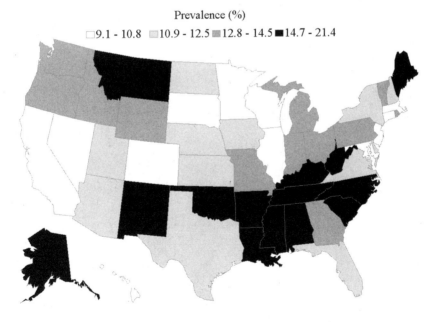

Prevalence (%)

9.1 - 10.8   10.9 - 12.5   12.8 - 14.5   14.7 - 21.4

SOURCE: Authors' calculations based on the 2006 ACS household sample.

Table 3.3 Disability Prevalence (%) by Demographic Group, 2006[a]

Survey and disability type	Total	Sex		Age group				Race/ethnicity[b]						Education			
		Men	Women	25–34	35–44	45–54	55–61	White	Black	Native American/ Alaskan Native	Asian	Some other race(s)	Hisp.	Less than HS	High school	Some coll.	Coll. or more
ACS																	
Any	12.6	12.4	12.9	7.0	9.8	15.3	22.2	12.3	17.3	22.2	6.0	12.0	10.3	23.5	15.3	12.4	5.6
Sensory	2.9	3.3	2.4	1.5	2.2	3.4	5.4	2.9	3.4	6.2	1.3	3.1	2.6	5.3	3.4	2.8	1.4
Physical	7.9	7.3	8.4	3.0	5.6	10.1	16.0	7.7	11.2	14.9	3.0	7.3	6.2	14.7	9.6	7.9	3.2
Mental	4.5	4.4	4.7	3.2	3.9	5.4	6.5	4.4	6.3	8.8	1.9	4.3	3.6	10.8	5.4	4.0	1.6
Self-care	2.2	2.0	2.5	0.9	1.6	2.9	4.3	2.1	3.6	4.5	0.8	2.1	1.7	4.8	2.7	2.1	0.8
Go-outside-home	3.2	2.8	3.6	1.7	2.5	3.9	5.6	3.0	4.8	6.1	1.9	3.0	2.6	7.4	3.9	2.8	1.1
Employment Disability	7.4	7.1	7.7	3.5	5.5	9.2	14.0	7.2	10.9	13.3	3.3	6.5	5.4	15.6	9.2	6.9	2.6
March CPS																	
Work limitation	8.4	8.2	8.6	3.9	6.5	10.5	15.5	8.2	13.5	NA	NA	NA	5.8	16.9	10.5	7.7	3.4

[a]Persons in the Armed Forces excluded.
[b]White Hispanics and black Hispanics are coded as Hispanic.
SOURCE: Calculations by the authors from the 2006 March CPS and the 2006 ACS.

Asian Americans report any disability in the ACS, compared to 17 percent for blacks/African Americans and 22 percent for Native Americans. The well-known negative association between education and disability is also evident. Those with less than a high school education are about five times more likely to report a work-limitation disability than those with a college degree, five times more likely to report a physical disability, and seven times more likely to have a mental disability. There are many possible explanations of the variation across education levels including nature of jobs held, lower levels of educational attainment among children and youth with disabilities, and relationships between education and nutrition, exercise, smoking, and medical care.

The patterns based on sex are less clear. Using the ACS data for 2006, prevalence of a disability among women is about 0.5 percentage points higher than among men. But there are large differences for specific disabilities. Men are 38 percent more likely to have a sensory disability (3.3 percent for men compared to 2.4 percent for women). In contrast, women are 28 percent more likely than men to report a "go-outside-home" disability (3.6 percent of women and 2.8 percent of men).[6]

The bottom row of Table 3.3 shows that variation in the prevalence of work limitations within these subgroups, as measured by the CPS, is similar to the variation in the prevalence of employment disability, as measured in the ACS, even though the prevalence of work limitations is slightly higher.

Prevalence Trends

The direction of long-term trends depends on which definition of disability is used (Figure 3.3 and Table 3.4). The four different measures presented here are the work-limitation measures from the March CPS and the NHIS, the ADL/IADL measure from the NHIS, and a longer term work-limitation measure from the March CPS. This longer term measure takes advantage of the rotating panel used for the CPS interviews—some respondents to each March survey are reinterviewed the following year. Longer term work-limitation prevalence is defined as the percentage of such respondents who reported a work limitation in both the current and the previous interview. The NHIS figures from

Figure 3.3 Disability Prevalence Rates for the Working-Age Population, by Data Source and Disability Measure, 1981–2007

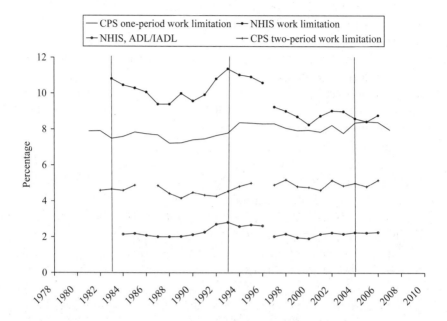

NOTE: There were extensive changes to the NHIS in 1997. Statistics from 1998 on-wards are not comparable to statistics from earlier years. Matched CPS data for the two period work limitation measure are not available in 1986, 1996, and 2007 due to changes in the sampling frame.
SOURCE: Calculations by the authors. See Table 3.4.

before 1997 are not comparable to the data gathered after that year be-cause of extensive changes to the NHIS in 1997. Also, CPS matched data are not available in 1986, 1996, or 2007 because of changes in the sampling frame that were implemented in those years.[7] All of the statistics presented are dated with the year in which the survey was conducted.[8]

Overall, none of the time series presents a definitive trend either upward or downward for disability rates. All but one—the NHIS work-limitation measure after 1997—show some slight upward trend. The CPS work-limitation measure is less than 8 percent in every year before 1994 and greater than 8 percent in 9 out of the 14 years since then. Simi-

Table 3.4 Disability Prevalence Statistics (%) for the Working-Age Population, 1981–2007

Survey year	March CPS		NHIS	
	One-period work limitation	Two-period work limitation[b]	Work limitation	ADL/IADL
1981	7.9	—	—	—
1982	7.9	4.6	—	—
1983	**7.5**	**4.7**	**10.8**	—
1984	7.6	4.6	10.5	2.2
1985	7.8	4.9	10.3	2.2
1986	7.7	—	10.0	2.1
1987	7.7	4.9	9.4	2.0
1988	7.2	4.4	9.4	2.0
1989	7.2	4.2	10.0	2.0
1990	7.4	4.5	9.6	2.1
1991	7.5	4.3	9.9	2.3
1992	7.7	4.3	10.8	2.7
1993	**7.8**	**4.5**	**11.4**	**2.8**
1994	8.4	4.8	11.0	2.6
1995	8.3	5.0	10.9	2.7
1996	8.3	—	10.6	2.6
1997[a]	8.3	4.9	9.3	2.0
1998	8.1	5.2	9.0	2.2
1999	7.9	4.8	8.7	2.0
2000	7.9	4.8	8.3	1.9
2001	7.8	4.6	8.7	2.2
2002	8.2	5.2	9.0	2.2
2003	7.8	4.9	9.0	2.2
2004	**8.4**	**5.0**	**8.6**	**2.3**
2005	8.4	4.8	8.4	2.2
2006	8.4	5.2	8.8	2.3
2007	8.0	—	—	—

NOTE: Years in bold are the trough years of the business cycle.

[a] There were extensive changes to NHIS in 1997. Statistics from 1998 onward are not comparable to statistics from earlier years.

[b] Matched CPS data for the two-period work-limitation measure are not available in 1986, 1996, and 2007 due to changes in the sampling frame.

SOURCE: Calculations by the authors from the 1981–2007 March CPS, 1983–1996 NHIS, and 1997–2006 NHIS (Person Files).

larly, the percentage of people with a longer term work limitation in the matched CPS data is less than 5 percent in every year before 1995 and greater than 5 percent in 5 out of the 11 years since then.[9]

Employment, income, and poverty statistics vary with the business cycle, as illustrated in Chapters 4, 5, and 6, respectively. Hence, in assessing trends in such statistics, it is important to consider comparable points in the business cycle, which can potentially affect the prevalence of work limitations as well. Workers who have been laid off for any reason might be more inclined to report a work limitation than they would if they were still working, especially if they have applied for, or even obtained, SSDI benefits (Autor and Duggan 2003; Lakdawalla, Bhattacharya, and Goldman 2004). If recession-induced increases in SSDI awards have an effect on prevalence trends, the effect might persist even as the economy recovers because only a tiny fraction of beneficiaries leave the rolls to return to work.

To assess the sensitivity of prevalence statistics to such effects, we examined the trends leading up to the three business cycle trough years in our sample period—1983, 1993, and 2004.[10] The statistics suggest a modest effect. For example, from 1989 (near the peak of the 1980s business cycle) to 1993 (the next trough), the one-period CPS work-limitation prevalence measure increased by 7.6 percent and the two-period measure increased by 9.4 percent, the NHIS work-limitation measure increased by 13.7 percent, and the NHIS ADL/IADL measure increased by 39.1 percent. A substantial share of the increase for each measure might reflect other factors, however, because all the measures were increasing during the 1980s expansion. Much smaller increases were observed for all four measures from the business cycle peak of 1999 to the trough of 2004.[11] We will return to this issue later when we consider the effect of the baby boom on prevalence statistics.

If prevalence statistics are sensitive to the business cycle, then assessments of long-term prevalence trends should only compare similar points in the business cycle. A comparison of the prevalence statistics from the three business cycle troughs within the time period examined suggests that there may have been some increase in disability prevalence rates (see Figure 3.4). From the 1983 trough to the 1993 trough, the one-period CPS measure increased by 3.9 percent and the NHIS work-limitation measure increased by 5.1 percent, but the two-period

Figure 3.4 The Prevalence of Work Limitations, Before and After Adjustment for Age, and Median Household Income, 1980–2007

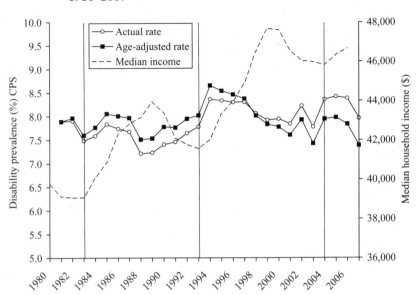

SOURCE: Calculations by the authors using March CPS 1981-2007. Since the CPS asks about income earned in the previous year, the median income series goes from 1980 until 2006. See Table 3.5.

CPS measure actually decreased by 2.6 percent. From the 1993 trough to the 2004 trough, the one-period CPS measure increased by 7.5 percent and the two-period CPS measure increased by 10.1 percent. The NHIS statistics are not comparable for these two years, because of the substantial revisions in 1997.

Aging of the Baby Boom Cohort

One possible cause of these increases in disability prevalence statistics for working-age people is the aging of the baby boom cohort. The oldest members of this large cohort were born in 1946 and turned age 34 in 1980. By 2006, they had turned 60, increasing the average age of the working-age population markedly during this period.

In contrast to the aggregate trends presented above, trends for those aged 55–61 in the CPS work-limitation prevalence statistics indicate a decline in disability prevalence since the early 1980s (Table 3.5). However, the prevalence rate for those aged 45–54 was almost the same in 1983 and 1993 but higher in 2004. It is the increase in the size of this group and the older group (which has far higher absolute levels of disability, despite the observed decline for the group) that explains the overall increase from 1993 to 2004. The prevalence rates for the two younger groups both rose slightly from 1983 to 1993 and were either lower or the same as for 1993 in 2004.

To control for the effect of aging on prevalence statistics, we produced one-period CPS work-limitation prevalence statistics adjusted for changes in the age distribution of the working-age population. To generate these statistics, we first produced prevalence statistics for five-year age groups in each year and then weighted them by their estimated population shares in 1981.[12] This series can be interpreted as representing what the current-year prevalence would be if the age distribution within the working-age population was the same as it was in 1981.

The age-adjusted prevalence rate was greater than the unadjusted series in the early 1980s as the baby boom cohort increased the share of young adults in the working-age population. It then decreased relative to the unadjusted series in the 1990s as the cohort aged (Figure 3.4).

Figure 3.4 also shows that the age-adjusted prevalence of work limitations increased somewhat from 1983 to 1993, but it declined slightly from 1993 to 2004. Finally, the figure shows that the age-adjusted work-limitation series is less sensitive to the business cycle than the unadjusted series. This is because the aging of the baby boom cohort contributed to the growth in unadjusted prevalence leading up to the trough years of 1993 and 2004. The effect of the adjustment is especially large for the last trough period observed; from 1999 to 2004, the unadjusted series increased by 5.5 percent, whereas the adjusted series increased by only 1.5 percent.

We also produced age-adjusted series for seven disability measures developed from the NHIS for the period from 1997 to 2006 (Table 3.6). The disability measures used are defined by Weathers (2009); see also Hendershot, Harris, and Stapleton (2009). This period only includes one of the three business cycle troughs, so it is not possible to make trough-

Table 3.5 Prevalence of Work Limitations by Age (%), and Age-Adjusted Prevalence (%), 1981–2007

Survey year	25–34	35–44	45–54	55–61	All ages	Age-adjusted
1981	4.0	5.9	10.3	16.9	7.9	7.9
1982	3.9	5.9	10.4	17.4	7.9	8.0
1983	**3.8**	**5.7**	**9.7**	**16.7**	**7.5**	**7.6**
1984	4.1	5.6	9.8	17.1	7.6	7.8
1985	4.1	6.0	10.2	17.6	7.8	8.1
1986	4.4	6.0	9.8	17.2	7.7	8.0
1987	4.4	6.2	9.5	17.0	7.7	8.0
1988	4.4	6.0	8.6	15.7	7.2	7.5
1989	4.0	6.3	9.0	16.0	7.2	7.5
1990	4.2	6.0	9.5	16.6	7.4	7.8
1991	4.4	6.3	9.4	15.8	7.5	7.8
1992	4.6	6.4	9.7	15.9	7.7	8.0
1993	**4.8**	**6.5**	**9.7**	**15.6**	**7.8**	**8.0**
1994	5.1	7.0	10.7	17.0	8.4	8.7
1995	4.7	7.3	10.6	16.7	8.3	8.5
1996	4.5	7.3	10.5	16.8	8.3	8.5
1997	4.3	7.1	10.6	16.9	8.3	8.4
1998	3.7	7.0	10.5	16.5	8.1	8.0
1999	3.8	6.7	10.0	16.2	7.9	7.8
2000	3.8	6.7	9.8	16.1	7.9	7.8
2001	3.7	6.2	10.2	15.5	7.8	7.6
2002	4.0	6.6	10.2	16.3	8.2	7.9
2003	3.8	6.2	9.9	14.4	7.8	7.4
2004	**4.3**	**6.5**	**10.5**	**15.3**	**8.4**	**8.0**
2005	4.4	6.6	10.4	15.4	8.4	8.0
2006	3.9	6.5	10.5	15.5	8.4	7.8
2007	3.7	5.6	10.3	14.9	8.0	7.4

NOTE: Years in bold are the trough years of the business cycle as calculated using the median household income from the March CPS of the following year. See Figure 3.4 and Burkhauser, Rovba, and Weathers (2009).

SOURCE: Calculations of the authors.

Table 3.6 NHIS Disability Prevalence and Age-Adjusted Disability Prevalence Statistics (%), 1997–2006

Year	Any disability		Sensory		Physical		Mental		Self-care		IADL		Work limitation	
	Actual	Age adj.	Actual	Age adj.	Actual	Age adj.	Actual	Age adj.	Actual	Age adj.	Actual	Age adj.	Actual	Age adj.
1997	16.4	16.4	2.1	2.1	10.2	10.2	3.3	3.3	0.6	0.6	1.8	1.8	9.7	9.7
1998	15.7	15.6	1.9	1.9	9.7	9.6	3.2	3.2	0.7	0.7	2.0	2.0	9.3	9.3
1999	15.1	14.8	2.1	2.1	8.9	8.7	2.6	2.6	0.8	0.7	1.8	1.8	9.4	9.2
2000	15.2	14.8	1.9	1.8	9.6	9.4	2.8	2.7	0.8	0.8	1.8	1.8	8.8	8.6
2001	17.1	16.5	2.2	2.1	10.8	10.4	3.4	3.4	1.0	1.0	2.3	2.2	9.5	9.1
2002	16.7	15.9	2.0	1.9	10.5	9.8	3.3	3.2	1.0	0.9	2.3	2.2	9.9	9.4
2003	17.1	16.2	2.0	1.8	11.1	10.4	3.4	3.3	1.0	1.0	2.3	2.1	9.9	9.3
2004	16.4	15.6	1.8	1.7	11.0	10.3	3.3	3.2	1.0	1.0	2.4	2.3	9.3	8.8
2005	16.4	15.5	2.1	1.9	10.9	10.1	3.2	3.1	1.0	1.0	2.3	2.1	9.4	8.7
2006	17.5	16.4	2.5	2.3	10.7	10.0	3.1	3.0	0.9	0.8	1.9	1.8	8.6	7.8

NOTE: Age-adjusted figures use 1997 population shares for the following age categories: 25–29, 30–34, 35–39, 40–44, 45–49, 50–54, 55–59, and 60–61.

SOURCE: Authors' calculations using the 1997–2006 NHIS Sample Adult files.

to-trough comparisons. We can, however, compare the business cycle peak year of 1999 to the year 2006, during which the economy appears to have been close to a business cycle peak. During this period, the decline in the age-adjusted NHIS work-limitation measure was larger than the decline in the unadjusted measure. These findings are consistent with the findings based on the CPS. Interestingly, however, all of the other unadjusted disability measures *increased* during the period. The increases were reduced by age adjustment but not reversed. Thus, based on the NHIS, the decline in the prevalence of disabilities captured by the work-limitation questions does not extend to other measures of disability, even after adjusting for changes in the age distribution of the working-age population. The NHIS findings for disability measures other than work limitation are broadly consistent with the NHIS findings through 2004 reported by the IOM.

Prevalence Trends by Demographic Group

The trends in the prevalence of work limitations within other demographic groups unadjusted for age (Table 3.7) are generally similar to the unadjusted aggregate trends we report in Table 3.5. Some interesting differences emerge, however. Comparing the business cycle troughs, the prevalence rate for women was eight percent lower than that for men in 1983, but it increased relative to the rate for men throughout the period and was only one percent lower by 2004. This trend likely reflects the growth of women in the labor force, which presumably increases their chance of reporting a condition limiting their ability to work. Hence, this increase may have had a positive effect on aggregate trends in the prevalence of work limitations throughout this period. The prevalence of work limitations among men did not change from 1993 to 2004; the increase in the aggregate prevalence rate between these recession troughs is entirely attributed to the increase for women. However, these series have not been adjusted for age. But because the age distributions for men and women changed together during this period, it is apparent that, relative to the aggregate age-adjusted series presented previously, the age-adjusted series for men would show larger declines in the prevalence of work limitations than the age-adjusted series for women.

Table 3.7 Work Limitation Prevalence Rates (%) by Demographic Subpopulation, 1981–2007

Survey year	Total	Sex		Race/ethnicity[a]			Education[b]			
		Men	Women	White	Black	Hispanic	Less than HS	High school	Some college	College or more
1981	7.9	8.2	7.6	7.3	13.7	7.0	16.3	6.6	5.3	2.9
1982	7.9	8.2	7.6	7.4	12.9	6.9	16.5	6.7	5.6	3.1
1983	**7.5**	**7.8**	**7.2**	**7.1**	**11.7**	**7.2**	**16.2**	**6.2**	**5.4**	**3.0**
1984	7.6	8.0	7.2	7.2	11.8	6.8	16.6	6.6	5.2	3.1
1985	7.8	8.2	7.5	7.2	13.2	8.1	17.3	7.0	5.6	2.9
1986	7.7	8.3	7.2	7.3	12.3	6.6	17.2	6.9	5.9	2.8
1987	7.7	8.2	7.2	7.2	12.4	7.1	17.7	7.0	5.3	2.8
1988	7.2	7.7	6.7	6.7	11.7	7.0	16.1	6.6	5.8	2.6
1989	7.2	7.6	6.9	6.9	11.1	6.3	16.9	6.7	5.5	2.6
1990	7.4	7.9	7.0	6.9	11.7	7.5	17.0	7.3	5.1	2.8
1991	7.5	7.7	7.2	6.9	11.9	7.3	16.8	7.4	5.6	3.0
1992	7.7	8.1	7.2	7.2	11.4	7.1	18.1	7.6	6.0	2.7
1993	**7.8**	**8.4**	**7.2**	**7.5**	**10.8**	**7.7**	**18.3**	**8.0**	**6.5**	**2.6**
1994	8.4	8.8	8.0	7.8	13.4	7.8	20.6	8.6	6.7	2.7
1995	8.3	8.5	8.2	7.7	13.4	7.8	19.3	9.1	6.9	3.0
1996	8.3	8.2	8.4	7.6	13.7	7.4	19.0	8.9	6.9	3.2

1997	8.3	8.3	8.4	7.8	13.3	7.0	18.7	8.9	7.3	3.2
1998	8.1	7.8	8.3	7.6	12.3	7.1	18.1	8.9	7.0	3.1
1999	7.9	8.0	7.9	7.4	12.9	7.2	17.3	9.0	7.1	3.1
2000	7.9	8.0	7.9	7.5	12.8	6.4	17.9	9.2	6.9	3.2
2001	7.8	7.7	8.0	7.5	12.3	6.1	17.6	9.3	7.1	2.9
2002	8.2	8.0	8.4	7.9	13.3	6.2	17.8	9.8	7.7	2.9
2003	7.8	7.6	7.9	7.3	13.2	6.2	16.5	9.6	7.2	2.9
2004	**8.4**	**8.4**	**8.3**	**8.1**	**13.5**	**6.2**	**17.6**	**10.1**	**8.0**	**3.3**
2005	8.4	8.4	8.5	8.2	13.1	6.5	17.5	10.3	7.7	3.4
2006	8.4	8.2	8.6	8.2	13.5	5.8	16.9	10.5	7.7	3.4
2007	8.0	7.7	8.3	8.0	11.8	5.7	15.7	10.2	7.6	3.2

NOTE: Persons in the Armed Forces are excluded. Years in bold are the trough years of the business cycle.

[a] White Hispanics and black Hispanics are coded as Hispanic.

[b] Beginning in survey year 1992, educational attainment questions in the CPS were changed to reflect credentials and degrees rather than grades (years) completed.

SOURCE: Authors' calculations using the March CPS for persons aged 25–61.

Although prevalence for blacks/African Americans is extraordinarily high relative to prevalence for whites, as we have already seen, it fluctuated during this period, from 66 percent higher in 1983 to 45 percent higher in 1993 and back to 66 percent higher in 2004. Prevalence also declined for Hispanics relative to whites, from 1 percent higher in 1983 to 23 percent lower in 2004.

Prevalence statistics by level of education are plotted in Figure 3.5. A 1992 change in the CPS educational attainment question—shifting emphasis from years of schooling toward attainment of a degree—means that statistics after that are not fully comparable with pre-1992 statistics. Nevertheless, this chart shows that work-limitation prevalence trends vary markedly by education level. There is a marked upward trend in prevalence for those who have completed high school and not college throughout the period, especially in the latter half. From 1993 to 2004, the prevalence rate for those with a high school degree increased

Figure 3.5 Prevalence of Work Limitations by Level of Education, 1981–2007

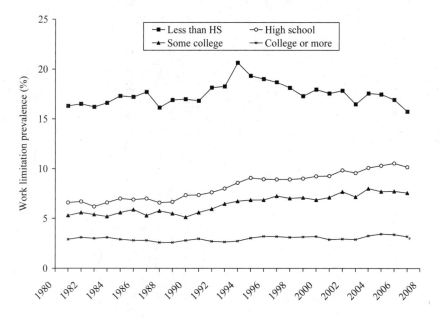

SOURCE: Calculations by the authors. See Table 3.7.

from 8.0 percent to 10.1 percent, and it increased for those with some college education from 6.5 percent to 8.0 percent. The prevalence trend was also upward for those with less than a high school education from 1983 to 1993, but it has been distinctly downward in more recent years, falling from 18.3 percent in 1993 to 17.6 percent in 2004. However, it is difficult to interpret these disparate trends because educational attainment varies across age cohorts, with more recent cohorts attaining higher levels of education. In other words, the age distribution varies across education groups (e.g., college graduates tend to be younger, on average, than those having less education), so the aging of the baby boomers is affecting these education groups differently. Even holding age constant, those within an education category during the latter part of the period differ in other important respects from those within the same category in the earlier part (e.g., a growing share of college graduates are female).

SUMMARY AND CONCLUSION

Disability prevalence, measured in various ways and using an array of data sets, differs considerably across states and demographic groups. We find very large differences in prevalence across racial groups; blacks/African Americans and Native Americans have prevalence rates that are much higher than those of other groups. Prevalence declines substantially with educational attainment—those with less than a high school education have rates five to six times the size of those for college graduates. Prevalence also increases with age—for most disability measures, those aged 55–61 have prevalence rates that are three to four times higher than those aged 25–34.

Perhaps the most important finding is that, after adjusting for the aging of the baby boom cohort, the prevalence of work limitations increased between the recession troughs of 1983 and 1993, but it declined slightly from 1993 to the next trough in 2004. A decline in the recent period is clearly evident for those aged 55–61, and the decline appears to have started in the 1980s. It is also clear that, after adjusting for age, prevalence of work limitations for men declined substantially from

1993 to 2004. The prevalence of work limitations among women increased relative to men, perhaps because of increases in female labor force participation.

Consistent with earlier studies, however, we did not find recent declines in disability prevalence for measures other than work limitations, even after controlling for the aging of the baby boom cohort. We did not examine whether trends in these measures vary by demographic group.

These statistics raise many interesting questions for future research. An inquiry into the sources of the extreme variation in disability prevalence across states might be very fruitful. The advent of the ACS presents a new opportunity to conduct research in this area. Possible explanations for the variation across states include, at a minimum, variation in demographic characteristics, state economies, and public policies.

It would also be valuable to gain a better understanding of why disability prevalence among blacks/African Americans relative to that of whites declined from 1983 to 1993. One possible explanation is that gains in educational attainment and economic opportunities for blacks/African Americans have reduced the relative levels of disability prevalence in the working-age population. It is also possible that part of the decline could be an artifact of the CPS sampling frame, which excludes the incarcerated population. As She and Stapleton (2009) shows, the prevalence of disabilities is much higher among the incarcerated than the household population, and disproportionately large numbers of inmates are blacks/African Americans. Hence, as incarceration rates increased during this period, disproportionately large numbers of blacks/African Americans with disabilities were removed from the CPS sampling frame, which could be part of the reason why prevalence rates did not increase for blacks/African Americans as they did for whites.

The finding of a decline in the prevalence of work limitations since the early 1990s also merits additional research. A first step would be to produce and examine age-adjusted changes in prevalence within demographic groups. Such series might still show that the prevalence of work limitations has declined relative to the prevalence of other types of disabilities. If so, it would be valuable to gain a better understanding of why these series diverged. It would also be helpful to know why the age-adjusted prevalence of work limitations increased in the 1980s but has since declined. Is there evidence linking prevalence to the expansion of eligibility criteria for SSDI after 1984 as suggested by Autor and Duggan (2003)? Did the 1990 Americans with Disabilities Act or the broader cultural changes underlying its enactment contribute to a decline in the reporting of work limitations among those with given impairments? Is there evidence that medical and technological advances during the 1990s—especially the rapid growth in the economic role of information technology—have reduced the chances that an individual with a given impairment will experience a work limitation?

Findings from the literature on trends in life expectancy also suggest an interesting direction for future research on disability prevalence. A recent review of this research by the Congressional Budget Office concluded that there are growing disparities in life expectancy across socioeconomic status (SES), even as the influence of race (at least for black women) declines (Manchester and Topoleski 2008). In brief, there is substantial evidence that, during the past few decades, life expectancy has been increasing substantially for those in relatively high SES groups, defined in various ways, while gains have been much more limited for relatively low SES groups. Some possible explanations for these findings are outlined in Manchester and Topoleski (2008) and include lifestyle factors such as smoking and obesity, and differential trends in access to health care, including access to new life-saving treatments. Research on life expectancy trends raises an interesting question about disability prevalence trends. Is it possible that disability prevalence is declining rapidly among high SES groups, while remaining high or even increasing for low SES groups? Perhaps reductions in smoking, the effects of medical and technological advances, and changes in the nature of the jobs held by those in high SES groups have substantially reduced the likelihood that they will experience disability onset while of working age. Those from lower SES groups might have experienced smaller reductions in disability, or even increases, because of smaller declines in smoking, relatively limited access to new medical technologies, declines in health insurance coverage, fewer benefits from advances in information technologies, and perhaps other factors. The variations in the work-limitation prevalence trends by educational attainment as reported in this chapter seem consistent with the hypothesis of a growing disparity in disability prevalence across SES groups for working-age people, but they are far from definitive.

Increases in the disparity of disability across these groups could have profound consequences for public policies, with higher SES groups experiencing a decline in the need for social insurance against the onset of disability, even as the needs of lower SES groups remain high or even increase. Similarly, most of those in relatively high SES groups might be able to extend their labor force participation well past the current full retirement age for Social Security (now 66) in response to policy changes that encourage later retirement, whereas many of those from lower SES groups might find it very difficult to do so.

Notes

1. Technological advances and changes to the environment may also play a role in decreasing disability rates among the elderly. Even if the risk of some disabilities may not have declined, the ability to cope with what once would have been thought of as a disabling condition might have changed. This idea is explored in Stewart et al. (2008), where they tested whether the availability of ramps, van transportation, and senior housing decreases self-reported measures of disability conditional on objective measures of functioning. Their work is mostly suggestive at this point, but they did find that increased use of van service may explain approximately 4 percent of the decline in disability grocery shopping among Boston-area elderly women from 1982 to 1999.
2. ADLs are defined as bathing, dressing, and getting around inside the home; IADLs are defined as shopping, cleaning, and going places outside the home. Both are considered predictors of long-term care needs.
3. These estimates were adjusted for sex, race, Hispanic origin, education, and employment.
4. The other states with self-reported work limitation rates below 6 percent are New Jersey, North Dakota, Minnesota, the District of Columbia, Hawaii, Utah, Maryland, Connecticut, Colorado, Illinois, Nebraska, Nevada, and Wisconsin.
5. Education is not technically a demographic characteristic, but since it is a largely static trait in the working-age population, we treat it as if it were.
6. The "go-outside-home" disability is the ACS IADL disability referred to by Weathers (2009).
7. The sampling frame was changed to reflect the most recent decennial census.
8. The dating of the employment, income, and poverty measures reported in Weathers and Wittenburg (2009); Burkhauser, Rovba, and Weathers (2009); and Burkhauser, Houtenville, and Rovba (2009) refers to the pre-survey year.
9. It is possible that changes in interview methodology could have contributed to

changes in prevalence during this period. This was a time of extensive innovation in the use of computer-assisted interviews, including, for example, the automated insertion of an individual's name into questions throughout the survey.

10. Weathers and Wittenburg (2009) provides evidence that these years are business cycle troughs. Although it is more common to make comparisons across business cycle peaks than across troughs, we chose to examine troughs throughout this book because only two peaks occurred from 1980 through 2006.

11. Although the business cycle peak prior to the 1983 trough is not observed in the data, if a recession induces an increase in measured prevalence, we would expect to see an increase from 1981 to 1983. Only the one-period CPS measure is available for that period, and it shows a decline. This seemingly contradictory evidence might, however, reflect the fact that SSDI awards did not increase during this period, despite the recession, because of administrative tightening of SSDI eligibility rules (Rupp and Stapleton 1995).

12. The eight age categories used are 25–29, 30–34, 35–39, 40–44, 45–49, 50–54, 55–59, and 60–61.

References

Autor, D. H., and M. G. Duggan. 2003. "The Rise in the Disability Rolls and the Decline in Unemployment." *Quarterly Journal of Economics* 118(1): 157–205.

Burkhauser, Richard V., Andrew J. Houtenville, and Ludmila Rovba. 2009. "Poverty." In *Counting Working-Age People with Disabilities: What Current Data Tell Us and Options for Improvement*, Andrew J. Houtenville, David C. Stapleton, Robert R. Weathers II, and Richard V. Burkhauser, eds. Kalamazoo, MI: W.E. Upjohn Institute for Employment Research, pp. 193–226.

Burkhauser, Richard V., Ludmila Rovba, and Robert R. Weathers II. 2009. "Household Income." In *Counting Working-Age People with Disabilities: What Current Data Tell Us and Options for Improvement*, Andrew J. Houtenville, David C. Stapleton, Robert R. Weathers II, and Richard V. Burkhauser, eds. Kalamazoo, MI: W.E. Upjohn Institute for Employment Research, pp. 145–192.

Crimmins, E. M., S. L. Reynolds, and Y. Saito. 1999. "Trends in Health and Ability to Work Among the Older Working-Age Population." *Journal of Gerontology: Social Sciences* 54B(1): S31–S40.

Crimmins, E. M., Y. Saito, and S. Reynolds. 1997. "Further Evidence on Recent Trends in the Prevalence and Incidence of Disability Among Older Americans from Two Sources: The LSOA and the NHIS." *The Journal of Gerontology: Social Sciences* 52B: S59–S71.

Cutler, D. M., M. B. Landrum, and K. A. Stewart. 2006. "Intensive Medical Care and Cardiovascular Disease Disability Reductions." NBER Working Paper no. 12184. Cambridge, MA: National Bureau of Economic Research.

Freedman, V. A., E. Crimmins, R. F. Schoeni, B. C. Spillman, H. Aykan, E. Kramarow, K. Land, J. Lubitz, K. Manton, L. G. Martin, D. Shinberg, and T. Waidmann. 2004. "Resolving Inconsistencies in Trends in Old-Age Disability: Report from a Technical Working Group." *Demography* 41(3): 417–441.

Freedman, V. A., L. G. Martin, and R. F. Schoeni. 2002. "Recent Trends in Disability and Functioning Among Older Adults in the United States: A Systematic Review." *Journal of the American Medical Association* 288(24): 3137–3146.

Goodman, N. J., and D. C. Stapleton. 2007. "Federal Program Expenditures for Working-Age People with Disabilities." *Journal of Disability Policy Studies* 18(2): 66–78.

Hendershot, Gerry E., Benjamin H. Harris, and David C. Stapleton. 2009. "Health and Functional Status." In *Counting Working-Age People with Disabilities: What Current Data Tell Us and Options for Improvement*, Andrew J. Houtenville, David C. Stapleton, Robert R. Weathers II, and Richard V. Burkhauser, eds. Kalamazoo, MI: W.E. Upjohn Institute for Employment Research, pp. 227–264.

Institute of Medicine. 2007. *The Future of Disability in America*. 2007. Committee on Disability in America, Marilyn J. Field and Alan M. Jette, eds. Washington, DC: National Academies Press.

Lakdawalla, D. N., J. Bhattacharya, and D. P. Goldman. 2004. "Are the Young Becoming More Disabled?" *Health Affairs* 23(1): 168–176.

Manchester, J., and J. Topoleski. 2008. "Growing Disparities in Life Expectancy." Washington, DC: Congressional Budget Office. http://digitalcommons .ilr.cornell.edu/ key_workplace/506/ (accessed June 6, 2008).

Manton, K. G., and X. Gu. 2001. "Changes in the Prevalence of Chronic Disability in the United States Black and Nonblack Population Above Age 65 from 1982 to 1999." *Proceedings of the National Academy of Sciences of the United States of America* 98(11): 6354–6359.

Rehabilitation Research and Training Center on Disability Demographics and Statistics. 2007. *2006 Disability Status Report*. Ithaca, NY: Cornell University, Rehabilitation Research and Training Center on Disability Demographics and Statistics.

Rupp, K., and D. Stapleton. 1995. "Determinants of the Growth in the Social Security Administration's Disability Programs—an Overview." *Social Security Bulletin* 58(4): 43–70.

Schoeni, R. F., V. A. Freedman, and R. B. Wallace. 2001. "Persistent, Consistent, Widespread, and Robust? Another Look at Recent Trends in Old-Age Disability." *Journal of Gerontology* 56B(4): S206–S218.

She, Peiyun, and David C. Stapleton. 2009. "The Group Quarters Population." In *Counting Working-Age People with Disabilities: What Current Data Tell Us and Options for Improvement*, Andrew J. Houtenville, David C. Stapleton, Robert R. Weathers II, and Richard V. Burkhauser, eds. Kalamazoo, MI: W.E. Upjohn Institute for Employment Research, pp. 353–380.

Stewart, K. A., M. B. Landrum, P. M. Gallagher, and D. M. Cutler. 2008. "Understanding Self-Reported Disability Among the Elderly." Unpublished manuscript.

Weathers, Robert R. II. 2009. "The Disability Data Landscape." In *Counting Working-Age People with Disabilities: What Current Data Tell Us and Options for Improvement*, Andrew J. Houtenville, David C. Stapleton, Robert R. Weathers II, and Richard V. Burkhauser, eds. Kalamazoo, MI: W.E. Upjohn Institute for Employment Research, pp. 27–67.

Weathers, Robert R. II, and David C. Wittenburg. 2009. "Employment." In *Counting Working-Age People with Disabilities: What Current Data Tell Us and Options for Improvement*, Andrew J. Houtenville, David C. Stapleton, Robert R. Weathers II, and Richard V. Burkhauser, eds. Kalamazoo, MI: W.E. Upjohn Institute for Employment Research, pp. 101–144.

4

Employment

Robert R. Weathers II
Social Security Administration

David C. Wittenburg
Mathematica Policy Research, Inc.

A major challenge in tracking the employment outcomes of working-age people (aged 25–61) with disabilities is that a large range of employment rate estimates exists in the literature and in government publications. The availability of multiple measures and the wide variation in employment rates across those measures creates confusion when communicating research findings on employment outcomes of people with disabilities to a broad audience.

This chapter provides a guide to interpreting and developing employment rate estimates for people with disabilities using data from four major sources: the American Community Survey (ACS), the Current Population Survey (CPS), the National Health Interview Survey (NHIS), and the Survey of Income and Program Participation (SIPP). We first describe how employment rate estimates vary when different disability concepts, employment reference periods, and data sources are used. We then show how the unique features of the ACS, CPS, NHIS, and SIPP can be used to describe different aspects of employment for various groups of people with disabilities, as defined in Weathers (2009).

Our findings demonstrate that different disability concepts, employment reference periods, and data sources result in a wide range of employment rate estimates for people with disabilities. We show that employment rate estimates are especially sensitive to the choice of disability concepts and employment reference period. Employment rates are relatively low if they are based on disability concepts that capture the interaction of an impairment with a social activity, especially work limitations, and/or are based on full-time work or employment in the most recent reference period. They are relatively high, however, when based on impairment disability concepts or any employment definition over longer reference periods. Employment rate estimates also vary across data sources, even when based on approximately the same disability concept or employment definition, but the range of the estimates is relatively small when compared to the range of estimates across disability concepts or employment definitions.

In the next section, we present background on how the federal government constructs employment measures for the U.S. population and for various segments of the population, and describe the challenges related to measuring employment for persons with a disability. We then describe the methods that we used to examine disability employment rates in the chapter and how those methods influence employment rate estimates. Next, we use the unique features from our four data sources to present several different types of employment rate estimates that will be of interest to policymakers. These include state differences, historical trends, and findings from the 2005 calendar year. We conclude with a summary of findings and directions for future research.

BACKGROUND

The U.S. Department of Labor's Bureau of Labor Statistics (BLS) regularly collects employment data on the U.S. population and several demographic subgroups. The BLS Web site contains data on the employment situation of adults, including employment and unemployment status, hours worked, and wages for the entire U.S. population, as well as detailed statistics stratified by age, race, sex, and ethnicity (see Bureau of Labor Statistics n.d.). The BLS uses data from the CPS to generate statistics for each of these subgroups and the data are often used to assess the general health of the economy and policy initiatives that provide economic support for subgroups that face potential financial risks, especially unemployed workers.

The BLS employment tabulations do not, however, include information on people with disabilities. Although the BLS is attempting to develop an accurate and reliable measure of the employment rate of people with disabilities in the CPS under Executive Order 13078 established in 1998, the lack of an official measure makes it difficult for policymakers to systematically track the employment progress of this population. The need for a more public reporting of employment rates for people with disabilities is particularly pressing given the large number of policies aimed at improving the employment outcomes of this population, including the Americans with Disabilities Act (ADA), the New Freedom Initiative, and several return-to-work programs and initiatives by the Social Security Administration (SSA), Center for Medicare & Medicaid Service, and the Department of Labor.

The BLS's efforts to create an official disability employment measure will be a major step forward to communicate information about the employment status of people with disabilities when it becomes available. Even when that happens, however, it will not provide a comprehensive definition that will cover the full range of potential disability measures for the diverse population of people with disabilities. Consequently, researchers and policymakers will continue to need to use alternative disability and employment concepts to address the full range of policy issues influencing the employment outcomes of people with disabilities.

One of the major challenges in estimating employment rates for people with disabilities is that both disability and employment are dynamic concepts that have several definitions. As noted in Weathers (2009), concepts of disability vary with respect to severity, duration, and effect on the ability to perform and participate in major life activities. These variations have important implications for developing employment rate measures because they require the interaction of an impairment with a social activity, especially work. They will also lead to lower employment rate estimates for people with disabilities relative to those that use broader based definitions of a person's impairment. Similarly, employment is a dynamic concept that can change over the course of a year. For example, persons who work part of the year could be defined as employed using an annual definition of work, but not employed if they were not working during the most recent reference week or month. Hence, employment rate estimates using a longer period of time and a less stringent definition of employment (e.g., part time instead of full time) will produce relatively larger estimates as compared to those using shorter intervals or more stringent employment definitions.

An additional challenge in developing employment rate estimates for people with disabilities is that the number and types of questions on employment, health, and functional limitations vary substantially across surveys. The CPS, for example, includes detailed information on employment but, as noted in Weathers (2009), contains few questions on health and functional status. In contrast, other surveys, such as the NHIS, include detailed information on health and functional limitation status but little on employment. Even when the same questions are available across surveys, there will likely be some differences in employment rate estimates because of variation in survey methodology (see Ballou and Markesich 2009) and the role that survey context plays in influencing health and employment responses.

The previous literature has drawn on several disability and employment concepts to examine aspects of employment of people with disabilities (Burkhauser, Houtenville, and Wittenburg 2003; Kaye 2003; McNeil 2000). As discussed in Weathers (2009), the use of multiple disability concepts is necessary to characterize outcomes across different subgroups. Similarly, alternative employment measures are necessary to characterize different aspects of employment, such as part- and full-time work. Finally, the way researchers construct these measures might depend on the availability of information in existing data sources.

METHODS

To illustrate the variation that exists within employment rate estimates for people with disabilities, we generate estimates for adults aged 25–61 using the available International Classification of Functioning, Disability and Health (ICF) concept described in Weathers (2009). This group has been used in several studies of people with disabilities because the age range falls at a time when most people have completed all of their schooling (including postsecondary schooling) but before the age of early retirement. The data sources covered in this chapter include the ACS, CPS, NHIS, and SIPP. Some, like the CPS, are limited insofar as disability is defined only as an activity limitation. For the ICF, we used an "NA" entry to indicate that information on a particular concept is not present in the survey. In developing trend estimates, we used data from the CPS covering 1980 to 2005 and from the NHIS covering 1987 to 1996.[1] In making comparisons across surveys, we used the most comparable year available across all data sources, 2002–2003. The use of a common year for employment estimates is especially important given the sensitivity of employment rates to macroeconomic conditions.

We chose the following three employment measures to represent the varying levels of attachment to the labor force:[2]

- Reference period employment, which counts people as employed if they had any reported hours in the most recent week in the ACS and CPS, two weeks in the NHIS, and within the last month in the SIPP;

- Any annual employment, which counts a respondent as employed if they worked at least 52 hours (one hour per week) during the previous calendar year; and

- Full-time annual employment, which counts a respondent as employed if they worked at least 35 hours per week and 50 weeks per year (including paid vacation, sick leave, and other paid leave).

The reference period represents work in the most recent period and, for the CPS, is the same one used by BLS.[3] The any annual employment definition measures any work activity during the past year and therefore produces the highest employment rate estimates. Unlike the other measures, this measure will capture all people who work sporadically during the year. Finally, the full-time annual measure captures people who have the strongest attachment to the labor force and, hence, will produce the lowest employment rate estimates.

The one notable measure reported by the BLS, but excluded from our list above, is the unemployment rate for people with disabilities. Although this rate generally is a very useful measure of labor force attachment, we view its use for measuring employment outcomes of people with disabilities as problematic because the denominator only includes those in the labor force (i.e., people who are working or actively looking for work), and a large number of people with disabilities are not in the labor force. When a person experiences the onset of a disability and leaves the labor force, the three employment rate measures discussed above go down, but the unemployment rate would be essentially unaffected because this person is no longer counted in either the numerator or denominator. The use of the unemployment rate measures is particularly problematic in evaluating how disability policies are promoting employment, including keeping people in the labor force, as well as returning people from disability programs to work (see Burkhauser, Houtenville, and Wittenburg 2003 for more details on this issue).

As summarized in Table 4.1, there is considerable variation across surveys in disability and employment information that researchers can use to examine different aspects of employment behavior across subgroups of people with disabilities. The ACS includes multiple questions on health, functional limitations, and employment, and it has the relative advantage of a large sample that can be used to track employment rates at the state level and for narrowly defined demographic groups such as Native Americans. The CPS is more limited in generating employment rates for just one subgroup (those with work limitations), but it is valuable for trend analysis because of its long history and also is sufficiently large to support state-level estimates.[4] The NHIS contains extensive health and functional limitation information and has the relative advantage of providing trend analyses of several subgroups of people with disabilities. Finally, the SIPP includes several questions on employment, health, and functional limitations, and it has the relative advantage of being able to track longitudinal employment rates of the different subgroups.

Our analysis below draws on information from each survey to depict the general sources of variation in employment rates for people with disabilities in the literature. We also point out how researchers can utilize the unique features of these surveys to examine the full spectrum of employment outcomes of people with disabilities. Our findings are based on previous estimates generated in Cornell University's user guide series (see Burkhauser and Houtenville 2006; Harris, Hendershot, and Stapleton 2005; Weathers 2005; Wittenburg and Nelson 2006).

Table 4.1 Summary of Employment and Disability Conceptualizations and Analysis Options by Data Source

	Employment definitions					Analysis options			
	Disability definition	Full-time annual	Any annual	Reference period	Trends	Longitudinal	SSA administrative data links	State estimates	Most recent data publicly available
ACS	6 definitions	Yes	Yes	Week	Limited currently	No	Planned for future links	Yes	2006
CPS	Work-limitation only	Yes	Yes	Week	Yes	Limited sample	Yes	Yes	2006
NHIS	More than 6 definitions possible	Yes	Yes, but asked as "any employment in year"	Two weeks (before 1997) Week (since 1997)	Yes	No	Yes, but limited match rate	No	2006
SIPP	More than 6 definitions possible	Yes	Yes	Month	Limited	Yes	Yes	No	2001

NOTE: The ACS is currently limited for trend analyses because it only includes two cross-sections of data. However, the ACS should be a viable source of information for future trend analyses. The ACS also is not currently linked to SSA administrative data, but there is a potential to link these data to the records in the future. The CPS can be used to produce a limited longitudinal sample over a one-year period by matching respondents across interviews (see Burkhauser and Houtenville 2006 for more details). The SIPP can be used to develop trend estimates, but it is limited in its capacity relative to the ACS, CPS, and NHIS because of changes to the SIPP questionnaire across several panels (see Wittenburg and Nelson 2006 for more details).

EXPLANATION OF DIFFERENCES IN REPORTED EMPLOYMENT RATES

This section demonstrates the variation that exists in employment rate estimates for people with disabilities by presenting statistics using alternative disability and employment concepts across surveys. We first present estimates across alternative disability and employment rate concepts using data from the SIPP, a useful comparison tool because it contains information that can construct multiple disability and employment concepts. Using a common disability and employment concept, we then compare annual employment rate estimates from the SIPP to those from the ACS, CPS, and NHIS to illustrate the variations that can exist across surveys. The findings provide insights on the magnitude of the difference that exists in employment rates depending on disability and employment definitions, as well as on data source.

Employment Period

Data from the 2001 SIPP show the variation that exists when three alternative employment reference periods (any annual, reference period, and full-time annual) are used to characterize the employment rates for a single subgroup—people who report work limitations (Figure 4.1). The any annual employment definition produces a much larger employment rate estimate than either the reference period (in this case May 2002) or the full-time annual measure (41 percent vs. 28 and 15 percent, respectively). Wittenburg and Nelson (2006) also reported that employment rates using any annual measures are approximately two times larger than those using the more restrictive full-time annual measures (see Table 4A.2 in Appendix 4A). By comparison, they found that employment rates also vary across reference period for people without any disabilities over the same time period from the SIPP, although the relative differences are smaller (91 percent work any annual, 82 percent work in the previous month, and 58 percent work full-time annual), especially within demographic subgroups that have high employment rates (e.g., males).[5] These findings indicate that a relatively large number of employed people with work limitations or other disabilities work either on a part-time or part-year basis.

Figure 4.1 Differences in Employment Rates by Reference Period for Adults (Aged 25–61) with Work Limitations

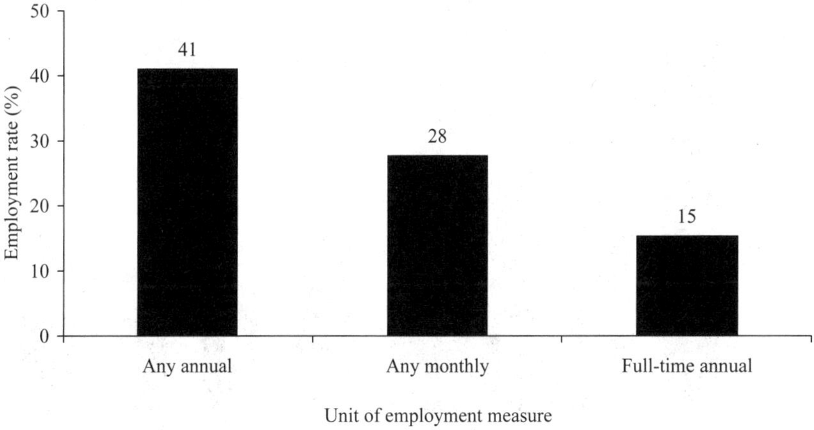

Unit of employment measure

NOTE: Any annual employment includes at least 52 hours or more worked from June 2001 through May 2002. Reference period includes positive reported earnings in May 2002. Full-time annual employment includes at least 35 hours or more of work and 50 weeks or more worked from June 2001 through May 2002.
SOURCE: Authors' calculation using the 2001 SIPP.

Disability Concept

There is also substantial variation in the employment rates across disability concepts in the 2001 SIPP (Figure 4.2). These data include measures to capture impairment (sensory, physical, and mental), participation restrictions (work limitation), and limitations on activities of daily living (ADL) and instrumental activities of daily living (IADL). Also included is a rate for "any disability," which includes any of the aforementioned disability concepts, and "no disability," which includes people who report none of the aforementioned disability concepts. The estimates for all disability groups are much lower than the estimate for the no disability group (91 percent), but the range across the disability groups is also very large, from 34 percent (IADL limitations) to 64 percent (sensory impairment). Employment rate estimates based on disability concepts that measure the interaction of an impairment with a social activity (i.e., participation and activity restriction concepts) produce lower estimates of employment rates than those that measure just

Figure 4.2 Differences in Any Annual Employment Rates by Disability Conceptualization for Adults (Aged 25–61)

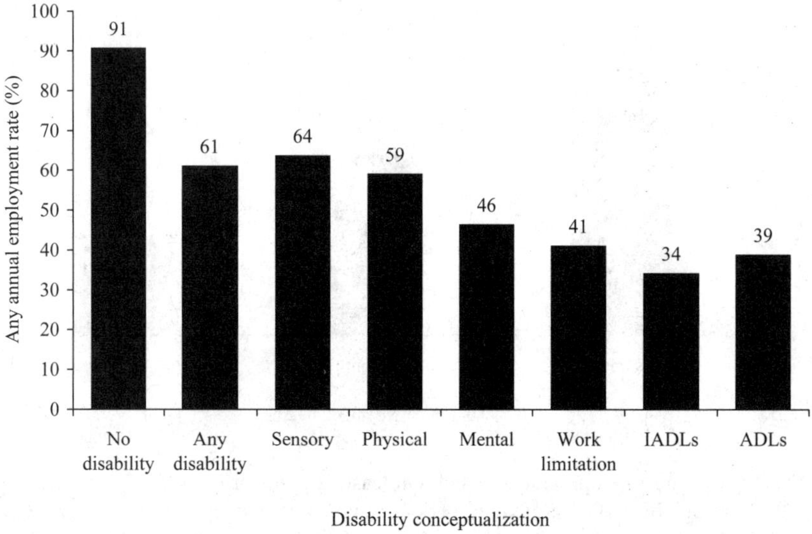

NOTE: Any annual employment includes at least 52 hours or more worked from June 2001 through May 2002. The disability conceptualizations are described in Weathers (2009). For a more detailed summary of the questions used to generate these estimates from the SIPP, see Wittenburg and Nelson (2006).

SOURCE: Authors' calculation using the 2001 SIPP.

an impairment. This finding is not surprising given that the types of limitations that affect social activities would likely restrict participation in work—especially, of course, "work limitations." Group differences in demographic composition (especially education) and health characteristics also contribute to variation in the employment rate differences across these groups (Houtenville et al. 2009).

Comparisons to Other Data Sources

Variation in employment rate estimates exists across surveys even when the same employment and disability concepts are used, probably because differences in survey methods and questionnaires influence responses to questions related to employment and disability (Figure 4.3).

Although the work-limitation concept is the same across surveys, the wording of this question varies across surveys, as does the survey design (see Weathers 2009). The annual employment rates derived from the surveys range from about 28 percent in the ACS and CPS to approximately 42 percent in the SIPP and NHIS. The differences in employment rate estimates are heavily influenced by the composition of the population reporting work limitations in each survey. As shown in Weathers (2009), the prevalence of work limitations is much higher in the SIPP and NHIS relative to the CPS and ACS, suggesting that the SIPP and NHIS surveys might capture a broader population with more work capacity. It is difficult to pinpoint the exact factors that result in different prevalence rates across surveys. We suspect the higher prevalence of work-limitation status in the SIPP and NHIS relative to the CPS and ACS exists because SIPP and NHIS respondents are more "tuned in" to reporting health difficulties because they are asked a long battery of questions on health and disability status, whereas the CPS and ACS only include a limited set of questions in this area.

Figure 4.3 Differences in Any Annual Employment Rates by Data Sources for Adults (Aged 25–61) with Work Limitations

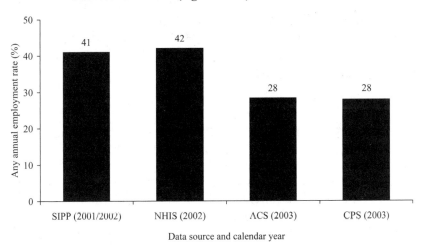

NOTE: See Table 4A.1 for details on employment rate measures for each survey.
SOURCE: Authors' calculations using the 2001 SIPP, 2002 NHIS, 2003 ACS, and 2003 CPS.

Summary of Differences

These findings underscore the challenges in communicating employment rates for people with disabilities because these estimates are sensitive to disability concept, employment reference period, and data source. Consequently, it is difficult to identify a single employment rate for people with disabilities that would be universally agreed upon by policymakers, researchers, and disability advocates because there are multiple conceptualizations of both disability status and employment. For example, our estimates above, which represent only a limited spectrum of choices for disability concepts and employment definitions, indicate that employment estimates for people with disabilities can range from 15 percent (full-time annual employment for people with work limitations) to 64 percent (any annual employment for people with sensory impairments). Furthermore, temporal changes in the definitions can undermine comparisons across time, even from the same survey. For example, Census Bureau publications on disability employment rates using SIPP data use different definitions for disability and employment in the 2001 SIPP and the 1996 SIPP (McNeil 2000; Steinmetz 2004), making it impossible to use these two publications for comparative purposes. As will be described in more detail below, there are multiple options for tracking the multi-faceted concepts of employment rates for people with disabilities across surveys. The best choice of disability concept, employment concept, and survey depends on the policy question being asked.

ANALYSIS OF DIFFERENT ASPECTS OF EMPLOYMENT OUTCOMES OF PEOPLE WITH DISABILITIES

In addition to the differences in disability and employment rate measures, the surveys vary with respect to different features that are used to examine various aspects of the disability employment rate. To illustrate some of the aspects of employment that can be tracked across surveys, we present a brief summary of the unique features and some basic employment estimates from each of these data sources that have been used in previous studies and/or could be used in future studies on employment outcomes. We start first by comparing employment rate estimates across the full range of disability concepts, employment reference periods, and data sources, building on our findings presented in Houtenville et al. (2009), Figures 3.1–3.3. To illustrate the potential uses of these estimates, we then examine employment rate trends (CPS and NHIS), recent employment rates for subgroups (ACS), state employment rates (ACS), estimates from longitudinal data (SIPP), and estimates from linked administrative data (CPS and SIPP). In each case, we present data on at least one of these employment rate measures from the available data.[6]

Comparisons of Employment Rates across Data Sources

Table 4.2 presents employment rate estimates across disability concepts and reference periods found in the ACS, CPS, NHIS, and SIPP. Not surprisingly, given our findings in Figure 4.1, the employment rates across all disability concepts are highest when the reference period is 52 or more hours per year. Consistent with our findings in Figure 4.2, within each of the data sets that capture all six disability concepts, employment rates are highest among those with sensory impairment, followed by those with physical impairment, mental impairment, work limitation, and finally, IADL or ADL limitations. Consistent with the findings shown in Figure 4.3, reported employment rates in the SIPP and NHIS are higher than those in the ACS and CPS. For example, among those with work limitations, the SIPP and NHIS reference period employment rates are more than 27 percent, and the ACS and CPS employment rates for the same measure are less than 20 percent.

Employment Trends from CPS and NHIS

A major advantage of the CPS and NHIS survey designs is that they represent repeated cross-sections, fielded in a consistent manner over long periods, and they can be used to track long-term trends in employment outcomes. Trend analysis is particularly important in tracking the economic progress of particular subgroups. Additionally, several studies have used constructed employment rate trends to evaluate the effects of policy changes, such as the ADA (Acemoglu and Angrist

Table 4.2 Summary of Differences in Employment Rates (%) by Employment Conceptualization, Disability Conceptualization, and Data Source for Adults (Aged 25–61)

	No disability	Any disability	Participation restriction		Activity limitation	Impairment		
			Work limitation	IADL	ADL	Mental	Physical	Sensory
Reference period								
ACS, 2003	79.5	39.3	18.9	17.9	18.3	28.2	33.8	49.9
CPS, 2003	81.4	19.6	19.6	NA	NA	NA	NA	NA
NHIS, 2002	83.3	47.3	29.8	18.3	14.1	37.1	43.8	58.6
SIPP, 2002	82.4	48.9	27.7	20.3	22.8	37.0	46.4	53.5
Any annual								
ACS, 2003	87.1	48.9	28.3	25.8	26.2	37.2	42.8	58.1
CPS, 2003	86.2	27.9	27.9	NA	NA	NA	NA	NA
NHIS, 2002	88.3	57.9	42.0	25.7	19.9	51.9	53.8	66.6
SIPP, 2002	90.6	61.1	41.0	34.1	38.8	46.3	59.0	63.7
Full-time annual								
ACS, 2003	59.6	24.5	9.1	9.0	9.4	15.0	20.3	34.5
CPS, 2003	65.3	9.4	9.4	NA	NA	NA	NA	NA
NHIS, 2002	62.8	29.8	16.3	9.3	6.2	21.3	27.2	43.4
SIPP, 2002	58.1	31.2	15.3	12.0	15.0	20.3	29.6	35.6

NOTE: Any annual employment includes 52 hours or more worked during the previous year. The SIPP estimates represent employment estimates from June 2001 through May 2002 from the 2001 SIPP. The NHIS estimates represent any annual employment estimates for calendar year 2002 from the 2002 NHIS. The ACS estimates represent any annual employment estimates for calendar year 2002 from the 2003 ACS. The CPS estimates represent any annual employment estimates for calendar year 2002 from the 2003 CPS.

SOURCE: Authors' calculations from the 2001 SIPP, 2002 NHIS, 2003 ACS, and 2003 CPS.

2001; Houtenville and Burkhauser 2004). The CPS has used the same work-limitation question from 1980 to the present, allowing users to construct annual estimates of employment over a 27-year period that covers almost three complete economic business cycles.[7] The NHIS also provides generally consistent measures of health, employment, and functional measures for trend analyses, but the survey has been redesigned over time. For this reason, we do not make comparisons in the NHIS during these redesign periods, which occurred in 1982 and 1996. Despite this limitation, the NHIS does include several years of data that can be used to construct trends analyses, which can be compared to CPS findings.

In Figure 4.4, we present relative employment rates, comparing the employment rate of men with disabilities to men without disabilities over a 25-year period (1980–2005) using the alternative disability concepts that are available over this period from the CPS and NHIS.[8] Each annual measure of the relative employment rate shows the gap in employment rates between men with and without disabilities. A relative rate of 100 would suggest that the employment rates of the two groups are the same, and any rate less than 100 suggests that employment rates are lower for men with disabilities relative to those without disabilities. By tracking trends in relative employment rates, we can measure how the gap in employment rates across men with and without disabilities is changing over time. This type of trend analysis is particularly powerful in understanding the general directions in disability policy, especially in how people with disabilities are faring relative to the general population.

Employment trends for two disability measures from the CPS are available over this 25-year period—the work limitation and one year work limitation (i.e., reported work limitation in two periods). There are also two disability measures from the NHIS (work limitation and impairment). For the NHIS comparisons using work limitations, there is a gap in the trends in 1996.

There are substantial differences in the relative employment rates across disability measures, which is consistent with the findings in the earlier tables that show the employment rates of broader disability definitions (e.g., impairment) are higher than those with more narrow definitions (e.g., longer term work limitations). The relative employ-

Figure 4.4   Relative Employment Rate for Any Annual Employment Measure (Adults Aged 21– 58)

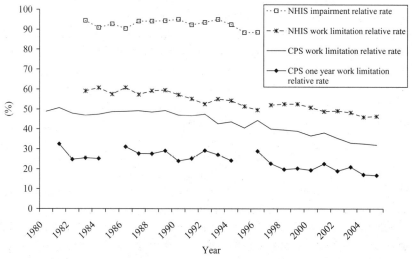

NOTE: Relative rates are the employment rate for persons with work limitations (impairments) divided by the employment rate for those without work limitations (impairments). The NHIS impairment measure is only available from 1983 to 1996 due to the NHIS redesign. Two different series (1983–1996, 1997–2006) for the NHIS work limitation measure are used because of differences that may have occurred related to the NHIS 1996 redesign.

SOURCE: Burkhauser et al. (2002) and authors' calculations using the CPS and the NHIS.

ment rates in 1996, a year in which comparable data exists across all measures, ranges from a high of 89 percent for the NHIS impairment measure to a low of 29 percent for the longer term work limitation in the CPS (Figure 4.4; see Table 4A.3 in Appendix 4A for detailed data).

Despite the overall differences in the level of these rates, the striking aspect of Figure 4.4 is the relative long-term decline in employment rates of people with disabilities across all comparable measures since the 1980s. The relative employment rates using the CPS work-limitation and long-term work-limitation measures dropped from 51 and 32 percent, respectively, in 1981 to 32 percent and 17 percent in 2005. In the NHIS, comparisons for work limitations and impairment definitions are limited to 10-year intervals, but the general direction of the relative rate measures is also downward. These findings are important because they illustrate the potential for using the NHIS and CPS for trend analysis and suggest the findings for trends in relative employment outcomes are not sensitive to the disability conceptualization.

The trends in Figure 4.4 also show the importance of making comparisons of employment rates across similar points in the business cycle, a point that was emphasized by Burkhauser et al. (2002). The relative employment rates across all disability measures increased in periods immediately following the recessions of 1991 and 2001. They declined during the economic expansions of the late 1980s and late 1990s, indicating that persons with disabilities tended to lose ground relative to those without disabilities during these periods.

Recent Employment Estimates from the ACS

The ACS has several features that make it one of the best sources for up-to-date estimates of employment rates of people with disabilities. First, its large sample allows users to produce reasonable estimates of narrowly defined subgroups (e.g., Native Americans) and small area estimates (e.g., estimates created for states and counties). Second, it allows users to create a broader set of disability measures than the CPS does and a broader set of employment measures than the NHIS does. Third, the data are available relatively quickly after being collected. The Census Bureau releases a wide variety of disability employment rate tables on its American Factfinder site approximately eight months after the last month of data collection in a given calendar year, and it also releases a Public Use Microdata Sample (PUMS) that contains the individual-level data necessary to construct customized tables. PUMS data allow users to describe the employment rate for subgroups of people with a disability at the national level as well as to construct customized state-level disability tables. The timely and easily accessible data drawn from the ACS is an improvement over the SIPP, which does not collect or release disability employment rate data on an annual basis. It is also an improvement over the NHIS, which releases a public-use data file soon after the annual data collection but does not produce easily accessible estimates on the employment rate of people with disabilities.

As can be seen in Table 4.3, which uses data from the 2006 ACS, 39 percent of those aged 25–61 with a disability were employed using the past week as our reference period compared to 81 percent of those without a disability. This results in a relative employment rate of 48 percent. The employment rate results are similar to those in the previous section—among the population with a disability, the employment rate is highest for those with sensory disabilities (50 percent), followed by physical impairments (33 percent), mental impairments (29 percent), work limitations (18 percent), ADL limitations (17 percent), and IADL limitations (17 percent). The levels and relative rates are somewhat higher when the any annual employment measure is used and somewhat lower when the full-time annual measure is used. The ordering across disability types, however, is similar. The lone exception is the lower employment rate for the full-time annual measure for those with a work limitation compared to those with an ADL limitation.

Table 4.3 also shows differences in the employment rate across sex, race, and education subgroups. Although the levels differ across sex (men have higher employment rate levels), the relative employment rate between those with and without a disability is almost identical, as shown in column 3. The employment rate ordering across the various disability types is also similar across groups.

State- and Local-Level Estimates from the ACS

Both the CPS and the ACS may be used to construct state-level estimates, but the U.S. Census Bureau recommends using the ACS for up-to-date employment rate data for all states and some smaller geographic areas. The 2006 ACS sample is large enough to produce estimates on geographic areas with a population of 65,000 or more, including 783 counties, 436 congressional districts, 621 metropolitan statistical areas (MSAs), all 50 states, and the District of Columbia. In future years, it will be able to support smaller area estimates by pooling adjacent years of data together.

A major advantage of the ACS is the ability to use broader disability concepts than are available in other sources to illustrate the substantial variation in the relative employment rates of people with disabilities to people without disabilities across states (Figure 4.5). The differences

Figure 4.5 Relative Reference Period Employment Rates of Adults (Aged 25–61), by State (2005)

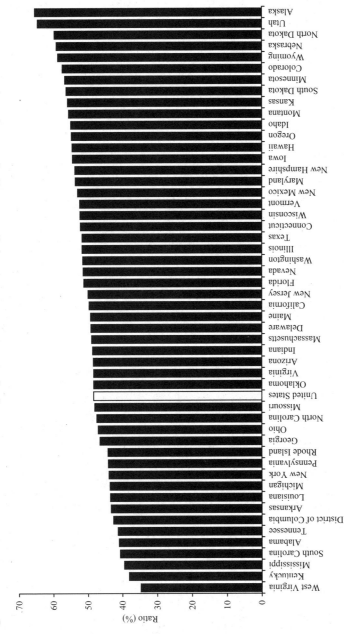

NOTE: Relative reference period employment rate calculated as the ratio of the employment rate of people who report "any disability" in the ACS, which includes any sensory impairment, physical impairment, mental impairment, ADL, IADL, or work limitation, relative to people who do not report any disability.

SOURCE: Authors' calculations using the 2006 ACS.

Table 4.3 Recent (2005) Employment Rates (%) for Demographic Groups from the ACS for the Working-Age Population (Aged 25–61)

Employment measure	No disability (1)	Any disability (2)	Relative employment rate [(1)/(2)] (3)	Sensory impairment (4)	Physical impairment (5)	Mental impairment (6)	ADL (7)	IADL (8)	Work limitation
All									
Reference week	81.4	39.4	48.4	50.3	33.5	29.0	17.8	17.3	18.4
Any annual	87.8	47.8	54.4	57.3	41.4	36.6	24.6	24.0	26.7
Full-time annual	60.1	23.6	39.3	34.3	19.6	14.7	9.1	7.9	8.0
Men									
Reference week	88.6	43.2	48.8	55.9	34.9	31.5	18.6	18.7	20.0
Any annual	94.7	51.9	54.9	63.3	43.5	39.5	25.9	25.8	28.9
Full-time annual	72.2	28.4	39.4	41.2	22.2	17.7	10.2	9.2	9.7
Women									
Reference week	74.4	35.9	48.2	42.8	32.3	26.7	17.1	16.3	17.0
Any annual	81.1	43.9	54.1	49.4	39.7	34.1	23.6	22.7	24.7
Full-time annual	48.3	19.2	39.7	25.2	17.4	11.9	8.2	6.9	6.5
White									
Reference week	82.1	39.7	48.4	51.2	33.4	29.2	17.6	17.6	18.6
Any annual	88.3	48.3	54.7	58.5	41.5	37.4	24.1	23.9	26.9
Full-time annual	60.7	23.7	39.0	35.2	19.5	14.3	8.4	7.1	7.6
Black									
Reference week	75.9	27.9	36.8	31.7	25.4	18.8	13.6	13.0	13.5

Any annual	85.5	37.8	44.2	41.0	34.7	27.5	21.3	20.0	21.6
Full-time annual	56.9	16.4	28.9	20.6	14.9	8.9	7.1	6.2	6.2
Hispanic									
Reference week	76.5	38.8	50.7	45.9	33.3	28.4	16.4	16.7	18.7
Any annual	83.6	48.4	57.9	54.7	42.0	36.6	23.0	23.6	27.7
Full-time annual	56.4	23.3	41.4	31.0	18.8	15.0	8.5	8.5	9.1
Native American									
Reference week	71.8	30.5	42.5	36.7	26.7	20.8	15.9	16.3	15.4
Any annual	81.6	41.5	50.9	47.3	35.0	31.0	24.6	23.5	24.0
Full-time annual	49.1	18.1	36.9	23.6	14.7	11.0	9.4	7.8	6.9
Asian									
Reference week	76.6	43.5	56.7	48.7	39.8	28.6	22.5	28.3	28.8
Any annual	82.9	52.7	63.6	55.9	47.4	35.6	30.6	38.2	38.5
Full-time annual	55.4	26.5	47.9	32.1	24.6	14.9	13.3	15.3	16.0
Less than high school									
Reference week	67.7	23.9	35.3	28.9	18.9	19.1	11.1	13.5	12.0
Any annual	76.8	32.5	42.3	36.6	26.8	26.4	16.1	18.3	18.6
Full-time annual	46.9	12.5	26.7	17.5	9.9	8.2	4.1	4.4	4.5
High school									
Reference week	78.7	35.6	45.3	46.5	29.9	27.0	15.1	15.7	16.5
Any annual	86.0	44.6	51.8	54.5	38.3	35.3	21.7	22.1	24.7
Full-time annual	59.3	21.1	35.5	31.7	17.1	13.3	7.4	6.4	7.0

(continued)

Table 4.3 (continued)

Employment measure	No disability (1)	Any disability (2)	Relative employment rate [(1)/(2)] (3)	Sensory impairment (4)	Physical impairment (5)	Mental impairment (6)	ADL (7)	IADL (8)	Work limitation
Greater than high school									
Reference week	83.8	47.7	56.9	59.5	41.9	35.1	23.4	21.5	23.7
Any annual	89.9	57.0	63.4	67.3	50.7	44.5	32.0	29.9	33.6
Full-time annual	62.0	29.7	47.8	41.8	25.5	18.5	12.6	10.8	10.6

SOURCE: Authors' calculations using the 2006 ACS.

in relative employment rates ranged from 35 percent (West Virginia) to 66 percent (Alaska). The primary reason for the large differences in the relative rates is the large differences in the employment rates of people with disabilities in these states. As shown in Table 4A.4 in Appendix 4A, West Virginia has the lowest employment rate for the any disability group (28 percent) nationally, and Alaska had one of the highest employment rates for the any disability group (51 percent). The federal government, and states themselves, can use these measures to both target and monitor their efforts for improving employment among people with disabilities. For example, does the large variation in relative employment rates suggest a potential area for improving state programs for people with disabilities by looking at the programs and policies of states that have relatively higher employment rates? When smaller area estimates eventually become available, states can target efforts at smaller geographic areas that may need disability employment support programs. By tracking consistently defined disability employment measures over time, states may identify progress toward reaching disability employment rate goals or identify a need to improve policies aimed at improving this rate.

Longitudinal Analysis from the SIPP

The primary advantage of using SIPP data for disability research is that it can be used to track longitudinal changes in characteristics and outcomes, such as changes in health, income, and employment. Tracking these changes is especially helpful in understanding the effects of events, such as the onset of a disability, on earnings. For example, Burkhauser and Wittenburg (1996) used SIPP data to compare the income and earnings of people who had reported a work limitation over multiple periods to individuals who had either had never reported such a limitation or had done so only recently. The longitudinal data also provides information on how employment varies throughout the year for people with disabilities.

To illustrate the potential for tracking outcomes longitudinally, we present data from the 2001 SIPP on changes in the health, employment, and program participation status of people who reported a work limitation in both wave 5 and wave 8, one year apart (Table 4.4).[9] More than 75 percent of the people who reported a work limitation in wave 5

Table 4.4 Longitudinal Analyses of Health and Employment Changes
from the SIPP for Adults (Age 25–61)

	No work limitation	Work limitation
Sample size	26,587	3,145
Population estimate	112,700,000	12,540,000
Changes in work limitation status (%)		
Work limitation in wave 5	0.0	100.0
Work limitation one year later	NA	75.6
No work limitation one year later	NA	24.4
Without work limitation in wave 5	100.0	0.0
Work limitation one year later	3.2	NA
No work limitation one year later	96.8	NA
Reference period (%)		
Employed (May 2002)	82.0	28.0
Employed one year later (May 2003)	75.6	22.0
Not employed one year later (May 2003)	6.4	6.0
Not employed (May 2002)	18.0	72.0
Employed one year later (May 2003)	5.8	6.1
Not employed one year later (May 2003)	12.2	65.9

NOTE: Because of attrition, there are respondents who do not have data in both time periods (May 2002 and May 2003). The amount of attrition is larger than in previous tables, but it most likely does not have a substantive effect on the findings.
SOURCE: Wittenburg and Nelson (2006), who used data from the 2001 SIPP.

also reported a work limitation one year later (in wave 8). These results suggest that at least three-quarters of the population with a work limitation are composed of people who have had the limitation for more than one year. Only 3.2 percent of those without a work limitation in wave 5 reported a work limitation one year later, but this seemingly small incidence of disability actually represents a large number of people (approximately 3.6 million people) because the total population without a disability is so large. However, this population is still much smaller than the overall base of all people with disabilities (approximately 12 million people).

Employment status also changes throughout the course of the year, which partly reflects the changing health status of people with disabilities. For example, 28 percent of those who report a work limitation in wave 5 were working in May 2002, and 22 percent were working in May 2003 (i.e., 78 percent of workers with a limitation who were working in May 2002 were also working a year later). Similarly, 72 percent of workers who reported a work limitation in wave 5 were not employed in May 2002, and 66 percent of those were not employed one year later. These findings underscore the dynamic nature of the disability process and how a person's health and employment status can change throughout the year.

Linked Administrative Data

Another advantage of the SIPP, CPS, and future versions of the ACS is that they include linked data to SSA records on program participation and earnings, which can be accessed on a restricted basis to examine long-term trends in program and employment outcomes.[10] The primary advantage of the matched data is that they combine survey responses for a nationally representative sample of survey respondents with lifetime program and earnings information from the SSA administrative records. The SSA administrative records include information on participation in SSI and SSDI programs and annual earnings from SSA-covered employment. Hence, researchers can use these data to observe in detail the program participation and earnings before, during, and after the respondent's interviews. The combination of survey and administrative data provides detailed characteristics of Social Security disability program applicants and recipients—family characteristics, health, labor market, and other program participation information (e.g., food stamps)—that is not possible with SSA administrative data alone.

In Table 4.5, we present descriptive information on trends in program participation and earnings of people with and without work limitations who were working during their first interview for the 1990, 1991, 1992, and 1993 SIPP panels (Stapleton, Wittenburg, and Maag 2005).[11] They pooled data from these panels to examine transitions into SSI and

Table 4.5 Longitudinal Analyses of Employment and Program Participation Using Matched SIPP and SSA Administrative Data for Adults (Aged 25–61)

	Year relative to first SIPP interview										
	−5	−4	−3	−2	−1	0	1	2	3	4	5
Employment rates (%)											
Men without limitations	92.5	93.6	94.7	96.0	97.1	100	96.7	95.1	93.8	92.8	91.6
Men with limitations	88.5	89.3	90.8	91.0	92.4	100	93.2	87.9	84.7	81.6	78.5
Women without limitations	84.5	86.4	88.9	91.2	93.9	100	94.4	91.9	90.2	89.1	87.7
Women with limitations	78.3	78.8	80.4	85.4	88.5	100	87.2	82.8	79.2	76.3	74.6
SSI/SSDI participation rates (%)											
Men without limitations	0.0	0.0	0.0	0.0	0.3	0.0	0.3	0.7	1.0	1.4	1.7
Men with limitations	0.8	0.8	0.8	0.5	0.4	0.0	3.0	5.8	8.0	10.4	11.1
Women without limitations	0.1	0.0	0.0	0.0	0.0	0.0	0.3	0.7	1.1	1.5	1.9
Women with limitations	1.1	0.9	0.8	0.5	0.4	0.0	2.4	4.8	6.9	9.8	10.6

NOTE: Stapleton, Wittenburg, and Maag (2005) defined employment and program participation using SSA administrative data. Employment is defined as any annual earnings, and program participation is defined as any participation in SSI or SSDI during the year.
SOURCE: Stapleton, Wittenburg, and Maag (2005), who used data from restricted access matched SSA data that were linked to the 1990, 1991, 1992, and 1993 SIPP panels.

SSDI as well as entries and exits from the labor market. They identified workers as those for whom Social Security earnings were reported for their base year (i.e., earnings that appeared in SSA's administrative files) but who did not receive SSA disability benefits. "Employment exits and re-entries" and "program entries and exits" were identified solely from the administrative data. A respondent was defined as being employed during a calendar year if, and only if, he or she had earnings in that year. An exit was defined as a change from positive calendar year earnings to zero earnings in the following year, and re-entry was defined as the opposite. Similarly, program entry (exit) was marked by a change in SSDI or SSI benefits from zero to positive (positive to zero) during a year.

Stapleton, Wittenburg, and Maag (2005) showed that there are important differences in earnings and program participation between people with and without disabilities before, during, and after their SIPP interviews. For example, workers with disabilities (regardless of sex) were less likely to be employed than their counterparts without disabilities in the five years leading up to the interview. In the year after the first SIPP interview, workers with disabilities experienced a sharper employment decline relative to those without disabilities, and a large gap between the two groups emerged by the fifth year after the interview. Additionally, very few employed workers in these panels had participated in SSDI or SSI before their base year, although participation did increase in the five years following their first SIPP interview. Program participation for workers with disabilities grew substantially in the five years after the base year—to approximately 12 percent, compared to about 2 percent for those without disabilities. Although many people with disabilities who were not employed in the fifth year had entered one of the disability programs, this analysis suggests that a substantial share had not.

DISCUSSION

Based on the information in this chapter, we found substantial differences in the employment rates both within and across national data sources. These differences may be driven by several factors, including 1) differences in the definition of disability, 2) differences in the definition of employment, and 3) differences in survey design.

Much confusion arises in the literature and public discourse about the employment of people with disabilities because of the variation in employment statistics that stems from these factors. In the absence of a common understanding of what "disability" means, or a standard for defining employment, the only way to minimize confusion is to more precisely describe the disability population referenced and the employment measure used. When CPS data are used, it is best to refer to the "population with a work limitation," rather than the "population with disabilities." In the ACS, when including both work and IADL limitations, it would be "the population with participation restrictions," or more generally, when using data on participation restrictions, activity limitations, and impairment, it would be the population with "any disability." A more precise definition of these terms and of the employment measure used should reduce confusion. In addition, information on relevant aspects of the survey design can provide context for estimates on the disability employment rate. Of course, this is burdensome. It is much easier to simply use the terms "disability" and "employment" without reference to specific definitions or a survey's context. To do so, however, is likely to be confusing at best and misleading at worst.

We also delineated the advantages and limitations of the different national data sources used to study different aspects of employment for the population with disabilities. The primary advantages of the ACS are that it produces timely information, has substantial employment information, and uses a set of disability measures that can capture a broadly defined group of people with disabilities, as well as more narrowly defined groups. The ACS is relatively new, however, and currently is limited in its ability to measure time trends because of ongoing improvements. In addition, the ACS is a repeated cross-section and does not track sample members over time. The CPS has the most extensive measures of employment, has the longest consistently measured time series of people with a health-related work limitation, and is able to track a sample of respondents over a one-year period. The primary drawback is that the CPS has a single disability measure (work limitation). The NHIS has an extensive set of disability measures, a fair amount of employment measures, and can produce consistent time series for certain periods of time (1983–1996 and 1997–2007). It is limited, however, in that it cannot produce state-level estimates and is a repeated cross-sectional survey that does not follow sample members over time. Finally, the SIPP has the most extensive combination of disability and employment measures among the national data sources, it may be used to follow individuals over a three-year period, and it has the capability to be linked to SSA administrative data. It is limited in that it is conducted only periodically, is not well suited to produce time series estimates, and is too small to support state-level estimates. Thus, users may be limited to specific data sources depending upon the particular aspect of the disability employment characteristics that are of interest, and they must make decisions on the source of data based upon advantages and limitations of each.

Fortunately, there are new enhancements that will substantially improve the existing data on employment for people with disabilities, which are discussed in more detail in Stapleton, Livermore, and She (2009). The creation of an official disability measure in the CPS is particularly noteworthy because the BLS will be able to regularly disseminate detailed employment statistics on the population with disabilities, as they do for other subpopulations. Additionally, the inclusion of more disability measures in the CPS will allow researchers to expand beyond the employment rate estimates for the work-limitation measure and estimate employment rates for alternative conceptualizations, including those that include functional limitations. These enhancements essentially build on the advantages these data sources already have for conducting disability research and create a basis for tracking lifetime employment outcomes. Armed with these enhanced data on employment outcomes, policymakers will have better information to administer programs and to identify potentially promising new policies that will improve the employment and economic self-sufficiency of people with disabilities.

Appendix 4A

Table 4A.1 Employment Definitions from National Data Sources

Measure/data source	Definitions
Employment: current employment	
ACS	LAST WEEK, did this person do ANY work for either pay or profit? Mark the "Yes" box even if the person worked for only 1 hour, or helped without pay in a family business or farm for 15 hours or more, or was on active duty in the Armed Forces. LAST WEEK, was the person TEMPORARILY absent from a job or business? (Yes, on vacation, temporary illness, labor dispute, etc.)
CPS	(Beginning in 1994) Last week, did [person] do any work for either pay or profit?
NHIS	(Prior to 1997) During the previous two weeks, did [person] work at any time at a job or business not counting work around the house? (Include unpaid work in the family farm/business.) Even though [person] did not work during those 2 weeks, did [person] have a job or business? . . . "Earlier you said that [person] has a job or business but didn't work last week or the week before. Was [person] . . . on layoff from a job?"
	(After 1996) Which of the following [were/was] [you/ subject name] doing last week? . . . "working for pay at a job or business" or "with a job or business, but not at work."
SIPP	The Labor Force Section of SIPP includes a summary measure of total personal earnings from all jobs. If a person has any earnings in the reference period, the respondent is considered employed.

(continued)

Table 4A.1 (continued)

Measure/data source	Definitions

Employment: any annual employment

ACS

At least 52 hours of work during the previous year. Determined by multiplying usual hours per week by the number of weeks worked in past 12 months, which are derived from the following questions. During the PAST 12 MONTHS, how many WEEKS did this person work? *Count paid vacation, paid sick leave, and military service.* During the PAST 12 MONTHS, in the WEEKS WORKED, how many hours did this person usually work each WEEK?

CPS

At least 52 hours of work during the previous year. Determined by multiplying usual hours per week, which are derived from the following questions, by the number of weeks worked in past 12 months. During [the previous calendar year] in how many weeks did [person] work even for a few hours? Include paid vacation and sick leave as work. In the weeks that [person] worked [the previous calendar year], how many hours did [person] usually work per week?

NHIS

Did {you/he/she}work for pay at any time in {last year in 4 digit format}?

SIPP

Usual hours worked during the month times the number of weeks worked during the month summed over the period June 2001–May 2002—if greater than or equal to 52 hours, the person worked sometime in the previous year. (Labor Force Section) Usual hours worked during the reference month includes hours at Job 1, Job 2, business 1, and business 2 and number of weeks worked during the reference month.

Employment: full-time annual employment

ACS

At least 50 weeks during the previous year and at least 35 hours per week, as determined from the following questions. During the PAST 12 MONTHS, how many WEEKS did this person work? *Count paid vacation, paid sick leave and military service.* During the PAST 12 MONTHS, in the WEEKS WORKED, how many hours did this person usually work each WEEK?

Table 4A.1 (continued)

Measure/data source	Definitions
CPS	At least 50 weeks during the previous year and at least 35 hours per week, as determined from the following questions. During [the previous calendar year] in how many weeks did [person] work even for a few hours? Include paid vacation and sick leave as work. In the weeks that [person] worked [the previous calendar year], how many hours did [person] usually work per week?
NHIS	Those answering 35 or greater hours and 12 months to the following questions. How many hours did {you/subject name} work LAST WEEK at all jobs or businesses? OR How many hours {do/does} {you/subject name} USUALLY work at all jobs or businesses? How many months in {last year in 4 digit format} did {you/subject name} have at least one job or business?
SIPP	If the average over the 12 month period of June 2001– May 2002 of the usual hours worked during the month is equal to or greater than 35 and the total number of weeks worked during the 12 month period was equal to or greater than 50, the person is considered to be full-time annual employed.

SOURCE: Adapted from Burkhauser and Houtenville (2006), Weathers (2005), Harris, Hendershot, and Stapleton (2005), and Wittenburg and Nelson (2006).

Table 4A.2 Employment Rates Using Alternative Employment Reference Periods and Disability Definitions for Adults (Aged 25–61) from the 2001 SIPP

Employed during	No disability	Any disability At least 1 of the 6	Participation restriction Work limitation	IADLs	Activity limitation ADLs	Impairments Mental	Physical	Sensory
All								
Reference period	82.4	48.9	27.7	20.3	22.8	37.0	46.4	53.5
Any annual	90.6	61.1	41.0	34.1	38.8	46.3	59.0	63.7
Full-time annual	58.1	31.2	15.3	12.0	15.0	20.3	29.6	35.6

SOURCE: Wittenburg and Nelson (2006), who used data from the 2001 SIPP.

Table 4A.3 Any Annual Employment of Working-Age Men (Aged 21–58) in the CPS and NHIS Data Using Alternative Definitions of Disability

	CPS Annual Socioeconomic Supplement						NHIS					
	Cross-sectional data			Matched data			Cross-sectional data[a]			Cross-sectional data		
	Work limitation			Two-period work limitation			Work limitation			Impairment		
Year	With	Without	Relative rate	With	Without	Relative rate	With	Without	Relative rate	With	Without	Relative rate
1980	47.1	96.3	48.9	—	—	—	—	—	—	—	—	—
1981	48.7	96.0	50.7	31.2	96.1	32.5	—	—	—	—	—	—
1982	45.3	94.5	47.9	23.5	94.6	24.8	—	—	—	—	—	—
1983	44.2	94.3	46.9	24.0	94.3	25.5	52.8	89.4	59.1	82.3	87.2	94.4
1984	45.3	95.5	47.4	24.1	95.5	25.2	55.6	91.6	60.7	81.7	89.9	90.9
1985	46.7	95.9	48.7	—	—	—	53.1	92.3	57.5	83.8	90.4	92.7
1986	47.0	96.1	48.9	29.8	95.9	31.1	55.9	92.0	60.8	81.1	89.7	90.4
1987	47.2	95.9	49.2	26.6	96.2	27.7	53.0	92.5	57.3	84.6	89.9	94.1
1988	46.6	96.1	48.5	26.5	95.9	27.6	55.1	93.1	59.2	86.1	91.6	94.1
1989	47.4	96.1	49.3	28.0	96.2	29.1	55.7	93.6	59.5	86.8	92.1	94.3
1990	45.0	95.8	47.0	22.9	95.5	24.0	52.9	92.5	57.2	86.2	90.7	95.0
1991	44.5	95.3	46.7	24.1	95.5	25.2	50.5	91.5	55.2	83.4	90.3	92.3
1992	45.0	94.7	47.5	27.5	94.2	29.2	47.9	91.1	52.6	83.1	88.9	93.5

(continued)

Table 4A.3 (continued)

1993	40.3	94.7	42.6	25.7	94.8	27.1	50.4	91.6	55.1	85.2	89.7	95.0
1994	41.4	95.0	43.6	22.9	94.5	24.2	50.0	92.2	54.3	83.0	89.8	92.4
1995	38.4	94.9	40.5	—	—	—	47.6	92.5	51.4	79.9	90.4	88.4
1996	42.1	95.1	44.3	27.4	94.9	28.9	46.1	92.9	49.6	79.6	89.8	88.6
1997	38.2	95.4	40.0	21.5	94.7	22.7	50.5	96.9	52.1	—	—	—
1998	37.6	95.3	39.5	18.9	95.4	19.8	51.1	97.2	52.6	—	—	—
1999	37.0	95.2	38.9	19.2	94.8	20.3	51.2	97.4	52.6	—	—	—
2000	34.7	94.9	36.6	18.4	94.7	19.4	49.4	97.0	50.9	—	—	—
2001	36.0	94.5	38.1	21.3	94.1	22.6	46.7	95.5	48.9	—	—	—
2002	33.1	93.4	35.4	17.7	93.3	19.0	46.6	94.7	49.2	—	—	—
2003	30.8	93.2	33.0	19.5	92.8	21.0	45.4	93.9	48.3	—	—	—
2004	30.4	93.3	32.6	15.9	92.4	17.2	43.0	93.4	46.0	—	—	—
2005	29.9	93.4	32.0	15.7	93.3	16.8	43.4	93.5	46.4	—	—	—

[a] NHIS changes in 1997 make work-limitation statistics from 1997 to 2005 not comparable to earlier statistics.
SOURCE: Authors' calculations using the CPS, 1981–2006, and NHIS, 1983–1996.

Table 4A.4 2006 ACS Reference Period Employment Rate for the Working-Age Population (Aged 25–61), by State

	No disability (1)	Any disability (2)	Relative employment rate = (2)/(1) (3)	Impairment					
				Sensory (4)	Physical (5)	Mental (6)	ADL (7)	IADL (8)	Work limitation (9)
All States	81.4	39.4	48.4	50.3	33.5	29.0	17.8	17.3	18.4
Alabama	80.2	33.0	41.1	42.4	27.3	24.1	14.8	13.1	12.2
Alaska	77.7	50.9	65.5	67.0	44.7	36.9	36.2	19.2	22.7
Arizona	80.0	38.9	48.6	47.7	33.9	28.4	17.1	16.5	18.4
Arkansas	81.4	35.3	43.4	45.3	27.5	25.4	9.0	10.7	14.5
California	78.9	39.2	49.8	50.7	34.4	28.8	17.8	18.6	19.1
Colorado	82.7	47.5	57.5	60.4	41.1	36.4	24.4	20.2	23.9
Connecticut	83.1	43.5	52.3	57.3	36.4	35.0	21.7	20.9	21.9
Delaware	83.2	41.0	49.3	51.7	35.7	37.1	19.5	13.8	15.9
District of Columbia	80.9	34.5	42.7	47.2	30.9	18.5	7.7	17.7	15.9
Florida	81.2	41.7	51.3	52.7	35.5	29.2	17.8	17.3	19.7
Georgia	80.8	37.8	46.7	47.5	31.5	27.5	16.8	14.4	16.2
Hawaii	79.2	43.3	54.7	41.9	37.2	30.8	21.1	22.9	28.1
Idaho	81.7	45.0	55.1	54.5	37.2	37.5	20.5	20.2	22.5
Illinois	81.0	42.0	51.8	54.5	35.4	31.6	19.3	19.0	21.7
Indiana	82.9	40.5	48.8	53.0	33.3	29.8	16.1	17.2	19.4
Iowa	86.9	47.4	54.6	61.3	40.9	41.6	24.2	22.1	25.0

(continued)

Table 4A.4 (continued)

	No disability (1)	Any disability (2)	Relative employment rate = (2)/(1) (3)	Impairment			ADL (7)	IADL (8)	Work limitation (9)
				Sensory (4)	Physical (5)	Mental (6)			
Kansas	84.8	47.5	56.0	58.3	40.8	39.2	25.9	27.8	24.6
Kentucky	81.0	31.0	38.2	40.5	25.5	17.9	13.9	10.8	11.5
Louisiana	78.4	34.2	43.6	43.3	29.4	25.9	16.0	14.9	15.6
Maine	85.0	42.0	49.4	57.5	33.0	34.3	20.2	11.6	18.8
Maryland	84.1	45.3	53.8	55.3	40.3	35.1	18.9	21.8	21.5
Massachusetts	84.1	41.3	49.1	53.6	37.1	32.5	23.2	21.8	20.6
Michigan	79.5	34.7	43.7	46.1	28.3	26.5	15.2	13.9	15.7
Minnesota	86.3	49.0	56.8	61.7	42.1	40.2	29.6	29.4	28.6
Mississippi	79.8	31.6	39.6	40.7	26.0	20.7	13.8	9.9	11.3
Missouri	83.3	40.2	48.2	45.0	33.6	30.5	15.2	16.6	19.5
Montana	84.2	46.9	55.7	64.2	36.4	34.4	21.6	17.5	23.1
Nebraska	86.4	51.1	59.2	67.6	45.3	43.9	17.0	20.3	25.2
Nevada	81.4	41.9	51.5	55.4	34.9	35.5	21.0	20.2	19.7
New Hampshire	86.6	46.7	53.9	66.0	41.0	37.0	28.0	28.4	23.7
New Jersey	82.1	41.1	50.1	51.0	36.1	29.6	18.9	21.8	19.7
New Mexico	78.9	41.9	53.1	52.5	35.2	31.8	18.7	19.0	20.5
New York	80.6	35.5	44.0	48.3	30.6	25.4	16.3	16.0	17.4

North Carolina	81.6	38.8	47.6	45.9	33.1	27.8	15.8	17.3	17.3
North Dakota	88.1	52.7	59.8	66.7	48.0	47.0	25.3	35.8	27.9
Ohio	82.5	39.0	47.2	50.7	32.8	29.8	20.3	20.3	18.5
Oklahoma	81.8	39.7	48.5	49.6	34.2	26.6	17.7	15.9	16.4
Oregon	80.8	44.4	54.9	55.8	39.4	33.4	18.3	18.0	22.4
Pennsylvania	82.7	36.6	44.2	51.3	30.7	26.2	16.5	17.6	16.7
Rhode Island	83.8	37.1	44.3	55.5	29.1	27.7	19.2	20.7	16.7
South Carolina	81.4	33.2	40.8	45.4	27.5	23.4	16.0	14.8	14.8
South Dakota	87.1	49.1	56.4	57.1	41.8	38.2	31.2	26.3	29.9
Tennessee	81.2	33.7	41.4	41.4	28.5	21.3	14.3	12.9	15.4
Texas	79.8	41.3	51.8	50.9	35.4	29.2	17.4	16.4	18.2
Utah	81.4	52.7	64.7	67.9	44.8	42.7	32.0	26.7	29.1
Vermont	86.6	45.5	52.5	56.4	36.2	35.5	28.9	21.9	20.0
Virginia	82.9	40.2	48.5	46.0	34.6	29.9	18.8	19.4	18.9
Washington	80.8	41.7	51.6	55.6	35.9	30.3	19.8	18.1	19.5
West Virginia	79.1	27.5	34.8	29.6	23.0	16.1	9.3	9.5	12.7
Wisconsin	85.9	45.0	52.4	58.6	38.4	37.5	24.1	19.9	23.6
Wyoming	84.8	49.9	58.8	68.5	36.9	37.5	20.7	17.2	24.4

SOURCE: Authors' calculations using the 2006 ACS.

Notes

1. The redesign of the NHIS that occurred in 1997, described in Chapter 2, makes it impossible to develop an accurate and reliable time series across the 1983–1996 period and the 1997 period forward. We chose to present work limitation data from the 1983–1996 period and 1997–2005 period in this chapter to illustrate the similarity in trends across the CPS and NHIS measures.
2. For specific employment definitions from each survey, see Table A4.1 in Appendix 4A.
3. We used a weekly reference period to report work from the CPS, ACS, and NHIS and a monthly period to report work from the SIPP. We chose the monthly period for the SIPP because most SIPP-based estimates are monthly, given the design of the survey.
4. The CPS can also be used to create panel estimates by linking respondents across different waves of the survey.
5. The "no disabilities" category Wittenburg and Nelson (2006) use is the same as that documented in Weathers (2009). It includes people without any reported participation restrictions, activity limitations, or impairments.
6. We did not have access to linked administrative data from the CPS. However, we do present estimates from the linked SIPP administrative data files from one of our prior studies.
7. Although some components of the March supplement of the CPS have changed over time, the employment and work-limitation measures have remained the same, and there does not appear to be a "seam" in the CPS data for these measures.
8. We focus on employment rates of men because there was a sharper decline in the employment rate of this group that can be readily identified in the tables. Burkhauser, Houtenville, and Wittenburg (2003) also compared employment rates of women with and without disabilities and found the same relative differences as they found for men. However, the relative employment rate differences for women were caused largely by the expansion in employment by women without disabilities, whereas the relative employment rate differences for men were caused by the decline in employment of men with disabilities, as will be discussed in more detail in this chapter.
9. This table updates the earlier analysis of Burkhauser and Wittenburg (1996).
10. Researchers can apply for access to the restricted files through Census's Center for Economic Studies program at www.ces.census.gov. The Census Bureau and the SSA are working on linking the ACS to SSA administrative data, but these linked data are not yet available to researchers. Some caution must be used in using linked files, because the match rates of survey to administrative records varies over time across both the CPS and SIPP. Finally, the NHIS data for 1994–1998 have been linked to SSA program participation data but not to earnings records. The match rate is much lower than that of the CPS and the SIPP, which substantially limits its value in conducting disability research, as described in Stapleton, Wittenburg, and Thorton (2009).

11. Stapleton, Wittenburg, and Maag (2005) also present analyses to examine specific transitions following business cycle changes that use more complex multivariate analyses.

References

Acemoglu, Daron, and Joshua Angrist. 2001. "Consequences of Employment Protection? The Case of the Americans with Disabilities Act." *Journal of Political Economy* 109(5): 915–957.

Ballou, Janice, and Jason Markesich. 2009. "Survey Data Collection Methods." In *Counting Working-Age People with Disabilities: What Current Data Tell Us and Options for Improvement*, Andrew J. Houtenville, David C. Stapleton, Robert R. Weathers II, and Richard V. Burkhauser, eds. Kalamazoo, MI: W.E. Upjohn Institute for Employment Research, pp. 265–298.

Bureau of Labor Statistics. n.d. "Economic News Release: Employment Situation." Washington, DC: U.S. Department of Labor. http://www.bls.gov/news.release/empsit.toc.htm (accessed October 30, 2009).

Burkhauser, Richard V., Mary C. Daly, Andrew J. Houtenville, and Nigar Nargis. 2002. "Self-Reported Work Limitation Data: What They Can and Cannot Tell Us." *Demography* 39(3): 541–555.

Burkhauser, Richard, and Andrew Houtenville. 2006. "A Guide to Disability Statistics from the Current Population Survey—Annual Social and Economic Supplement (March CPS)." Ithaca, NY: Cornell University, Rehabilitation Research and Training Center on Disability Demographics and Statistics.

Burkhauser, Richard V., Andrew Houtenville, and David C. Wittenburg. 2003. "A User's Guide to Current Statistics on the Employment of People with Disabilities." In *The Decline in Employment of People with Disabilities: A Policy Puzzle,* David C. Stapleton and Richard V. Burkhauser, eds. Kalamazoo, MI: W.E. Upjohn Institute for Employment Research, pp. 23–86.

Burkhauser, Richard V., and David C. Wittenburg. 1996. "How Current Disability Transfer Policies Discourage Work: Analysis from the 1990 SIPP." *Journal of Vocational Rehabilitation* 7(1): 9–27.

Harris, Benjamin, Gary Hendershot, and David Stapleton. 2005. "A Guide to Disability Statistics from the National Health Interview Survey." Ithaca, NY: Cornell University, Rehabilitation Research and Training Center on Disability Demographics and Statistics.

Houtenville, Andrew J., and Richard V. Burkhauser. 2004. "Did the Employment of People with Disabilities Decline in the 1990s, and Was the ADA Responsible? A Replication and Robustness Check of Acemoglu and Angrist (2001)—Research Brief." Ithaca, NY: Cornell University, Rehabilitation Research and Training Center for Economic Research on Employment Policy for Persons with Disabilities.

Houtenville, Andrew J., Elizabeth Potamites, William A. Erickson, and S. Antonio Ruiz-Quintanilla. 2009. "Disability Prevalence and Demographics." In *Counting Working-Age People with Disabilities: What Current Data Tell Us and Options for Improvement*, Andrew J. Houtenville, David C. Stapleton, Robert R. Weathers II, and Richard V. Burkhauser, eds. Kalamazoo, MI: W.E. Upjohn Institute for Employment Research, pp. 69–99.

Kaye, H. Stephen. 2003. "Employment and the Changing Disability Population." In *The Decline in Employment of People with Disabilities: A Policy Puzzle*, David C. Stapleton and Richard V. Burkhauser, eds. Kalamazoo, MI: W.E. Upjohn Institute for Employment Research, pp. 217–258.

McNeil, John. 2000. "Employment, Earnings, and Disability." Paper presented at the 75th Annual Conference of the Western Economic Association International, held in Vancouver, BC, June 29–July 3, 2000. http://www.census.gov/hhes/www/disability/emperndis.pdf (accessed June 17, 2008).

Stapleton, David C., Gina A. Livermore, and Peiyun She. 2009. "Options for Improving Disability Data Collection." In *Counting Working-Age People with Disabilities: What Current Data Tell Us and Options for Improvement*, Andrew J. Houtenville, David C. Stapleton, Robert R. Weathers II, and Richard V. Burkhauser, eds. Kalamazoo, MI: W.E. Upjohn Institute for Employment Research, pp. 381–418.

Stapleton, David, David C. Wittenburg, and Elaine Maag. 2005. "A Difficult Cycle: The Effect of Labor Market Changes on the Employment and Program Participation of People with Disabilities." Cornell University, Ithaca, NY. Rehabilitation Research and Training Center for Economic Research on Employment Policy for Persons with Disabilities. http://digitalcommons.ilr.cornell.edu/editcollect/172/ (accessed September 23, 2008).

Stapleton, David C., David C. Wittenburg, and Craig Thornton. 2009. "Program Participants." In *Counting Working-Age People with Disabilities: What Current Data Tell Us and Options for Improvement*, Andrew J. Houtenville, David C. Stapleton, Robert R. Weathers II, and Richard V. Burkhauser, eds. Kalamazoo, MI: W.E. Upjohn Institute for Employment Research, pp. 299–352.

Steinmetz, Erika. 2004. "Americans with Disabilities: 2002." Current Population Reports, P70–107. Washington, DC: U.S. Census Bureau.

Weathers, Robert R. II. 2005. "A Guide to Disability Statistics from the American Community Survey." Ithaca, NY: Cornell University, Rehabilitation Research and Training Center on Disability Demographics and Statistics.

———. 2009. "The Disability Landscape." In *Counting Working-Age People with Disabilities: What Current Data Tell Us and Options for Improve-*

ment, Andrew J. Houtenville, David C. Stapleton, Robert R. Weathers II, and Richard V. Burkhauser, eds. Kalamazoo, MI: W.E. Upjohn Institute for Employment Research, pp. 27–67.

Wittenburg, David, and Sandi Nelson. 2006. "A Guide to Disability Statistics from the Survey of Income and Program Participation." Ithaca, NY: Cornell University, Rehabilitation Research and Training Center on Disability Demographics and Statistics.

5

Household Income

Richard V. Burkhauser
Cornell University

Ludmila Rovba
The Analysis Group, Inc.

Robert R. Weathers II
Social Security Administration

The economic well-being of households in market economies like the United States is most easily measured by income. So it is not surprising that U.S. statistical agencies have been tracking household income and its sources for representative samples of the American population with the Decennial Census since 1940 and annually with the Current Population Survey (CPS) since 1968. These data are used by the research and public policy communities to measure average income, income distribution (income inequality), and the share of the population with very low income (poverty rates). The data are also used to track changes in these values over time and to assess how income differs among subpopulations based on family structure, race, ethnicity, and age (DeNavas-Walt, Proctor, and Smith 2008). It is surprising, however, how little progress has been made in using such measures to track the economic well-being of working-age people with disabilities and how it has changed over time.

In this chapter, we use data from the CPS to examine the economic well-being of people with disabilities. We focus on the CPS because it is the primary data set that annually examines the economic well-being of people with disabilities, measures long-term economic well-being trends of this population, and it alone has used the same set of questions to capture both the income and disability status of working-age people since 1981. We also evaluate the economic well-being of people with disabilities using the new American Community Survey (ACS) because it offers a far richer set of questions to capture this population.

Our analysis of the CPS compares how working-age men (aged 21–58) with and without work limitations have fared over the last two business cycles of the twentieth century.[1] In so doing, we also show the dramatic shifts from private to public sources of income, particularly to Social Security Disability Insurance (SSDI) and Supplemental Security Income (SSI) benefits. These shifts are evident when the standard, single-period work-limitation measure of this population is used in the CPS data. It is even more pronounced when a two-period measure (having a work limitation in two consecutive Demographic Supplements to the CPS, hereafter the "March CPS") is used because it better captures the population with longer term, severe disabilities that government transfer programs like SSDI and SSI were designed to protect.

As discussed in Weathers (2009), a major limitation of the CPS data is that its measure of disability is whether a work limitation is reported. To show the sensitivity of the results, we compare levels of income for people with disabilities using the work-limitation-based disability measure in the CPS with results using a work-limitation-based measure of disability in the ACS. This comparison illustrates how income levels can change when broader definitions of disability are used. The comparison also shows that the income difference between those with and without disabilities, using the same definition of work limitation, do not change much between the two data sets. But income differences are much larger across the various definitions of disability captured in the ACS. When we use the broadest definition of working-age people with disabilities captured in the ACS, we find that this population is much better off than the subset of that population that report work limitations. Nonetheless, the income of this broader population with disabilities is still far below that of working-age people who do not report a disability. Finally, using the full power of the much larger samples collected by the ACS, we show that substantial differences in the relative economic well-being of those with and without disability persist across sex, race, educational attainment, and state.

USING THE CPS TO CAPTURE THE POPULATION
WITH DISABILITIES

The March CPS is a nationally representative, annual cross-sectional survey of approximately 150,000 noninstitutionalized civilians. It is collected by the Census Bureau and the Bureau of Labor Statistics (BLS) and is the main source of official U.S. employment and income statistics.

Since 1981, the CPS has consistently included a work-limitation question. Because a subsample of the March respondents is reinterviewed in the following March, the CPS allows researchers to create matched samples containing a second round of information on these individuals. Thus, researchers can measure the household income of people with work limitations as well as the sources of that income, in the same way that these values are officially measured for other at-risk populations.[2]

A major drawback of the CPS, however, is that it has very limited information on disability. Researchers must rely on its work-limitation questions alone to capture working-age people with disabilities. Nonetheless, the CPS has been widely used in the economics literature to look at the employment and/or economic well-being of working-age people with disabilities (Acemoglu and Angrist 2001; Autor and Duggan 2003; Bound and Waidmann 1992, 2002; Burkhauser, Daly, and Houtenville 2001; Burkhauser et al. 2002; Daly and Burkhauser 2003; Houtenville and Burkhauser 2005; Hotchkiss 2003, 2004; Jolls and Prescott 2005).

Although any self-reported disability questions must be used with caution, particularly if the answers are sensitive to the respondent's socioeconomic environment (as discussed in detail in Weathers 2009), the CPS is the only data set available for those interested in tracing the long-term economic outcomes of working-age people with disabilities.

We will follow convention in the literature by looking at the yearly household income of working-age men with and without disabilities adjusted for household size. Hence, our unit of analysis is the household (all those living in the house). Using a one-period measure of disability, we look at the yearly household income of men in the year prior to the

March survey and the sources of that income. We assumed that income is shared equally in the household and the household size adjusted income of each household member is equal to the total household income divided by the number of members of the household to the 0.5 power.[3] Income is adjusted for inflation using the Urban Consumer Price Index (CPI-U) estimated by the BLS. Unless otherwise indicated, all incomes reported are adjusted for household size and for inflation to 2004 dollars.

We look at the yearly household income of men in the year prior to the March CPS response. We only consider a respondent to have a longer term disability if he also reported a work limitation in the previous March. This two-period measure of disability is superior to the one-period measure because it brackets the yearly income measure being used, and it better captures those most likely to be targeted by public programs.

THE ECONOMIC WELL-BEING OF WORKING-AGE MEN WITH AND WITHOUT DISABILITIES

Although the United States economy has grown substantially, the long periods of economic growth that have substantially improved the economic well-being of the average American (as measured by median household income; Figure 5.1) have also been punctuated by periods of recessions and drops in economic well-being. We were able to use the CPS data to examine the incomes of men with and without disabilities from 1980 to 2005, a period that contains two complete business cycles.

Table 5.1 reports the mean household size-adjusted income for working-age men with and without work limitations from 1980 through 2005 using both a one- and a two-period measure of work limitations. Inter-temporal comparisons of household incomes are sensitive to the years over which the comparisons are made, and mean income is sensitive to the business cycle. Mean household income rises during periods of economic growth, only to fall as the economy goes into recession. As can be seen in Table 5.1, underlying business conditions affect the

Figure 5.1 Real Median Household Income (in 2007 Dollars) in the United States, 1967–2007

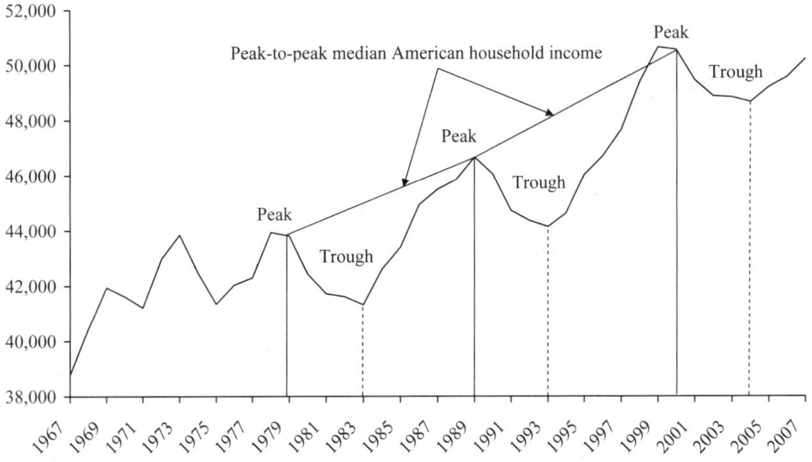

SOURCE: DeNavas-Walt, Proctor, and Smith (2008).

mean household income of working-age men both with and without work limitations over this period. To disentangle the impact of short-run business conditions from longer term economic trends on the relative incomes of these two populations, we looked at similar points in the business cycle over the entire period. Ideally, we would compare business cycle peaks, but the starting period of our sample just misses the 1979 peak. Hence, in our discussion of Table 5.1, we examined the two complete business cycles defined by the three business cycle troughs in 1983, 1993, and 2004.[4]

The recessionary trough of 1983 marked the low point in mean income over the entire period. It was followed by seven years of rising mean income to a business cycle peak in 1989. But this was followed by four years of decline in mean income to a business cycle trough in 1993. Using our one-period measure of work limitations, we found that the household income of men without work limitations rose in real terms over the entire business cycle of the 1980s (i.e., 1983 to 1993) from $38,264 to $42,394, while the household income of men with work limitations remained almost stationary, going from $23,720 to $23,599.

Table 5.1 Mean Household Size-Adjusted Income (in 2004 Dollars) for Working-Age Men (Aged 21–58) with and without Work Limitations from the March CPS

Year	One-period sample				Two-period sample			
	Total	With (1)	Without (2)	Ratio (1)/(2)	Total	With (1)	Without (2)	Ratio (1)/(2)
1980	37,721	24,119	38,681	0.62	—	—	—	—
1981	36,988	24,305	37,865	0.64	38,243	21,278	38,920	0.55
1982	36,519	23,640	37,376	0.63	37,916	21,473	38,589	0.56
1983	**37,346**	**23,720**	**38,264**	**0.62**	**38,284**	**21,333**	**38,923**	**0.55**
1984	38,438	24,281	39,450	0.62	40,357	22,477	41,033	0.55
1985	39,331	24,715	40,398	0.61	—	—	—	—
1986	40,959	25,438	42,086	0.60	42,427	22,277	43,289	0.51
1987	41,592	26,223	42,655	0.61	43,889	24,345	44,650	0.55
1988	42,233	25,576	43,384	0.59	43,896	24,042	44,674	0.54
1989	42,813	26,173	43,981	0.60	44,634	23,077	45,483	0.51
1990	41,540	24,766	42,710	0.58	43,635	22,861	44,516	0.51
1991	40,771	25,245	41,898	0.60	42,692	21,146	43,538	0.49
1992	40,700	24,771	41,930	0.59	42,509	23,889	43,380	0.55
1993	**41,009**	**23,599**	**42,394**	**0.56**	**43,106**	**22,415**	**44,114**	**0.51**
1994	41,638	24,245	42,984	0.56	44,542	22,370	45,520	0.49

1995	41,846	24,758	43,092	0.57	—	—	—	—
1996	42,325	24,930	43,632	0.57	44,039	23,228	44,927	0.52
1997	43,891	24,803	45,234	0.55	45,860	21,944	47,017	0.47
1998	45,368	26,064	46,782	0.56	47,266	23,254	48,345	0.48
1999	46,655	26,615	48,144	0.55	48,505	24,132	49,686	0.49
2000	46,710	25,183	48,250	0.52	48,757	23,214	49,937	0.46
2001	46,409	25,072	47,902	0.52	48,553	22,109	49,782	0.44
2002	45,412	24,581	46,809	0.53	47,388	22,660	48,417	0.47
2003	45,744	24,568	47,306	0.52	47,931	21,359	49,201	0.43
2004	**44,674**	**25,333**	**46,108**	**0.55**	**47,976**	**23,241**	**49,157**	**0.47**
2005	45,112	24,424	46,562	0.52	47,569	23,001	48,725	0.47

NOTE: Years in bold are trough years in the business cycle.
SOURCE: Authors' calculations using the March CPS, 1981–2006.

This resulted in a decline in the relative mean household income of working-age men with work limitations from 62 to 56 percent of that for men without work limitations. Note that the decline in the relative income of men with work limitations began during the growth period of the 1980s—well before the decline in overall income after the business cycle peak year of 1989 and the passage of the Americans with Disabilities Act in 1990.

Seven years of economic growth between 1993 and 2000 increased the mean household income of men with and without work limitations. By the trough year of 2004, the income of men with and without work limitations was substantially above their 1993 lows. Nonetheless, the decline in the relative income of men with work limitations that began in the 1980s continued over the growth period of the 1990s, hitting a low of 52 percent of those without work limitations in 2000 (Table 5.1). This percentage stayed roughly constant as mean household income fell for men with and without work limitations between 2000 and 2003. It then rose to 55 percent in 2004, as the mean household income of men with work limitations actually rose while the mean household income of men without work limitations continued to fall. However, in 2005, the last year of our income data, the mean household income of men with work limitations was once again 52 percent of that for men without work limitations.

The general trends portrayed for those with disabilities, measured by the one-period work limitations measure, are not dramatically different from those found with the two-period work limitation measure. But there are differences. As expected, the mean household income of working-age men with longer term work limitations is lower in every year than that of both their counterparts in the one-period population and their counterparts without longer term work limitations. In 1983, the relative household income of men with a longer term work limitation was 55 percent of the value for their counterparts without such limitations. This ratio trended downward over the rest of the business cycle and was 51 percent by 1993. It continued to trend downward over the next 10 years and hit a low of 43 percent in 2003 before rising to 47 percent in 2004 as the mean household income of men with longer term work limitations rose, while the corresponding value remained roughly constant for those without such limitations (see Table 5.1). It remains to be seen if this higher relative value will continue, but it did so in 2005.

Although the mean household income of men with work limitations increased over the last two business cycles of the twentieth century, it has steadily fallen relative to the much greater growth in the mean household income of working-age men without work limitations.

The median household income for these populations is illustrated in Table 5.2. Although the levels are lower over the entire period, the trend is similar. Using the one-period definition, the median household income of working-age men with work limitations declined substantially relative to that of men without work limitations over the 1980s business cycle, but then it was relatively stable at this low ratio during the 1990s. But unlike for mean household income, the rise in median household income over the 1990s was insufficient to make up for its fall over the 1980s. So the median household income of men with work limitations ($19,592) was slightly lower in 2004 than it was in 1983 ($19,606), while the median income for men without limitations in 2004 ($39,900) was substantially greater than it was in 1983 ($35,357).

While the median household income of men with longer term work limitations in 2004 ($18,305) was slightly greater than it was in 1983 ($17,440), its growth was much smaller than that of men without work limitations ($42,943 in 2004 versus $36,474 in 1983) over the same period, and the ratio of these income values fell from 48 to 43 percent over the entire period.

Sources of Income

The relative importance of various sources of household income for men with and without disabilities (using the one-period work limitation measure of disability) has changed over these two business cycles. In Table 5.3, we disaggregate mean total household income (unadjusted for household size) into five income components to show not only the dramatic decline in the importance of their own labor earnings as a share of total income but also which sources of income offset this decline. The mean income value for each source is reported in Table 5.4.

The share of income from the five sources—own labor earnings, labor earnings of other household members, own public disability trans-

Table 5.2 Median Household Size-Adjusted Income (in 2004 Dollars) for Working-Age Men (Aged 21–58) with and without Work Limitations from the March CPS

Year	One-period sample				Two-period sample			
	Total	With (1)	Without (2)	Ratio (1)/(2)	Total	With (1)	Without (2)	Ratio (1)/(2)
1980	35,516	20,214	36,413	0.56	—	—	—	—
1981	34,595	20,243	35,642	0.57	36,293	17,184	36,928	0.47
1982	33,969	19,750	34,816	0.57	35,536	17,527	36,315	0.48
1983	**34,423**	**19,606**	**35,357**	**0.55**	**35,734**	**17,440**	**36,474**	**0.48**
1984	35,398	20,028	36,432	0.55	37,708	19,347	38,465	0.50
1985	36,256	20,242	37,108	0.55	—	—	—	—
1986	37,358	21,295	38,511	0.55	38,776	18,872	39,609	0.48
1987	38,251	21,552	39,246	0.55	40,962	20,575	41,591	0.49
1988	38,632	20,505	39,658	0.52	40,709	18,663	41,441	0.45
1989	38,620	20,982	39,755	0.53	40,728	18,295	41,461	0.44
1990	37,439	19,919	38,670	0.52	39,837	19,155	40,658	0.47
1991	36,940	19,895	38,006	0.52	39,016	17,060	40,000	0.43
1992	36,624	19,631	37,872	0.52	38,451	18,471	39,314	0.47
1993	**36,444**	**18,660**	**37,829**	**0.49**	**38,706**	**18,321**	**39,791**	**0.46**
1994	37,019	18,373	38,271	0.48	39,685	17,330	40,594	0.43

1995	36,973	19,273	38,385	0.50	—	—	—	0.41
1996	37,507	18,757	38,796	0.48	39,790	16,606	40,518	0.40
1997	38,673	18,651	40,032	0.47	40,890	16,818	42,059	0.40
1998	40,055	19,952	41,501	0.48	42,310	18,159	43,407	0.42
1999	40,690	20,415	42,159	0.48	42,873	18,205	44,042	0.41
2000	40,795	19,635	42,306	0.46	42,826	19,149	43,816	0.44
2001	40,501	19,235	41,832	0.46	42,692	16,745	44,102	0.38
2002	39,260	19,219	40,685	0.47	41,296	16,064	42,327	0.38
2003	39,599	19,500	41,095	0.47	42,013	17,468	43,162	0.40
2004	**38,373**	**19,592**	**39,900**	**0.49**	**42,011**	**18,305**	**42,943**	**0.43**
2005	38,616	18,592	39,950	0.47	41,281	17,878	42,373	0.42

NOTE: Years in bold are trough years in the business cycle.
SOURCE: Authors' calculations using the March CPS, 1981–2006.

Table 5.3 Share (%) of Various Sources of Household Income for Working-Age Men (Aged 21–58) with and without Work Limitations from the March CPS (one-period sample)

Year	Own earnings			Earnings of other household members			Own public disability transfers			All other public transfers in household			All other sources of household income		
	With (1)	Without (2)	Ratio[a] (3)	With (4)	Without (5)	Ratio (6)	With (7)	Without (8)	Ratio (9)	With (10)	Without (11)	Ratio (12)	With (13)	Without (14)	Ratio (15)
1980	28.02	57.11	0.49	35.29	28.84	1.22	8.03	0.08	—	13.20	2.60	5.07	15.45	11.37	1.36
1981	29.80	56.66	0.53	33.49	29.24	1.15	7.89	0.09	—	12.30	2.53	4.85	16.52	11.48	1.44
1982	25.80	54.88	0.47	36.90	30.34	1.22	7.19	0.08	—	12.98	3.08	4.21	17.13	11.62	1.47
1983	**25.89**	**54.25**	**0.48**	**36.68**	**30.83**	**1.19**	**6.92**	**0.08**	—	**12.98**	**2.87**	**4.53**	**17.54**	**11.97**	**1.46**
1984	26.80	54.81	0.49	35.19	30.55	1.15	7.54	0.06	—	12.63	2.25	5.61	17.84	12.33	1.45
1985	27.35	54.98	0.50	37.23	30.79	1.21	7.26	0.05	—	12.47	2.18	5.72	15.69	12.00	1.31
1986	26.83	54.24	0.49	38.32	31.75	1.21	7.20	0.05	—	12.92	2.12	6.10	14.73	11.84	1.24
1987	26.04	53.48	0.49	35.87	31.71	1.13	7.70	0.08	—	12.76	1.96	6.51	17.63	12.77	1.38
1988	24.69	54.11	0.46	36.06	31.47	1.15	7.87	0.07	—	14.93	1.87	7.96	16.46	12.47	1.32
1989	24.68	52.54	0.47	36.53	32.41	1.13	7.59	0.06	—	13.51	1.92	7.03	17.69	13.06	1.35
1990	23.15	52.25	0.44	38.28	32.39	1.18	8.03	0.08	—	13.10	2.17	6.05	17.44	13.11	1.33
1991	23.47	51.95	0.45	38.37	32.99	1.16	8.34	0.08	—	14.31	2.41	5.95	15.51	12.58	1.23
1992	22.54	51.79	0.44	38.35	33.25	1.15	8.87	0.10	—	14.01	2.57	5.45	16.23	12.29	1.32
1993	**20.96**	**52.20**	**0.40**	**37.65**	**33.24**	**1.13**	**9.72**	**0.08**	—	**14.82**	**2.54**	**5.84**	**16.86**	**11.95**	**1.41**
1994	22.79	53.27	0.43	38.06	33.20	1.15	9.73	0.08	—	13.13	2.34	5.62	16.29	11.10	1.47
1995	23.06	54.01	0.43	37.71	33.07	1.14	10.30	0.10	—	13.58	2.31	5.87	15.35	10.51	1.46
1996	24.00	53.28	0.45	37.96	33.59	1.13	10.44	0.08	—	11.91	2.13	5.60	15.69	10.92	1.44
1997	20.05	52.94	0.38	39.17	32.98	1.19	11.89	0.08	—	13.09	1.91	6.85	15.80	12.08	1.31
1998	20.22	53.01	0.38	40.65	33.23	1.22	10.43	0.08	—	11.25	1.77	6.36	17.44	11.91	1.46

1999	19.74	52.69	0.37	40.86	33.68	1.21	10.68	0.09	—	11.32	1.77	6.38	17.39	11.76	1.48
2000	18.24	53.69	0.34	40.55	33.65	1.20	11.68	0.10	—	11.27	1.74	6.48	18.26	10.82	1.69
2001	20.70	54.49	0.38	38.76	33.54	1.16	11.36	0.10	—	13.15	1.84	7.13	16.03	10.02	1.60
2002	18.09	54.41	0.33	42.99	33.94	1.27	11.36	0.12	—	12.93	2.11	6.12	14.63	9.42	1.55
2003	17.27	53.50	0.32	40.83	34.29	1.19	12.08	0.10	—	14.84	2.05	7.23	14.98	10.05	1.49
2004	**17.00**	**53.85**	**0.32**	**41.51**	**34.18**	**1.21**	**11.96**	**0.11**	—	**13.49**	**1.85**	**7.28**	**16.03**	**10.00**	**1.60**
2005	16.09	52.94	0.30	42.34	34.34	1.23	12.43	0.12	—	13.38	1.78	7.53	15.77	10.83	1.46

NOTE: Years in bold are trough years in the business cycle.

[a] The ratio is with/without for each category.

SOURCE: Authors' calculations using the March CPS, 1981–2006.

Table 5.4 Mean Real Income (in 2004 Dollars) from Various Household Income Sources for Working-Age Men (Aged 21–58) with and without Work Limitations from the March CPS (one-period sample)

Year	Own earnings			Earnings of other household members			Own public disability transfers			All other public transfers in household			All other sources of household income			Total household income		
	With (1)	W/out (2)	Ratio[a] (3)	With (4)	W/out (5)	Ratio (6)	With (7)	W/out (8)	Ratio (9)	With (10)	W/out (11)	Ratio (12)	With (13)	W/out (14)	Ratio (15)	With (16)	W/out (17)	Ratio (18)
1980	10,725	34,513	0.31	13,506	17,431	0.77	3,075	47	—	5,053	1,574	3.21	5,914	6,869	0.86	38,273	60,434	0.63
1981	11,410	33,446	0.34	12,826	17,261	0.74	3,023	53	—	4,710	1,496	3.15	6,325	6,775	0.93	38,293	59,031	0.65
1982	9,816	32,116	0.31	14,039	17,757	0.79	2,737	44	—	4,938	1,804	2.74	6,517	6,800	0.96	38,047	58,520	0.65
1983	9,786	32,379	0.30	13,864	18,401	0.75	2,614	47	—	4,906	1,712	2.87	6,630	7,146	0.93	37,801	59,684	0.63
1984	10,311	33,596	0.31	13,537	18,725	0.72	2,901	38	—	4,860	1,379	3.52	6,865	7,561	0.91	38,473	61,299	0.63
1985	10,741	34,385	0.31	14,622	19,258	0.76	2,850	32	—	4,897	1,363	3.59	6,161	7,502	0.82	39,271	62,540	0.63
1986	10,722	35,421	0.30	15,317	20,730	0.74	2,878	33	—	5,164	1,383	3.73	5,886	7,732	0.76	39,968	65,299	0.61
1987	10,583	35,259	0.30	14,574	20,906	0.70	3,130	50	—	5,185	1,292	4.01	7,163	8,419	0.85	40,636	65,925	0.62
1988	9,823	35,998	0.27	14,347	20,938	0.69	3,132	46	—	5,940	1,247	4.76	6,548	8,295	0.79	39,790	66,524	0.60
1989	9,966	35,648	0.28	14,754	21,987	0.67	3,066	43	—	5,458	1,305	4.18	7,144	8,863	0.81	40,388	67,845	0.60
1990	8,972	34,297	0.26	14,837	21,259	0.70	3,112	51	—	5,078	1,423	3.57	6,758	8,607	0.79	38,758	65,636	0.59
1991	9,110	33,358	0.27	14,894	21,183	0.70	3,237	54	—	5,555	1,544	3.60	6,019	8,077	0.75	38,815	64,216	0.60
1992	8,645	33,250	0.26	14,706	21,348	0.69	3,401	62	—	5,371	1,649	3.26	6,223	7,889	0.79	38,346	64,198	0.60
1993	7,643	33,927	0.23	13,730	21,603	0.64	3,543	49	—	5,403	1,648	3.28	6,147	7,769	0.79	36,464	64,996	0.56
1994	8,433	34,995	0.24	14,086	21,811	0.65	3,601	56	—	4,859	1,535	3.16	6,029	7,291	0.83	37,009	65,688	0.56
1995	8,750	35,469	0.25	14,308	21,717	0.66	3,907	64	—	5,151	1,520	3.39	5,826	6,904	0.84	37,941	65,674	0.58
1996	9,200	35,490	0.26	14,551	22,375	0.65	4,002	56	—	4,567	1,416	3.22	6,016	7,274	0.83	38,335	66,611	0.58
1997	7,642	36,472	0.21	14,928	22,724	0.66	4,531	56	—	4,989	1,317	3.79	6,024	8,325	0.72	38,114	68,893	0.55
1998	8,056	37,722	0.21	16,193	23,643	0.68	4,156	56	—	4,482	1,259	3.56	6,947	8,476	0.82	39,835	71,155	0.56
1999	8,018	38,794	0.21	16,591	24,800	0.67	4,337	69	—	4,599	1,306	3.52	7,061	8,657	0.82	40,605	73,627	0.55
2000	7,080	39,521	0.18	15,737	24,773	0.64	4,533	72	—	4,375	1,281	3.42	7,088	7,968	0.89	38,813	73,614	0.53

2001	7,986	39,893	0.20	14,949	24,550	0.61	4,381	75	—	5,072	1,351	3.76	6,184	7,337	0.84	38,571	73,205	0.53
2002	6,861	39,061	0.18	16,308	24,364	0.67	4,308	88	—	4,905	1,518	3.23	5,550	6,762	0.82	37,932	71,794	0.53
2003	6,616	38,919	0.17	15,641	24,942	0.63	4,626	76	—	5,684	1,493	3.81	5,738	7,314	0.78	38,305	72,745	0.53
2004	**6,697**	**38,227**	**0.18**	**16,355**	**24,264**	**0.67**	**4,714**	**80**	—	**5,316**	**1,315**	**4.04**	**6,315**	**7,098**	**0.89**	**39,396**	**70,984**	**0.55**
2005	6,113	38,010	0.16	16,091	24,655	0.65	4,723	86	—	5,084	1,275	3.99	5,992	7,778	0.77	38,002	71,805	0.53

NOTE: Years in bold are trough years in the business cycle.

[a] The ratio is with/without for each category.

SOURCE: Authors' calculations using the March CPS, 1981–2006.

fers, all other public transfers, and all other private income—and their mean levels are sensitive to the business cycle. But long-term patterns clearly emerge.

Over the two business cycles, for men with work limitations there is a dramatic drop in the share of income from own labor earnings. As can be seen in Table 5.3 (column 1), own earnings fell as a share of income from 25.9 percent in 1983 to 21.0 percent in 1993, the end of the first cycle. It then continued to fall to 17.0 percent in 2004, the end of the second cycle. The share of income from own labor earnings in households of men without limitations also fell, but much less so over this period. So, as can be seen in column 3, the share of labor earnings of men with work limitations dropped relative to the share for men without work limitations. The ratio between the two fell from 48 percent in 1983 to 40 percent in 1993 to 32 percent in 2004.

Additional information on changes in the importance of income from different sources in households of men with and without work limitations can be found in Table 5.4. Over the same time period, and using the one-period measure of work limitations, the mean labor earnings for men with limitations (column 1) fell, while the corresponding mean for men without limitations rose (column 2). The ratio of the mean for men with work limitations to that for men without work limitations declined remarkably, from 30 percent in 1983 to 23 percent in 1993 to just 18 percent in 2004 (column 3).

The share of income coming from the labor earnings of other household members in the households of men with work limitations increased substantially over this same period (Table 5.3, column 4). This was also the case in households of men without work limitations (column 5), but the ratio between the two (column 6) shows that the pace of the increase was more rapid for men with work limitations in the 1980s and more rapid for men without work limitations in the 1990s. Thus, the share of household income from the labor earnings of others in the household for men with work limitations initially fell relative to that of men without work limitations (through 1993) and then returned to its 1982 level by 2004. Over the entire period, the labor earnings of others remained a more important source of income in the households of men with work limitations than in those of men without disabilities.

Mean labor earnings fell for other members of households of men with work limitations over the 1980s, rose in the 1990s, and were substantially higher in 2004 than in 1983 (Table 5.4, column 4). In contrast, the mean labor earnings of other household members of working-age men without work limitations (column 5) rose over the entire period. As a result, the ratio of these two values (column 6) fell dramatically in the 1980s but remained about the same over the 1990s. Hence, over the entire period the ratio fell from 75 percent in 1983 to 67 percent in 2004. Even so, the labor earnings of other household members in households of men with work limitations rose over the entire period, replacing a substantial share of the decline in own earnings for this group.

The major public source of income that replaces the earnings of men with work limitations—their own income from SSDI and SSI— was 7.9 percent of household income in 1981 (Table 5.3, column 7). There were significant administrative efforts to cut the SSDI and SSI rolls in 1982 and 1983, and this share of income fell to 7.2 percent in 1982 and to a series low of 6.9 percent in 1983. But legislation ending these administrative practices stemmed this decline in 1984, and a further loosening of the eligibility rules in 1985, especially for those with mental conditions, was followed by a return of own SSDI and SSI benefits as a share of household income in 1990 to its pre-1981 level and to 9.7 percent by 1993. Own SSDI and SSI income continued to increase as a share of household income to 11.9 percent in 1997. It then fell for two years, but as the economic expansion ended in 2000, own SSDI and SSI income started to grow, reaching a high of 12.4 percent in 2005. Over the business cycle trough years of 1983, 1993, and 2004, own disability transfers from SSDI and SSI grew from 7.2 to 9.7 to 12.0 percent of the household income for men with work limitations. Thus mean income from own SSDI and SSI benefits (Table 5.4, column 7) rose substantially over this period in the households of men with work limitations, whereas both share and income from this source for men without work limitations was trivial in all years (column 8 in Tables 5.3 and 5.4).

Autor and Duggan (2006) and Duggan, Singleton, and Song (2007) provide empirical evidence, after controlling for compositional changes, that three factors led to the increases in SSDI and SSI benefits over this period: the changes in the screening rules discussed above; a rise in the after-tax SSDI replacement rate for low-skill workers; and the projected change in the normal retirement age from 65 to 67, set in motion by the Amendments to the Social Security Act of 1983.[5]

As can be seen in columns 10 and 11 of Table 5.3, the share of income from other public transfer programs rose in the households of men with work limitations and fell in the households of men without work limitations over this period, resulting in a rise in the relative importance of this source of income for men with work limitations from 4.53 in 1983 to 7.28 in 2004 (column 12).

The mean income from other public transfers for men with work limitations rose in the 1980s and fell slightly in the 1990s (Table 5.4, column 10). In contrast, other public transfers in the households of men without work limitations (column 11) fell over both business cycles. The ratio of mean income from other public transfers grew over the entire period from 2.9 in 1983 to 4.0 in 2004 (column 12). Overall, mean income from all government sources for this population (column 7 plus column 10) rose from $7,520 in 1983 to $8,946 in 1993 to $10,030 in 2004, a rise of more than 33 percent over the entire period. In contrast, the mean income from all government sources in the household of working-age men without work limitations fell from $1,759 in 1983 to $1,395 in 2004.

As can be seen in columns 13 and 14 of Table 5.3, there was a modest decline (rise) in the share of all other private sources of income (rents, dividends, etc.) in the households of working-age men with (without) work limitations in the 1980s. In the 1990s, there was a decline in the share of this income source, especially for men without work limitations. Hence, other sources of private income, which were always a larger share of the household income of working-age men with work limitations, took on more importance relative to their income share in the households of working-age men without work limitations, as seen in column 15.

The mean income from all other private sources of income in the households of working-age men with work limitations fell modestly in the 1980s and rose slightly in the 1990s, resulting in little change over the period ($6,630 in 1983 versus $6,315 in 2004; Table 5.4, column 13). The pattern in households of working-age men without work limitations (column 14) was different, up in the 1980s and down in the

1990s, but the overall change was about the same, a modest decrease from $7,146 in 1983 to $7,098 in 2004. Nonetheless, the ratio of this source of private income also fell over the entire period, as did that of all other private sources of income.

The information in Tables 5.3 and 5.4 provides several important insights into the dramatic transformation in the sources of income in households of men with work limitations over the last two business cycles. First, their labor earnings, which were never the primary source of their household income, have dramatically declined in real dollars, as a share of household total income, and relative to the households of men without work limitations.

Second, there has been a rapid rise in the importance of SSDI and SSI income in the households of men with work limitations, especially relative to own labor earnings. In 1983, own labor earnings accounted for 3.7 times as much of their household's income as did own SSDI and SSI benefits. By 1993, this relationship had fallen to 2.2 times as much. In 2004, it was only 1.4 times as much. Own SSDI and SSI benefits increased as a share of income in the households of men with work limitations by 73 percent between 1983 and 2004.

Third, the rise in the importance of labor earnings from other household members has also been substantial for men with work limitations, relative to both own labor earnings and especially when compared to the households of men without work limitations. In 1983, own labor earnings for men with work limitations accounted for 71 percent as much household income as did the labor earnings of other household members. This value had fallen to 56 percent by 1993 and only 41 percent by 2004. In contrast, the labor earnings of other household members increased as a share of income in the same households by 13 percent between 1983 and 2004. Over this same period, the share of household income provided by the labor earnings of other household members in the households of men without work limitations declined.

Fourth, in the households of men with work limitations, the share of mean household income coming from all private sources fell from 80 percent in 1983 to 75 percent in 2004, with most of the decline coming from the drop in their own labor earnings. In contrast, the share of household income from private sources remained essentially constant

(97 percent) in the households of men without work limitations over the same period.

Fifth, the labor earnings of men with work limitations have fallen from $9,786 in 1983 to $6,697 in 2004, a decline of $3,089. Increases in income from total public sources over that same period have only amounted to $2,510 ($7,520 in 1983 to $10,030 in 2004), replacing only about 81 percent of the decline in earnings. Increases in the earnings of other household members have more than made up the gap between the decline in own earnings and the rise in public income, resulting in a modest rise in household income from $37,801 in 1983 to $39,396 in 2004. But this rise pales in comparison to the increase in the household income of men without work limitations, which rose from $59,684 to $70,984 over the same period.

Tables 5.5 and 5.6 present similar information for working-age men with and without a longer term work limitation, using the two-period work limitation measure instead of the one-period measure used for Tables 5.3 and 5.4. Not surprisingly, the share of own labor earnings in the household income of men with longer term work limitations is smaller than the corresponding share for men with one-period work limitations. The long-term trends, however, are very similar for both groups.

The labor earnings of men with longer term work limitations were just 13 percent of their household's total income in the 1983 recession trough, but they fell even further, to 11 percent, in the 1993 trough and to just 6 percent in the 2004 trough. In contrast, the share of own labor earnings in household income of men without work limitations remained about the same. As a result, the relative share for those with work limitations as compared with those without work limitations fell from 23 percent in 1983 to 11 percent in 2004 (Table 5.5, column 3).

The share of income contributed by other household members in the households of men with longer term work limitations increased over the period but fell relative to the share contributed by the other household members of men without longer term limitations (Table 5.5, columns 4–6).

As was the case in the one-period measure, the major public source of income growth for men with longer term work limitations came from SSDI and SSI benefits. They rose from 11.9 percent of total household income in 1983 to 14.6 percent in 1993 to 19.0 percent in 2004 (Table 5.5, columns 7–9). In contrast, the share of income coming from all other transfer programs fell over the period from 17.2 percent in 1983 to 18.2 percent in 1993 to 14.5 percent in 2004 (Table 5.5, column 10). Hence, some of the increase in the public share of income coming from SSDI and SSI benefits, especially in the 1990s, appears to represent a shift toward federally funded disability programs and away from other public programs (e.g., state welfare and unemployment insurance programs or Workers Compensation). The share of all other private income in the households of men with longer term work limitations fell over the 1980s but rose over the 1990s; for households of men without limitations, it first rose and then fell. Over the entire period, the importance of this source of income in the households of men with longer term work limitations rose relative to its importance in households of men without limitations (columns 13–15).

For men with longer term work limitations, own labor earnings was never a major source of household income, and this share decreased across the two business cycles. The major public source of income growth has come from SSDI and SSI benefits. In most years prior to 1987, the share of own earnings in the household income of men with longer term work limitations approximately equaled or even exceeded the share coming from own SSDI and SSI benefits. Since then, the share coming from own labor earnings has fallen, while the share provided by own SSDI and SSI has grown. By 1993, SSDI and SSI benefits provided 135 percent as much as own labor earnings to the household income of men with longer term work limitations. By 2004, this had increased to 306 percent (Table 5.6).

The values shown in Table 5.7, derived from the values in Tables 5.3 and 5.5, provide a more focused look at how dramatically the own earnings of men with work limitations fell as a share of household income over the last two business cycles. As can be seen in column 1, the share of own earnings in household income based on the one-period work measure fell 4.9 percentage points between 1983 and 1993. This decline was offset, to some degree, by a rise in the share of labor earnings from other household members (1.0 percentage point). Because the share of all other sources of private income also fell slightly (0.7 percentage points), the total income from private sources fell by 4.6

166

Table 5.5 Share (%) of Various Sources of Household Income for Working-Age Men (Aged 21–58) with and without Longer Term Work Limitations in the Matched CPS Data (two-period sample)

Year	Own earnings With (1)	Without (2)	Ratio (3)	Earnings of other household members With (4)	Without (5)	Ratio (6)	Own public disability transfers With (7)	Without (8)	Ratio (9)	All other public transfers in household With (10)	Without (11)	Ratio (12)	All other sources of household income With (13)	Without (14)	Ratio (15)
1980	—	—	—	—	—	—	—	—	—	—	—	—	—	—	—
1981	19.60	57.44	0.34	33.15	28.67	1.16	13.04	0.11	—	17.25	2.34	7.38	16.97	11.45	1.48
1982	12.38	55.58	0.22	38.55	29.24	1.32	13.34	0.12	—	16.53	3.01	5.49	19.20	12.06	1.59
1983	**12.62**	**54.38**	**0.23**	**39.26**	**30.60**	**1.28**	**11.90**	**0.11**	—	**17.23**	**2.86**	**6.03**	**18.98**	**12.05**	**1.58**
1984	11.15	54.41	0.20	41.07	30.76	1.34	11.86	0.10	—	16.82	2.22	7.59	19.11	12.51	1.53
1985	—	—	—	—	—	—	—	—	—	—	—	—	—	—	—
1986	15.73	54.82	0.29	38.07	30.57	1.25	12.35	0.08	—	18.33	2.20	8.32	15.51	12.33	1.26
1987	12.59	53.47	0.24	42.54	30.94	1.37	13.06	0.11	—	14.49	1.88	7.69	17.32	13.60	1.27
1988	11.20	55.09	0.20	35.48	30.37	1.17	12.30	0.13	—	22.73	1.94	11.74	18.30	12.47	1.47
1989	13.18	54.14	0.24	36.20	30.65	1.18	14.25	0.12	—	17.34	1.92	9.05	19.04	13.18	1.44
1990	12.10	52.91	0.23	40.22	31.61	1.27	13.71	0.13	—	16.41	2.11	7.76	17.56	13.24	1.33
1991	13.11	52.92	0.25	42.66	31.81	1.34	14.44	0.12	—	15.79	2.42	6.52	14.02	12.73	1.10
1992	10.08	52.16	0.19	41.54	32.76	1.27	13.74	0.14	—	15.93	2.59	6.14	18.71	12.35	1.51
1993	**10.78**	**52.56**	**0.21**	**40.02**	**32.26**	**1.24**	**14.58**	**0.13**	—	**18.21**	**2.47**	**7.38**	**16.41**	**12.59**	**1.30**
1994	9.60	53.05	0.18	42.32	33.06	1.28	15.10	0.14	—	15.92	2.31	6.88	17.06	11.43	1.49
1995	—	—	—	—	—	—	—	—	—	—	—	—	—	—	—
1996	14.76	54.04	0.27	36.56	32.33	1.13	15.38	0.15	—	14.98	2.29	6.53	18.32	11.20	1.64
1997	9.63	52.69	0.18	40.06	32.61	1.23	17.04	0.14	—	15.87	1.98	8.02	17.40	12.58	1.38
1998	9.31	54.10	0.17	40.32	32.05	1.26	16.68	0.14	—	15.17	1.77	8.58	18.52	11.94	1.55
1999	7.57	53.04	0.14	48.36	32.38	1.49	15.98	0.17	—	13.29	1.80	7.38	14.79	12.61	1.17

2000	8.63	54.22	0.16	41.80	32.97	1.27	17.44	0.16	—	13.25	1.76	7.52	18.88	10.89	1.73
2001	8.44	54.25	0.16	40.87	32.80	1.25	18.25	0.19	—	14.74	1.99	7.41	17.70	10.78	1.64
2002	8.09	55.28	0.15	43.13	33.02	1.31	16.98	0.16	—	15.22	2.10	7.26	16.57	9.44	1.75
2003	9.08	53.89	0.17	40.47	33.37	1.21	17.10	0.18	—	16.40	2.12	7.73	16.95	10.44	1.62
2004	**6.21**	**54.69**	**0.11**	**40.71**	**33.23**	**1.23**	**18.98**	**0.23**	—	**14.52**	**2.04**	**7.11**	**19.59**	**9.81**	**2.00**
2005	8.12	53.92	0.15	42.29	33.02	1.28	18.81	0.21	—	15.16	1.84	8.23	15.62	11.00	1.42

NOTE: Years in bold are trough years in the business cycle.
[a] The ratio is with/without for each category.
SOURCE: Authors' calculations using the March CPS, 1981–2006.

Table 5.6 Mean Real Income (in 2004 Dollars) from Various Household Income Sources for Working-Age Men (Aged 21–58) with and without Longer Term Work Limitations in the Matched CPS Data (two-period sample)

Year	Own earnings			Earnings of other household members			Own public disability transfers			All other public transfers in household			All other sources of household income			Total household income		
	With (1)	W/out (2)	Ratio (3)	With (4)	W/out (5)	Ratio (6)	With (7)	W/out (8)	Ratio (9)	With (10)	W/out (11)	Ratio (12)	With (13)	W/out (14)	Ratio (15)	With (16)	W/out (17)	Ratio (18)
1980	—	—	—	—	—	—	—	—	—	—	—	—	—	—	—	—	—	—
1981	6,764	35,310	0.19	11,439	17,624	0.65	4,500	65	—	5,952	1,437	4.14	5,855	7,039	0.83	34,510	61,475	0.56
1982	4,346	33,896	0.13	13,538	17,830	0.76	4,684	71	—	5,806	1,837	3.16	6,741	7,354	0.92	35,114	60,987	0.58
1983	**4,370**	**33,656**	**0.13**	**13,593**	**18,937**	**0.72**	**4,120**	**65**	—	**5,966**	**1,769**	**3.37**	**6,573**	**7,458**	**0.88**	**34,623**	**61,886**	**0.56**
1984	4,183	35,293	0.12	15,415	19,953	0.77	4,450	66	—	6,311	1,437	4.39	7,172	8,114	0.88	37,530	64,864	0.58
1985	—	—	—	—	—	—	—	—	—	—	—	—	—	—	—	—	—	—
1986	5,565	37,176	0.15	13,473	20,731	0.65	4,371	54	—	6,487	1,495	4.34	5,490	8,360	0.66	35,387	67,816	0.52
1987	4,940	37,386	0.13	16,691	21,636	0.77	5,124	75	—	5,685	1,317	4.32	6,797	9,510	0.71	39,238	69,924	0.56
1988	4,344	38,149	0.11	13,765	21,031	0.65	4,774	90	—	8,818	1,341	6.57	7,101	8,639	0.82	38,801	69,251	0.56
1989	4,610	38,051	0.12	12,662	21,537	0.59	4,984	81	—	6,065	1,347	4.50	6,659	9,261	0.72	34,980	70,277	0.50
1990	4,313	36,482	0.12	14,334	21,794	0.66	4,886	87	—	5,848	1,458	4.01	6,259	9,126	0.69	35,640	68,948	0.52
1991	4,337	35,499	0.12	14,117	21,339	0.66	4,777	82	—	5,224	1,625	3.22	4,640	8,537	0.54	33,093	67,081	0.49
1992	3,781	34,882	0.11	15,580	21,904	0.71	5,153	92	—	5,974	1,735	3.44	7,018	8,260	0.85	37,507	66,872	0.56
1993	**3,756**	**35,837**	**0.10**	**13,947**	**21,999**	**0.63**	**5,080**	**88**	—	**6,346**	**1,682**	**3.77**	**5,720**	**8,582**	**0.67**	**34,849**	**68,187**	**0.51**
1994	3,394	37,309	0.09	14,953	23,252	0.64	5,336	101	—	5,626	1,628	3.46	6,029	8,039	0.75	35,337	70,328	0.50
1995	—	—	—	—	—	—	—	—	—	—	—	—	—	—	—	—	—	—
1996	5,242	37,287	0.14	12,988	22,308	0.58	5,463	101	—	5,322	1,582	3.36	6,509	7,727	0.84	35,524	69,004	0.51
1997	3,287	38,042	0.09	13,672	23,549	0.58	5,815	100	—	5,417	1,429	3.79	5,938	9,087	0.65	34,130	72,206	0.47
1998	3,282	39,843	0.08	14,218	23,606	0.60	5,882	104	—	5,351	1,303	4.11	6,530	8,795	0.74	35,263	73,650	0.48

1999	2,859	40,448	0.07	18,266	24,692	0.74	6,037	132	—	5,020	1,373	3.66	5,587	9,614	0.58	37,769	76,259	0.50
2000	3,102	41,508	0.07	15,024	25,242	0.60	6,269	119	—	4,762	1,349	3.53	6,786	8,334	0.81	35,943	76,552	0.47
2001	2,885	41,382	0.07	13,968	25,021	0.56	6,237	142	—	5,036	1,518	3.32	6,050	8,222	0.74	34,176	76,284	0.45
2002	2,776	40,696	0.07	14,795	24,309	0.61	5,825	121	—	5,220	1,543	3.38	5,685	6,953	0.82	34,301	73,621	0.47
2003	2,997	40,862	0.07	13,362	25,306	0.53	5,644	135	—	5,414	1,609	3.36	5,597	7,915	0.71	33,014	75,828	0.44
2004	**2,143**	**41,383**	**0.05**	**14,057**	**25,141**	**0.56**	**6,554**	**175**	—	**5,013**	**1,544**	**3.25**	**6,763**	**7,419**	**0.91**	**34,530**	**75,663**	**0.46**
2005	2,824	40,386	0.07	14,714	24,737	0.59	6,546	160	—	5,274	1,380	3.82	5,436	8,241	0.66	34,794	74,904	0.46

NOTE: Years in bold are trough years in the business cycle.

[a]The ratio is with/without for each category.

SOURCE: Authors' calculations using the March CPS, 1981–2006.

Table 5.7 Change in the Share (percentage points) of Household Income of Working-Age Men (Aged 21–58) with Work Limitations by Source over the 1980s and 1990s Business Cycles from the March CPS

Sources	One-period sample			Two-period sample		
	1983–1993	1993–2004	1983–2004	1983–1993	1993–2004	1983–2004
	(1)	(2)	(3)	(4)	(5)	(6)
Private	-4.64	-0.93	-5.57	-3.65	-0.70	-4.35
Own labor earnings	-4.93	-3.96	-8.89	-1.84	-4.57	-6.41
Others' labor earnings	0.97	3.86	4.83	0.76	0.69	1.45
Other private	-0.68	-0.83	-1.51	-2.57	3.18	0.61
Public	4.52	0.91	5.55	3.58	0.71	4.37
Own SSDI/SSI	2.68	2.24	5.04	2.68	4.40	7.08
Other public	1.84	-1.33	0.51	0.98	-3.69	-2.71

SOURCE: Calculated from values presented in Tables 5.3 and 5.4. Public and private do not sum to zero due to rounding.

percentage points over the 1980s business cycle. This decline was offset by a 2.7 percentage point increase in the share of income coming from own SSDI and SSI benefits and a 1.8 percentage point increase in the share of income from other public transfers.

Over the 1990s, the share of household income coming from own labor earnings for this same group fell another 4.0 percentage points (Table 5.7, column 2). But the share of coming from private sources as a whole only declined by 0.9 percentage points in this period because the share of labor earnings of other household members grew by 3.9 percentage points and the share from all other private income sources fell by 0.8 percentage points. Public transfers from own SSDI and SSI benefits continued to grow as a share of household income (2.2 percentage points), but that increase was substantially offset by a decline (1.3 percentage points) in the share of household income coming from all other public transfers.

During the last two business cycles (1983–2004) combined, the share of own earnings in the household incomes of men with one-period work limitations dropped dramatically—by 8.9 percentage points (column 3). But the decline in the share of income from all private sources dropped less precipitously (5.6 percentage points) because the share of labor earnings of other household members grew by 4.8 percentage points. The major source of the rise in public income offsetting the loss in private income came from the 5.0 percentage point increase in the share of income from own SSDI and SSI payments.

There is a similar pattern for men with longer term disabilities. Over the entire period (Table 5.7, column 6), own labor earnings fell as a share of household income by 6.4 percentage points, and own SSDI and SSI payments increased by 7.1 percentage points. Once the increase in the labor earnings of others and other private income as a source of household income is factored in, total private income fell by 4.4 percentage points. Hence, regardless of which measure of disability is used, the households of men with disabilities were much more dependent on public transfers in 2004 than was the case in 1983.

INCOME LEVELS USING BROADER
DISABILITY DEFINITIONS

The ACS is a continuous data collection effort by the Census Bureau, started on a small scale in 2001. By 2003, the ACS collected information from more than 500,000 households, and by 2006, the sample had grown to about 3 million. The ACS sample is now many times larger than the number of sample households included in the CPS. Like the CPS, the ACS asks about work limitations of household members, but it also asks questions about other disabilities. For further discussion of the value of the ACS for disability research, see Weathers (2009) and Weathers (2005).

In the CPS, income is reported for the previous calendar year; for the ACS, income is reported for the previous 12 months. Because the ACS is administered throughout the calendar year, the income reporting periods differ across sample members in the annual ACS file. The Census Bureau indexes the values so that they are representative of the survey year.[6] Definitions of the income measures in each of the surveys are presented in Appendix 5A.

Comparing Income Using Work Limitation in the CPS and ACS

Median household income and median household size-adjusted income for working-age people (men and women, aged 25–61) estimated from the 2004 March CPS (income year 2003) and the corresponding estimates from the 2003 ACS (income year 2003) are presented in Table 5.8.[7]

Not surprisingly, the median income values for those with any disability, which includes those reporting any of the six types of limitation (including a work limitation) in the ACS but only those reporting a work limitation in the CPS, are substantially different because the ACS captures a much broader population with disabilities. However, ACS medians based on the work-limitation measure alone are remarkably similar to CPS medians: $28,000 in the ACS and $27,955 in the CPS. The corresponding size-adjusted medians are also very similar: $17,487 in the ACS and $17,967 in the CPS. There are far greater differences in median income across alternative subpopulations of men with disabili-

Table 5.8 **Median Household Income and Median Household Size-Adjusted Income (2003 dollars) Estimates for Working-Age Persons (Aged 25–61) with and without Disabilities, by Data Source and Disability Definition**

Measure and data source	No disability	Disability	Ratio[a]	Work limitation	IADL	ADL	Mental	Physical	Sensory
Median household income									
2003 ACS	60,000	34,600	0.58	28,000	28,600	28,000	27,400	32,100	38,000
2004 CPS[b]	61,999	27,955	0.45	27,955	NA	NA	NA	NA	NA
Median household size-adjusted income									
2003 ACS	35,796	21,304	0.60	17,487	17,615	17,667	17,321	20,207	23,415
2004 CPS[b]	36,770	17,967	0.49	17,967	NA	NA	NA	NA	NA

[a] The (disability)/(no disability) ratio.
[b] The 2004 CPS collects income data for the 2003 calendar year.
SOURCE: Weathers (2005).

ties in the ACS data. Medians for the broadest ACS definition are substantially larger than for the work limitation definition, likely reflecting the fact that many of those identified as having "any disability" do not report a work limitation.

Although the ACS, with its more nuanced questions and larger sample size, will likely be the data set of choice for most future research on the economic well-being of working-age people with disabilities, with respect to both levels and trends, it cannot replace the CPS as the only data set providing consistent information since 1980. The work-limitation measures in the ACS, as shown in Table 5.8, yield remarkably similar median income estimates to those found in the CPS. This allows researchers to be more confident that these two data sets are capturing the same population when their work limitation definitions of disability are used to evaluate the economic well-being of working-age people with disabilities.

ACS Income Statistics by Sex, Race, Education, and State

Because of the broad set of disability questions and large sample size in the ACS, detailed income statistics can be generated for important subgroups using alternative measures of those with disabilities. Using data from the 2006 ACS, Table 5.9 presents median household income and median household size-adjusted income for working-age people (aged 25–61) with and without any disability, defined by inclusion in any of the six ACS disability subgroups, as well as for subgroups defined by sex, race, and education. There are large differences between those with and without disabilities. The median household income for persons with any disability was $37,000, compared with $66,500 for those without any disability; thus, the median household income of persons with a disability was only 56 percent of the median for persons without one. Although the magnitude of income changes when size-adjusted income is used, the relative value is almost the same—58 percent. There are differences among subgroups defined by sex, race, or education, and median income levels are consistently higher for those who have a sensory or physical impairment as compared to other disability groups.

The ACS can also provide more detailed income data at the state level using alternative measures of working-age people with and without disabilities. Using data from the 2006 ACS, Table 5.10 presents median household size-adjusted income of those with and without disabilities as well as for those in each disability subgroup by state and for the District of Columbia. For all states, the median income of people with disabilities is substantially below that of people without disabilities. But the differences vary widely, as depicted in Figure 5.2. Median household size-adjusted income for those with disabilities in the District of Columbia is only 30.6 percent of that for those without disabilities, well below that in any state. Among the states, the value ranges from a low of 50.6 percent in Kentucky to a high of 79.7 percent in Utah.

DISCUSSION AND CONCLUSIONS

Using data from the CPS and ACS we looked at levels and long-term trends in the economic well-being of working-age men with and without disabilities and how the sources of that economic well-being have changed over the last two business cycles (1983–1993 and 1993–2004). The real household (size-adjusted) income of men with work limitations stagnated between 1983 and 2004, while it rose substantially for men without such limitations, thus widening the income gap between the two. The median income of men with a one-period work limitation was 55 percent as large as the median income of men without a work limitation in 1983, but fell to 49 percent by 2004. The two-period work limitation population began with an even lower—48 percent—relative median income in 1983 and fell to 43 percent by 2004.

Dramatic changes also occurred in the sources of household income of men with disabilities both in the level of income gained from individual sources and its importance as a share of income relative to those without disabilities. First, and foremost, the importance of own labor earnings of men with work limitations, which were never the primary source of income in their households, dramatically declined in real dollars, as a share of household total income, and relative to their importance in the households of men without work limitations. Second, there

Table 5.9 2006 Median Household Income and Median Household Size-Adjusted Income (2006 dollars) for Persons with and without Disabilities (Aged 25–61) by Demographic Subgroups

Description	No disability	ACS disability	Ratio[a]	Sensory	Physical	Mental	ADL	IADL	Work limitation
All									
Household income	66,500	37,000	0.56	39,800	34,900	30,000	30,400	30,704	30,500
Adjusted income	39,598	22,910	0.58	24,700	21,779	18,764	19,024	18,850	19,021
Men									
Household income	68,700	39,200	0.57	43,000	36,000	32,100	31,200	31,700	31,800
Adjusted income	40,500	24,324	0.60	26,870	22,600	20,207	19,500	19,550	19,800
Women, Age 25–61									
Household income	65,000	35,000	0.54	35,010	33,600	28,100	30,000	30,000	29,800
Adjusted income	38,184	21,500	0.56	21,600	21,131	17,500	18,668	18,385	18,336
White									
Household income	70,300	40,000	0.57	43,200	37,200	32,100	33,100	32,710	32,600
Adjusted Income	42,410	25,000	0.59	27,210	23,688	20,435	20,943	20,435	20,577
Black									
Household income	49,000	26,000	0.53	25,600	25,000	21,120	21,700	22,800	22,200
Adjusted Income	29,698	16,000	0.54	16,044	15,600	13,250	13,500	13,789	13,741
Hispanic									
Household income	50,000	33,500	0.67	33,500	31,600	29,600	28,320	28,900	29,800
Adjusted income	26,163	18,694	0.71	18,861	17,764	16,466	16,166	16,234	16,750

Native American									
Household income	48,000	28,100	0.59	30,000	27,950	22,600	28,100	24,400	24,000
Adjusted income	27,482	17,436	0.63	18,244	17,352	14,000	15,762	15,011	15,146
Asian									
Household income	79,000	53,000	0.67	50,000	53,400	45,500	50,000	51,600	50,000
Adjusted income	44,050	29,445	0.67	28,284	30,022	25,000	26,550	28,284	27,414
Less than high school education									
Household income	40,000	24,900	0.62	25,000	23,000	22,600	23,000	24,500	22,400
Adjusted income	21,511	14,779	0.69	15,000	14,000	13,733	13,845	14,491	13,600
Greater than high school education									
Household income	79,000	48,000	0.61	52,500	45,000	38,500	39,004	38,000	39,000
Adjusted income	47,500	30,406	0.64	33,850	29,000	24,826	24,826	23,960	24,789

[a] The (ACS disability)/(no disability) ratio.
SOURCE: Authors' calculations from the 2006 ACS PUMS file.

Table 5.10 2006 State-Level Estimates of Median Household Size-Adjusted Income (2006 dollars), Working-Age Population (Aged 25–61)

State	No disability	Disability	Ratio[a]	Sensory	Physical	Mental	ADL	IADL	Work limitation
All States	39,598	22,910	0.57	24,700	21,779	18,764	19,024	18,850	19,021
Alabama	34,500	18,940	0.55	20,750	18,000	15,966	16,681	16,000	15,750
Alaska	43,879	31,678	0.72	35,907	27,150	27,250	34,701	31,841	27,235
Arizona	37,355	23,971	0.64	23,622	23,274	21,824	23,135	21,377	21,939
Arkansas	31,466	18,385	0.58	21,131	17,050	15,000	13,576	14,400	14,849
California	41,569	26,558	0.64	27,713	25,491	22,173	21,362	21,593	22,748
Colorado	42,500	26,905	0.63	29,698	25,385	23,094	21,189	21,567	21,779
Connecticut	49,999	30,321	0.61	37,335	27,078	21,600	27,000	22,769	24,480
Delaware	44,398	26,304	0.59	30,000	24,042	24,597	23,759	22,000	22,000
District of Columbia	53,160	16,263	0.31	18,385	16,019	12,000	10,324	14,142	13,700
Florida	37,194	24,000	0.65	25,288	22,800	20,751	20,500	20,265	20,754
Georgia	37,500	21,420	0.57	23,000	20,050	18,668	18,102	17,956	17,678
Hawaii	44,907	29,353	0.65	35,350	28,666	23,789	20,888	22,910	25,527
Idaho	33,446	22,274	0.67	22,000	22,910	18,407	19,767	20,648	18,031
Illinois	41,200	25,189	0.61	26,000	24,060	21,920	21,064	20,718	21,100
Indiana	37,066	22,700	0.61	25,500	21,651	17,567	18,235	17,961	18,700
Iowa	37,400	22,500	0.60	25,324	21,265	16,327	21,246	16,263	17,257
Kansas	38,049	21,300	0.56	24,249	20,150	16,200	19,163	18,314	18,455
Kentucky	34,927	17,678	0.51	18,850	16,859	12,471	14,637	12,875	13,856

Louisiana	33,944	20,082	0.59	19,799	19,658	17,378	17,678	17,805	16,829
Maine	37,597	21,920	0.58	26,905	20,785	17,667	17,106	13,378	16,900
Maryland	50,250	31,000	0.62	31,678	30,187	27,648	26,770	27,100	25,825
Massachusetts	50,000	26,163	0.52	31,537	25,250	20,785	21,066	20,700	20,785
Michigan	39,386	22,632	0.58	25,000	21,500	18,417	17,146	18,173	19,163
Minnesota	43,948	27,506	0.63	33,234	25,550	23,476	26,296	24,600	22,769
Mississippi	30,193	16,108	0.53	16,971	14,924	13,625	12,162	13,506	12,924
Missouri	36,100	21,637	0.60	22,944	19,870	18,000	17,491	18,071	17,800
Montana	32,870	20,153	0.61	24,000	19,514	15,146	19,514	14,656	15,473
Nebraska	36,900	22,486	0.61	26,000	21,213	18,591	21,213	15,415	17,494
Nevada	40,000	28,426	0.71	31,820	27,224	24,254	21,680	22,981	22,981
New Hampshire	46,669	28,500	0.61	32,909	29,874	21,355	24,950	24,950	22,800
New Jersey	49,992	30,604	0.61	30,426	28,868	25,223	25,000	25,000	27,153
New Mexico	32,000	22,000	0.69	22,627	21,939	18,000	18,475	19,050	19,050
New York	42,426	22,650	0.53	25,057	21,284	16,971	18,550	17,840	19,092
North Carolina	35,500	20,657	0.58	21,991	20,000	17,400	17,150	17,840	17,250
North Dakota	36,062	19,799	0.55	23,000	19,799	19,000	13,950	15,600	18,000
Ohio	38,013	21,355	0.56	24,507	20,082	17,250	17,782	18,470	17,678
Oklahoma	32,600	20,600	0.63	21,016	19,764	15,556	16,674	16,800	16,674
Oregon	37,500	24,042	0.64	27,000	24,466	18,000	18,385	19,300	20,577
Pennsylvania	39,723	22,250	0.56	25,152	21,311	18,100	18,850	18,533	18,187
Rhode Island	44,090	25,050	0.57	25,178	24,884	20,290	18,000	19,000	21,517
South Carolina	34,295	20,207	0.59	20,506	19,500	18,013	18,783	18,455	17,395

(continued)

Table 5.10 (continued)

State	No disability	Disability	Ratio[a]	Sensory	Physical	Mental	ADL	IADL	Work limitation
South Dakota	34,930	22,627	0.65	26,300	21,300	16,949	29,500	19,750	19,000
Tennessee	35,000	18,187	0.52	19,600	16,971	14,549	15,300	15,698	15,698
Texas	35,000	21,391	0.61	22,500	20,365	17,973	17,536	17,665	17,956
Utah	35,796	28,521	0.80	29,791	28,085	25,000	25,271	25,314	24,042
Vermont	38,983	24,749	0.64	28,510	22,979	18,246	21,392	17,378	16,758
Virginia	45,091	26,096	0.58	28,200	24,537	21,850	22,013	22,401	21,213
Washington	42,426	25,456	0.60	29,840	24,798	20,000	20,435	19,427	20,000
West Virginia	32,043	17,032	0.53	16,971	16,476	13,314	13,750	14,300	14,400
Wisconsin	39,664	22,780	0.57	26,460	21,920	18,157	19,942	19,587	18,943
Wyoming	38,749	26,941	0.70	27,761	25,456	24,500	22,585	23,267	20,572

[a] The disability/no disability ratio.
SOURCE: Authors' calculations from the 2006 ACS PUMS file.

181

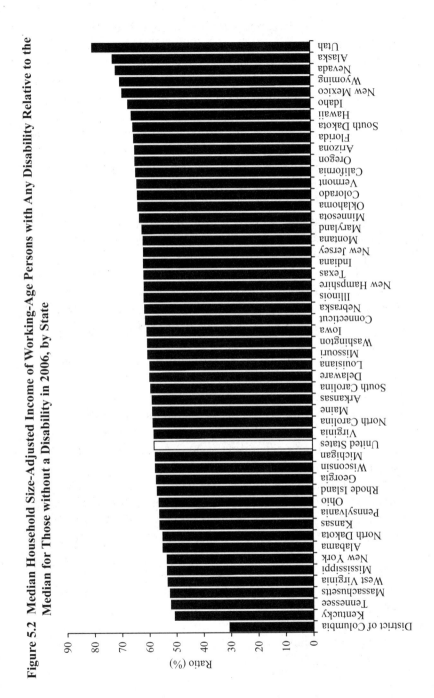

Figure 5.2 Median Household Size-Adjusted Income of Working-Age Persons with Any Disability Relative to the Median for Those without a Disability in 2006, by State

has been a rapid rise in the importance of own SSDI and SSI income as a share of household income of men with work limitations, especially relative to own labor earnings. Third, the rise in the importance of labor earnings from other household members as a share of the household income of men with work limitations has also been substantial and larger than in the households of men without limitations, especially relative to own labor earnings. Fourth, in the households of men with work limitations, the share of household income from all private sources fell over the period examined, with most of the decline coming from a drop in own labor earnings. In contrast, the share of income from private sources for men without work limitations rose over the same period. Finally, the labor earnings of men with work limitations have fallen by more than the increase in income from all public sources over that same period. The increases in the labor earnings of other household members have offset the decline in own labor earnings, thus preventing total household income from falling over the last two business cycles. But this modest growth in household incomes pales next to the substantial increase in the household income of men without work limitations over the same period.

Because no other data set has consistently used the same questions to capture the population with disabilities, only the CPS provides information that can trace the economic well-being of working-age people as far back as 1980. But recent improvements in data now allow us to better capture the working-age population with disabilities and its economic well-being. Using data from the 2003 ACS (income year 2003), we are able to compare the ACS measure of the population with work limitations with that of the 2004 March CPS (income year 2003). We found that the results are remarkably close—there is little difference in the median household income of these similarly defined populations. However, there is considerable difference in median household income across alternatively defined disability populations captured in the ACS data. The broadest population with disabilities captured in the survey has a much higher median household income than does the population with work limitations. This is not too surprising given the heterogeneous nature of disability and the fact that a large share of those in the broadest disability population do not report work limitations. But even this broader population has a median household income considerably below that of people without such disabilities.

The ACS provides researchers with a much broader range of measures of the working-age population with disabilities, and in this way is superior to the CPS in capturing social outcomes for working-age people with disabilities. Eventually, the ACS will allow researchers to trace changes in the economic well-being of those with and without disabilities over time. But the CPS will remain the one data set that allows researchers to trace patterns in economic well-being both absolutely and relative to those without disabilities back to the 1980s. It is critical that work-limitation questions remain in the ACS so that researchers will be able to link findings on this population with those based on long-term CPS-based results.

Appendix 5A

Definitions of Disability and Income

Table 5A.1 Definitions of Disability and Income

Measure/data source	Definitions
Disability: one-period work limitation	
March CPS	The CPS March Supplement asks "[d]oes anyone in this household have a health problem or disability which prevents them from working or which limits the kind or amount of work they can do? [If so,] who is that? (Anyone else?)" Those who answer yes to this question are considered to report a work limitation.
ACS	Because of a physical, mental, or emotional condition lasting 6 months or more, does this person have any difficulty in doing any of the following activities: b. Working at a job or business?
Disability: two-period work limitation	
March CPS	A portion of the March Supplement participants are asked about work limitations in two consecutive years. Those who report work limitations in two consecutive years (March to March) are considered to report a two-period work limitation. The years 1986 and 1996 are not applicable because the Census Bureau changed the sampling frame and the thus housing units were not consecutively interviewed. Also note, the CPS follows housing units, not the people in the households, so that matched files do not contain movers.
ACS	Not available.
Instrumental activity of daily living (IADL)	
March CPS	Not available.
ACS	Because of a physical, mental, or emotional condition lasting 6 months or more, does this person have any difficulty in doing any of the following activities: a. Going outside the home alone to shop or visit a doctor's office?

Activities of daily living (ADL)

March CPS   Not available

ACS   Because of a physical, mental, or emotional condition lasting 6 months or more, does this person have any difficulty in doing any of the following activities: b. Dressing, bathing, or getting around inside the home?

Mental impairments

March CPS   Not available.

ACS   Because of a physical, mental, or emotional condition lasting 6 months or more, does this person have any difficulty in doing any of the following activities: a. Learning, remembering, or concentrating?

Physical impairments

March CPS   Not available

ACS   Does this person have any of the following long lasting conditions: b. A condition that substantially limits one or more basic physical activities such as walking, climbing stairs, reaching, lifting, or carrying?

Sensory impairments

March CPS   Not available.

ACS   Does this person have any of the following long lasting conditions: a. Blindness, deafness, or a severe vision or hearing impairment?

(continued)

Table 5A.1 (continued)

Measure/data source	Definitions
Income sources	
March CPS	The CPS collects data on 23 sources of income for each person: 1) labor earnings, 2) self-employment income, 3) farm income, 4) public assistance and welfare, 5) unemployment compensation, 6) workers' compensation, 7) veteran's benefits, 8) Supplemental Security Income program, 9) Social Security Old Age, Survivors and Disability program, 10) educational assistance, 11) dividends, 12) interest income, 13) rental income, 14) alimony, 15) child support, 16, 17) two sources of private retirement income, 18,19) two sources of private disability income, 20, 21) two sources of private survivor's income, 22) financial assistance from outside the household, and 23) any other income. Capital gains or capital losses, taxes, and the value of noncash benefits (such as Food Stamps and housing subsidies) are not considered in this measure of income. If a person lives with a family, add up the income of all family members. (Nonrelatives, such as housemates, do not count.)
ACS	Asks the person to list the amount of income that each person in the household age 15 and older received from the following sources: 1) wages, salary, commissions, bonuses, or tips from all jobs (before deductions for taxes, bonds, dues or other items); 2) self-employment income from own nonfarm businesses or farm businesses, including proprietorships and partnerships (net income after business expenses); 3) interest, dividends, net rental income, royalty income, or income from real estate and trusts; 4) Social Security or Railroad Retirement; 5) Supplemental Security Income (SSI); 6) any public assistance or welfare payments from the state or local welfare office; 7) retirement, survivor or disability pensions (not including Social Security); and 8) any other sources of income received regularly such as Veterans' (VA) payments, unemployment compensation, child support, or alimony (not including lump sum payments such as money from an inheritance or the sale of a home).

Household income

March CPS   The sum of income for each household member age 15 and older in the household unit.

ACS   The sum of income for each household member age 15 and older in the household unit.

Household size

March CPS   Author's calculations using the household sequence number.

ACS   Number of persons in the household variable in ACS PUMS household file.

Household size-adjusted income

March CPS   Household income divided by the square root of household size. See Citro and Michael (1995) page 176 for further information.

ACS   Household income divided by the square root of household size. See Citro and Michael (1995) page 176 for further information.

SOURCE: Adapted from Burkhauser and Houtenville (2006) and Weathers (2005).

Notes

1. We focus on working-age men in this paper only because of space limitations, but the story for working-age women is similar. Despite the increased labor force participation of women over the period we examine (1980–2005), the labor earnings of men continue to be the most important source of married-couple household income. Thus, the differences between the economic well-being of households of working-age women with and without disabilities, although similar in direction, are smaller in magnitude than the ones for working-age men with and without disabilities.

2. For example, each year the Census Bureau provides official yearly income, poverty, and employment values by sex, race/ethnicity, and age based on March CPS data. It does not provide such values, however, for working-age people with disabilities. Burkhauser, Houtenville, and Rovba (2009) uses CPS data to provide the first such multi-year estimates of poverty, using the official Office of Management and Budget poverty line criteria, for the working-age population with disabilities.

3. This is a standard way of controlling for differences in household size in the economic well-being literature and is a variation of the Office of Management and Budget method of determining poverty levels for households of different sizes.

4. A business cycle trough is defined as the year in which household mean income hit its lowest absolute level over the cycle. This method of choosing comparison years only approximates the official National Bureau of Economic Research measure of business cycle peaks and troughs using overall economic growth. This is done for ease of exposition; the results do not change substantively if an alternative comparison of business cycles is chosen.

5. See Daly and Burkhauser (2003) and Berkowitz and Burkhauser (1996) for histories of Social Security disability policies over these years.

6. For example, the 2003 ACS was administered to a portion of its survey respondents in June 2003, and they were asked about their incomes from June 2002 to May 2003. The Census Bureau indexes the values so that they are comparable to those collected by 2003 ACS survey respondents interviewed in December 2003.

7. Because the ACS is collected over the entire year and the March CPS is collected only in March, it is not possible to precisely produce estimates from the two surveys for exactly the same period.

References

Acemoglu, Daron, and Joshua Angrist. 2001. "Consequences of Employment Protection? The Case of the Americans with Disabilities Act." *Journal of Political Economy* 109(5): 915–957.

Autor, David, and Mark Duggan. 2003. "The Rise in Disability Recipiency and the Decline in Unemployment." *The Quarterly Journal of Economics* 118(1): 157–205.

———. 2006. "The Growth in the Social Security Disability Rolls: A Fiscal Crisis Unfolding." NBER Working Paper no. W12436. Cambridge, MA: National Bureau of Economic Research.

Berkowitz, Edward D., and Richard V. Burkhauser. 1996. "A United States Perspective on Disability Programs." In *Curing the Dutch Disease: An International Perspective on Disability Policy Reform*, Leo J. M. Aarts, Richard V. Burkhauser, and Philip P. deJong, eds. Aldershot, Great Britain and Brookfield, VT: Ashgate Publishing Ltd., pp. 71–91.

Bound, John, and Richard V. Burkhauser. 1999. "Economic Analysis of Transfer Programs Targeted on People with Disabilities." In *Handbook of Labor Economics,* Vol. 3C, Orley Ashenfelter and David Card, eds. Amsterdam, New York, and Oxford: Elsevier Science, North Holland, pp. 3417–3528.

Bound, John, and Timothy Waidmann. 1992. "Disability Transfers, Self-Reported Health, and the Labor Force Attachment of Older Men: Evidence from the Historical Record." *The Quarterly Journal of Economics* 107(4): 1393–1419.

———. 2002. "Accounting for Recent Declines in Employment Rates Among the Working-Aged Disabled." *Journal of Human Resources* 37(2): 231–250.

Burkhauser, Richard V., Mary C. Daly, and Andrew J. Houtenville. 2001. "How Working-Age People with Disabilities Fared over the 1990s Business Cycle." In *Ensuring Health and Income Security for an Aging Workforce*, Peter P. Budetti, Richard V. Burkhauser, Janice M. Gregory, and H. Allan Hunt, eds. Kalamazoo, MI: W.E. Upjohn Institute for Employment Research, pp. 291–346.

Burkhauser, Richard V., Mary C. Daly, Andrew J. Houtenville, and Nigar Nargis. 2002. "Self-Reported Work Limitation Data: What They Can and Cannot Tell Us." *Demography* 39(3): 541–555.

Burkhauser, Richard V., and Andrew J. Houtenville. 2006. "A Guide to Disability Statistics from the Current Population Survey—Annual Social and Economic Supplement (March CPS)." Ithaca, NY: Cornell University, Rehabilitation Research and Training Center on Disability Demographics and Statistics.

Burkhauser, Richard V., Andrew J. Houtenville, and Ludmila Rovba. 2009. "Poverty." In *Counting Working-Age People with Disabilities: What Current Data Tell Us and Options for Improvement*, Andrew J. Houtenville, David C. Stapleton, Robert R. Weathers II, and Richard V. Burkhauser, eds. Kalamazoo, MI: W.E. Upjohn Institute for Employment Research, pp. 193–226.

Citro, Constance F., and Robert T. Michael, eds. 1995. *Measuring Poverty: A New Approach*. Washington, DC: National Academies Press.

Daly, Mary C., and Richard V. Burkhauser. 2003. "The Supplemental Security Income Program." In *Means Tested Transfer Programs in the United States*, Robert Moffitt, ed. NBER Conference Report Series. Chicago: University of Chicago Press, pp. 79–139.

DeNavas-Walt, Carmen, Bernadette D. Proctor, and Jessica C. Smith. 2008. "Income, Poverty and Health Insurance Coverage in the United States: 2007." U.S. Census Bureau Current Population Reports P60-235. Washington, DC: Government Printing Office.

Duggan, Mark, Perry Singleton, and Jae Song. 2007. "Aching to Retire? The Rise in the Full Retirement Age and Its Impact on the Social Security Disability Rolls." *Journal of Public Economics* 91(7): 1327–1350.

Hotchkiss, Julie L. 2003. *The Labor Market Experience of Workers with Disabilities: The ADA and Beyond*. Kalamazoo, MI: W.E. Upjohn Institute for Employment Research.

———. 2004. "A Closer Look at the Employment Impact of the Americans with Disabilities Act." *Journal of Human Resources* 39(4): 887–911.

Houtenville, Andrew J., and Richard V. Burkhauser. 2005. "Did the Employment of Those with Disabilities Fall in the 1990s and Was the ADA Responsible? A Replication of Acemoglu and Angrist (2001)—Research Brief." Ithaca, NY: Cornell University, Research and Rehabilitation Training Center for Economic Research on Employment Policy for Persons with Disabilities.

Jolls, Christine, and J. J. Prescott. 2005. "Disaggregating Employment Protection: The Case of Disability Discrimination." Harvard Public Law Working Paper no. 106. Cambridge, MA: Harvard Law School.

Weathers, Robert R., II. 2005. "A Guide to Disability Statistics from the American Community Survey." Ithaca, NY: Cornell University, Rehabilitation Research and Training Center on Disability Demographics and Statistics.

———. 2009. "The Disability Landscape." In *Counting Working-Age People with Disabilities: What Current Data Tell Us and Options for Improvement*, Andrew J. Houtenville, David C. Stapleton, Robert R. Weathers II, and Richard V. Burkhauser, eds. Kalamazoo, MI: W.E. Upjohn Institute for Employment Research, pp. 27–67.

6
Poverty

Richard V. Burkhauser
Cornell University

Andrew J. Houtenville
New Editions Consulting, Inc.

Ludmila Rovba
The Analysis Group, Inc

Every year, the *Economic Report of the President* provides information on the median income and poverty status of families and individuals in the United States. This is one of many government reports that use statistics generated by the Census Bureau from the March Demographic Supplement of the Current Population Survey (March CPS) on these closely watched measures of overall U.S. social policy success. As illustrated in Figure 6.1, median income has risen over time, but it is quite sensitive to changes in economic growth, decreasing during economic downturns and rising with recoveries. These fluctuations roughly trace out the last two full business cycles of the twentieth century (1983–1993 and 1993–2004).

While the starting and ending years of a business cycle are to some degree arbitrary, we take advantage of the clear trend in median income shown in Figure 6.1 to define our peak and trough years. Because employment and income lag changes in economic growth, these years do not necessarily match business cycles defined by changes in macroeconomic growth. Measured in this way, each cycle begins with an increase in median income from the previous cycle's trough year to a business cycle peak, followed by a drop to the next trough and the beginning of the next cycle. During this period, median income in each successive trough was higher than in the previous one.

Figure 6.1 Median Family Income and Poverty Rate of Families and Persons, 1979–2005

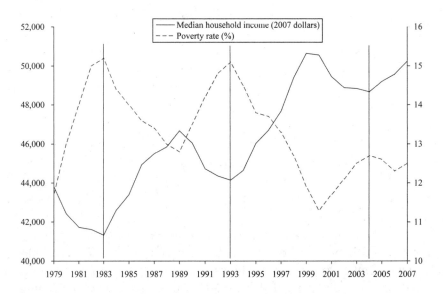

SOURCE: DeNavas-Walt, Proctor, and Smith (2008).

Although there was substantial growth in median income over both these cycles, those in the lower part of the income distribution gained more during the 1990s business cycle than they did in the 1980s cycle, as indicated by Census Bureau's official poverty rate statistics (Figure 6.1), which are also compiled from the yearly CPS Reports. The poverty rate was 15.2 percent in 1983 and fell to 12.8 percent in 1989 before rising to 15.1 percent in 1993. Thus, while yearly median income rose over the 1980s, there was little change in the share of the population in poverty. This was not the case in the 1990s. Seven years of economic growth resulted in a fall in the poverty rate to 11.3 percent in 2000, its lowest level over the two business cycles. Although the poverty rate increased over the slack early years of the 2000s to 12.7 percent in 2004, it was still considerably below the 1993 trough year rate.

The March CPS data indicate that the yearly poverty rates of the working-age population (aged 25–61) were consistently below those of the overall population (regardless of age), but they also follow the same business cycle trends (Table 6.1, column 1).[1] Table 6.1 also shows poverty rates by sex and race subgroups. While poverty rates fell and then rose over the business cycle of the 1980s for all groups, a comparison of the 1993 rates with those from 1983 shows only modest declines for most groups and little change in the relative poverty of the higher risk groups to their lower risk counterparts (i.e., women to men and non-whites to whites). But this subpopulation pattern changed dramatically over the 1990s. Absolute poverty rates fell for all groups, but the risk of poverty fell substantially more for the two high-risk subgroups.

This chapter will focus on an economically at-risk population not analyzed by those who officially measure economic well-being or poverty—working-age people with disabilities. We first briefly review the issues related to capturing this population, both conceptually and operationally, in the data sets discussed in Weathers (2009), as well as the limitations faced in using the CPS to do so. We then estimate the poverty rate captured in the CPS population with disabilities—those who report work limitations—and compare it both with the poverty rates for those with work limitations identified in other data sets as well as disability groups defined by alternative concepts and questions. The American Community Survey (ACS) offers researchers a much richer mix of concepts and questions in which to capture a population with disabilities and its poverty rate. Variation in poverty rates across alternative concepts of the disability population within the ACS was found to be much greater than variation in poverty rates across surveys for those with work limitations.

Next, we focus on the real strength of the CPS for poverty research—its ability to support poverty rate estimates for persons with and without disabilities based on the same set of questions in every year since 1980. Using these data, we are able to focus on trends in the relative risk of poverty for people with work limitations and show that this economically at-risk population had a substantially different experience over the last two business cycles of the twentieth century than other at-risk groups.

Because the CPS asks the same set of work-limitation questions one year apart to a subset of its cross-sectional population, we are also able to show that the levels of poverty of those with longer term dis-

Table 6.1 Poverty Rate for Selected Economically At-Risk Working-Age Populations (Aged 25–61)

Income year	All (1)	Sex			Race		
		Women (%) (2)	Men (%) (3)	Relative (2)/(3)	Nonwhite (%) (4)	White (%) (5)	Relative (4)/(5)
1979	8.06	9.97	6.04	1.65	19.05	5.73	3.32
1980	9.44	11.48	7.27	1.58	21.73	6.69	3.25
1981	10.26	12.48	7.92	1.58	22.07	7.57	2.92
1982	11.39	13.56	9.10	1.49	23.69	8.49	2.79
1983	**11.49**	**13.45**	**9.43**	**1.43**	**24.13**	**8.48**	**2.84**
1984	10.86	12.91	8.71	1.48	22.53	7.87	2.86
1985	10.45	12.58	8.23	1.53	21.05	7.66	2.75
1986	10.08	12.36	7.71	1.60	20.84	7.17	2.91
1987	9.60	11.54	7.57	1.53	20.88	6.47	3.23
1988	9.40	11.24	7.49	1.50	20.23	6.33	3.20
1989	9.27	11.20	7.24	1.55	19.50	6.30	3.09
1990	9.77	11.63	7.81	1.49	20.63	6.57	3.14
1991	10.35	12.36	8.25	1.50	21.12	7.10	2.98
1992	10.58	12.50	8.58	1.46	21.63	7.18	3.01
1993	**11.23**	**13.23**	**9.14**	**1.45**	**22.39**	**7.55**	**2.97**
1994	10.77	12.48	9.00	1.39	21.35	7.29	2.93
1995	10.20	11.87	8.46	1.40	20.40	6.65	3.07
1996	10.19	12.04	8.28	1.45	19.79	6.73	2.94
1997	9.74	11.72	7.68	1.53	18.12	6.64	2.73

1998	9.43	11.18	7.60	1.47	17.33	6.47	2.68
1999	8.66	10.18	7.07	1.44	15.50	6.05	2.56
2000	8.46	9.85	7.01	1.41	14.96	5.91	2.53
2001	8.94	10.31	7.51	1.37	15.25	6.32	2.41
2002	9.48	10.89	8.01	1.36	16.15	6.55	2.46
2003	9.76	11.11	8.37	1.33	16.50	6.75	2.44
2004	**10.06**	**11.47**	**8.60**	**1.33**	**16.18**	**7.23**	**2.24**
2005	9.88	11.50	8.20	1.40	16.45	6.77	2.43

NOTE: Bold years are business cycle troughs.
SOURCE: Authors' calculations based on the March CPS, 1980–2006.

abilities (those reported in both interviews) are even higher than for those identified as having a disability in a single interview. The last section of this chapter focuses on research that has used data from the 1996 Survey of Income and Program Participation (SIPP), a true panel data set that interviews individuals at four-month intervals over four years to investigate the relationship between those with longer term disabilities and their risk of longer terms in poverty. We argue that the SIPP is the best currently available data set for those interested in comparing the poverty experiences of those with more permanent disabilities.

DATA AND MEASUREMENT

The March CPS is a nationally representative sample of approximately 150,000 civilians living in 50,000 U.S. households. While its income data have been collected since survey year 1968 (income year 1967—the March CPS collects income information for the previous calendar year), the work-limitation measure has only been available since survey year 1981. Nonetheless, this variable allows us to capture the economic well-being of people with and without work limitations over the last two business cycles of the twentieth century (1983–1993 and 1993–2004).

To avoid attribution of cyclical fluctuations to secular trends, we make comparisons of poverty rates at similar points in the business cycles. Although we use data from all years since 1980, our focus is on the trough years of 1983, 1993, and 2004. By examining these years, we implicitly control for the state of the business cycle. Business cycles are usually compared across peak-to-peak years. The peaks for the 1980s and 1990s business cycles are 1979, 1989, and 2000, but the CPS data on work limitations begin in 1980. Hence, to capture two complete business cycles for those with and without work limitations, we compare the trough years. Comparisons for 1980, 1989, and 2000 (near peak and peak years) yield similar results for changes in poverty rates, but at lower poverty levels. We chose 2004 as the end point of the 1990s business cycle because median income rose in 2005 and poverty rates fell.

We focus on men and women aged 25–61 who self-report a work limitation. Focusing on this age range allows us to avoid confusing changes in economic well-being associated with a disability from those associated with initial transitions into the labor force due to education or job shopping at younger ages and retirement at older ages.

Because a subsample of the March CPS respondents is reinter-viewed in the following March, the CPS allows researchers to create matched samples containing a second round of information on these individuals. We use this aspect of the CPS to create a two-period work-limitation measure—people who report a work limitation in two con-secutive March CPS surveys.

Although most statistics in this chapter are based on the CPS, statis-tics based on the 2003 ACS, the 2002 National Health Interview Survey (NHIS), and the 2002 SIPP are also presented.

The March CPS has consistently asked a work-limitation question since 1981. We define two work-limitation groups based on this ques-tion: those reporting a work limitation in the current March CPS and the subsample of those with "longer term" work limitations (those who report a work limitation in both interviews). The CPS allows research-ers to produce poverty rates for groups of people with work limitations in the same way that poverty rates are officially measured for other at-risk populations.

As discussed in Weathers (2009) and Burkhauser, Rovba, and Weathers (2009), a major drawback of the CPS is that it has very limited information on disability. Nonetheless, the March CPS has been widely used in the economics literature to look at the employment and/or eco-nomic well-being of people with disabilities and is the only data set able to trace the long-term economic outcomes of working-age people with disabilities.

The Census Bureau maintains official poverty thresholds for fami-lies of different sizes (including those who live alone—a one-person family). The Office of Management and Budget (OMB) defines the of-ficial poverty thresholds for each type of family and how income should be measured to determine whether a family lives in poverty. These thresholds do not vary geographically, but they are updated annually for inflation with the Consumer Price Index for urban families (CPI-U). The official poverty definition counts money income before taxes and excludes capital gains and noncash benefits (e.g., public housing, food stamps, etc.). By excluding in-kind transfers, the OMB guidelines understate their value to families. But to the degree that recipients would not purchase them at their market price, using their market value would overstate their value. Likewise, the failure to account for tax payments overstates and the failure to capture tax credits (e.g., the Earned Income Tax Credit) understates the family's disposable income. The guidelines also do not adjust for special needs that a family might have, such as assistive devices, accommodations, and services that might be used to address a family member's impairment.[2] These and other problems with the OMB guidelines for measuring poverty make it a less than perfect measure. Nevertheless, we use the OMB method because it is the official method the Census Bureau uses to estimate the politically most important measure of economic progress of at-risk populations in the United States. It is also the measure most referenced in public policy debates on poverty.

The CPS is the data set used by the Census Bureau to estimate the official poverty rate and the one primarily applied in this chapter. The ACS offers income data that is comparable to that of the CPS and has the added feature of a much greater sample size. Hence, it can provide more precise measures of income and poverty at the national, state, and local levels. The SIPP, with its smaller sample sizes, produces less precise estimates, but its more detailed questions with respect to program participation make it better able to capture the bottom of the income distribution. All three of these data sets provide excellent information on income and poverty. The data provided to researchers in the public-use NHIS is much less precise in this regard because income is only provided in brackets, and poverty rates are based on income information not available to researchers.

Throughout the analyses, we disaggregate the population with disabilities into broad, and frequently overlapping, subgroups based on sex, race, age, and education. Specifically, we compare the poverty rates of men and women, whites and nonwhites, individuals aged 25–44 and 45–61, and individuals with less than a high school degree, a high school degree, and more than a high school degree. Small sample sizes prohibit us from making more detailed comparisons.

The CPS age, race, and sex questions are straightforward. We divide individuals into whites and all others (nonwhites). Education is derived from two questions. Prior to 1992, the CPS asked, "[W]hat is the highest grade or year of regular school [person] has ever attended? Did [person] complete that grade (year)?" In 1992, the CPS switched from this "grade/years attended" characterization of education to a "credential" characterization: "[W]hat is the highest level of school [person] has completed or the highest degree [person] has received?" To provide continuity, we converted these credentials to years completed using standard assumptions. Educational attainment is captured in similar ways in the ACS and SIPP.

COMPARING POVERTY ACROSS DATA SETS AND CONCEPTS OF DISABILITIES

Before evaluating long-term trends in the poverty rates of people with work limitations, we compare the poverty rates of the population with work limitations found by using the CPS data with other nationally representative data sets that use a similar work-limitations measure. In addition to the March 2004 CPS (income year 2003) and the matched March 2003–2004 CPS (income year 2003), we look at the 2003 ACS, the 2002 NHIS, and the 2002 SIPP. As discussed above, these last three surveys also ask a work-limitation question and have enough information about income to determine whether a person is in poverty using the OMB definition. But as discussed in Weathers (2009), unlike the CPS, these nationally representative surveys also allow for the identification of the population with disabilities using alternative disability concepts and questions. They do not, however, provide the long continuous time series that the CPS provides.[3]

Poverty rates of people with work limitations are reported for the five data sets in Table 6.2. In all cases, those not identified as having any type of disability have dramatically lower poverty rates than those who report a disability of some sort. The robustness of the estimates for work-limitation disability across data sets is quite remarkable given the differences in work-limitation and income questions and in the year

Table 6.2 Poverty Rates (%) of People with Disabilities (Aged 25–61), by Data Source and Disability Measure

	No disability	Any disability	Participation restriction		Activity limitation	Impairment		
			Work limitation	IADL	ADL	Mental	Physical	Sensory
2004 March CPS	8.0	28.8	28.8	—	—	—	—	—
2003/4 Matched CPS	6.3	29.0	29.0	—	—	—	—	—
2003 ACS	7.7	23.7	29.6	29.7	28.9	30.8	25.0	20.8
2002 NHIS	7.5	21.2	26.5	32.3	30.1	29.8	22.1	20.7
2002 SIPP	6.5	18.8	26.0	26.3	25.1	24.9	19.1	17.6

NOTE: IADL, instrumental activities of daily living.

SOURCE: Weathers (2005) for ACS, Wittenburg and Nelson (2006) for SIPP, Harris, Hendershot, and Stapleton (2005) for NHIS, and authors' calculations for CPS, 2003–2004.

analyzed. The table also reports poverty rates for alternatively defined working-age populations with disabilities, such as those with physical or mental impairments. (For more detailed information on how these alternatively defined populations with disabilities are defined in each data set, see Weathers 2009.) Poverty rates vary much more across alternative definitions of the disability population than across data sets using the same definition. People with physical and sensory impairments have lower poverty rates than those with mental impairments, activity limitations, or participation restrictions, consistent with their higher employment rates (Weathers and Wittenburg 2009) and their higher mean income (Burkhauser, Rovba, and Weathers 2009).

Hence, while the population with disabilities captured using our work-limitation measure in the CPS is different from that captured using alternative definitions of disability, the differences in the poverty rates are in the expected direction. And, the poverty rate found in the CPS population with work limitations is very close to the poverty rate found for working-age people with work limitations in the other data sets featured in Table 6.2.

In addition to the richness of information on disability markers in the ACS, the survey's very large sample size allows researchers to capture characteristics of the working-age population with disabilities at the state level. The poverty rates shown in Table 6.3 by state and disability measure are based on the 2003 ACS.

Poverty rates for people with disabilities vary widely across states, but this variation partly reflects wide variation in poverty rates for those without disabilities. The relative poverty rates for those with a disability (using the ACS "any disability" measure) relative to those without a disability also vary widely, however, as illustrated in Figure 6.2. At the low end, Utah residents with any disability are somewhat more than twice as likely as those without a disability to live in poverty; at the high end, Nebraskans with disabilities are almost five times as likely to live in poverty.

Poverty rates are highly correlated across disability, and of all the possible combinations of disability measures, the highest correlation (0.92) is between the poverty rates of those with work limitations and those with physical disabilities. This strong correlation might reflect the fact that people with physical disabilities comprise the greatest

Table 6.3 2003 ACS Poverty, by State and Disability Measure, Persons Aged 25–61

State	No disability	Any disability	Ratio[a]	Work limitation	Specific disability				
					IADL	ADL	Mental	Physical	Sensory
All states	7.7	23.7	3.08	29.6	29.7	28.9	30.8	25.0	20.8
Alabama	9.8	30.1	3.07	36.1	29.5	31.1	34.9	30.2	23.5
Alaska	6.4	13.8	2.16	18.3	18.9	18.4	18.1	14.3	13.6
Arizona	10.5	22.8	2.17	28.6	28.5	26.8	28.6	23.6	17.2
Arkansas	9.1	25.8	2.84	31.2	30.0	32.6	31.5	26.5	17.5
California	9.1	21.8	2.40	25.7	25.0	28.3	27.7	22.5	20.1
Colorado	5.5	18.3	3.33	24.8	22.1	27.5	23.3	20.6	13.2
Connecticut	4.9	19.1	3.90	27.1	33.4	26.2	22.8	22.7	13.3
DC	4.7	17.6	3.74	23.5	18.6	19.5	21.6	17.4	17.4
Delaware	12.7	30.7	2.42	33.6	37.1	25.4	36.8	33.6	28.0
Florida	8.7	22.6	2.60	29.2	28.6	30.7	29.5	23.7	21.1
Georgia	7.6	25.9	3.41	32.0	32.7	30.0	31.4	26.1	22.2
Hawaii	7.0	21.5	3.07	28.8	27.6	30.4	31.3	26.0	21.1
Idaho	8.6	20.9	2.43	27.7	22.3	20.3	26.9	19.6	19.1
Illinois	6.8	22.9	3.37	29.4	29.6	27.8	33.0	24.2	19.9
Indiana	5.8	20.8	3.59	27.6	26.8	21.8	30.3	21.6	18.4
Iowa	5.7	20.9	3.67	28.7	33.0	25.2	29.3	21.7	16.4
Kansas	5.4	20.8	3.85	30.6	29.2	37.6	30.7	23.4	17.6
Kentucky	10.2	30.6	3.00	37.1	34.2	30.6	37.0	31.8	31.2
Louisiana	11.9	31.3	2.63	39.5	44.3	37.9	38.7	31.3	27.2

Maine	5.7	21.5	3.77	27.9	28.5	22.6	29.0	22.4	18.6
Maryland	4.7	18.6	3.96	24.2	21.8	22.1	23.3	19.8	15.7
Massachusetts	5.4	23.8	4.41	28.9	32.1	30.0	34.2	24.7	23.4
Michigan	6.4	22.9	3.58	29.5	30.1	27.8	29.7	24.2	21.2
Minnesota	4.0	18.8	4.70	26.2	22.6	20.6	22.5	20.2	7.8
Mississippi	10.9	31.3	2.87	36.3	38.3	39.1	39.1	33.6	28.2
Missouri	6.0	22.6	3.77	27.0	30.9	28.5	30.3	24.3	15.2
Montana	8.8	23.2	2.64	28.4	22.0	25.6	32.3	24.5	20.5
Nebraska	5.4	26.1	4.83	33.5	30.3	35.8	35.8	28.3	26.3
Nevada	7.5	21.8	2.91	28.3	25.4	30.7	24.0	21.8	25.3
N. Hampshire	4.5	17.3	3.84	23.4	24.5	14.0	23.7	18.4	16.5
New Jersey	5.3	19.0	3.58	23.8	22.8	25.3	26.5	19.7	21.0
New Mexico	11.3	31.3	2.77	40.0	44.7	50.7	41.0	32.6	30.1
New York	8.6	26.5	3.08	31.7	32.3	29.8	34.3	27.6	22.1
North Carolina	7.9	24.3	3.08	31.5	30.0	28.1	28.5	26.2	22.7
North Dakota	6.6	21.9	3.32	30.5	27.1	23.7	25.2	27.1	11.4
Ohio	6.8	24.1	3.54	30.1	32.6	29.0	33.2	26.1	20.9
Oklahoma	9.6	25.5	2.66	30.4	30.9	28.0	30.1	27.0	26.9
Oregon	8.9	23.2	2.61	28.7	31.1	28.2	33.3	22.4	14.5
Pennsylvania	6.2	24.1	3.89	28.9	27.8	25.8	30.8	24.9	20.9
Rhode Island	5.5	26.0	4.73	31.0	27.6	30.6	33.9	27.9	28.8
South Carolina	8.2	26.2	3.20	28.7	27.2	22.8	33.3	28.2	19.7
South Dakota	6.4	19.2	3.00	24.1	18.2	17.3	26.8	19.7	16.7

(continued)

Table 6.3 (continued)

State	No disability	Any disability	Ratio[a]	Specific disability					
				Work limitation	IADL	ADL	Mental	Physical	Sensory
Tennessee	7.7	26.1	3.39	32.5	31.2	35.7	34.5	28.5	20.2
Texas	10.6	24.5	2.31	30.1	32.7	32.3	32.3	26.5	24.5
Utah	7.3	15.2	2.08	22.3	23.0	22.9	18.2	16.7	15.2
Vermont	4.9	22.3	4.55	29.4	33.0	28.1	23.1	23.6	13.4
Virginia	4.6	20.3	4.41	25.8	23.0	24.5	25.0	22.3	14.6
Washington	7.3	22.5	3.08	31.3	35.8	29.7	32.1	24.2	16.1
West Virginia	12.1	28.4	2.35	34.4	35.7	31.8	38.9	28.8	24.8
Wisconsin	5.9	20.5	3.47	26.2	31.9	21.5	29.6	21.6	23.6
Wyoming	6.2	17.6	2.84	25.3	23.8	27.7	25.5	19.0	16.1

[a] The (any disability)/(no disability) ratio.
SOURCE: Weathers (2005).

Figure 6.2 Poverty Rate of Working-Age Persons with any Disability Relative to the Poverty Rate for Those without a Disability in 2003, by State

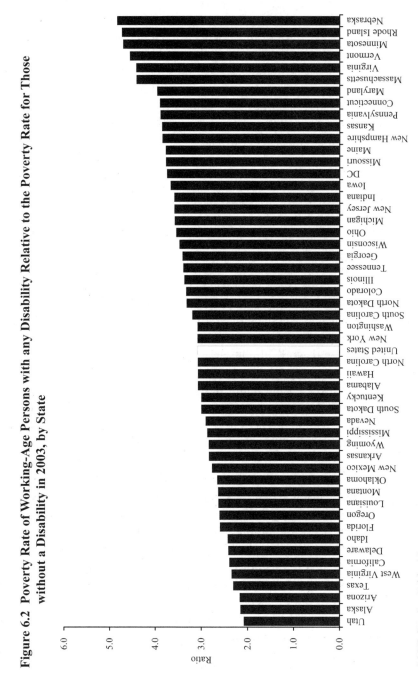

SOURCE: See Table 6.3.

proportion of those reporting work limitations, as shown in Weathers (2009). The poverty rates of those with work limitations are least correlated with those with sensory impairments, but the correlation is still quite high (0.68). These findings suggest it is reasonable to use a work-limitation measure of disability to capture differences in the poverty rates of people with disabilities across states for much the same reasons that Burkhauser et al. (2002) suggest it is reasonable to capture variations in employment rates across time.

POVERTY TRENDS OVER THE LAST TWO BUSINESS CYCLES

While the ACS, the NHIS, and the SIPP have more nuanced questions about disability, they cannot replace the CPS as the only data set that provides information on the employment and economic well-being of a consistently defined disability population since 1981. Table 6.4 documents the fluctuations in the poverty rate of people with and without one-period work limitations over the business cycles of the 1980s and 1990s. The poverty rates of both groups follow the business cycle, rising between 1980 and 1983, the first business cycle trough year we consider. Both populations' poverty rates were sensitive to the ebb and flow of economic activity over the next two business cycles (1983–1993 and 1993–2004), fluctuating in a similar manner over these years.

However, the net changes in the poverty rates for the two groups differ over these business cycles. The poverty rate of people with work limitations rose between 1983 and 1993, whereas that of their counterparts without work limitations fell. While the poverty rates of both groups fell in the 1990s, the relative risk of poverty for those with work limitations rose. In 1983, people with work limitations were 2.8 times more likely to be in poverty than their counterparts without work limitations. At the end of the 1980s business cycle, in 1993, their relative risk had risen to 3.3, and it had reached 3.4 by 2004.

While overall median income rose in 2005 (Figure 6.1) and the poverty rate of people without work limitations fell, the poverty rate of people with work limitations continued to rise. Thus, the relative risk of poverty for people with work limitations was even greater in the first year of our most recent business cycle.

The same pattern can be seen among people with two-period work limitations, although this population experienced consistently higher levels of poverty (Table 6.4). In 1983, people with two-period work limitations were 3.1 times more likely to be in poverty than were their counterparts without such longer term work limitations. By 1993, their relative risk had risen to 4.2, and it was essentially the same in 2004.

Demographic Factors Driving the Growth in Poverty

The change in the average poverty risk of people with work limitations is the consequence of changes in the poverty rates of many demographic subgroups. Some fared better than others over the 1980s and 1990s business cycles. Table 6.5 shows the poverty rates of various subgroups by work-limitation status.

As Table 6.5 indicates, among both people with and without work limitations, poverty rates were higher for women than for men, for those with less education relative to those with more, for nonwhites than for whites, and for younger than for older working-age persons. This pattern is not surprising and simply indicates that the risk of poverty varies across many demographic characteristics for both those with and without work limitations. But it also demonstrates that compositional changes within the overall working-age populations with and without work limitations can influence overall poverty trends.

The growth in the absolute and relative poverty rates of those with and without work limitations within each demographic subgroup varied over the two decades (Table 6.5). Over the 1980s, most subgroups within the population with work limitations experienced an increase in their poverty rate while the opposite was true of the subgroups without work limitations. Hence, the relative risk of poverty rose for most subgroups within the population with work limitations (with the exception of those with less than a high school education).[4]

The poverty rate of people with and without work limitations was lower at the end of the business cycle of the 1990s than it was at the beginning, as was the poverty rate of most of the subgroups. But the

Table 6.4 Poverty Rate for Working-Age (Aged 25–61) Populations with Work Limitations

Income Year	One-period (cross-sectional CPS)			Two-period (matched CPS)		
	With (%)	Without (%)	Relative	With (%)	Without (%)	Relative
	(1)	(2)	(1)/(2)	(3)	(4)	(3)/(4)
1980	25.61	8.06	3.18	—	—	—
1981	27.22	8.81	3.09	30.29	7.38	4.11
1982	27.72	10.07	2.75	27.19	8.74	3.11
1983	**28.61**	**10.10**	**2.83**	**27.72**	**8.91**	**3.11**
1984	28.00	9.41	2.98	26.51	8.34	3.18
1985	27.33	9.04	3.02	—	—	—
1986	27.09	8.68	3.12	26.50	7.31	3.63
1987	27.35	8.22	3.33	28.25	6.53	4.33
1988	26.69	8.06	3.31	24.06	6.43	3.74
1989	27.26	7.83	3.48	29.47	6.32	4.66
1990	28.72	8.24	3.49	28.96	6.67	4.34
1991	28.14	8.88	3.17	29.93	7.14	4.19
1992	29.12	9.02	3.23	30.41	7.74	3.93
1993	**31.28**	**9.40**	**3.33**	**31.73**	**7.64**	**4.15**
1994	30.35	9.00	3.37	30.56	7.19	4.25
1995	28.20	8.57	3.29	—	—	—
1996	29.49	8.45	3.49	30.86	6.84	4.51
1997	28.78	8.07	3.56	30.65	6.50	4.72
1998	29.30	7.72	3.80	29.05	5.88	4.94

1999	27.20	7.06	3.85	27.82	6.13	4.54
2000	28.07	6.79	4.13	29.63	5.62	5.28
2001	27.51	7.28	3.78	25.46	5.62	4.53
2002	29.38	7.80	3.77	30.22	6.12	4.94
2003	28.85	8.02	3.60	29.00	6.44	4.50
2004	**28.49**	**8.37**	**3.40**	**26.94**	**6.42**	**4.20**
2005	29.65	8.07	3.67	—	—	—

NOTE: Bold years are business cycle troughs.
SOURCE: Authors' calculations based on the March CPS, 1980–2006.

Table 6.5 Poverty Rates of People with and without Work Limitations, by Sex, Education, Race, and Age

Category	1983			1993			2004		
	Work limitation			Work limitation			Work limitation		
	With (%)	Without (%)	Relative[a]	With (%)	Without (%)	Relative	With (%)	Without (%)	Relative
All	28.61	10.10	2.83	31.28	9.40	3.33	28.49	8.37	3.40
Men	24.15	8.17	2.96	28.23	7.31	3.86	26.40	6.98	3.78
Women	33.26	11.91	2.79	34.51	11.39	3.03	30.49	9.72	3.14
<H.S.	39.19	23.43	1.67	44.31	27.25	1.63	42.24	23.49	1.80
H.S.	22.87	9.41	2.43	27.11	10.14	2.67	28.55	9.88	2.89
>H.S.	16.15	4.93	3.27	20.66	4.78	4.32	19.13	4.80	3.99
White	22.60	7.40	3.05	25.82	6.01	4.30	24.58	5.69	4.32
Nonwhite	47.75	21.69	2.20	43.94	19.95	2.20	36.21	14.22	2.55
Age 25–44	31.79	11.41	2.79	33.64	10.96	3.07	32.19	9.95	3.23
Age 45–61	26.48	7.44	3.56	29.21	6.24	4.68	26.33	6.20	4.25

[a] The (with)/(without) ratio.
SOURCE: Authors' calculations based on the March CPS (1984, 1994, and 2005).

poverty risk of most of the subgroups with work limitations rose relative to their counterparts without work limitations. That is, the dramatic
growth in the 1990s consistently increased the relative risk of poverty
for those with work limitations relative to those without work limitations in their demographic subgroup. Furthermore, the relative poverty
of the most economically at-risk subpopulations all increased (women,
the more poorly educated, nonwhites, and those aged 25–44). At the
same time, except for whites, who remained about the same, the relative
poverty of all less economically at-risk subpopulations decreased.

Hence, the dramatic improvement among the other economically
at-risk subpopulations in the 1990s (Table 6.1) also occurred for those
with work limitations in the 1990s. But for the more at-risk subpopulations with work limitations, these gains were lower relative to their
counterparts without such work limitations.

Decomposition of Absolute Overall Poverty Increase over the 1980s and 1990s

As shown in Table 6.4, the overall poverty rate of working-age
people with work limitations increased by 2.7 percentage points over
the 1980s business cycle and then declined by 2.8 percentage points
over the 1990s cycle. The data presented in Table 6.5 suggest that these
changes may be due both to changes in the composition of this population as well as to changes in poverty rates within subpopulations. The
data also suggest that the relative importance and characteristics of
these forces may have been quite different in the 1980s and 1990s.

To quantify the relative influence of compositional changes and
subgroup-specific increases in poverty over both the 1980s and 1990s
business cycles, we first divided the working-age population with work
limitations into 24 mutually exclusive subgroups, based on male, female, white, nonwhite, ages 25–44, ages 45–61, less than high school,
high school, and more than high school differences.[5]

To estimate the relative influence of compositional versus subgroup-
specific changes in poverty on the overall poverty rate of people with
work limitations over the 1980s and 1990s business cycles, a decomposition technique was used that breaks percentage point changes in
the poverty rates into two components: 1) those due to the change in
the composition of the population, and 2) those due to the change in

subgroup poverty rates. The overall poverty in any given year (P') is the sum of subgroup poverty rates (P'_g) weighted by subgroup population shares (S'_g) over all subgroups ($g = 1, 2 \ldots G$). This calculation requires mutually exclusive subgroups. The change in overall poverty rates from one year (t) to another year (t') is:

$$P^{t'} - P^t = \sum_{g=1}^{G}\left(P_g^{t'}S_g^{t'}\right) - \sum_{g=1}^{G}\left(P_g^t S_g^t\right).$$

To facilitate decomposition, this change can be rewritten as:

$$P^{t'} - P^t = \sum_{g=1}^{G}\left(\left(S_g^{t'} - S_g^t\right)\left(P_g^t - P^t\right)\right) + \sum_{g=1}^{G}\left(\left(P_g^{t'} - P_g^t\right)S_g^{t'}\right)$$

$$= \sum_{g=1}^{G}\left(\Delta S_g P_g^t\right) + \sum_{g=1}^{G}\left(\Delta P_g S_g^{t'}\right).$$

In other words, the impact of the change in subgroup composition (the first term) is the weighted sum of changes in subgroup population shares (ΔS_g) over all subgroups, where each subgroup is weighted by the deviation of its initial poverty rate from the initial overall poverty rate (P_g^t). A rise (fall) in a population share of a subgroup with an above-average poverty rate will increase (decrease) the overall poverty rate. The change attributed to changes in subgroup poverty rates (the second term) is the weighted sum of changes in subgroup poverty rates (ΔP_g) over all subgroups, where each subgroup is weighted by its population share in the second year ($S_g^{t'}$). A decline in the poverty rate of any subgroup will reduce the overall poverty rate.

The results of the decomposition for both business cycle periods are reported in Table 6.6. Between 1983 and 1993, the poverty rate among all people with work limitations increased by 2.67 percentage points (row 1, column 3), of which 0.05 percentage points were due to compositional change and 2.62 percentage points to changes in the absolute within-subpopulation poverty rate. That is, if the population shares in 1993 had remained exactly the same as in 1983, the poverty rate of people with work limitations would have increased by 2.62 rather than 2.67 percentage points. Hence, over the 1980s, increases (decreases) in the share of those subgroups that experienced relatively high (low) increases in their absolute within-subgroup poverty rate added to the impact of the overall poverty rate, but this shift in population shares was a very minor factor.

Likewise, in the 1990s, the gross overall poverty rate decrease of 2.79 percentage points (Table 6.6, row 1, column 6) overstates the pure poverty rate decrease of 0.92 percentage points because compositional changes accounted for a decrease of 1.86 percentage points. Although this decline in the underlying poverty rate is certainly an improvement over the compositionally adjusted percentage point increase of 2.62 in the 1980s, it is far less than is implied by simply comparing the overall decline in the 1990s with the overall increase in the 1980s. Compositional changes played a much greater role in the 1990s than they did in the 1980s.

The findings from Table 6.6 for working-age people with work limitations are summarized in the first row of Table 6.7. In 1983 their poverty rate was 28.6 percent. By 1993, their unadjusted poverty rate grew to 31.3 percent. Adjusting for compositional change, using a 1983 population base, we found that the underlying poverty rate changes slightly to 31.2 percent. In contrast, compositional changes mattered much more between 1993 and 2004. In this period, the unadjusted poverty rate fell to 28.5 percent in 2004, but using a 1993 base, the adjusted poverty rate fell only to 30.4 percent. Hence, as previously discussed, unlike the 1980s business cycle, the change in poverty over the 1990s business cycle was mostly due to compositional change. Adjusted for composition effects over the entire period, the underlying poverty rate of people with work limitations was higher in 2004 (30.1 percent, Table 6.7) than it was in 1983 (28.6 percent).

We did the same analysis for people without work limitations (row 2, Table 6.7). Their adjusted poverty rate was 10.0 percent in 1993, slightly higher than their unadjusted rate of 9.4 percent. Likewise, when we assumed no change in the composition of the population without work limitations between 1993 and 2004, their poverty rate would have been 8.5 percent, only slightly higher than the unadjusted rate of 8.4 percent. But unlike people with work limitations, when we controlled for composition effects over the entire period, the poverty rate of people without limitations still fell from 10.1 percent in 1983 to 9.1 percent in 2004.

Table 6.6 Decomposition of the Percentage Point Change in the Poverty Rate of People Reporting Work Limitations, by Changes in Absolute Population Shares and Poverty Rates, and by Sex, Age, Race, and Education (24 Mutually Exclusive Groups)

| | 1983–1993 | | | 1993–2004 | | |
| | Attributed to changes in | | | Attributed to changes in | | |
Group	Pop. share (1)	Poverty rate (2)	Total change (1)+(2)	Pop. share (3)	Poverty rate (4)	Total change (3)+(4)
Total Population	0.05	2.62	2.67	−1.86	−0.92	−2.79
Men, 25–44, white, < H.S.	0.00	0.33	0.33	−0.18	−0.09	−0.27
Men, 25–44, white, H.S.	−0.03	0.31	0.29	0.07	0.06	0.13
Men, 25–44, white, > H.S.	−0.15	−0.04	−0.19	0.47	0.17	0.63
Men, 25–44, nonwhite, < H.S.	0.14	−0.06	0.08	−0.22	−0.13	−0.35
Men, 25–44, nonwhite, H.S.	0.35	−0.64	−0.29	0.01	0.23	0.23
Men, 25–44, nonwhite, > H.S.	−0.06	0.19	0.13	0.00	−0.18	−0.18
Men, 45–61, white, < H.S.	0.10	0.29	0.39	0.01	0.10	0.11
Men, 45–61, white, H.S.	0.31	0.47	0.78	−0.16	0.25	0.09
Men, 45–61, white, > H.S.	−0.28	0.53	0.25	−0.32	−0.39	−0.71
Men, 45–61, nonwhite, < H.S.	−0.04	0.34	0.31	−0.16	−0.20	−0.37
Men, 45–61, nonwhite, H.S.	−0.01	0.20	0.19	0.10	−0.18	−0.09
Men, 45–61, nonwhite, > H.S.	−0.07	−0.11	−0.18	−0.37	0.32	−0.05
Women, 25–44, white, < H.S.	−0.10	0.23	0.13	−0.27	0.01	−0.27
Women, 25–44, white, H.S.	0.01	0.09	0.10	0.03	0.02	0.04

Women, 25–44, white, > H.S.	-0.25	0.49	0.24	0.05	-0.11	-0.06
Women, 25–44, nonwhite, < H.S.	0.09	-0.11	-0.02	-0.26	-0.07	-0.34
Women, 25–44, nonwhite, H.S.	0.26	-0.08	0.18	-0.02	-0.11	-0.13
Women, 25–44, nonwhite, > H.S.	0.05	0.04	0.09	0.10	-0.31	-0.21
Women, 45–61, white, < H.S.	-0.15	0.39	0.24	-0.16	0.04	-0.11
Women, 45–61, white, H.S.	0.18	0.07	0.25	-0.16	0.42	0.25
Women, 45–61, white, > H.S.	-0.12	-0.05	-0.18	-0.51	0.04	-0.47
Women, 45–61, nonwhite, < H.S.	-0.25	-0.29	-0.54	-0.08	-0.18	-0.26
Women, 45–61, nonwhite, H.S.	0.04	-0.04	0.00	0.13	-0.23	-0.10
Women, 45–61, nonwhite, > H.S.	0.01	0.08	0.09	0.06	-0.37	-0.31

SOURCE: Authors' calculations based on the March CPS (1984–2005).

Table 6.7 Actual and Compositionally Adjusted Poverty Rates for Working-Age People with and without Work Limitations, 1983, 1993, and 2004

Group	1983		1993		2004		
	Actual		Actual	Adjusted (1983 base)	Actual	Adjusted (1993 base)	Adjusted (1983 base)
Work limitations (%)	28.61	31.28	31.23	28.49	30.36	30.07
No work limitations (%)	10.10	9.40	10.01	8.37	8.48	9.12
Relative[a]	2.83	3.33	3.12	3.40	3.58	3.30

[a] The (work limitations)/(no work limitations) ratio.

SOURCE: Authors' calculations based on the March CPS (1984, 1994, and 2005).

When comparing the rise in the relative risk of poverty for people with work limitations over these two periods, as shown in the third row of Table 6.7, we found that controlling for composition effects resulted in slightly lower increases over the 1980s business cycle, but it raised the reported increases over the 1990s business cycle. When we controlled for compositional effects over the entire period, the relative poverty rate of people with work limitations grew from 2.8 in 1983 to 3.3 in 2004. See Figure 6.3 for relative poverty rates for all years.

Figure 6.3 Trends in the Ratio of Actual and Compositionally Adjusted Poverty Rates of Working-Age People with and without Work Limitations, 1980–2005

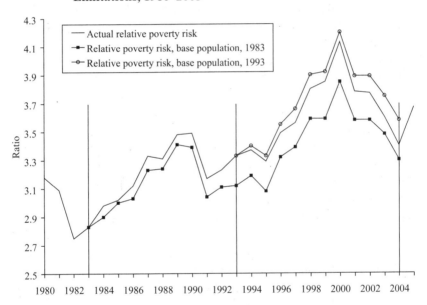

SOURCE: Author's calculations based on the March CPS (1981–2006).

POVERTY EXPERIENCE OF THOSE WITH LONGER TERM WORK LIMITATIONS

The development of panel data sets has allowed researchers to look at poverty dynamics in a way that is not possible with cross-sectional data. Although a large empirical literature—documenting the duration in poverty and its determinants based primarily on data from the Panel Study of Income Dynamics and the SIPP—has shown that the likelihood of falling into poverty at some point during your lifetime is surprisingly high, the vast majority of those who do so exit fairly rapidly. Nonetheless, a small segment of those entering poverty remain poor for long periods of time.[6] But with few exceptions, this literature has not focused on the experience of people with disabilities in this regard.[7] The literature that does exist focuses on spell length and finds that the onset of a disability increases the likelihood of falling into poverty and decreases the likelihood of exiting.

Most recently She and Livermore (2007) used four years of data from the 1966 SIPP to look at the poverty experience of persons with and without disabilities. Rather than using spell analysis, they instead focused on the number of months a person reports having a work limitation and showed that those who report a work limitation over the four-year period are much more likely to spend some time in poverty than those who do not. They then disaggregated the population with disabilities based on the number of months they report a work limitation over the four-year period and found that the greater the number of months with a work limitation, the greater the number of months they are in poverty. They tested the sensitivity of their results using the alternative concepts of disability discussed in Table 6.2, and found similar results. Finally they showed that the share of the working-age population in poverty rises when they compared those in poverty in a given year to those in poverty for at least 36 months of the 48-month period.

These findings suggest that not only has the relative risk of poverty increased over the 1990s in the United States for people with disabilities, but that in the 1990s, people with longer term disabilities were much more likely to be in poverty.

DISCUSSION AND CONCLUSION

The business cycle of the 1990s not only greatly increased the economic well-being of the median American, but it did so for the most economically at-risk populations that missed the gains from economic growth over the 1980s business cycle. This chapter shows that (working-age) people with work limitations, a little-recognized, economically at-risk population, not only missed the rewards of this growth but did relatively less well than other at-risk populations during the 1990s.

Using the same Census Bureau measure of poverty developed to track the progress of other economically at-risk populations in the CPS data, we first defined and then measured the poverty rate of people with disabilities (as identified with a work-limitation survey question) and compared it with the poverty rate found in other data sets using the same work-limitation concept of disability. We found very little difference in outcomes. The poverty rate found using other concepts of disability are different, but regardless of the measure used, rates for people with disabilities were substantially higher than rates for those without disabilities.

When looking at variation in poverty across states, the poverty rates for the ACS work-limitation measure of disability were highly correlated with the poverty rates for the other ACS disability measures. The ACS, with its more nuanced questions on disability and its much larger sample size, is a richer data set than the CPS for investigating current levels of poverty for people with disabilities, especially at the state level. However, the CPS remains the only data set capable of providing information on long-term trends in the poverty rates of this population relative to those without disabilities.

Using the CPS data to do so, we found that the poverty rate of people with work limitations increased both absolutely and relative to that of others over the 1980s business cycle. While their poverty rates fell over the 1990s business cycle, their poverty rates relative to those without work limitations continued to rise.

When compositional effects were controlled for, the underlying poverty rate increase for people with work limitations over the 1980s business cycle was less than the unadjusted poverty rate for the same group. That is, the absolute and relative increases in poverty found in the unadjusted CPS numbers overstated the magnitude of the increase in poverty caused by nondemographic factors, but the difference is small. Over the 1990s business cycle, the underlying poverty rate decrease was less than the unadjusted poverty rate. But in this case, the compositional changes were much larger. They were responsible for almost two-thirds of the decrease in the uncontrolled poverty rate.

Thus, the improvement in the uncontrolled poverty rate of people with work limitations over the 1990s business cycle, implied by comparing it with the uncontrolled change in the 1980s business cycle, grossly overstated the actual improvement in the underlying poverty rate change over these two business cycles. Once compositional changes are accounted for, the slight reduction in their underlying poverty rate during the 1990s business cycle was not enough to offset the underlying rise in their poverty rate over the 1980s business cycle. Hence, the underlying risk of poverty for people with work limitations was actually higher in 2004 than in 1983.

This is in contrast to the compositionally adjusted poverty rate of their counterparts without work limitations, which fell from 1983 to 2004. In addition, when composition effects were controlled for both those with and without work limitations, we found that the relative increase in the poverty risk measured by unadjusted statistics somewhat overstated the increase in risk for the 1980s, but understated it for the 1990s.

Finally, the findings of She and Livermore (2007) show that not only were people with disabilities more likely to be in poverty than their counterparts without disabilities in the 1990s, but that this likelihood was much greater the more months they reported having a work limitation.

Stapleton and Burkhauser (2003) and Burkhauser and Stapleton (2004) provide evidence of the dramatic decline in the employment of people with disabilities in the United States over the 1990s. They argued that changes in the social environment, rather than in the severity of the impairments of people with disabilities, are the primary cause for this decline. We suggest other negative outcomes of such changes in the social environment—a dramatic increase in the poverty rate of people with disabilities relative to people without disabilities and a decline in poverty rates in the 1990s that is mostly explained by compositional changes rather than any real decline in the within-subgroup poverty risks of people with work limitations.

Like other researchers, we used the less than ideal work-limitation variable from the CPS to follow a critical economic outcome for people with disabilities because it is the only data set available to capture long-term trends in this population. But to argue that nothing can be said about trends in the economic well-being of people with disabilities over the last 25 years because the data for making these observations are not ideal is to make *perfect* the enemy of *good*. The CPS data provide plausible estimates of the trends in the relative poverty of working-age people with work limitations. And as we have shown, the trends are discouraging.

It is time for the federal government to officially track the economic well-being of people with disabilities, to investigate the causes for the dramatic increase in their relative poverty risk over the past two business cycles and the lack of progress in reducing their absolute poverty risk over this same period, and to initiate evidence-based policies to increase the employment of people with disabilities and reduce their risk of poverty.

Notes

1. Unless otherwise indicated, the discussion in this chapter refers only to the working-age population, and all statistics presented are for those aged 25–61.
2. See Citro and Michael (1995) for a more detailed critique of the official poverty measure. See She and Livermore (2007) for a critique of this measure in the context of capturing the poverty rate for people with disabilities.
3. The User Guide Series of the Rehabilitation Research and Training Center on Disability Demographics and Statistics (StatsRRTC) analyzes demographic trends and economic well-being of people with disabilities using these and other data sources; see Employment and Disability Institute (n.d.).
4. Tables showing the population shares across all subgroups are available from the authors.
5. Tables reporting each subgroup's population share and poverty rate in 1983, 1993, and 2004, as well as their percentage point change in size and poverty rate between 1983–1993, 1993–2004, and 1983–2004, are available from the authors.
6. See Rank and Hirschl (2001) and commentaries on Rank and Hirschl by Burkhauser (2001) and Wiseman (2001). See McKernan and Ratcliffe (2002a) for a review of the U.S. poverty dynamics literature.

7. See McKernan and Ratcliffe (2002a, 2002b) and Ribar and Hamrick (2003) for exceptions.

References

Burkhauser, Richard V. 2001. "What Policymakers Need to Know about Poverty Dynamics." *Journal of Policy Analysis and Management* 20(4): 757–758.

Burkhauser, Richard V., Mary C. Daly, Andrew J. Houtenville, and Nigar Nargis. 2002. "Self-Reported Work Limitation Data: What They Can and Cannot Tell Us." *Demography* 39(3): 541–555.

Burkhauser, Richard V., Ludmila Rovba, and Robert R. Weathers II. 2009. "Household Income." In *Counting Working-Age People with Disabilities: What Current Data Tell Us and Options for Improvement*, Andrew J. Houtenville, David C. Stapleton, Robert R. Weathers II, and Richard V. Burkhauser, eds. Kalamazoo, MI: W.E. Upjohn Institute for Employment Research, pp. 145–192.

Burkhauser, Richard V., and David C. Stapleton. 2004. "The Decline in the Employment Rate for People with Disabilities: Bad Data, Bad Health, or Bad Policy?" *Journal of Vocational Rehabilitation* 20(3): 185–201.

Citro, Constance F., and Robert T. Michael, eds. 1995. *Measuring Poverty: A New Approach*. Washington, DC: National Academies Press.

Daly, Mary C., and Richard V. Burkhauser. 2003. "The Supplemental Security Income Program." In *Means Tested Transfer Programs in the United States*, Robert Moffitt, ed. NBER Conference Report Series. Chicago: University of Chicago Press, pp. 79–139.

DeNavas-Walt, Carmen, Bernadette D. Proctor, and Jessica C. Smith. 2008. Income, Poverty and Health Insurance Coverage in the United States: 2007. U.S. Census Bureau Current Population Reports P60-235. Washington, DC: Government Printing Office.

Employment and Disability Institute. n.d. "Disability Statistics." Ithaca, NY: Cornell University, Employment and Disability Institute. http://www.ilr .cornell.edu/edi/disabilitystatistics/ (accessed November 10, 2008).

Harris, Benjamin H., Gerry E. Hendershot, and David C. Stapleton. 2005. "A Guide to Disability Statistics from the National Health Interview Survey." Ithaca, NY: Cornell University, Rehabilitation Research and Training Center on Disability Demographics and Statistics.

McKernan, Signe-Mary, and Caroline Ratcliffe. 2002a. "Transition Events in the Dynamics of Poverty." Research report. Washington, DC: The Urban Institute.

———. 2002b. "Events That Trigger Poverty Entries and Exits." Research report. Washington, DC: The Urban Institute.

Rank, Mark R., and Thomas A. Hirschl. 2001. "The Occurrence of Poverty Across the Life Cycle: Evidence from the PSID." *Journal of Policy Analysis and Management* 20(4): 737–756.

Ribar, David C., and Karen S. Hamrick. 2003. Dynamics of Poverty and Food Sufficiency. Economic Research Service, Food Assistance and Nutrition Research Report 33. Washington, DC: U.S. Department of Agriculture.

———. Forthcoming. "Long-Term Poverty and Disability Among Working-Age Adults." *Journal of Disability Policy Studies.*

She, Peiyun, and Gina A. Livermore. 2007. "Material Hardship, Poverty, and Disability Among Working-Age Adults." *Social Science Quarterly* 88(4): 970–989.

Stapleton, David C., and Richard V. Burkhauser, eds. 2003. *The Decline in Employment of People with Disabilities: A Policy Puzzle.* Kalamazoo, MI: W.E. Upjohn Institute for Employment Research.

Weathers, Robert R., II. 2005. "A Guide to Disability Statistics from the American Community Survey." Ithaca, NY: Cornell University, Rehabilitation Research and Training Center on Disability Demographics and Statistics. http://digitalcommons.ilr.cornell.edu/edicollect/123 (accessed June 6, 2008).

———. 2009. "The Disability Data Landscape." In *Counting Working-Age People with Disabilities: What Current Data Tell Us and Options for Improvement*, Andrew J. Houtenville, David C. Stapleton, Robert R. Weathers II, and Richard V. Burkhauser, eds. Kalamazoo, MI: W.E. Upjohn Institute for Employment Research, pp. 27–67.

Weathers, Robert R., II, and David C. Wittenburg. 2009. "Employment." In *Counting Working-Age People with Disabilities: What Current Data Tell Us and Options for Improvement*, Andrew J. Houtenville, David C. Stapleton, Robert R. Weathers II, and Richard V. Burkhauser, eds. Kalamazoo, MI: W.E. Upjohn Institute for Employment Research, pp. 101–144.

Wiseman, M. 2001. "A Note on Poverty and the Life Course." *Journal of Policy Analysis and Management* 20(4): 759–760.

Wittenburg, David, and Sandi Nelson. 2006. "A Guide to Disability Statistics from the Survey of Income and Program Participation." Ithaca, NY: Cornell University, Rehabilitation Research and Training Center on Disability Demographics and Statistics. http://digitalcommons.ilr.cornell.edu/edicollect/1 (accessed June 6, 2008).

7

Health and Functional Status

Gerry E. Hendershot
Private Consultant

Benjamin H. Harris
Brookings Institution

David C. Stapleton
Mathematica Policy Research, Inc.

Information on the health and functional status of people with disabilities (and the broader population) is fundamental to our understanding of who is at risk for disability, the mental and physical challenges they face, their well-being and support needs, how well they are served by current policies, and the likely consequences of policy change. This chapter describes the data available to support these information needs and presents statistics from the main data source, the National Health Interview Survey (NHIS).

We begin with a review of the conceptualization and definition of health and function. This is followed by a discussion of subjective and objective approaches to measuring health and function and a review of evidence on the statistical relationship between health and function. We then present descriptive statistics from the 2002 and 2006 NHIS. We conclude with a discussion of the strengths and limitations of current data.

DEFINITIONS OF HEALTH AND FUNCTIONING

The nature of the relationship between health and disability is complex and much debated. At one extreme, disability is a health condition to be prevented or medically treated; at the other extreme, it is a socially constructed discriminatory institution, a part of the social environment with no real relationship to health. An early, and still very useful, discussion of the differing views of the relationship between health and disability, and their implications for social policy, can be found in Bickenbach (1993). Altman (2001) and Jette and Badley (2002) provide more recent reviews.

Consistent with the earlier chapters in this book, we adopt the conceptual framework of the World Health Organization's (WHO) International Classification of Functioning, Disability and Health (ICF).

In the ICF, "functioning" refers to human activity at the levels of the body, the person, and the community (participation in life situations). As discussed by Weathers (2009), "disability" refers to problems in functioning at three levels: 1) impairments (body), 2) activity limitations (person), and 3) participation restrictions (community). Functioning and disability occur in three contexts: 1) health, 2) the environment (broadly defined), and 3) personal characteristics (e.g., sex, age, etc.).

Conceptually, the ICF views health, environment, personal factors, and functioning as an interacting causal system; that is, changes in each part of the system can cause changes in the other parts. Disability is not the result of a health condition, but rather the result of an array of conditions involving health, other personal characteristics, and the environment. Further, causality can run from disability to health, personal factors, and even the environment. A person with a disability might have problems accessing health care, obtaining an education, or living in certain environments; hence, their health, education, and environment can all be influenced by their disability.

The nature and strength of the relationships between health and disability are empirical questions, about which there is a large research literature. For instance, it is well established that some health conditions (e.g., spinal cord injury) can cause loss of function and that disability can increase the risk of some "secondary" health conditions (e.g., urinary tract infection).

As a classification system (as opposed to a theoretical framework), the ICF explicitly excludes consideration of the context of personal factors and provides only a short list for the environment context. Nor does the ICF classify factors in the health context, but that is because the ICF is intended to be a companion to the WHO's International Classification of Diseases (ICD) and its clinical modifications, which classify medically diagnosed health conditions in great detail.

The official WHO definition of health, however, is much broader than the ICD: "a state of complete physical, mental, and social well-being and not merely the absence of disease, or infirmity" (WHO 1946). In this larger sense, the ICF is a classification of health, hence its full official name, International Classification of Functioning, Disability and Health. In this chapter, however, "health" will have the narrower meaning unless otherwise indicated. A disability is not a health condition, but health and disability are interrelated in a complex fashion. In this regard, the ICF typifies the view of health and disability on which recent discussions of the issue are converging. A framework that clearly distinguishes health from disability allows for more thoughtful consideration of the relationships between them. A recent report from the Surgeon General of the United States (U.S. Department of Health and Human Services 2005) captures the spirit of this viewpoint well and is worth quoting at length:

> Disability is not an illness. The concept of health means the same for persons with or without disabilities: achieving and sustaining an optimal level of wellness—both physical and mental—that promotes a fullness of life. For persons with disabilities, as for those without disabilities, to be healthy, it means having the tools and knowledge to help promote wellness and knowing the risk factors that can promote illness and the protective factors that can prevent it. For persons with all kinds of disabilities it also means knowing that conditions secondary to a disability—from pain to depression and from urinary tract infections to heightened susceptibility to acute illnesses—can be treated successfully. Health also means that persons with disabilities can access appropriate, integrated, culturally sensitive and respectful health care that meets the needs of a whole person, not just a disability.

Measuring Health and Functioning with Objective Tests and Subjective Reports

However health and functioning may be defined conceptually, if the goal is to produce reliable population estimates of statistics on incidence, prevalence, correlates, and trends, they must be measured.

Broadly speaking, there are two approaches to measuring health and functioning in population-based sample surveys: subjective measurement and objective measurement, or more precisely, measurement based on the reports of survey respondents and measurement based on examination by health professionals or the administration of standardized medical tests.

Objective measures of health and function are generally regarded as more accurate than subjective measures (although, as we shall see, that is not always the case). On the other hand, objective measures tend to be much more expensive than their subjective counterparts because they require staff with specialized skills and training, and they often use complex, costly equipment. For these reasons, most surveys of health and function rely heavily, often exclusively, on subjective measures. Where objective measures are used at all, they tend to be simple measures and limited to a subsample of the study population.

Objective measures

In the United States, objective measures of health and functioning are limited primarily to the National Health and Nutrition Examination Survey (NHANES), conducted by the National Center for Health Statistics (NCHS), part of the Centers for Disease Control and Prevention (CDC). NHANES uses specially designed Mobile Examination Centers (MEC) to collect data in sampled geographic areas. Staff members in these centers administer objective tests and examinations to representative samples of the civilian, noninstitutionalized population in each selected area. They also administer standardized questionnaires on health and functioning to sample persons in their homes, as discussed below.

Some examinations and tests are conducted at the MEC, and blood and urine are collected for later laboratory tests. The particular examination and laboratory components included in the survey change periodically. The components in use during the 2005–2006 data collection period are described at the NHANES Web site and are listed here:[1]

Blood and Urine
Venipuncture
Bone Markers
Diabetes Profile
Infectious Disease Profile
Miscellaneous Laboratory Assays
Kidney Disease Profile
Nutritional Biochemistries &
   Hematologies
Sexually Transmitted Disease Profile
Tobacco Use

Environmental Health Profile
Audiometry
Body Composition
Body Measurements
Cardiovascular Fitness
Ophthalmology
Oral Health
Physical Activity Monitor
Physician's Exam
Vision
Blood Lipids

Most of these examinations and tests measure health, in the narrow ICD sense, not function; only the audiometry and vision tests would produce results that could be coded to the ICF (as hearing and seeing functions). In other data collection years, the NHANES has included other objective measures of function that could be coded to the ICF, such as walking (length of time to walk a measured distance), climbing (walking up an inclined treadmill), and balancing (standing without shoes for 15 seconds with eyes open or closed on standard or compliant support surfaces).

Other population-based sample surveys have incorporated simple objective measures of health and function. A new survey planned by the Social Security Administration (SSA)—the National Study of Health and Activity (NSHA)—would have advanced that methodology significantly. The plan was to collect information from a nationally representative sample that would simulate the information used in the medical determination of eligibility for benefits from two SSA programs: Social Security Disability Insurance (SSDI) and Supplemental Security Income (SSI).

A pilot study for the NSHA pioneered some new methods for objective measures of health and function in the context of a population-based survey, but in the end it was not implemented as a full scale national study. There were issues of escalating costs, shifting policies, and survey methods that proved too difficult to overcome. A review of the NSHA experience by a committee of the Institute of Medicine concluded that substantially more time and research (and probably more money) would be required to field a survey that could accomplish the objectives of the NSHA (Wunderlich, Rice, and Amado 2002). Although the use of objective health measures was not the only methodological problem faced by the NSHA (screening for sample persons with serious disabilities was also a problem), it certainly was a factor in its demise, thus demonstrating the difficulty of using objective measures of health and function in surveys.

Subjective measures

Because of the costs and other difficulties associated with objective measures of health and function, most large population-based surveys rely on subjective, respondent-reported measures. They are used almost exclusively, although sometimes they are used in conjunction with objective measures. NHANES uses both types. In addition to its many objective measures, discussed above, it also uses subjective measures based on interviews of sample persons in their homes, face-to-face or by phone, using standardized, computerized questionnaires.

Many of NHANES interview questions are similar or identical to questions used in the NHIS, another survey on health and function conducted by the NCHS. The NHIS has no objective measures of health and function, relying entirely on subjective respondent reports. It was one of the first large population-based surveys that focused on health and function, and it has been in continuous operation since 1957. Because of its long history and wide use, it is well-known in the United States and abroad, and its design and content have influenced many other health surveys, such as NHANES.

Just as we used NHANES to illustrate use of objective measures in surveys, we will use NHIS to illustrate subjective measures.[2] For present purposes, it is enough to know that the NHIS collects information annually on health and function by means of standardized, computerized, face-to-face interviews with a large, nationally representative sample of the civilian, noninstitutionalized population of the United States.

In the NHIS, as currently designed, some questions apply to all persons in sample families, some to a randomly selected adult in the family, and some to a randomly selected child. Because this volume focuses on the working-age population, the child questionnaire will not be discussed. For the family questionnaire, proxy respondents are allowed; that is, an adult family member answers questions about themselves and any adult family members not present. For the sample adult questionnaire, self-response is required (except in a few, strictly limited situations).

Health and function information are obtained in both the family and adult questionnaires, although the approaches differ in the two instruments. Two approaches are used: 1) asking directly about specific health conditions (the condition approach); and 2) asking about specific functions and disabilities, and then, if a disability is reported, asking about the conditions that cause the disability (the person approach). In the family questionnaire, only the person approach is used, but both approaches are used in the adult questionnaire.

Relationship between objective and subjective measures of health and their implications for NHIS design

The current NHIS approach to measuring health was influenced by a series of methodological studies of the accuracy of the health information obtained in the survey. As noted above, objective measures of health and function are generally regarded as more accurate than subjective measures. To assess the accuracy of respondent reports of health conditions, NHIS compared those responses to information about health conditions obtained from their medical records for the same persons. It was assumed that medical records are based on objective tests and examinations.

In a review of such studies on the NHIS and other surveys, Jabine (1987) concluded that respondents grossly underreport chronic health conditions, by as much as 80 percent for some conditions; that is, respondents often fail to report conditions that are recorded in their medical records. Reporting was more complete when sample persons responded for themselves than when proxy respondents reported for them, and it was also more complete when additional questions were asked about specific conditions. Studies undertaken since the Jabine review (such as Edwards et al. 1994) have confirmed these results.

During the redesign of the NHIS questionnaire to its present form and content (first implemented in 1997), it was decided to greatly reduce the number of conditions about which questions were asked, a decision based largely on the evidence that subjective respondent reports of medical conditions are inaccurate. Furthermore, the remaining direct questions about conditions and symptoms were limited to the adult questionnaire, because condition reporting is more complete for self-response, which is required by the adult questionnaire. Finally, for those conditions about which direct questions are asked, the number and specificity of the questions was increased.

In addition to the condition approach, the redesigned NHIS continued to use questions on health and function based on the person approach. In both the family and adult surveys, questions are asked about "limitations" (family questionnaire) or "difficulty" (adult questionnaire) in performing selected functions. For each limitation or difficulty reported, further questions are asked about the name and date of onset of the health conditions underlying the disability. The NHIS questions on disability are described in greater detail in Harris, Hendershot, and Stapleton (2005).

Compared to earlier permutations, the current design of the NHIS collects and reports information on fewer, and less detailed, health conditions.[3] For those conditions, however, the current NHIS was designed to improve the accuracy of the information it collects. Because no study comparing self-reports with medical records has yet been conducted using data from the current NHIS design, it is not yet known if the attempt to improve accuracy was successful.

Relationship between objective and subjective measures of function

This discussion of the NHIS and subjective measures of health and function has focused largely on health, with less attention to function and disability. That is partly because there are good published descriptions of the NHIS measures of function and disability (e.g., Harris, Hendershot, and Stapleton 2005). There are relatively few comprehensive studies of the correspondence of objective and subjective measures of function, but we will cite two recent studies.

In a study by Sayers et al. (2004), 150 community-dwelling (living in households and some other noninstitutional settings) older adults responded to a series of questions about their mobility function and then attempted to walk 400 meters. The authors found that a walking score based on responses to three subjective questions—ability to walk a quarter mile without rest, difficulty walking a mile, and ability to walk all the aisles of a supermarket—predicted inability to complete the 400-meter walk with 97 percent specificity (i.e., correctly identified 97 percent of those who did complete the walk) and 46 percent sensitivity (i.e., correctly identified 46 percent of those who did not complete the walk). The authors noted that, with this degree of predictive ability, some studies of mobility in large populations could use self-reports instead of objective tests of walking function.

In a Dutch study of elderly men (Hoeymans et al. 1996), physical function was objectively measured by tests of balancing, walking, rising from a chair, and rotating the shoulders. Subjective physical function was measured using subjects' reports on their level of function in walking, instrumental activities of daily living (IADL), and activities of daily living (ADL). There were statistically significant but modest correlations between composite scores of the objective and subjective measures. Correlations were higher between the objective walking test and subjective IADLs, and between objective shoulder movement and subjective ADLs.

Studies such as these indicate that subjective measures of function are related to objective measures, and for some functions, such as walking, subjective measures predict performance on objective measures so well that they can be substituted for objective measures.

Composite or global measures of subjective health and functioning

The measures discussed thus far are for particular aspects or types of health and functioning, such as specific health conditions (e.g., cancer) or types of disability (e.g., walking limitations). In addition to such measures, there has long been an interest in single measures of overall health and functional status. Such measures are sometimes useful for summarizing population health and function as well as for simplifying communication and debate. Some summary measures combine many data elements into a single measure, often by means of complex algorithms; such measures are sometimes referred to as "composite" measures or "indices." Other summary measures are based on responses to a few questions, sometimes only one question; such measures are sometimes referred to as "global" measures.

Throughout its history, the NHIS has included a global measure of health based on one question: "Would you say (subject's name) health in general is excellent, very good, good, fair, or poor?" The "subject's name" is filled in if the respondent is not the sample person, but is acting as a proxy. (This question is asked on the family questionnaire, for which a proxy respondent is allowed.) Many other surveys have included some version of this question; such measures are sometimes identified as general self-rated health (GSRH).

As simple as the GSRH is, it repeatedly has been shown to be a good predictor of objective health outcomes, such as morbidity, hospitalization, and mortality. A recent review of the literature on GSRH measures as predictors of mortality by DeSalvo et al. (2006) identified 22 studies that met their criteria for inclusion in their meta-analysis. Some of the most important criteria were that the studies had to be community based (living in households and some other noninstitutional settings), have a prospective (longitudinal) design, and report an adjusted relative risk statistic.

After conducting a meta-analysis of the data from the 22 studies, the authors concluded, "In this meta-analysis, we found a statistically significant relationship between worse GSRH and an increased risk of death. Study participants' responses to a simple, single-item GSRH question maintained a strong association with mortality even after adjustment for key covariates such as functional status, depression, and comorbidity. Additionally, this relationship persisted in studies with a long duration of follow-up, for men and women, and irrespective of country origin."

Since its inception, the NHIS has used a composite measure of functioning and disability—activity limitation—in its official publications. The NHIS definition of activity limitation approximately corresponds to the ICF definition of participation restriction. There have been changes in the operational definition of activity limitation over the years, most importantly in the 1997 NHIS redesign, but the *concept* has remained constant: an activity limitation is a respondent-reported, health-related limitation in ability to perform major life activities, such as play (preschool children), school (school-aged children), work (working-age adults), and independent living (adults past retirement age). For respondents who report none of these limitations, a question is asked about limitation in "any other activity."

The NHIS activity limitation measure combines responses to a number of different questions in a single variable with four levels of functional limitations: unable to perform major activity, limited in major activity, limited in other activity, and no limitation.[4]

The statistical relationship between health and function

The NCHS publishes annual reports based on the NHIS, and they include standard tables showing national estimates of a wide range of health and functioning statistics for the data year, including statistics on the summary measures, GSRH and activity limitation. Three annual reports are published, each based on one of the three questionnaires used, that is, for all persons, adults, and children. For the most recent editions of those reports see, respectively, Adams, Dey, and Vickerie (2007), Pleis and Lethbridge-Çejku (2007), and Bloom, Dey, and Freeman (2006).

NCHS also releases public use files of the NHIS microdata (without personal identifiers). Some data that might increase the risk of disclosure (such as state identifiers) are not released, but they may be analyzed under special arrangements.

Because the NHIS has measures, both detailed and summary, on both health and function, it can be used to analyze the statistical relationships between the two types of measures. As noted above, health and function are distinct concepts, and their statistical relationship is an empirical question. Unfortunately, statistics relating health to function are not included in the official annual reports mentioned above; however, some special studies have related health and function using the NHIS. There are two broad study types—studies that relate specific medical conditions or types of conditions to function and disability and studies that relate global or composite measures of health to function and disability.

Studies of specific medical conditions and NHIS activity limitations are found in the work of LaPlante (1989, 1996). He has used both the "person" approach and the "condition" approach when analyzing health and disability. The person approach examines the conditions that are reported by the respondent as the cause(s) of a previously identified activity limitation. LaPlante notes that the medical conditions most often reported to be a cause of an NHIS activity limitation among persons with a limitation are diseases of the musculoskeletal and circulatory systems and orthopedic impairments.

The condition approach examines reports of activity limitations among those who have first reported a specific medical condition or type of condition. Following this approach, LaPlante has estimated the risk of an NHIS activity limitation associated with different conditions, that is, the proportion of people with a specific condition who have an activity limitation. Viewed this way, the conditions that put people at the highest risk for activity limitation are mental retardation, absence of leg(s), and lung or bronchial cancer. These conditions do not account for a very large number of persons with activity limitations, however, because their prevalence is low.

The work by LaPlante used data from before 1997, when the data collected made it possible to classify health conditions in considerable detail. Since the redesign of the NHIS implemented in 1997, it is still possible to analyze relationships between health conditions and disability but not for the full range of conditions covered in the LaPlante studies. For instance, the annual publication *Health, United States* (National Center for Health Statistics 2006) includes a table that shows the proportion of persons with activity limitations caused by six selected conditions: mental illness, fractures or joint injury, lung, diabetes, heart or other circulatory, and arthritis or other musculoskeletal, with the last category accounting for the largest proportion of disabilities. The condition categories now used in the NHIS are based on the names of conditions reported by respondents, and they do not necessarily correspond to ICD condition categories.

We turn now to the second broad type of study in health and disability: analysis of the relationship (i.e., correlation) between disability and health, usually identified with global or composite health measures. The GSRH from the NHIS can be related to the NHIS activity limitation measure. This is a simple and straightforward approach to answering the question, "to what extent are health and disability statistically related?" Ries and Brown (1991) combined data from the 1984–1988 NHIS to analyze the relationship of general health to activity limitation and the factors affecting that relationship. Multiple years were used so that statistics for small groups could be estimated reliably.

Ries and Brown present extensive tabulations of health and activity limitations, using several measures of health, disaggregated by age, sex, race, income, geographic region, and place of residence (central city, suburban, or rural). For present purposes, however, we will examine only the overall, gross relationship between GSRH and activity limitation. For comparison, we have computed comparable statistics for the 2006 NHIS from the public use data file.

Table 7.1 shows that, from 1984 to 1988, about 95 percent of persons with no activity limitation were in good, very good, or excellent health, and only 5 percent were in fair or poor health. Among persons with an activity limitation, however, only 57 percent were in good, very good, or excellent health, and more than 40 percent were in fair or poor health. Compared to people without activity limitations, people with those limitations were almost nine times more likely to be in fair or poor health. This confirms what common sense and other evidence tell us—there is a statistical relationship between health and disability. At the same time, however, it is just as important to note that the majority of people with activity limitations are reported to be in good or excellent health—evidence that health and disability, although empirically

Table 7.1 Health Status of the Working-Age Population (Aged 18–64) by NHIS Activity Limitation Status, 1984–1988 and 2006

Health status	No limitation	Any limitation
Survey years 1984–88		
Good, very good, excellent	95.1	57.0
Fair/poor	4.9	43.0
Survey year 2006		
Good, very good, excellent	95.3	55.8
Fair/poor	4.7	44.2

NOTE: The NHIS activity limitation concept used for these tabulations differs from the "any disability" definition used in later tables, but it is the same as that used by Ries and Brown in their tabulations. The operational definition used for the 2006 data necessarily differs from that used by Ries and Brown because the NHIS question used in 2006 enumerates more types of activity limitations than questions in an earlier period, but there is no evidence that the change in the question had a substantial impact on prevalence.
SOURCE: NHIS 1984–1988; Ries and Brown (1991); NHIS 2006, tabulated for this chapter.

related, are different concepts between which people make meaningful distinctions.

Surprisingly, despite the 1997 redesign of the NHIS and other changes between 1984–1988 and 2006, the estimates for 2006 are nearly identical to those of 1984–1988, evidence that the statistical relationships and conceptual distinctions of health and disability are robust over time.

Numerous other ongoing or fairly recent federal surveys of the household population also collect health and functioning information. Livermore and She (2007) provide a review of health and disability content in all federal surveys. Three of these surveys are designed specifically to collect health information; all include information about functioning, and all use subjective measures. The Behavioral Risk Factor Surveillance System (BRFSS), sponsored by the CDC, is designed to collect uniform, state-specific data on the preventive health practices and risk behaviors of adults (National Center for Chronic Disease Prevention and Health Promotion 2006). The Medical Expenditure Panel Survey, co-sponsored by the Agency for Healthcare Research and Quality (AHRQ), is designed to provide comprehensive information about health care use and costs in the United States (Ezzati-Rice, Rohde, and Greenblat 2008). The National Comorbidity Survey (NCS 1990–1992) and the NCS Replication Survey (NCS-R 2001–2002), sponsored by the Substance Abuse and Mental Health Services Administration, are designed to determine the prevalence and correlates of mental illness among adults.

DESCRIPTIVE STATISTICS ON HEALTH AND FUNCTIONING FROM THE NHIS

The *Guide to Disability Statistics from the National Health Interview Survey* (Harris, Hendershot, and Stapleton, 2005; hereafter, the *Guide*) includes statistics from the 2002 NHIS on the topics covered in other chapters of this volume, including health. As described by Weathers (2009), for purposes of the *Guide*, six types of disability were conceptualized and operationally defined: three impairment categories (sensory, physical, and mental), two personal activity limitation categories (ADL and IADL), and one participation restriction category (employment). We refer to the personal activity limitations as ADL/IADL limitations, to distinguish them from the NHIS definition of activity limitation, which, as discussed previously, encompasses participation restrictions. See Weathers (2009) and the *Guide* for detailed definitions of these categories. As a summary measure, persons were classified as having a disability if they had one or more of the six types of disability.

The *Guide* presents an extensive set of statistics on the 2002 prevalence of disability for the working-age, household population classified by age, race, sex, and other social and economic variables. It also investigates the occurrence of multiple disabilities (comorbidity), as well as the relationship of disability and a variety of health and health-related measures. The reader is referred to the *Guide* for those statistics, which amplify the statistics on disability in the official NHIS publications already cited. In this chapter, we present selected 2002 statistics from the *Guide* and the same statistics based on the 2006 NHIS, the latest data publicly available at the time of writing. The 2006 NHIS statistics not only update the statistics in the *Guide*, they also enable us to comment on stability and change in the statistics over the four-year period.

A word of caution is in order about making comparisons between estimates for different years of the NHIS. Although the methodology of the NHIS is quite stable, some changes do occur from time to time in questionnaire design, field procedures, processing, and estimation procedures. Such changes can result in a spurious appearance of change in population health when, in fact, no change has occurred. One change in methods did occur between the 2002 and 2006 NHIS that may affect comparison of estimates for those years. The procedure for estimating population statistics from the NHIS sample in 2002 used population information based, ultimately, on the 1990 Decennial Census. Beginning in 2003 and thereafter, the estimation procedure used data from the 2000 Census.

Disability Prevalence

In Table 7.2 we present estimates of the prevalence of six types of disability in the working-age household population (aged 18–64), based on the 2006 NHIS.[5] An estimated 15.7 percent of the working-age household population had at least one of these six types of disability in 2006—approximately 29 million people. This includes more than 18 million with physical impairments, almost 6 million with mental impairments, 4 million with sensory impairments, and almost 17 million with a work restriction.

A summary of the *Guide's* disability tabulations for 2002 appears in Weathers (2009, Table 2.1). The 2006 estimate for the percentage of the working-age household population with any disability is a full percentage point lower than the 2002 estimate (15.7 percent versus 16.7 percent). There are no statistically significant declines in any of the specific disability categories except work restriction; the prevalence of work restrictions declined from 9.9 percent to 9.0 percent. It appears that the decline in the percentage with any disability reflects the stronger economy and the sensitivity of the prevalence of self-reported work restrictions to the business cycle, with prevalence rising somewhat during recessions and declining somewhat during expansions (see Weathers 2009, for evidence on this point). Although in theory, self-reports of other types of disabilities could be countercyclical, the other disability measures reported did not decline during this expansionary period.

Many NHIS respondents report more than one disability type. The bottom half of Table 7.2 shows the percentage of persons reporting each disability type who report each of the other disability types. For example, the first number in the column under sensory impairments indicates that only 50.3 percent of those with a sensory impairment *only* have a sensory impairment. In addition, 37.7 percent also have a physical impairment, 15.6 percent have a mental impairment, and so on. Not surprisingly, almost all those with an activity limitation reported an impairment of some sort. Perhaps surprisingly, however, more than a quarter (27.6 percent) of those who reported a work restriction did not report an impairment or an ADL or IADL limitation. This might mean that a substantial share of those who report a work restriction do not have a significant impairment (e.g., they have a health condition that does not

Table 7.2 NHIS Measures of Disability Prevalence in the Working-Age Household Population, 2006

			Disability type					
			Impairments			Activity limitations		Participation restrictions
Disability type		Any	Sensory	Physical	Mental	ADLs	IADLs	Work
% of household population		15.7	2.2	10.1	3.2	1.0	2.1	9.0
Number of persons (thousands)		29,023	3,976	18,585	5,851	1,842	3,892	16,668
Sample size		3,316	411	2,125	684	212	482	1,991
% with disabilities		100.0	13.7	64.0	20.2	6.3	13.4	57.4
Multiple disability types								
One disability type only (%)			50.3	38.4	32.7	3.3	1.8	27.6
Impairments	Sensory		100.0	8.1	10.6	15.6	14.5	8.7
	Physical		37.7	100.0	52.6	82.2	79.9	62.3
	Mental		15.6	16.6	100.0	23.3	22.7	18.9
Activity limitations	ADLs		7.2	8.2	7.3	100.0	37.1	10.4
	IADLs		14.2	16.7	15.1	78.4	100.0	22.5
Participation restrictions	Work		36.5	55.9	54.0	94.2	96.3	100.0

SOURCE: Calculations by the authors.

impair a body function, but certain types of work would interact with the condition to cause an impairment), or that the impairment questions fail to capture a substantial share of those with impairments that are substantial enough to contribute to a work restriction (e.g., persons with significant cognitive or intellectual impairments).

Many respondents report impairments in two or more of the impairment categories. Most notably, more than half (52.6 percent) of those with mental impairments also have a physical impairment, and 10.6 percent have sensory impairments. In some cases these impairments might be independent, but we suspect that in many cases they either have a common origin (e.g., as the consequence of a disease, accident, or congenital problem), or one impairment is an underlying cause of another (e.g., when a severe physical or sensory impairment contributes to a serious affective disorder or other psychiatric disorder).

People who report physical impairments and mental impairments appear to be at approximately equal risk for ADL or IADL limitations and work restrictions. People who report sensory impairment, as a group, appear to be at somewhat lower risk for such limitations and restrictions.

Self-Reported Health Status

Distributions for self-reported health at the time of interview are presented in Table 7.3. This global measure of health is based on a single NHIS question that asks if the sample person's health is excellent, very good, good, fair, or poor. The categories excellent and very good have been combined in this table, as have the categories fair and poor. The percent distributions are shown for working-age persons with and without disabilities, including any of the six types of disability and each of those types individually.

These statistics are consistent with the finding already noted: disability is strongly related to poorer health, but substantial numbers of persons with disabilities are in good health. In both data years, the type of disability most strongly associated with poor health is difficulty in performing personal care activities (ADLs), followed by needing the help of another person in performing routine activities (IADLs).

Although the distributions by health are very similar in the two data years, as we would expect, it is noteworthy that the percentage of re-

Table 7.3 Percent Distribution of Working-Age Adults by Respondent-Reported Health Status According to Type of Disability, Survey Years 2002 and 2006

Health status	Total household population	Disability type							
				Impairments			Activity limitations		Participation restrictions
		None	Any	Sensory	Physical	Mental	ADLs	IADLs	Work
Survey year 2002									
Excellent/very good	66.9	74.2	27.7	37.4	21.8	26.5	9.9	12.3	17.8
Good	23.7	21.8	33.5	31.0	31.8	26.0	20.9	24.1	31.1
Fair/poor	9.4	3.9	38.6	31.1	46.3	47.0	69.2	63.2	50.8
Don't know	0.1	0.1	0.2	0.4	0.2	0.5	0.0	0.4	0.3
Survey year 2006									
Excellent/very good	65.1***	72.7***	24.6***	32.7	19.0*	21.2**	9.3	11.0	15.5*
Good	24.9***	23.1***	34.5	30.5	32.4	26.5*	16.4	20.8	31.0
Fair/poor	9.9	4.1	40.7	36.8	48.4	52.2	74.2	68.2	53.2
Don't know	0.1	0.0	0.2	0.0	0.2	0.1	0.0	0.0	0.2

NOTE: * indicates statistically significant from 2002 at the 0.10 level, **at the 0.05 level, and ***at the 0.01 level.
SOURCE: Calculations by the authors.

spondents reporting fair or poor health increased over the four-year period in every category of disability. The change in some disability categories is not statistically significant because the number of sample cases is small—for example, the change in the sensory disability category, which has small numbers, is not significant; however, the consistency of the change across disability categories suggests that it is real. It seems unlikely that the change in estimation procedures implemented in 2003 accounts for these apparent changes between 2002 and 2006 because a methodological study demonstrated that this change had virtually no effect on the overall estimate of the percentage of people responding they were in excellent or very good health (Barnes and Schiller 2007). Part of the change probably reflects the aging of the workforce—in 2006, the oldest of the baby boomers reached 60 years of age. This is an intriguing finding, but more research would be required, holding age and other characteristics of the disability population constant, to determine whether the change in reported health represents a real trend in health status.

Change in Health during the Past Year

In addition to the question about current health status, respondents were asked if their health had changed during the past year. The response categories included no change, a change for the better, and a change for the worse. This is another way to get a global indication of health with a question that is straightforward and easily understood.

As a group, people with disabilities are not only more likely to report fair or poor health than people without disabilities, but are also more likely to have recently experienced deterioration in their health (Table 7.4). In 2006, only 4 percent of those with no disability reported a decline in health from the previous year, whereas 27 percent of those with a disability did. Just as those with ADL or IADL limitations are the most likely to be in poor health, they are also the most likely to have reported a decline in their health (46 percent and 40 percent, respectively). To some extent, these higher rates of reported decline might reflect the experience of disability onset, but it seems likely that they also reflect the fact that people with disabilities are at greater risk for a decline in their health.

Table 7.4 Percent Distribution of Working-Age Adults by Change in Health Status in the Past Year, According to Type of Disability, Survey Years 2002 and 2006

Change in health status	Total household population	Disability type							
				Impairments			Activity limitations		Participation restrictions
		None	Any	Sensory	Physical	Mental	ADLs	IADLs	Work
Survey year 2002									
Better	18.2	17.9	19.9	20.0	17.4	14.7	17.5	18.3	20.5
About the same	73.8	77.6	53.2	58.9	49.5	46.3	43.2	41.8	48.8
Worse	7.7	4.2	26.5	20.6	32.8	38.5	38.7	39.2	30.3
Don't know	0.3	0.3	0.4	0.5	0.3	0.5	0.7	0.7	0.5
Survey year 2006									
Better	18.6	18.5	18.9*	16.6	17.4	15.1	13.9	15.9	18.2*
About the same	73.8	77.5	53.9	58.6	49.7	46.3	39.4	43.1	49.8
Worse	7.3**	3.7	26.6	24.6	32.4	37.8	45.9	39.6	31.2
Don't know	0.3	0.3	0.5	0.3	0.5	0.8	0.8	1.4	0.8

NOTE: * indicates statistically significant from 2002 value at 0.10 level, and ** at the 0.05 level.
SOURCE: Calculations by the authors.

The differences between 2002 and 2006 with respect to reported changes in health in the preceding year are too small to be statistically significant for most disability categories, and they are not consistent in direction across those categories.

The findings with respect to both current health and recent changes in health are broadly similar. Compared to people with no disabilities, people with disabilities appear less healthy, although a substantial number of people with disabilities are healthy. Also, people with disabilities in personal care activities (ADLs) or other routine activities (IADLs) are less healthy than people with other types of disability.

Obesity

Growth in the prevalence of obesity has been so rapid that public health researchers and the popular press often refer to the "obesity epidemic." The concern is appropriate and realistic because being overweight increases the risk of many health conditions. Furthermore, it is well known that persons with disabilities are more likely than others to be overweight. The causes of the latter relationship are complex; obesity can contribute to disability, and low levels of exercise, resulting from impairments, can contribute to obesity. In addition, there may be many indirect effects. Because obesity among persons with disabilities is an important public health problem, statistical monitoring of its prevalence is also important and statistics on this were included in the *Guide* and are updated in this chapter.

Earlier in this chapter, we discussed the relative strengths and weaknesses of objective and subjective measures of health and function. Those concerns are especially relevant in considering measures of being overweight. Studies have compared body measurements given subjectively by sample persons with objective measures of the same persons. Not surprisingly, those studies have found a tendency for subjective reports by respondents to underreport weight. This tendency is stronger among women than men, but men are more likely than women to overreport height (see, for example, Ezzati et al. 2006). Thus, statistics on the most commonly used measure of obesity, body mass index (BMI), are biased downward when they are based on self-reports.[6] At the same time, however, these statistics can be good guides to the relative levels of obesity between groups and over time.

Table 7.5 shows the distribution of working-age adults by BMI category, according to disability categories. The BMI categories are those commonly used by medical researchers: underweight, normal weight, overweight, mild obesity, moderate obesity, and severe obesity. There are two striking patterns in Table 7.5. First, in both survey years, people with disabilities were substantially more likely than those without disabilities to be overweight or obese. That is true for both disabilities of any kind ("any disability") and for each particular type of disability, although differences for the specific types of disability are mostly too small to be statistically significant.

Second, the prevalence of obesity (mild, moderate, or severe) increased between 2002 and 2006, both among people without disabilities and among people with disabilities. The percent with severe obesity among persons with any disability increased by about 40 percent and increased in each of the specific types of disability shown, except ADLs. The general increase in obesity seen here is consistent with an increase in obesity reported in official NHIS statistics. NHIS reweighted the 2002 estimates using the new estimation procedure introduced in 2003 to avoid a statistical artifact (Barnes and Schiller 2007). The growth in obesity and the strong relationship between obesity and disability are a cause for serious public health concern.

Conditions Underlying Disability

As noted earlier, the current NHIS asked direct and detailed questions about selected health conditions, and the NCHS then regularly reports statistics on the relationship of those conditions to disability. Although the "condition approach" is used less now than before 1997, the "person approach" is still used, but less detail is obtained about conditions reported. When a person is reported to have a disability, the respondent is asked to name the conditions causing the disability, which is then coded by the interviewer using a short, preprinted list of standard condition labels.

That information was used in the *Guide* to tabulate the frequency with which conditions on the short list were mentioned in connection with disabilities. Table 7.6 summarizes the results for both 2002 and 2006, and a more detailed table for 2006 appears in Appendix 7A.[7] Table 7.6 shows the five underlying conditions most frequently reported

Table 7.5 Percent Distribution of Working-Age Adults by Body Weight, According to Type of Disability, Survey Years 2002 and 2006

| | Total household population | Disability type | | | | | | | |
| | | | | Impairments | | | Activity limitations | | Participation restrictions |
BMI category[a]		None	Any	Sensory	Physical	Mental	ADLs	IADLs	Work
Survey year 2002									
Underweight	1.2	1.1	1.4	1.2	1.4	2.4	5.2	3.2	1.7
Normal	38.4	40.3	28.7	26.8	24.3	34.0	27.0	27.9	29.2
Overweight	32.9	33.5	29.7	32.9	28.4	29.9	21.7	23.2	28.2
Mild obesity	14.5	13.7	19.0	20.6	19.8	15.2	16.8	17.2	19.1
Moderate obesity	5.1	4.3	9.0	10.5	10.6	7.8	10.3	11.5	9.7
Severe obesity	3.0	2.2	7.1	5.6	9.8	6.1	11.6	10.9	7.3
Missing	4.9	4.9	5.2	2.4	5.5	4.6	7.4	6.2	4.7
Survey year 2006									
Underweight	1.5***	1.5***	1.7	2.1	1.4	2.5	3.4	3.5	2.1
Normal	35.8***	37.6***	26.6*	27.6	23.1	29.2*	25.2	24.2	26.8
Overweight	32.8	33.8	27.7	29.4	26.8	25.7	20.0	23.7	27.9
Mild obesity	15.4**	14.7***	18.7	21.5	18.4	18.4	17.6	19.3	18.1
Moderate obesity	5.8***	5.0***	10.4	9.2	12.4	11.1*	12.8	11.6	11.0
Severe obesity	3.9***	2.7**	10.1***	7.4	12.9**	8.8	11.5	11.3	9.3**
Missing	4.7	4.7	4.8	2.8	5.0	4.3	9.5	6.5	4.8

[a] Body Mass Index (BMI) categories: underweight, less than 18.5; normal, 18.5–24.9; overweight, 25.0–29.9; mild obesity 30.0–34.9; moderate obesity, 35.0–39.9; and severe obesity, 40.0 or more. * indicates statistically significant from 2002 at 0.10 level, ** at the 0.05 level, and *** at the 0.01 level.

by those with a disability, overall and by disability type. In interpreting these estimates, it is important to keep in mind that they are for prevalence of conditions reported to underlie a disability. They are not estimates for the total prevalence of the conditions. Respondents having these conditions but not reporting them as underlying a disability are not included in the counts.

Of conditions associated with a disability, arthritis and back or neck problems are reported most frequently or second most frequently for a disability of any kind and for all but one specific type of disability in both years.[8] The exception is mental disability, for which "depression or anxiety" was the leading cause in 2002 and runner-up in 2006. The association between mental disability and "depression and anxiety" is not surprising because the operational measure of mental disability is a score based on a series of questions about symptoms of depression and anxiety—the association between "mental disability" and "depression and anxiety" is, in a sense, tautological, at least as they are operationalized in the *Guide* and in this chapter. Hence, it might be that the statistics for mental disability understate the extent to which other conditions underlie the disability.

It is also noteworthy that depression and anxiety show up among the top five conditions related to "any disability" and to most of the specific types of disability (especially in 2002, less so in 2006). Although the questions about conditions related to disability are intended to elicit causes, it seems likely that many respondents report conditions arising from the disability as well as conditions underlying the disability. It would be difficult to otherwise explain how depression and anxiety could be a cause, for instance, of a sensory disability.

CONCLUSION

Information on the health and functional status of both people with disabilities and the broader population is fundamental to our understanding of disability on many levels. Such data are needed to understand the extent to which impairments and health conditions put people at risk for disability. It is also needed to understand the mental and physical

Table 7.6 Top Five Conditions Causing Disability According to Type of Disability, Survey Years 2002 and 2006

| | Disability type | | | | | | |
| | | Impairments | | | Activity limitations | | Participation restrictions |
Any	Sensory	Physical	Mental	ADLs	IADLs	Work
Survey year 2002							
Back or neck	Arthritis	Arthritis	Depression, anxiety	Back or neck	Arthritis	Back or neck
Arthritis	Back or neck	Back or neck	Back or neck	Arthritis	Back or neck	Arthritis
Fractures, bone injury	Depression, anxiety	Fractures, bone injury	Arthritis	Other nervous	Depression, anxiety	Depression, anxiety
Depression, anxiety	Lung	Other musculoskeletal	Lung	Depression, anxiety	Other nervous	Fractures, bone injury
Other musculoskeletal	Vision or Seeing	Depression, Anxiety	Fractures, Bone injury	Lung	Other musculoskeletal	Lung
Survey year 2006							
Arthritis	Arthritis	Arthritis	Arthritis	Arthritis	Arthritis	Arthritis
Back or neck	Back or neck	Back or neck	Depression, anxiety	Back or neck	Back or neck	Back or neck
Other musculoskeletal	Fractures, bone injury	Other musculoskeletal	Back or neck	Other nervous	Other nervous	Depression, anxiety
Fractures, bone injury	Vision or seeing	Fractures, bone injury	Fractures, bone injury	Depression, anxiety	Depression, anxiety	Fractures, bone injury
Depression, anxiety	Lung	Depression, anxiety	Other musculoskeletal	Lung	Other musculoskeletal	Other musculoskeletal

challenges that people with disabilities face and their support needs. Finally, health is an important dimension of well-being for anybody, but especially for people with disabilities.

The NHIS is a rich source of information about the health and health conditions of people with disabilities in the household population, both currently and over the survey's long history. Much of what is known about the health and functional status of the household population comes from this survey. The NHIS statistics presented in this chapter document the conditions underlying several types of disability captured in the NHIS, at least as reported by respondents. They also demonstrate that the majority of people with disabilities consider themselves to be in good to excellent health, but they are also more likely than others to report that their health is fair or poor and are more likely to have experienced a deterioration in health in the past year. They also show that obesity is much more common among those with disabilities than it is among those without disabilities and that the prevalence of obesity in this population is growing.

Although the NHIS data are quite rich, they are also limited in very important respects, reflecting the difficulty and expense associated with collection of health data. The NHIS data are based on self-reports and are thus likely to be very subjective. Objective data, based on direct measurement by trained specialists, would be more reliable, but are enormously expensive to collect. The NHANES collects substantial objective health data, but very little information about disability. It would be desirable to have a better understanding of the relationship between objective and subjective health measures, and how both relate to disability. Occasional data collection for the purpose of improving our understanding of self-reported health data would be very valuable. The NHIS can no longer be used to analyze the extent to which people with very specific health conditions are at risk for disability, and the value of earlier analyses of this sort were limited by the poor quality of the condition reports. In the absence of such information, it is very difficult to learn how various environmental factors, including public policies, reduce or increase the risk of disability associated with specific conditions. Although it would be very desirable to have such information, the earlier NHIS experience indicates that the quality of detailed, unconditional self-reported information is too poor to make their collection worthwhile.

The NHIS can be used to examine the disability experience of those with a much smaller set of more broadly defined conditions. If the 1997 redesign was successful, the accuracy of the reports of these conditions is higher than the accuracy for the more detailed conditions used prior to 1997. We have not examined the extent to which people having each of these more broadly defined conditions experience disability. Although such analysis would be interesting, its value in regard to which health conditions put working-age people at greatest risk for disability is limited by the broad nature of the condition categories and lack of information on the accuracy of NHIS self-reports with regard to these conditions.

The historical experience with the NHIS suggests that the only way to substantially improve information about the extent to which medical conditions put people at risk for disability is through collection of clinical data on specific conditions. That could be accomplished through expansion of the biometric measures and disability information collected for NHANES or through other expansions in the collection of biometric and clinical data. In the absence of an expanded effort, this important gap in our knowledge will continue to be substantial.

As pointed out in the introduction to this book, state-level statistics on people with disabilities are important because of the impact of each state's policy and economic environment for the well-being of this population. Unfortunately, sample sizes in the NHIS are not large enough to provide reliable information about the health and health conditions of people with disabilities in individual states or metropolitan areas. Such statistics can be constructed reliably for a few large states only. Statistics in other states can be produced by pooling the NHIS across years. Access to the data with state identifiers is restricted, however, and such statistics have not been produced. Furthermore, estimates based on pooled data have limited usefulness for modeling trends; at best, they will identify trends over very long periods only.

The BRFSS offers an opportunity to monitor the health and health conditions of this population at the state level. The BRFSS has substantial methodological limitations that could undermine its value for this purpose, however. The random digit dial methodology might lead to relatively low response rates among people with disabilities; declining response rates overall might bias trend statistics; and comparability of statistics across states is limited by state-to-state variation in data collection methodologies. Efforts to strengthen our ability to measure state-level trends in the health, health conditions, and functional limitations could potentially make an important contribution to disability statistics.

The NHIS only includes health information about the household population—those living in housing units that are in the NHIS sampling frame. Periodic surveys of two institutional populations, nursing home residents and prison and jail inmates, produce substantial health information on these two significant populations, but nothing comparable is available for those in other types of institutional and noninstitutional group quarters, including group quarters that are designed for people with disabilities (see She and Stapleton 2009). Some residents of noninstitutional group quarters are captured in the NHIS, but inclusion of those living in a specific residence depends on field procedures, the training of field staff, and the extent to which field staff follow appropriate procedures (see Ballou and Markesich 2009).

We are also concerned that the NHIS either omits, or fails to identify, a substantial share of persons with intellectual and developmental disabilities (IDD). The National Health Interview Survey on Disability (NHIS-D) was used successfully to estimate many useful statistics about this population, but it was an *ad hoc* survey. In an attempt to determine if the current annual NHIS could provide at least basic prevalence estimates for IDD, Hendershot et al. (2005) attempted to apply the IDD definitions developed for the NHIS-D analyses to data from the 2001 NHIS. They found that estimates of mental retardation (MR) prevalence from the NHIS were only about one-third as large as the estimates from the NHIS-D, and NHIS estimates for developmental disabilities were less than one-tenth of the estimates from the NHIS-D. Clearly, the NHIS, in its present configuration, is not useful for making national estimates of IDD.

The IDD population is unusual, but not unique, in that it is both small (about 1.5% of the population) and is defined, for program purposes, by very precise and numerous conditions, making it difficult to capture in a survey. For such a disability population, periodic special surveys or supplements might be required, although we believe that with the addition of relatively few questions, the performance of the

NHIS as a source of IDD estimates could be greatly improved. Those questions would be on conditions causing limitations in activity, including direct questions about MR-related conditions and learning problems; functional limitations in use of expressive or receptive language, learning, and self-direction; and whether family members have MR or developmental disability.

Perhaps the most practical approach to addressing the limitations of health data for people with disabilities is to conduct occasional population surveys designed to obtain more detailed information about some aspect of population health and functioning. The NCS and NCS-R, designed to measure the prevalence, severity, and correlates of mental illness in the household population, are important examples. Such surveys can potentially be used to gain a better understanding of the extent to which individuals with specific conditions and comorbidities are at risk for activity limitations. They can also be helpful in the interpretation of findings from the NHIS and be used to support improvements to the NHIS.

Appendix 7A

Conditions Underlying Disability, Survey Year 2006 (%)

Table 7A.1 Conditions Underlying Disability, Survey Year 2006 (%)

| Conditions | Any disability | Disability type | | | Activity limitations | | Participation restrictions |
| | | Body | | | | | Work limitation |
		Sensory	Physical	Mental	ADLs	IADLs	
Vision or seeing	3.3	3.8	8.4	7.9	5.0	3.8	8.7
Hearing	1.0	1.2	2.1	3.0	0.8	1.2	5.4
Arthritis	29.3	29.0	34.2	29.5	27.0	39.2	27.4
Back or neck	26.6	28.8	28.4	24.0	25.7	35.2	22.7
Fractures, bone injury	10.9	10.9	12.5	9.4	11.4	14.1	9.4
Other injury	3.6	3.8	4.2	4.8	4.4	4.6	4.3
Heart	5.8	8.5	10.6	12.6	6.9	7.7	6.2
Stroke	2.0	3.0	5.6	5.6	1.8	2.5	3.7
Hypertension	5.5	6.7	8.9	12.2	5.6	7.6	4.1
Diabetes	5.1	6.2	9.3	10.3	5.5	7.3	4.0
Lung	7.8	9.2	13.0	13.0	8.0	10.1	8.3
Cancer	1.7	2.3	2.8	3.0	1.7	2.4	0.8
Birth defect	0.7	1.1	1.9	2.2	0.5	0.7	1.4
Mental retardation	0.8	1.4	5.4	9.8	1.0	0.9	1.5
Other developmental	0.9	1.3	3.5	7.0	0.7	1.3	0.8
Senility	0.1	0.2	0.8	0.0	0.1	0.0	0.1
Depression, anxiety	10.5	12.9	16.3	13.3	26.9	11.7	7.8
Weight	5.1	4.4	6.9	8.4	5.6	6.4	4.3

Other circulatory	2.0	2.3	2.5	2.9	2.3	2.5	2.0
Other endocrine	0.8	1.0	1.1	0.3	0.0	1.1	0.4
Other nervous	7.4	9.9	17.4	23.7	10.0	9.8	5.8
Digestive	1.7	2.2	2.5	1.4	2.1	2.3	1.4
Genitourinary	1.1	1.5	2.7	2.6	1.1	1.5	0.9
Skin	0.1	0.2	0.5	1.0	0.1	0.2	0.0
Blood	0.2	0.4	0.2	0.3	0.3	0.3	0.0
Tumors, cysts	0.3	0.5	0.2	0.3	0.7	0.3	0.3
Alcohol and drug	0.0	0.1	0.0	0.0	0.2	0.1	0.0
Other mental	0.8	0.6	0.5	0.7	0.7	1.0	0.2
Effects from surgery	0.4	0.6	1.4	0.8	0.2	0.4	0.3
Old age	0.2	0.1	0.0	0.0	0.2	0.1	0.2
Fatigue	0.1	0.1	0.0	0.0	0.0	0.1	0.0
Pregnancy-related	0.6	0.3	0.2	0.4	0.0	0.8	0.1

SOURCE: Calculations by the authors.

Notes

1. See National Center for Health Statistics (2008).
2. For descriptions and critical assessments of other surveys that rely on respondent reports, consult the series of Guides to Disability Statistics published by the Employment and Disability Institute at Cornell University at digitalcommons.ilr.cornell.edu/edicollect/. Descriptions of the NHIS are accessible from many sources (see, for instance, Harris, Hendershot, and Stapleton 2005).
3. The current NHIS includes three circulatory conditions (coronary, hypertension, and stroke), five respiratory conditions (emphysema, asthma, hay fever, sinusitis, and chronic bronchitis), three cancers (breast, cervical, and prostate), diabetes, ulcers, kidney disease, arthritis, chronic joint symptoms, pain in four categories (migraine headache, neck, lower back, face/jaw), hearing trouble, vision trouble, absence of natural teeth, negative feelings (sadness, hypertension, worthlessness, everything an effort), nervousness, and restlessness (see Pleis and Lethbridge-Çejku 2007).
4. For more detail on the NHIS definition of activity limitation and other measures of functioning in the NHIS, see Appendix II in Adams, Dey, and Vickerie 2007.
5. Comparable statistics for the 2002 population appear in the Guide.
6. BMI is a measure of weight that is standardized for height: BMI = weight (kg)/height^2 (m^2).
7. A detailed table for 2002 appears in the Guide.
8. Comparable results are reported by the NCHS in Health US, 2006. The high prevalence of arthritis and back and neck conditions reflects the fact that the statistics are for the prevalence of conditions associated with a disability, not all conditions.

References

Adams, Patricia F., Achintya N. Dey, and Jackline L. Vickerie. 2007. "Summary Health Statistics for the U.S. Population: National Health Interview Survey, 2005." Hyattsville, MD: National Center for Health Statistics. *Vital and Health Statistics* 10(233). http://www.cdc.gov/nchs/data/series/sr_10/sr10_233.pdf (accessed June 18, 2008).

Agency for Healthcare Research and Quality. 2007. "Medical Expenditure Panel Survey." Washington, DC: U.S. Department of Health and Human Services. http://www.meps.ahrq.gov/mepsweb (accessed September 24, 2008).

Altman, Barbara. 2001. "Disability Definitions, Models, Classification Systems, and Applications." In *Handbook of Disability Studies*, Gary L. Albrecht, Katherine D. Seelman, and Michael Bury, eds. Thousand Oaks, CA: Sage Publications, pp. 97–122.

Ballou, Janice, and Jason Markesich. 2009. "Survey Data Collection Methods." In *Counting Working-Age People with Disabilities: What Current Data Tell Us and Options for Improvement*, Andrew J. Houtenville, David C. Stapleton, Robert R. Weathers II, and Richard V. Burkhauser, eds. Kalamazoo, MI: W.E. Upjohn Institute for Employment Research, pp. 265–298.

Barnes, Patricia, and Jeannine S. Schiller. 2007. "Early Release of Selected Estimates Based on Data from the 2006 National Health Interview Survey." Hyattsville, MD: National Center for Health Statistics. http://www.cdc.gov/nchs/about/major/nhis/about200706.htm (accessed June 18, 2008).

Bickenbach, Jerome E. 1993. *Physical Disability and Social Policy*. Toronto: University of Toronto Press.

Bloom, Barbara, Achintya N. Dey, and Gulnur Freeman. 2006. "Summary Health Statistics for U.S. Children: National Health Interview Survey, 2005." Hyattsville, MD: National Center for Health Statistics. *Vital and Health Statistics* 10(231). http://www.cdc.gov/nchs/data/series/sr_10/sr10_231.pdf (accessed June 18, 2008).

DeSalvo, Karen B., Nicole Bloser, Kristi Reynolds, Jiang He, and Paul Muntner. 2006. "Mortality Prediction with a Single General Self-Rated Health Question." *Journal of General Internal Medicine* 21(3): 267–275.

Edwards, W. S., D. M. Winn, V. Kurlantzick, S. Sheridan, S. Retchins, and J. G. Collins. 1994. "Evaluation of National Health Interview Survey Diagnostic Reporting." Hyattsville, MD: National Center for Health Statistics. *Vital and Health Statistics* 2(120). http://www.cdc.gov/nchs/data/series/sr_02/sr02_120.pdf (accessed September 29, 2008).

Ezzati, M., H. Martin, S. Skjold, S. Vander Hoorn, and C. J. Murray. 2006. "Trends in National and State-Level Obesity in the U.S.A. after Correction for Self-Report Bias: Analysis of Health Surveys." *Journal of the Royal Society of Medicine* 99(5): 250–257.

Ezzati-Rice, Trena M., Frederick Rohde, and Janet Greenblatt. 2008. "Sample Design of the Medical Expenditure Panel Survey Household Component, 1998–2007." Methodology Report #22. Washington, DC: Agency for Healthcare Research and Quality.

Harris, Benjamin H., Gerry E. Hendershot, and David C. Stapleton. 2005. "Guide to Disability Statistics from the National Health Interview Survey." Ithaca, NY: Cornell University, Rehabilitation Research and Training Center on Disability Demographics and Statistics. http://digitalcommons.ilr.cornell.edu/edicollect/186/ (accessed June 6, 2008).

Hendershot, Gerry E., Sheryl A. Larson, K. Charlie Lakin, and Robert Doljanac. 2005. "Problems in Defining Mental Retardation and Developmental Disability: Using the National Health Interview Survey." *DD Data Brief* 7(1): 1–11.

Hoeymans, Nancy, Edith J. Feskens, Geertruids A. van den Bos, and Daan Kromhout. 1996. "Measuring Functional Status: Cross-Sectional and Longitudinal Associations between Performance and Self-Report." *Journal of Clinical Epidemiology* 49(10): 1103–1110.

Jabine, Thomas. 1987. "Reporting Chronic Conditions in the National Health Interview Survey: A Review of Tendencies from Evaluation Studies and Methodological Test." Hyattsville, MD: National Center for Health Statistics. *Vital and Health Statistics* 2(105). http://www.cdc.gov/nchs/data/series/sr_02/sr02_105.pdf (accessed June 18, 2008).

Jette, Alan M., and Elizabeth M. Badley. 2002. "Conceptual Issues in the Measurement of Work Disability." In *The Dynamics of Disability: Measuring and Monitoring Disability for Social Security Programs*, Gooloo S. Wunderlich, Dorothy P. Price, and Nicole L. Amado, eds. Washington, DC: National Academies Press, pp. 183–210.

Kessler, Ronald C., Patricia A. Berglund, Meyer D. Glantz, Doreen S. Koretz, Kathlene R. Merikangas, Ellen E. Walters, and Alan M. Zaslavsky. 2004. "Estimating the Prevalence and Correlates of Serious Mental Illness in Community Epidemiological Surveys." In *Mental Health United States, 2002*, R. W. Manderscheid and M. J. Henderson, eds. Rockville, MD: Substance Abuse and Mental Health Services Administration, pp. 155–164.

Kessler, Ronald C., Wai T. Chiu, L. Colpe, Olga Demler, Kathlene R. Merikangas, Ellen E. Walters, and Philip S. Wang. "The Prevalence and Correlates of Serious Mental Illness in the National Comorbidity Survey Replication." In *Mental Health, United States, 2004*, R. W. Manderscheid and J. T. Berry, eds. Rockville, MD: Substance Abuse and Mental Health Services Administration, pp. 134–148.

LaPlante, Mitchell P. 1989. "Disability Risks of Chronic Illness and Impairments." Disability Statistics Report no. 2. San Francisco: National Institute on Disability and Rehabilitation Research, Disability Statistics Program.

———. 1996. "Health Conditions and Impairments Causing Disability." Disability Statistics Abstract no. 16. Washington, DC: U.S. Department of Education.

Livermore, Gina A., and Peiyun She. 2007. "Limitations of the National Disability Data System." Ithaca, NY: Cornell University, Rehabilitation Research and Training Center on Disability Demographics and Statistics.

National Center for Chronic Disease Prevention and Health Promotion. 2006. "Behavioral Risk Factor Surveillance System Operational and User's Guide, Version 3.0." Atlanta, GA: Centers for Disease Control and Prevention. http://ftp.cdc.gov/pub/Data/Brfss/userguide.pdf (accessed February 10, 2009).

National Center for Health Statistics. 2006. "Health, United States, 2006, with

Chartbook on Trends in the Health of Americans with Special Feature on Pain." Hyattsville, MD: National Center for Health Statistics.

————. 2008. "NHANES 2005–2006." Hyattsville, MD: National Center for Health Statistics. http://www.cdc.gov/nchs/about/major/nhanes/nhanes2005-2006/nhanes05_06.htm (accessed October 20, 2007).

Pleis, John R., and Margaret Lethbridge-Çejku. 2007. "Summary Health Statistics for U.S. Adults: National Health Interview Survey, 2005." Hyattsville, MD: National Center for Health Statistics. *Vital and Health Statistics* 10(232). http://www.cdc.gov/nchs/data/series/sr_10/sr10_232.pdf (accessed June 18, 2008).

Ries, Peter, and Scott Brown. 1991. "Disability and Health: Characteristics of Persons by Limitation of Activity and Assessed Health Status, United States, 1984–88." *Advance Data: From Vital and Health Statistics of the National Center for Health Statistics*, no 197. Hyattsville, MD: National Center for Health Statistics. http://www.cdc/gov/nchs/data/ad/ad197.pdf (accessed June 18, 2008).

Sayers, S. P., J. S. Brach, A. B. Newman, T. C. Heeren, J. M. Guralnik, and R. A. Fielding. 2004. "Use of Self-Report to Predict Ability to Walk 400 Meters in Mobility-Limited Older Adults." *Journal of the American Geriatrics Society* 52(12): 2099–2103.

She, Peiyun, and David C. Stapleton. 2009. "The Group Quarters Population." In *Counting Working-Age People with Disabilities: What Current Data Tell Us and Options for Improvement*, Andrew J. Houtenville, David C. Stapleton, Robert R. Weathers II, and Richard V. Burkhauser, eds. Kalamazoo, MI: W.E. Upjohn Institute for Employment Research, pp. 353–378.

U.S. Department of Health and Human Services. 2005. "The Surgeon General's Call to Action to Improve the Health and Wellness of Persons with Disabilities." Washington, DC: U.S. Department of Health and Human Services, Office of the Surgeon General.

Weathers, Robert R. II. 2009. "The Disability Data Landscape." In *Counting Working-Age People with Disabilities: What Current Data Tell Us and Options for Improvement*, Andrew J. Houtenville, David C. Stapleton, Robert R. Weathers II, and Richard V. Burkhauser, eds. Kalamazoo, MI: W.E. Upjohn Institute for Employment Research, pp. 27–67.

World Health Organization (WHO). 1946. *Constitution of the World Health Organization*. Geneva: World Health Organization

Wunderlich, G. S., D. P. Rice, and N. L. Amado, eds. 2002. *The Dynamics of Disability*. Washington, DC: Institute of Medicine, National Research Council.

8
Survey Data Collection Methods

Janice Ballou
Jason Markesich
Mathematica Policy Research, Inc.

Prior chapters of this book have delved into the major national surveys providing specific types of information about people with disabilities. The purpose of this chapter is to review the survey methods that are used to obtain this information, prioritize methodological issues that need to be addressed, and provide guidelines for designing surveys to collect information about or from people with disabilities.

Guidelines Needed for Survey Methods

Survey data are a critical source of information to support the development and management of programs and policies for people with disabilities. The methods used to collect this information may, however, exclude the very people whose input is most relevant and introduce bias into population estimates. Therefore, it is critical to provide guidelines to promote the full inclusion of people with disabilities as part of national surveys. The contents of this chapter are based on a systematic effort to organize, prioritize, and recommend considerations for disability data collection.

The main objective of the review of methodological issues related to disability research, and the presentation of possible solutions for making surveys more accessible to persons with disabilities, is to improve the quality of the data that are used for public policy decision making and program needs assessments and evaluation. There is no dearth of topics that can be discussed to improve disability data collection, and this chapter will focus on those that have been identified as essential.

Use of Information

By outlining the methodological components that need to be considered prior to launching a survey, as well as the multiple trade-offs that need to be considered, the time and money invested in conducting disability research is likely to yield higher quality, more useful information. For those who are designing surveys, this chapter will provide a road map of the methodological considerations needed to expand the inclusion of people with disabilities in surveys and to identify the steps in the research process where vigilance can reduce total survey error. The discussion of survey best practices will also provide quality criteria that disability researchers can use to evaluate the data being used for analysis. As will be underscored in this chapter, a starting point for quality data collection is a review of the documentation that is available from prior research. With that in mind, the authors of this chapter in collaboration with others produced *Surveying Persons with Disabilities: A Source Guide* (Markesich, Cashion, and Bleeker 2006), which outlines key methodological topics and identifies relevant resources.

Survey Methodology Information

Information about survey methodology is valuable to both those who use and those who produce data. For a user to have confidence in information about disability issues or people with disabilities, he or she needs detailed methodological documentation. There are multiple sources that can be used to develop an inventory of key questions that need to be asked about data to ensure this confidence. An easily obtained source, and one that is used to guide federal surveys, is the Office of Management and Budget's (OMB) *Questions and Answers When Designing Surveys for Information Collections*.[1] Table 8.1 shows an abbreviated listing of the minimal information that should always be referenced by data users so they have some basic information to assess survey quality. Too often data users assume that, just because survey data are available, they have passed some type of quality review, but this is not necessarily the case. To prevent the use of data of uncertain quality or, worse yet, of unknown quality when no documentation is provided, data users should find and review the information listed in Table 8.1. Those who are in the process of developing surveys can use

Table 8.1 Basic Information for Survey Quality

Essential information
Dates of data collection
Number interviews completed
Sample frame(s)
Respondent selection criteria
Proxy documentation
Data collection mode(s)
Response rate[a]
Cooperation rate[a]
Length of interview
Useful information
Full questionnaire
Questionnaire topic modules
Question wording and position (item #) of key analytic variables
Interviewer characteristics
Interviewer training (general)
Interviewer training (survey specific)
Editing guidelines
Coding guidelines
Missing information

[a] The American Association for Public Opinion Research provides documentation on how to calculate response rates and cooperation rates in Standard Definitions: Final Dispositions of Case Codes and Outcome Rates for Surveys. See AAPOR (2008) for full documentation on the formula for these calculations plus a response rate calculator for easy and accurate computation.

this list to inform decisions that need to be made to design a quality survey.

IDENTIFYING SURVEY METHOD PRIORITIES FOR DISABILITY RESEARCH

We set out to identify items for a research agenda to improve the quality of disability data collection and to develop a prioritized list of recommendations to address the key research gaps to inform best practices (Ballou and Markesich 2006). To accomplish this task, we convened a planning group comprised of individuals with relevant experience in disability research and survey methods[2] to participate in a modified Delphi approach.[3]

The group discussions focused on the inclusion of persons with disabilities and how, at every stage in the survey research process, there are gaps in information about whether or not inclusion affects data quality. Although the current state of information can provide suggestions for best practices and standard procedures, without systematic and scientific research there are still unanswered questions at each phase of the survey process. However, it is clear that those conducting surveys can impact data quality, depending on the decisions that are made about the accommodations used to maximize the inclusion of people with disabilities.

The challenges of conducting research with persons who have disabilities or disability-related issues have been addressed in multiple venues by a range of different organizations.[4] Although a key disability research issue is how to define and identify people with disabilities, the planning group decided it was beyond the scope of its effort and deferred to the ongoing deliberations related to the International Classification of Functioning, Disability and Health (ICF).[5]

SURVEY BEST PRACTICES

Survey data collection is a multi-phase process, with each phase requiring necessary attention to obtain the best quality information while at the same time reducing the potential for measurement error. This section has a review of what we know and what we still need to learn about best practices for conducting research with and about people with disabilities. The discussion follows the typical steps in the data collection process, beginning with guidelines for decisions related to the survey research design. Included are best practice suggestions for survey implementation: sample design, proxy decisions, questionnaire development, data collection, and interviewer training. A convenient reference for these guidelines is presented in Table 8.2.

Table 8.2 Guidelines for Best Practices and Disclosure Considerations

Survey process	Methods considerations/decisions
Research design	Participatory action research (PAR)
	Purpose of survey
	Statistical
	Program needs assessment, evaluation
	Analysis plan: key subgroups; descriptive statistics
	Quantitative, qualitative
	Primary, secondary (e.g., survey data, administrative records)
Sample	Unit sample frame: general population random digit dial or participant list
	Intentional exclusions (e.g., institutional and other non-household populations)
	Respondent selection: household inventory, last birthday, nonrandom, proxy guidelines
	Eligibility screening
Proxy decisions	Interviewer judgment
	Questionnaire screening assessment
Questionnaire design	Established items (ADL, IADL, ICF)
	New items: cognitive testing, pretesting
	Wording: understandability, cognitive difficulty, reading level
	Format: screening, skip patterns, visual assistance (e.g., smiley faces, storyboards)
	Context: items precede others, overall questionnaire focus
	Match conceptual with measurement/operational
	Respondent burden
	Translation
Data collection	Quantitative
	Mode: in person, mail, telephone, Web-based
	Single or multimode
	Plans for alternative modes; accessibility
	Qualitative
	Focus groups
	Cognitive interviews
	Case studies/individual interviews
Interviewer training	Standard interviewer training
	Specific guidelines for people with disabilities

Research Design

The initial step in the survey process is to develop a research design that identifies the main purpose for conducting the research and a step-by-step plan that will be used to collect the relevant data. The overriding need identified by the planning group was the inclusion of people with disabilities when research is conducted with them or about issues related to people with disabilities. This approach is known as participatory action research (PAR), and the focus is to have people with disabilities involved right from the beginning of the research process so they can contribute to identifying research objectives, developing the survey instrument, planning approaches to increase the participation of people with disabilities, assisting in survey administration (possibly as interviewers), and conducting analysis and interpreting the findings. There is useful information about methods that have been used to improve inclusion of people with disabilities, particularly in the presentations at the "Best Practices for Surveying People with Disabilities" conference,[6] which are summarized in Kroll et al. (2007), but there is minimal scientific research on the effect of PAR contributions. One example that underscores the value of including people with disabilities is described in Certain Unalienable Rights (New Jersey Governor's Task Force 1987). Thirteen services, not found in any other process, were identified in focus groups of people with disabilities.

More examples based on scientific research are needed to address and document the value of PAR. In particular, distinctions should be made between PAR needs related to surveys of the general population, such as the American Community Survey (ACS) or the Behavioral Risk Factor Surveillance System, and those related to surveys of disability populations, such as the Social Security Administration's (SSA) National Beneficiary Survey, which is a recent survey of the SSA's disability program beneficiaries. The purpose of the survey and the targeted survey population (general population or disability only) should be key factors guiding survey design decisions.

Sample Design

Sample design decisions for surveys that are being used to report and analyze information about people with disabilities involve choices that impact the inclusion of people with disabilities at two stages in this process: 1) the sample frame or unit coverage decision and 2) the within-unit or respondent selection. Also, similar to the overall research design guidelines, sample design planning is directly related to the survey objective and the population of interest. The planning group identified two sample design categories: 1) samples for general population surveys and 2) samples of individuals with particular types of disabilities used for research related to program evaluation, consumer satisfaction, and needs assessments.

Sampling frame

A key research choice related to sample frames is the deliberate exclusion, for practical or other reasons, of nonhousehold units—institutions, nursing homes, group homes, assisted-living facilities, and other nontraditional, multi-person dwelling units—which can be problematic for inclusion in sampling frames, as are homeless people. Since many people with disabilities reside in these types of living situations, this exclusion prevents them from participating in surveys. Compounding the exclusion issue is the dynamic nature of tenure in some types of housing. Whereas some people with disabilities may permanently reside in nonhousehold locations, others may move in and out of a variety of locations depending on the nature of the disabling condition (She and Stapleton 2009). The mode of data collection—in person, mail, telephone, or Web—also determines the sampling frame choice, so information about which mode is the most or least inclusive of people with disabilities would be useful.

For general population probability samples, the most inclusive sample frame is an in-person household listing, but use of such a frame can be prohibitively expensive. Major improvements in U.S. Postal Service documentation support a mail sample frame as an inclusive alternative (Blumberg and Luke 2008; Link et al. 2007). Although there are documented coverage issues related to both telephone and Web-based sample frames, minimal information is available about the extent of their exclusion of people with disabilities.

There are other inclusion considerations for nonprobability sampling frames, including lists of participants in a particular program or of those who are targeted to receive local or regional services. For practical reasons, targeted or regional surveys use sampling frames that are easily accessible. These are commonly lists from organizations, such as centers for independent living and other disability consumer organizations. The planning group noted that an important research need is to develop sampling frames to meet this gap in coverage. In particular, it was noted that people with mental retardation and developmental disabilities are likely to be excluded from available disability service organization lists because they are less likely to participate in these programs. Even when a program list is supposed to include all participants, the quality of the contact information can be problematic. To reduce exclusion because of inaccurate or missing contact information, online databases, directory assistance, and other techniques should be used to locate individuals and obtain accurate information.

Respondent selection

The next inclusion challenge is the selection of individuals who will participate in the survey. At the core of this process are two important research questions: 1) Who is eligible to participate; and 2) how will the eligible participant be selected? Possible respondent selection approaches are interviewing the first contact within the sample unit, selecting the person in the household who has had the last birthday, and doing a full household listing and then using a random process for selection. Whatever the method, people with disabilities may be excluded because someone—a household member or an interviewer—determines that the person with a disability is not eligible or competent to respond. This can result in a proxy being selected to represent the person with a disability.

Additional research is needed on the use of screening questions as an inclusion method. They are used when researchers want to improve the representation of people with disabilities by using a general population sampling frame rather than a list of people with disabilities, which can have the previously described bias problems. To determine eligibility to participate in a survey designed only for people with disabilities, screening questions are used. However, there are multiple inclusion considerations with this approach that can affect survey quality. A basic decision is the question or series of questions to be used to identify particular disabilities. Also, there is the potential for social desirability response bias related to having the sample member (or a proxy) self-identify as having a disability.[7] Social desirability bias is of more concern when these questions are asked at the beginning of the contact, before the respondent has developed trust and rapport with the interviewer.

One way to monitor the exclusion of people with disabilities is to review the disposition codes that should be used in every survey to identify the outcome of the contact with each sample unit. The American Association for Public Opinion Research provides the most comprehensive method of describing disposition categories (AAPOR 2008). For example, included in the "Eligible, Non-interview" codes is the classification "physically or mentally unable/incompetent," while classifications for "institutions" and "group quarters" are included in the "Not Eligible" group of codes. In an ongoing survey, analysis of the cases or recontacting of sample members with these codes could provide useful information about exclusion. The planning group also recommended expanding the current AAPOR codes and introducing new ones that would provide additional information about reasons for exclusion.

Suggesting best practices for sample design is challenging because there is minimal research that informs decisions on how to address recognized issues related to people with disabilities. More information is needed on the extent of the coverage problem and who is most likely to be excluded. For example, random digit dial (RDD) surveys are generally believed to underrepresent persons with disabilities because some may have limitations using a telephone. Research focusing only on Washington State suggests that RDD surveys do not underrepresent adults with disabilities (Kinne and Topolski 2005). Overall, issues related to coverage are getting more attention because of ongoing communication changes, such as increased cell phone use and Internet access. As we learn more about coverage and other measurement issues that incorporate various modes of data collection, we will be able to inform discussions and decisions about maximizing the inclusion of people with disabilities in surveys. Meanwhile, it is most important for disability researchers to recognize sampling issues that might result in survey measurement error. Documentation and disclosure of the sampling methods are essential, so data users know as much as possible about the population included, and more importantly, excluded from a study. Getting the advice of sampling statisticians can also provide valuable information related to statistical power and sample design effects. Appropriate research designs are needed to address the sample design inclusion issues identified by the planning group. The sample frame is the entry point into the data collection process, so any error or bias introduced there has major consequences on survey quality.

Proxies

Among the topics that the planning group identified as being a top priority was the use of proxies to respond for sample members who have disabilities. Its main recommendation was to learn more about the effects of both proxy and assistant respondents on data quality.[8] Generally, the rationale for using proxy respondents is to minimize either unit nonresponse (exclusion of a sample member from the survey) or item nonresponse (missing data when a question is not answered). Although there is useful information about the use of proxies, for both people with and without disabilities, this information is typically based on secondary analysis of data that had previously been collected rather than experimental research designed explicitly to assess the potential measurement error associated with proxy responses. General guidelines based on current information suggest the following: proxy respondents are more likely to report a sample member has poor health but less likely to report a disability (Hendershot, Colpe, and Hunt 2003); factual questions are more likely to have proxy and self-report agreement than subjective or attitudinal questions; and proxies who are in close proximity to the selected sample member, such as a parent or a spouse, are more likely to give responses that correspond to what the sample member would say. In particular, among sample members with disabilities, individuals with mental retardation (intellectual disabilities) or learning disabilities are more likely to require a proxy than those with other types of disabilities.

Although further research is necessary on the data quality consequences of using a proxy, it is possible to suggest best practices for researchers who want to establish proxy guidelines to manage the potential error from nonresponse. The primary goal should always be to minimize the use of proxy respondents. To do this, researchers should take advantage of the various technology options that are available to make surveys more inclusive for people with disabilities such as planning telecommunication assistance to offer to those with hearing impairments.[9] Another basic best practice is documentation of when a proxy has been used, the relationship of the proxy respondent to the sample member, and the reason why a proxy interview was conducted as opposed to a self-interview. Figure 8.1 illustrates how the 2001 Canadian Participation and Activity Limitation Survey records proxy information.[10]

Interviewers play a key role in proxy decisions; therefore, the survey design should include an explicit training plan for proxy selection and instructions for when, or if, a proxy respondent is eligible. Several methods can be used to assess if a person with a disability is capable to respond for him- or herself. One is a subjective approach that depends on interviewer judgment, training to guide this judgment, and cues to look for in response patterns and other behavioral indicators. Another is a somewhat more objective approach where a "score" on a series of questions and answers assists the interviewer in determining the sample member's ability to participate (Ciemnecki et al. 2006).

Methods used to analyze the quality of proxy and self-reports include comparisons of self-reports and proxy reports with administrative information (Wright et al. 2007), test/retest research designs where proxy and self-respondents are contacted again to compare the two sets of results (Lee, Mathiowetz, and Tourangeau 2004), and secondary analysis of databases that compares proxy and self-respondent answers (Todorov 2003; Todorov and Kirchner 2000). There are a number of self- and proxy response comparisons, but the research is inconclusive.

Additional experimental research is needed to identify what is gained and what is lost with respect to data quality when proxies are substituted for the selected respondent. For example, a test/retest research design was developed to learn more about the differences in proxy and self-responses. Interviewers first collected baseline information from self-responders and proxies before returning to ask similar questions 14 days later (Lee, Mathiowetz, and Tourangeau 2004). The result was three groups that could be used for an analysis of proxies compared to self-responders: time 1/time 2 self-reports; time 1/time 2 proxy reports;

Figure 8.1 Canadian Proxy Questions

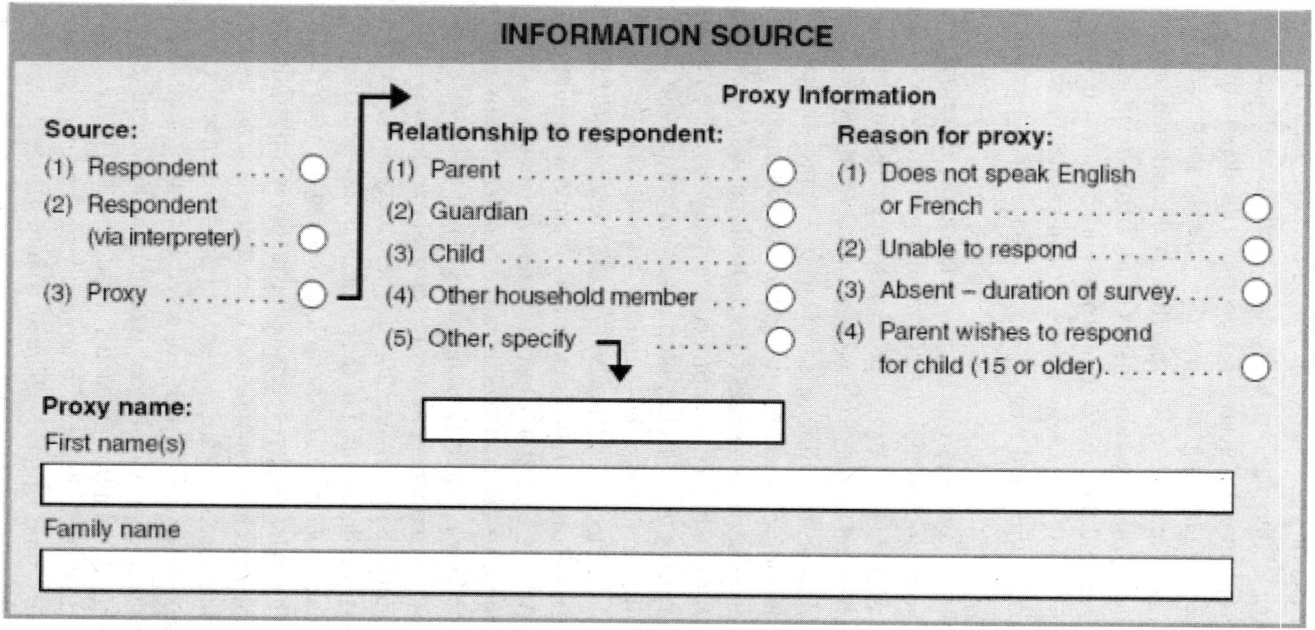

INFORMATION SOURCE

Source:

(1) Respondent · · · · · ○

(2) Respondent
    (via interpreter) · · · · ○

(3) Proxy · · · · · · · ○

Proxy Information

Relationship to respondent:

(1) Parent · · · · · · · ○

(2) Guardian · · · · · · ○

(3) Child · · · · · · · · ○

(4) Other household member · · · · ○

(5) Other, specify · · · · · ○

Reason for proxy:

(1) Does not speak English
    or French · · · · · ○

(2) Unable to respond · · · · ○

(3) Absent – duration of survey · · ○

(4) Parent wishes to respond
    for child (15 or older) · · · · ○

Proxy name:

First name(s)

Family name

and time 1/time 2 mix of proxy and self-reports. Not only did this study provide multiple results to inform various data quality dimensions, it identified several suggestions to improve future studies as well. In particular, the researchers speculate that using the last birthday method for respondent selection may have had an effect on the response to a core item in the first wave of data collection. Approximately 16 percent of proxies and self-reports responded in the same way to the question: Do you consider yourself (target person) to have a disability?

Questionnaire Design

The planning group did not focus on questionnaire design primarily because, as noted before, of the numerous efforts related to developing concepts and questions used to identify the overall incidence of people with specific types of disabilities. However, because questionnaire design can contribute to survey measurement error and nonresponse, it is useful to provide researchers with some guidelines related to this phase of the survey process.

Disability researchers have expressed interest in identifying a standard set of questionnaire items that can be added to ongoing national surveys or used for new surveys being developed. Also, the Census Bureau (Stern and Brault 2005) and Bureau of Labor Statistics (BLS) (McMenamin 2006) have conducted methodological research and recently committed to using a common set of questions in the ACS and the Current Population Survey (CPS; see Stapleton, Livermore, and She 2009). Having the ability to identify disability subpopulations at relatively low cost using a standard set of questions can expand analysis opportunities. Interest in adding disability questions to other surveys is also growing. For example, the National Bureau of Economic Research's Shared Capitalism Research Project has already added the question, "Do you have a health problem or impairment lasting six months or more that limits the kind or amount of work, housework, or other major activities you can do?" on its employee survey. Without the inclusion of this single question, the experiences of employed people with disabilities could not have been reported (Shure et al. 2006).

Both to frame the discussion of the choices when developing questionnaire items and to provide inclusion guidelines for best practices, it is useful to review the following four issues that can contribute to measurement error or differences in measurement when designing and using survey items related to disabilities: 1) question wording and response choices, 2) type of question (e.g., open-ended, close-ended, screening, or mark-all-that-apply list), 3) question context, and 4) questionnaire format. Each of these issues has to be considered when developing any questionnaire, but they take on heightened importance when designing a disability survey because researchers need to be vigilant for measurement errors related to social desirability bias and how people with disabilities perceive their abilities. Also, useful measurements of disabilities need to consider both duration (how long has the person had the disability) and extent of severity (e.g., visual problems can range from permanent total blindness to conditions that can be corrected by glasses, surgery, or other types of devices).

Question wording and response choices

Some examples of surveys used for national disability statistics are the National Health Interview Survey (NHIS), the 2000 Decennial Census, the ACS, the Survey of Income and Program Participation (SIPP), and the CPS (see Weathers 2009). Many of the questions in these surveys ask for yes/no responses. However, the response choice decision may be more complex for a person with a disability. The selection of an answer might often be subject to interpretation, depending on his or her views about the severity of disability, its duration, or whether he or she is experiencing a "good" or "bad" period with respect to a chronic condition.

Beatty (2007) provides another example of a measurement issue related to how questions are asked. He pretested the question "Are you limited in any way, in any activities because of any impairment or health problem?" and found that, in multiple cases, people who "unambiguously" had physical and sensory disabilities, responded to this question with a "no" answer. He also observed that researchers treat disabilities as an objective fact when the reality is more complex. According to Beatty, people with disabilities view their limitations as a "gap" between what they want and can potentially do, and what they can actually do. This gap is not static; it changes due to a variety of factors and circumstances in their environment that can support or hinder an activity (Beatty 2007).

As common disability questions are introduced to the ACS and the CPS, and perhaps eventually added to other major surveys, it will be important to study the extent to which they fail to identify individuals that might be considered to have disabilities for some purposes and to mistakenly include some individuals with conditions that would rarely be considered a disability (e.g., readily corrected vision problems).

Type of question

Research conducted by the National Science Foundation (NSF) illustrates how different question types can affect responses. The NSF uses two different types of questions to measure disabilities among the same population: the 2002 Survey of Earned Doctorates (SED; Figure 8.2) and the Survey of Doctorate Recipients (SDR; Figure 8.3). The SED uses a self-administered questionnaire with a yes/no screening question to identify people with disabilities. When a person self-identifies as having a disability, he or she is given five types of disabilities plus an "other" category to describe the disability. The SDR also uses a self-administered questionnaire, but it does not use the word disability or a yes/no response. Rather, the question asks the respondent to rank the degree of difficulty for two sensory and two physical activities. An analysis of data that compares the answers to each type of question from the same group of respondents showed that a higher percentage of people reported some type of difficulty in the SDR than reported a disability in the SED (Ballou et al. 2006).

Question context and format

The experience of Statistics Canada shows how the context of the questionnaire overall, not just a specific item or set of questions, may contribute to measurement error. Currently, there are two core disability questions that are asked on its major surveys. Although the wording of the questions used for the disability rate is the same, the results differ depending on the overall survey topic (Table 8.3). The highest percentage of disability occurs when these questions are asked on the Canadian Community Health Survey (31.3 percent) and the lowest on the Par-

Figure 8.2 Disability Questions from the June 2002 Survey of Earned Doctorates

C10.   Are you a person with a disability?

    1. Yes ☐   ⟶   **GO TO C11**

    2. No ☐   ⟶   **SKIP TO C12**

C11.   (IF YES) Which of the following categories describes your disability(ies)?

    Mark (X) one or more

        a. ☐ Blind/Visually Impaired

        b. ☐ Deaf/Hard of Hearing

        c. ☐ Physical/Orthopedic Disability

        d. ☐ Learning/Cognitive Disability

        e. ☐ Vocal/Speech Disability

        f. ☐ Other – Specify

SOURCE: Survey of Earned Doctorates, n.d.

ticipation and Activity Limitation Survey (14.8 percent). Although additional research is planned to learn more about the reasons for the variation in results, the prime consideration is that, within the context of the Canadian Community Health Survey, people think more about how their health contributes to what they can and cannot do (Stobert 2006).

An example of how several dimensions of questionnaire design can influence response, in particular the questionnaire format, is outlined in Stern's (2001) comparison of the results of the 2000 Decennial Census and the Census 2000 Supplementary Survey (C2SS). Stern notes that, although the disability-related questions were similar, the format of the questions and the mode of data collection resulted in a smaller percentage of people with a "go-outside-home" disability reported in the C2SS as compared with the 2000 Census. Stern speculates that these results could be due to the following four differences:1) layout

Figure 8.3 Disability Questions from the 2003 Survey of Doctorate Recipients

E18. What is the USUAL degree of difficulty you have with . . .

Mark (X) one answer for each item.

	None	Slight	Moderate	Severe	Unable to Do
1. SEEING words or letters in ordinary newsprint (with glasses/contact lenses if you usually wear them)......	1 ☐	2 ☐	3 ☐	4 ☐	5 ☐
2. HEARING what is normally said in conversation with another person (with hearing aid, if you usually wear one)..	1 ☐	2 ☐	3 ☐	4 ☐	5 ☐
3. WALKING without human or mechanical assistance or using stairs....................	1 ☐	2 ☐	3 ☐	4 ☐	5 ☐
4. LIFTING or carrying something as heavy as 10 pounds, such as a bag of groceries................	1 ☐	2 ☐	3 ☐	4 ☐	5 ☐

E19. ☐ ⟶ **Mark (X) this box if you answered "None" to all the activities in question E18, and go to question E21.**

E20. What is the earliest age at which you first began experiencing any difficulties in any of these areas?

AGE ☐☐ OR ☐ ⟶ SINCE BIRTH

SOURCE: Survey of Earned Doctorates, n.d.

Table 8.3 Example of Disability Rates for Those Aged 16 and Over for Major 2001 Canadian Surveys

Survey type	Survey results (%)
Census	18.5
Survey of Labor and Income Dynamics	20.5
Canadian Community Health Survey	31.3
Participation and Activity Limitation Survey (all)	14.8

Questions used to create disability rates:

1) Does this person have any difficulty hearing, seeing, communicating, walking, climbing stairs, bending, learning, or doing any similar activities?
    Yes, often
    Yes, sometimes
    No
2) Does a physical condition or mental condition or health problem reduce the amount or kind of activity this person can do:
    a. At home?
    b. At work or school?
    c. In other activities, for example, transportation or leisure?
    Yes, often
    Yes, sometimes
    No

NOTE: The same question wording was used in the different survey contexts.

of the 2000 Decennial Census enumerator form (used for interviewer-assisted responses) varied from the self-administered mailback forms, 2) text on the enumerator form was bolded and check boxes were located in a different place than on the mailback form, 3) presentation of the information related to question skip instructions was in italics on the enumerator form and in parentheses on the mailback form, and 4) the enumerator form had a column break in the middle of the disability questions.

As noted in these examples, additional research is needed to identify how different dimensions of the questionnaire can contribute to measurement error. Disability researchers need to further investigate the effects of the wording of questions to develop best practices related to questionnaire design.

Data Collection

Accessibility to alternative data collection modes is another area to explore to promote full participation of people with disabilities in surveys. A benefit of expanding alternative modes is the reduction of both unit and questionnaire item nonresponse as described in the sample design section. Although most of the planning group's discussion was related to maximizing accessibility in the modes used for quantitative research, it was also suggested that there is a need to learn more about using qualitative data collection techniques.

Quantitative data collection modes

Three research needs related to alternative modes of data collection should be addressed prior to making recommendations for surveys that include people with disabilities: 1) the effect of the data collection mode on the quality of the data, 2) the resources available to survey organizations to offer multiple modes, and 3) the availability and usefulness of alternative modes to the sample members who have disabilities.

In the past, most surveys used a single mode of data collection (e.g., in-person interviews, telephone interviews, mail, or Web-based, self-administered questionnaires) because there had been minimal research conducted on the advantages and disadvantages of using a mixed-mode approach. However, ongoing concerns about sampling frame coverage, particularly for telephone surveys, and reductions in response rates have increased the attention of researchers (de Leeuw 2005; Link et al. 2007). Currently, information about the impact of using mixed-mode designs on data quality and other dimensions of survey data collection operations is inconclusive, but as the general information about modes expands, it can inform data collection related to individuals with disabilities.

Although offering multiple modes of data collection on every survey can be expensive, most organizations have the technology available to provide these alternatives. However, it is often challenging to develop survey procedures to recognize and accommodate people with disabilities using the appropriate technologies, and there is minimal information about best practices to meet this operational inclusion issue. Individuals with hearing, visual, or cognitive disabilities may benefit from having the option of selecting a preferred data collection mode. For example, Web-based survey innovations, such as a video of an interviewer using American Sign Language, would be more inclusive for people with hearing impairments, and a visual presentation of symbols such as "smiley" faces (Culbert 2002) or storyboards could be used for people with cognitive impairments. Creative data collection solutions exist and can be particularly effective when information is being collected from specific populations with identified disabilities.

A useful example of how research can inform the development of appropriate data collection modes is a project conducted for the New Jersey Commission for the Blind and Visually Impaired. Initially, sample members were mailed a survey packet with options for four self-administered formats (large-print, Braille, computer disk, or audiotape). Even with these options, the response rate was low and an analysis indicated that the respondents differed from those in the total population. When a toll-free telephone number was offered as a fifth option, response rates increased by 10 percent. Low utilization of the audiotape and computer disk resulted in the decision to omit these options in subsequent data collection rounds (Murray 2004).

Even when data collection mode options are in place, people with disabilities need to be able to access them. An analysis of the 1998 and 1999 CPS found that people with disabilities are much less likely to have some types of technology available to them than those without disabilities. For example, access to household computers (24 percent for people with disabilities versus 52 percent for those without disabilities) and the Internet at home (7 percent versus 26 percent; Kaye 2000). Both of these technologies could be used to expand the modes of data collection. Although the actual percentages may have changed since these data were reported, it seems likely that a technological gap continues to exist between individuals with and without disabilities. These examples underscore the need for additional research to inform recommendations about how the mode of data collection affects survey accessibility.

Qualitative methods

Another approach to include people with disabilities is to use qualitative techniques such as individual, unstructured interviews; cognitive interviews; and focus groups. The key advantage of qualitative methods is the flexibility to adapt to the needs of people with particular disabilities. Examples include using Communications Access Realtime Translation (CART),[11] signing for people with hearing impairments, visual presentations (storyboards, scenarios), or assisted response (the use of a personal assistant or job coach) for people with mental retardation or learning disabilities. There is anecdotal information about the benefit of using qualitative methods, but little systematic research has been conducted in this area. La Plante et al. (2004) used focus groups with 100 people with disabilities during a questionnaire development phase. The response from these groups resulted in a shift in the underlying concept of questions about day-to-day activities from the traditional focus on what people cannot do to an assessment of the different ways similar activities could be accomplished. Another example comes from a pretest when a structured interview using a questionnaire elicited no response from a person with a disability. When a qualitative approach was used with the same person, however, it became clear that the person did not have a cognitive impairment, was knowledgeable about his health, and could talk about it in a conversation—what he could not do was respond to structured questions (Beatty 2007).

Whether a researcher is considering qualitative or quantitative research, mode of data collection is a core issue related to inclusion. The planning group discussed research that could provide the information needed to address this issue and recommended that research could begin with studies that focus on people with particular disabilities in order to identify their responses using various modes. While there are lessons to be learned from the research being conducted on the overall issue of the consequences of mixed-mode data collection on survey quality, a valuable extension of this research would be to focus on people with disabilities.

Recommendations for best practices are based on available information and practical solutions that have already been applied. For surveys of populations where there are known disabilities, such as a consumer study of people with hearing impairments, alternative modes should be in place. For general population surveys, it is helpful to train interviewers to identify or ask about accommodations, provided that survey organizations have the resources available to make these accommodations. For example, a simple, but important, improvement is training interviewers to identify the tone that signals a text telephone device in a household so that the sample member can be recontacted using the appropriate technology.

Interviewers

Related to data collection, the planning group noted the importance of the role of the interviewer in obtaining quality information. A set of guidelines for the selection and training of interviewers who conduct research with sample populations of people with disabilities is a priority action for best practices. Specifically, the planning group recommended developing a comprehensive interviewer training guide that focuses on the following three things: 1) sensitizing interviewers to issues faced by the respondents who have a range of disabilities; 2) training interviewers on how to overcome communication, stamina, and cognitive barriers; and 3) providing techniques that support interviewers to reduce stress and burnout. In addition, related to the theme of best practices that are inclusive, the planning group suggested that researchers learn more about using persons with disabilities as interviewers. Experimental studies comparing interviews conducted by individuals who have disabilities with those who do not will provide an opportunity for a PAR-centered research approach in addition to expanding information about response quality when interviews are conducted by individuals with disabilities.

Interviewer training

Current information about interviewer training that focuses on ensuring full participation of persons with disabilities is minimal. Of note are two sources that provide a foundation for the development of a standard interviewer training guide: "Training Temporarily Able-Bodied Survey Interviewers" (Glazier 2007) and "Removing the Barriers: Modifying Telephone Survey Methodology to Increase Self-Response Among People with Disabilities" (Ciemnecki and CyBulski 2007).

Table 8.4 provides a summary of the key guidelines included in the sensitivity training module that Glazier developed for in-person interviewers who will be collecting data from persons with disabili-

Table 8.4 In-Person Interviewer Sensitivity Training Guidelines

1) Always treat the person with a disability as a person and maintain eye contact with him or her.

2) Do not to make assumptions about the person's mental or physical capacities that could be unwarranted or insulting.

3) Keep in mind who the actual respondent is and focus attention on him or her in situations where there is a third party, proxy, or interpreter present.

4) Free the room of other distracting influences (like a noisy TV or radio, pets, playing children); suggest closing doors where it will help ensure privacy and/or cut down on background noise.

5) Position yourself at the respondent's eye level when interviewing someone in a wheelchair.

6) Repeat the question and response options as necessary, without taking on a condescending tone. Take notice of the respondent's demeanor and facial expressions; if he or she appears confused, offer to repeat the questions and response categories.

SOURCE: Glazier (2007).

ties. Ciemnecki and CyBulski have developed a training program for overcoming barriers to interviewing persons with disabilities over the telephone. The training program consists of a question-by-question review of the instrument, sensitivity exercises, and a discussion of contact protocols and refusal avoidance techniques. It also incorporates modules on how to overcome communication, stamina, and cognitive challenges, including the following:

- Communication challenges (e.g., speech and hearing impairments): use a normal tone of voice and do not restrict conversations to single-syllable words; use controls on headsets to amplify incoming and outgoing sounds; do not pretend to understand something—go back and build from the point at which responses were understood.

- Stamina challenges (e.g., mental and physical fatigue): be cognizant of behaviors that might suggest the respondent is too fatigued to continue with the interview; ask whether the respondent needs a call back, and set appointments for times when the respondent is more alert.

- Cognitive challenges (e.g., emotional disturbance, difficulty processing questions and responses, and confusion about the purpose of the interview): learn nonbiased, nondirective probing methods (silence, repeating the question and response categories, and stressing generality and subjectivity); use active listening skills and remain patient during the course of the interview.

Interviewer morale

Training that emphasizes the needs of respondents with disabilities is at the core of best practices for quality interviewing. Researchers can also maximize the benefits of having a well-trained staff by being attentive to interviewer needs. They need to know that the usual production standards (hours per completed interview) are not as important as taking time to ensure that the respondent understands the question and response categories, is comfortable with the interview process, and has ample time to formulate a response (Ciemnecki and CyBulski 2007). A method to reduce compassion fatigue and burnout felt by people who are exposed to difficult circumstances experienced by others is to schedule periodic debriefings so that the interviewing staff can discuss their experiences, provide support for one another, and receive encouragement from supervisors (Markesich and Ballou 2006). Another advantage of interviewer debriefing is that they can identify opportunities to improve future questionnaires (e.g., through simple, clear wording that reduces the need for repetition).

Persons with disabilities as interviewers

Using interviewers who have disabilities is another way to promote a PAR-centered research approach. The survey research literature, although inconclusive, has information about the effects on data quality when interviewers and respondents are matched on sex and race. But there is little research on the feasibility of using persons with disabilities as interviewers or the impact it would have on data quality. Available information suggests that persons with disabilities can be trained to conduct interviews with their peers, and they may obtain improved responses compared to interviewers without disabilities (Bonham et al. 2004; Perry and Felce 2004).

Bonham et al. provide a description of Maryland's "Ask Me!" project (Arc of Maryland n.d.), including information about the recruitment and training of people with disabilities to be interviewers, the in-person data collection procedures and modifications made to accommodate interviewers with various disabilities, and the results of the survey, including an analysis of data quality. Although this research did not have comparison information for people without disabilities, the documentation is useful for those considering using people with disabilities as interviewers.

Perry and Felce (2004) describe the experience of using one person with a mild intellectual disability to conduct quality of life interviews with his peers and include a comparison with data collected by an interviewer without a disability. They found that the inter-rater reliability was high on two of the three measures included in the research. However, where there was low inter-interviewer agreement, greater satisfaction, choice, or importance was reported on 13 items for the interviewer without a disability and on 10 items for the interviewer with the impairment.

SUMMARY AND RECOMMENDATIONS

This chapter summarizes the best practices for disability survey methods identified by a planning group comprised of disability and survey researchers. It is a road map of best practices that should be used to improve the quality of disability surveys and notes where available research is inconclusive. Use of the recommendations summarized below will improve disability surveys and systematically provide documentation that can be incorporated into the growing body of knowledge. Federal agencies, through the request for proposal process and the Government Performance and Results Act, have the mechanisms to encourage the use of these best practices. Conducting the research proposed in this chapter and summarized below will further inform recommended best practices and increase confidence in establishing standards for methods used to conduct surveys with or about people with disabilities.

Recommended Best Practices

Include people with disabilities

PAR must be considered. Although there is limited research to document the differences in research conducted with and without the participation of people with disabilities, current evidence suggests data quality can be improved by including people with disabilities. Researchers should be vigilant about addressing the need to include people with disabilities in all phases of the survey process.

Use available resources

Surveying Persons with Disabilities: A Source Guide (Markesich, Cashion, and Bleeker 2006) provides a starting point for any disability research project. Although the research included in the collection of sources may not be definitive, these citations provide extensive information related to the methodological issues associated with surveying persons with disabilities and include documentation on approaches that have been used to improve accessibility.

Plan your research

Using the guidelines listed in Table 8.2, researchers must keep in mind the key steps in the process that can impact data quality, particularly for research about and with people who have disabilities. At a minimum, reviewing these guidelines can help in making thoughtful and deliberate decisions about survey methods. In addition, information in this chapter identifies steps in the survey process where particular attention is needed to improve measurement quality.

Train interviewers

Current research identifies what interviewers should know to make sure they have the tools needed to communicate with people who have disabilities. This training should include recognition of types of disabilities, criteria for the selection of proxies, and options that can be used when interviewing people with disabilities, such as alternate wording of questions and qualitative approaches that may differ from interviews with people who do not have disabilities.

Provide documentation

The information presented in Table 8.1 shows what is needed to provide full disclosure of survey methods. It is feasible to provide complete and easily accessible documentation on disability survey information, and doing so has the added benefit of describing how various methods improve survey quality. This documentation is also essential for analysis to assist researchers in evaluating data quality.

Perfecting Best Practices

Meta-analysis of current research

A useful next step would be to conduct a meta-analysis that synthesizes data on similar topics. A systematic analysis of information would identify consistent research results that can be used to set best practice standards with increased confidence and to target the knowledge gaps that require research.

Conduct methodological and experimental research

We described examples of research that is needed to inform a set of best practices for surveying persons with disabilities in our discussion of the steps in the survey process: sampling, questionnaire design, and data collection methods. A goal of the planning group was to establish priorities for future research. This was a tremendous challenge because there are multiple issues that need to be addressed. Information from a meta-analysis could provide guidance on future research priorities.

Educating researchers, both those using data for analysis and those designing surveys to obtain data from and about people with disabilities, will result in improved disability information. One of the major changes needed in disability research is the inclusion of people with disabilities in all phases of the process. Being attentive to the methods used to collect survey information will increase the confidence that the data used for a range of public policy and service provision decisions more accurately represents people with disabilities.

Notes

1. See Office of Management and Budget (2006a).
2. Members of the group (and their affiliations at the time of the meetings) were Barbara Altman, Paul Beatty, and Jennifer Madans, National Center for Health Statistics; Marjorie Goldstein, Institute for AIDS Research and Center for Drug Use and HIV Research at the National Development and Research Institutes; Gerry Hendershot, consultant in Disability and Health Statistics; Corrine Kirchner, American Federation for the Blind; Thilo Kroll, University of Dundee; Douglass Kruse, Program for Disability Research at Rutgers University; Charlie Lakin, Institute on Community Integration at the University of Minnesota; Andrew Houtenville and David Stapleton, StatsRRTC members participating from Cornell; and Janice Ballou, Anne Ciemnecki, Karen CyBulski, and Jason Markesich from Mathematica Policy Research, Inc. The group met by conference call on October 7, 2005, and November 8, 2005. Between meetings, the members completed a questionnaire and exchanged other information related to best practices on surveying persons with disabilities.
3. The Delphi Method is based on a structured process for collecting and distilling knowledge from a group of experts by means of a series of questionnaires interspersed with controlled opinion feedback (Adler and Ziglio 1996).
4. Examples of other organized efforts to study and improve disability research include The Washington Group (ongoing meetings with an international focus whose goal is to define and develop question wording to identify people with disabilities); research and conferences of the World Health Organization's ongoing International Classification of Functioning, Disability and Health; the Institute of Medicine and National Research Council's Workshop on Functional Capacity and Work (June 1998) and Workshop on Survey Measurement of Work Disability (May 1999); 2000 National Center for Health Statistics review "Inclusion of Disabled Populations in Social Surveys: Review and Recommendations"; and the Interagency Committee on Disability Research, Interagency Subcommittee on Disability Statistics, "Workshop on Best Practices for Surveying People with Disabilities" (April 2004). The Committee to Review the Social Security Administration's Disability Decision Process Research produced a text, *The Dynamics of Disability: Measuring and Monitory Disability for Social Security Programs*, that has useful insights on disability research methods (Mathiowetz 2002a,b).
5. See World Health Organization (n.d.).
6. The Interagency Committee on Disability Research, Interagency Subcommittee on Disability Statistics, "Workshop on Best Practices for Surveying People with Disabilities" was held in Washington, DC, on April 19–20, 2004. This conference focused on providing information about how researchers were addressing the needs related to conducting disability research. Kroll et al. (2007) summarizes the presentations from this conference.
7. Social desirability, or the need to present oneself favorably, is a possible reason that respondents give biased or inaccurate responses. There are some questions in

which the respondent may become uncertain on how to answer because there is a perceived norm that defines or directs the answer that is most likely to be approved or considered positive. For example, a person with a disability may consider his or her condition as undesirable and not want to give this information to an interviewer.

8. Assisted interviews are means of facilitating self-response without relying on a proxy. Sample members respond for themselves, but another person, familiar with the respondent's abilities, is present who may occasionally help interpret or in other ways assist so the respondent can answer a question.

9. With changing technology, there are various assisted listening devices that can be used by people with hearing impairments to participate in telephone interviews. These include telephone typewriters (TTY), instant messaging, and video relay services.

10. Statistics Canada conducts the Participation and Activity Limitation Survey (PALS) to identify Canadians whose day-to-day activities may be limited.

11. CART facilitates communication for people who are deaf or hard of hearing. Also known as realtime captioning, CART is a word-per-word translation of spoken English onto a laptop or notebook computer by use of realtime software and a steno machine. Set-up time is moderate and the CART reporter usually provides the necessary equipment.

References

Adler, Michael, and Erio Ziglio. 1996. *Gazing Into the Oracle: The Delphi Method and Its Application to Social Policy and Public Health.* London: Jessica Kingsley Publishers.

American Association for Public Opinion Research (AAPOR). 2008. Standard Definitions: Final Dispositions of Case Codes and Outcome Rates for Surveys. http://www.aapor.org/uploads/Standard_Definitions_04_08_Final.pdf (accessed June 19, 2008).

Arc of Maryland. n.d. Ask Me! Project. http://www.thearcmd.org/programs/ask_me.html (accessed August 12, 2007).

Ballou, Janice, David Edson, Cheryl De Saw, and Jennifer McGovern. 2006. "Crafting Questions about Disabilities: Learning More about How the Question Determines the Answer." In 2006 Proceedings of the American Statistical Association. Alexandria, VA: American Statistical Association. http://www.amstat.org/Sections/Srms/Proceedings/y2006/y2006.html (accessed November 30, 2007).

Ballou, Janice, and Jason Markesich. 2006. "Toward a Research Agenda for Best Practices." Presented at the ISDS State of the Art conference, "Developing Improved Disability Data," held in Washington, DC, July 12–13.

Beatty, Paul. 2007. "Improvement of Survey Data Collection Methods."

Presentation at the StatsRRTC State of the Science conference, "The Future of Disability Statistics: What We Know and Need to Know," held in Washington, DC, October 5–6.

Blumberg, Stephen J., and Julian V. Luke. 2008. "Wireless Substitution: Early Release of Estimates from the National Health Interview Survey, July–December 2007. Hyattsville, MD: National Center for Health Statistics. http://sss.ced.gov/nchs/nhis.htm (accessed May 13, 2008).

Bonham, Gordon Scott, Sarah Basehart, Robert L. Schalock, Cristine Boswell Marchand, Nancy Kirchner, and Joan M. Rumenap. 2004. "Consumer-Based Quality of Life Assessment: The Maryland Ask Me! Project." *Mental Retardation* 42(5): 338–355.

Ciemnecki, Anne, Kirsten Barrett, Karen CyBulski, Jason Markesich, Matt Sloan, and Debra Wright. 2006. "Comparison of Two Methods for Proxy Respondent Decision." Paper presented at the StatsRRTC State of the Science conference, "The Future of Disability Statistics: What We Know and Need to Know," held in Washington, DC, October 5–6.

Ciemnecki, Anne, and Karen CyBulski. 2007. "Removing the Barriers: Modifying Telephone Survey Methodology to Increase Self-Response Among People with Disabilities." In *Towards Best Practices for Surveying People with Disabilities: Lessons Learned from the Field.* Vol. 1, Thilo Kroll, David Keer, Paul Placek, Juliana Cyril, and Gerry Hendershot, eds. Hauppauge, NY: Nova Science Publishers, pp. 13–31.

Culbert, Susan. 2002. "A Reliability and Validity Study of the Self-Perceived Satisfaction Scale: A Brief Summary." Department of Psychology Working Paper. Burlington, VT: University of Vermont.

de Leeuw, Edith. 2005. "To Mix or Not to Mix Data Collection Modes in Surveys." *Journal of Official Statistics* 21(2): 233–253.

Glazier, Raymond. 2007. "Training Temporarily Able-Bodied Survey Interviewers." In *Towards Best Practices for Surveying People with Disabilities: Lessons Learned from the Field.* Vol. 1, Thilo Kroll, David Keer, Paul Placek, Juliana Cyril, and Gerry Hendershot, eds. Hauppauge, NY: Nova Science Publishers, pp. 89–103.

Hendershot, Gerry E., Lisa J. Colpe, and Peter C. Hunt. 2003. "Persons with Activity Limitations: Non-Response and Proxy Response in the U.S. National Health Interview Survey on Disability." *Research in Social Science and Disability* 3: 41–54.

Kaye, H. Stephen. 2000. "Computer and Internet Use Among People with Disabilities." Disability Statistics Report no.13. Washington, DC: U.S. Department of Education, National Institute on Disability and Rehabilitation Research.

Kinne, Susan, and Tari D. Topolski. 2005. "Inclusion of People with Disabilities in Telephone Health Surveillance Surveys." *American Journal of Public Health* 95(3): 512–517.

Kroll, Thilo, David Keer, Paul Placek, Juliana Cyril, and Gary Hendershot, eds. 2007. *Towards Best Practices for Surveying People with Disabilities: Lessons Learned from the Field.* Hauppage, NY: Nova Science Publishers, 2007.

La Plante, Mitchell, H. Stephen Kaye, Joseph Mullan, and Alice Wong. 2004. "Including People with Disabilities in Questionnaire Development: A Best Practice in Improving the Validity of Survey Measures." Paper presented at the Interagency Committee on Disability Research conference, "Best Practices for Surveying People with Disabilities," held in Washington, DC, April 19–20.

Lee, Sunghee, Nancy Mathiowetz, and Roger Tourangeau. 2004. "Perceptions of Disability: The Effect of Self- and Proxy Response." *Journal of Official Statistics* 20(4): 671–686.

Link, Michael, Michael Battaglia, Martin Frankel, Larry Osborn, and Ali H. Mokdad. 2007. "Comparing Mixed-Mode Address-Based Surveys with Random Digit Dialing for General Population Surveys." Paper presented at the American Association for Public Opinion Research conference, "Of Polls and Policy," held in Anaheim, CA, May 17–20.

Markesich, Jason, and Janice Ballou. 2006. "Interviewer Debriefing on Surveying Persons with Disabilities." Final Report. Princeton, NJ: Mathematica Policy Research.

Markesich, Jason, James Cashion, and Martha Bleeker. 2006. "Surveying Persons with Disabilities: A Source Guide." Princeton, NJ: Mathematica Policy Research. http://digitalcommons.ilr.cornell.edu/cgi/viewcontent.cgi?article =1222&context=edicollect (accessed September 25, 2008).

Mathiowetz, Nancy. 2002a. "Methodological Issues in the Measurement of Work Disability" In *The Dynamics of Disability: Measuring and Monitoring Disability for Social Security Programs*, Gooloo S. Wunderlich, Dorothy P. Rice, and Nicole L. Amado, eds. Washington, DC: National Academies Press, pp. 211–240.

———. 2002b. "Survey Design Options for the Measurement of Persons with Work Disabilities." In *The Dynamics of Disability: Measuring and Monitoring Disability for Social Security Programs*, Gooloo S. Wunderlich, Dorothy P. Rice, and Nicole L. Amado, eds. Washington, DC: National Academies Press, pp. 281–302.

McMenamin, Terence. 2006. "Updates and Perspective on Existing National Data." Paper presented at the ISDS State of the Art conference, "Developing Improved Disability Data," held in Washington, DC, July 12–13.

Murray, Patrick. 2004. "Multi-Mode Surveys with Visually Impaired Consumers." Paper presented at the Interagency Committee on Disability Research conference, "Best Practices for Surveying People with Disabilities," held in Washington, DC, April 19–20.

New Jersey Governor's Task Force on Services for Disabled Persons. 1987. "Certain Unalienable Rights: The Final Report of the Governor's Task Force on Services for Disabled Persons." Trenton, NJ. New Jersey Governor's Task Force on Services for Disabled Persons.

Office of Management and Budget. 2006a. "Questions and Answers When Designing Surveys for Information Collections." Washington, DC: Office of Management and Budget. http://www.whitehouse.gov/omb/inforeg/pmc_survey_guidance_2006.pdf (accessed November 12, 2008).

———. 2006b. "Standards and Guidelines for Statistical Surveys." Washington, DC: Office of Management and Budget. http://www.whitehouse.gov/omb/inforeg/statpolicy/standards_stat_surveys.pdf (accessed June 19, 2008).

Perry, Jonathan, and David Felce. 2004. "Initial Findings on the Involvement of People with an Intellectual Disability in Interviewing Their Peers about Quality of Life." *Journal of Intellectual and Development Disability* 29(2): 164–171.

She, Peiyun, and David C. Stapleton. 2009. "The Group Quarters Population." In *Counting Working-Age People with Disabilities: What Current Data Tell Us and Options for Improvement*, Andrew J. Houtenville, David C. Stapleton, Robert R. Weathers II, and Richard V. Burkhauser, eds. Kalamazoo, MI: W.E. Upjohn Institute for Employment Research, pp. 353–380.

Shure, Lisa, Douglas Kruse, Joseph Blasi, and Peter Blanck. 2006. "Corporate Culture and the Experiences of Employees with Disabilities." Paper presented at the Society for Industrial and Organizational Psychology Annual Conference, held in Dallas, TX, May 5–7.

Stapleton, David C., Gina A. Livermore, and Peiyun She. 2009. "Options for Improving Disability Data Collection." In *Counting Working-Age People with Disabilities: What Current Data Tell Us and Options for Improvement*, Andrew J. Houtenville, David C. Stapleton, Robert R. Weathers II, and Richard V. Burkhauser, eds. Kalamazoo, MI: W.E. Upjohn Institute for Employment Research, pp. 381–418.

Stern, Sharon. 2001. "Counting People with Disabilities: How Survey Methodology Influences Estimates in Census 2000 and the Census 2000 Supplemental Survey." Washington, DC: U.S. Census Bureau, Housing and Household Economic Statistics Division.

Stern, Sharon, and M. Brault. 2005. "Disability Data from the American Community Survey: A Brief Examination of the Effects of a Question Redesign in 2003." Washington, DC: U.S. Census Bureau, Housing and Household Economic Statistics Division.

Stobert, Susan. 2006. "Measuring Disability at Statistics Canada." Presentation at the ISDS State of the Art conference, "Developing Improved Disability Data," held in Washington, DC, July 12–13.

Survey of Earned Doctorates. n.d. Arlington, VA: National Science Foundation. http://www.nsf.gov/statistics/nsf04303/pdf/sectc.pdf (accessed September 11, 2008).

Todorov, Alexander. 2003. "Cognitive Procedures for Correcting Proxy-Response Biases in Survey." *Applied Cognitive Psychology* 17(2): 215–224.

Todorov, Alexander, and Corinne Kirchner. 2000. "Bias in Proxies' Report of Disability: Data from the National Health Interview Survey on Disability." *American Journal of Public Health* 90(8): 1248–1253.

Weathers, Robert R. II. 2009. "The Disability Data Landscape." In *Counting Working-Age People with Disabilities: What Current Data Tell Us and Options for Improvement*, Andrew J. Houtenville, David C. Stapleton, Robert R. Weathers II, and Richard V. Burkhauser, eds. Kalamazoo, MI: W.E. Upjohn Institute for Employment Research, pp. 27–67.

World Health Organization. n.d. "International Classification of Functioning, Disability, and Health (ICF)." Geneva: World Health Organization. http://www.who.int/classifications/icf/en/ (accessed November 13, 2008).

Wright, Debra, Matt Sloan, Kirsten Barrett, and Gina Livermore. 2007. "Quality of Self and Proxy Responses on a National Survey of Persons with Disabilities." Paper presented at the American Association for Public Opinion Research conference, "Of Polls and Policy," held in Anaheim, CA, May 17–20.

9

Program Participants

David C. Stapleton
David C. Wittenburg
Craig Thornton
Mathematica Policy Research, Inc.

In this chapter we review the data available for studying working-age (aged 18–64)[1] participants in the largest federal and federal-state programs that serve people with disabilities, including Social Security Disability Insurance (SSDI), Supplemental Security Income (SSI), Medicare, Medicaid, state vocational rehabilitation (VR) services, and disabled veterans benefits programs. These data are increasingly important as the number of people covered by these programs and the corresponding expenditures continue to grow. Federal expenditures to support working-age people with disabilities in these programs represented more than 11 percent of all federal outlays in 2002, and that share is growing as the population ages.[2] In an era of substantial federal budget deficits, policymakers, administrators, advocates, and others have an obligation to monitor and improve these programs, and that can only be done with accurate and detailed information.

Currently, the most widely available data about participants comes from the statistics published by the four federal agencies with responsibility for these programs—the Social Security Administration (SSA), the Centers for Medicare and Medicaid Services (CMS), the Rehabilitation Services Administration (RSA), and the Department of Veterans Affairs (DVA). These statistics include basic information about the numbers of program participants, their state of residence, their basic demographic characteristics, and expenditures for their support.

There are also substantial data contained in agency administrative records and in surveys that can inform effective program monitoring and improvement. The key feature of these data is that they are available for individual program participants and can therefore be used to study how people with different types of characteristics react to alternative program incentives and options. The administrative records contain a fairly limited set of variables because the agencies tend to collect only data required to administer the programs, but records are generally available for thousands, if not millions, of people. In contrast, the survey data are generally available for smaller sets of individuals, but they can contain a very rich set of information about such important concepts as participation, attitudes, expectations, family circumstances, and day-to-day activities, as illustrated in the earlier chapters of this book.

The challenge facing the agencies, researchers, and others interested in disability policy is to use the available data effectively and to identify the best ways to augment the available data. Federal agencies have made very important advances, including developing longitudinal analytical files from administrative data, collecting more accurate information on program participation in major population surveys, conducting more detailed surveys of program participants themselves, matching survey records to administrative records, and matching administrative records across federal agencies.

To help researchers make use of the advances that have been made and to help guide the agencies in their continuing efforts, this chapter reviews the published statistics, administrative data, and surveys that contain information for participants in each of the major programs. The chapter also reviews the important limitations of the available data. Of particular importance is the lack of good information about people who are not participating but who are potentially eligible for services. For example, we know very little about participation rates because we do not have adequate information to identify people who are eligible but who do not apply for benefits. Another important area for improvement is expansion of state-level statistics to support assessments of how well these programs are meeting the needs of each state's working-age population with disabilities and to facilitate analysis of how changes in a state's policies or a state's economy affect participants, participation rates, and program expenditures. Finally, there is only limited information on the dynamics of participation—how people enter, leave, and re-enter these programs—and on the duration of program participation.

To illustrate the current status of and potential for state-level data, we provide new statistics on the extent to which working-age people with self-reported disabilities in each state participate in the major disability programs. Even though such comparisons fall short of being "participation rates" because many people with self-reported disabilities do not meet all eligibility criteria for any given program, the statistics nevertheless demonstrate that participation in the major disability programs relative to the size of the working-age population with disabilities varies enormously across states, and they are suggestive of numerous additional state-level statistics that could potentially be produced with existing data. These comparisons are the starting points for other analyses using individual-level survey and administrative data that could be used to address the gaps in knowledge noted above about participation rates, state differences, and the dynamics of program participation.

As the development of these data sources continues, continuation of lawmaker and agency executive support for efforts to generate accurate detailed information about program participants is essential. The emergence of new data sources and the extensive efforts of several program administrators offer hope that future data sources can provide a better guide for improving disability policy. We conclude our paper with a brief review of some of the most important new developments and some suggestions for the next steps.

EXISTING DATA ON PROGRAM PARTICIPANTS

In this section we describe current data on working-age participants in the major federal and federal-state programs that serve people with disabilities, under the oversight of SSA, CMS, RSA, and DVA.

In each section, we briefly describe the relevant agency programs, summarize the statistics that are published by the agency, discuss the agency's efforts to make individual-level data available to outside researchers, identify major federal surveys that collect program participation data for the agency's programs, and describe the agency's own efforts to survey its program's participants. We conclude the section with a brief discussion of data from other programs that provide assistance to people with disabilities. Discussion of efforts to improve the quality of program participation data is deferred to the "Data Initiatives" section of this chapter.

Each agency holds extensive administrative data on participants in its programs. These data have great value for management, policy analysis, and research. When maintained over long periods, administrative files can contain historical program information about every participant. The content of that information is often extremely rich and often includes extensive longitudinal information that is critical for understanding the dynamics of program participation. Each agency publishes substantial statistics on its program participants, including many state-level statistics. All of them also provide restricted access to administrative data.

Administrative data have important limitations for studying program participation, however. If there is no important programmatic reason for collecting a specific piece of information, the information will not be collected at all, or if collected, is likely to be of poor quality because it is not a priority for the agency. Comparable data are not available for nonparticipants, including eligible nonparticipants and those who are potentially eligible. Administrative data from any single agency contain little information about participation in multiple programs, even though multiple program participation is relatively common for this population.

The limitations of administrative data on program participants are partially addressed through surveys. Several large national surveys capture some information on participants in programs that serve working-age people with disabilities (Table 9.1). Survey data on program participants have their own significant limitations, however. Some program participants are excluded from participation in major surveys because of data collection methodologies or sample definitions (see Ballou and Markesich 2009). Respondents are often confused about which programs they participate in, and some report inaccurate information for other reasons. Increased use of direct deposit options for income support programs has meant that survey respondents can no longer verify their participation in a program by reference to their most recent check. Because most surveys are cross-sectional, they capture information about

Table 9.1 Summary of Program Participation Information in Federal Household Surveys

Survey	SSDI	SSI	Medicare	Medicaid	Veterans' Comp.	Veterans' Pension	Veterans' Comp. or Pension.	Veterans' Health	Vocat. Rehab.	Workers' Comp.	Unempl. Insurance	TANF	Food Stamps	Other
American Community Survey (ACS)	✓	✓	c	c			✓–	c				✓–	✓	
Current Population Survey (CPS)	✓	✓	✓	✓	✓	✓	✓	✓–		✓	✓	✓		
Health and Retirement Survey (HRS)	✓	✓	✓	✓	✓		✓	✓–		✓	✓	✓–	✓	
National Health Interview Survey (NHIS)	✓	✓	✓	✓			✓–	✓		✓–	✓–	✓	✓–	
1994–95 Disability Supplement (NHIS-D)	✓	✓	✓	✓			✓–	✓	✓	✓–	✓–	✓	✓–	
Survey of Income and Program Participation (SIPP)	✓	✓	✓	✓	✓	✓	✓	✓	✓	✓	✓	✓	✓	Energy, housing, general assistance
National Beneficiary Survey (NBS)[a]	✓	✓	✓	✓			✓	✓–	✓	✓	✓	✓–	✓	Energy
Medicare Current Beneficiary Survey (MCBS)[b]	✓	✓	✓	✓			✓	✓						

NOTE: A minus sign (−) next to a check mark indicates that the specific benefit identified by the column header is included in a single response category with one or more other benefits.

[a] The NBS sampling frame includes SSDI and SSI beneficiaries only.

[b] The MCBS sampling frame includes Medicare enrollees only.

[c] The ACS will add a health insurance question in 2008.

current program participation but little or nothing about the history of program participation. The broad objectives of these surveys limit inclusion of questions relevant to research on program participation, such as questions about the nature and severity of medical conditions and functional limitations that might be critical to program eligibility or other barriers to work. Agencies partially address these limitations by conducting surveys of program participants, in varying degrees.

Social Security Administration

The SSA administers the two most significant income support programs for working-age people with disabilities. SSDI is the disability component of the larger Old Age, Survivor, and Disability Insurance (OASDI) program, commonly known as Social Security, and pays benefits to workers with substantial work histories whose monthly earnings have fallen below a threshold (the "substantial gainful activity" level) because of an impairment that will last for at least one year or result in death. The SSI program is means tested and provides income support to individuals with low or zero earnings because of a significant impairment, regardless of work history.[3]

In 2005, 9.7 million working-age people (aged 18–64) received benefits from SSDI, SSI, or both (Figure 9.1). That is equivalent to 44 percent of the ACS estimate of 22.2 million working-age people with disabilities in the household population for that year (Appendix 9A).

SSA produces extensive statistics on working-age beneficiaries of these two programs in numerous publications that are available on its Web site, and many of these are available at the state level (Table 9.2, top panel). Statistics for the two programs are typically published separately. Some publications do, however, include statistics on "concurrent beneficiaries" (i.e., people who participate in both programs).

SSA also publishes state-level statistics on the employment and earnings of working-age SSI recipients.[4] Because SSI is a means-tested program, participants are required to report their earnings, and SSA validates their reports. SSA does not collect comparable data on SSDI beneficiaries because it is not a means-tested program. SSA does, however, have historical data on the annual earnings of virtually every person who has ever held a job covered by OASDI or Medicare. These data are

**Figure 9.1 Estimates of the Number of Working-Age Household
Population (Aged 18–64) with Disabilities and Number of
Program Participants, 2005**

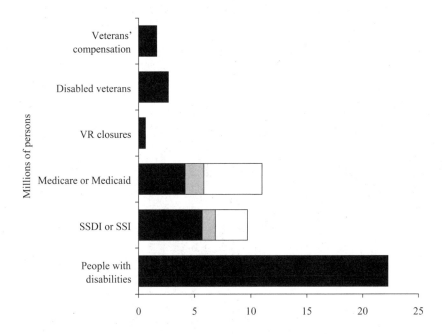

NOTE: For SSDI or SSI, SSDI only is black, both SSDI and SSI is gray, and SSI
only is white. For Medicare or Medicaid, Medicare only is black, both Medicare and
Medicaid is gray, and Medicaid only is white. "VR closures" is the number of cases
closed by state VR service agencies. "Disabled veterans" is the estimated number of
disabled working-age veterans in the household population. "Veterans compensation"
is the estimated number of working-age recipients of veterans' compensation. VR
closure statistics are conceptually not comparable to participant statistics for other
programs because they represent a flow of participants through a relatively short-term
program rather than the stock of participants in a long-term program.
SOURCE: Source information is provided in Appendix 9A.

Table 9.2 Summary of Sources for Program Statistics and Data on Working-Age Participants in SSA Disability Programs

Published statistics	
	Summary of statistics available by state
Social Security Disability Insurance (SSDI)	
Annual Statistical Report on Social Security Disability Insurance (2005)	Participation rate (SSDI beneficiaries as a percentage of the population aged 18–64), age and sex, entitlement category (disabled workers, widow[er]s and adult children), major diagnostic group, SSDI payment amount, concurrent beneficiaries, beneficiary filings for workers compensation or other public disability benefits, awards, terminations, and suspension or termination because of work. http://www.socialsecurity.gov/policy/docs/statcomps/di_asr/
Supplemental Security Income (SSI)	
SSI Annual Statistical Report (2005)	Participation by age and category (aged, blind, disabled), percent of resident population, monthly payments by age and category (aged, blind, disabled), concurrent participation by type of beneficiary (workers, widow[ers], adult children), and average monthly SSDI payment; SSI payment; noncitizen participants by category (aged, blind, disabled) and age; diagnostic group; participation in work incentives programs; applications (by age); awards (by age); statistics on state-administered SSI supplements (2002–2004). http://www.socialsecurity.gov/policy/docs/statcomps/ssi_asr/
Administrative records data available to non-agency researchers	
	Access
Social Security Disability Insurance (SSDI)	
OASDI Public–Use Microdata (2001) State, sex, age, and type of benefit	Available to all users in Statistical Analysis Software: http://www.socialsecurity.gov/policy/docs/microdata/mbr/index.html

Benefits and Earnings Public-use File (2004). Two linkable files—one with benefit information, the other with longitudinal earnings information	http://www.socialsecurity.gov/policy/docs/microdata/earn/index.html
Supplemental Security Income (SSI)	
SSI Public-Use Microdata File (2001) Information used to decide who receives SSI benefits	Available to all users at www.socialsecurity.gov/policy/docs/microdata/ssr/index .html

Federal surveys identifying SSDI and SSI recipients in the household population

American Community Survey (ACS)	1994–95 NHIS Disability Supplement (NHIS-D)
Current Population Survey (CPS)	Survey of Income and Program Participation (SIPP)
Health and Retirement Survey (HRS)	Medicare Current Beneficiary Survey (MCBS)—identifies SSDI recipients only
National Health Interview Survey (NHIS)	

Recent agency survey of SSDI and SSI participants

National Beneficiary Survey (NBS)	Survey conducted to support the Ticket to Work evaluation. Information on demographics, health, activity limitations, service receipt, work activity, income, and non-SSA benefits.

NOTE: All URLs accessed September 15, 2007.

provided to SSA by the Internal Revenue Service, are often referred to as the "IRS earnings data," and are housed in SSA's Master Earnings File. SSA holds the data under confidentiality restrictions that are even more stringent than those for other SSA data because of their source.[5] SSA also holds quarterly earnings New Hires data that employers must report to state labor agencies under the federal-state unemployment insurance (UI) program. States were initially required to submit these data to support efforts of the Office of Child Support Enforcement. SSA has also started to use the data to identify SSI beneficiaries who have failed to report earnings and might therefore be receiving benefit overpayments. Currently they cannot be used for other purposes, including research. Well-designed state-level statistics on beneficiary employment and earnings based on either of these sources would be of considerable interest to consumers of disability statistics.

SSA produces national statistics on the disability determination process, and six of its nine service performance targets in 2006 were disability determination process measures.[6] These statistics refer to applicants for SSDI and SSI benefits, rather than the beneficiary population. In 2005, about 2.5 million people filed claims for SSDI and 2.3 million for SSI, including many who filed claims for both.[7] SSA does not publish state statistics on determinations. SSA has, however, made state-level data on applications and awards available to researchers, and those data are now in the public domain, although they are not readily available.[8]

State data are of considerable interest to researchers and others for numerous reasons. One important reason is that SSA-funded state agencies—Disability Determination Services—play a critical role in the process. A second reason is that extraordinarily long processing times for many applicants have focused attention on the determination process. This reason also explains the presence of so many statistics from this process in the Agency's service performance measures. State leaders have an interest in how the applicants are faring, and the success of SSA efforts in their states to improve the timeliness and accuracy of disability determinations. A third reason is interest in studying the extent to which variation in application rates, allowance rates, and processing times can be attributed to economic, policy, and other environmental factors that vary across states. Finally, prior research using state-level data has demonstrated that the number of applications responds nega-tively to exogenous changes in allowance rates.[9] Similar analyses might also demonstrate that exogenous increases in processing times reduce application rates.

SSA researchers have recently produced the first national estimates of the number of working-age people who would be eligible for SSDI, SSI, or both were they to experience disablement (Rupp, Davies, and Strand 2008). SSA does not routinely publish state-level statistics on the population that is potentially eligible for SSDI benefits—that is, workers with sufficient work histories in jobs covered by OASDI to gain "disability insured" status. National disability insured statistics and state-level statistics on the number of workers with earnings subject to the OASDI payroll tax, and the amount of taxable earnings, are avail-able in the *Annual Statistical Supplement to the Social Security Bulletin* (SSA 2007a),[10] and county-level data appear in the annual publication *Earnings and Employment Data for Workers Covered Under Social Se-curity and Medicare, by State and County* (SSA 2008).

SSA improved state-level SSDI statistics in several small but im-portant ways from 2000 to 2005. These improvements include the addi-tion of information on beneficiary filings for workers compensation and other public disability benefits, and on benefit suspensions and termina-tions due to work. At the same time, however, changes in age categories during this period limit the utility of published state-level data for as-sessing trends.

SSA does not generally make its administrative data files available to outside researchers except to conduct SSA-sponsored research. There are two exceptions, however. First, SSA has released a public-use file containing the earnings history and a limited number of characteristics for a 1 percent sample of OASDI beneficiaries who were on the rolls in December 2004 (Table 9.2, second panel, Benefits and Earnings Public Use File, 2004). Second, SSA has created and made available a public-use file on SSI recipients in December 2001. SSA has made special ef-forts to protect the confidentiality of its beneficiaries in these files, and these efforts might introduce random error in the data.

All major federal surveys that collect extensive socioeconomic data on the working-age population have questions on SSDI and SSI partici-pation (Table 9.2, third panel), which means they can be used to produce statistics about participants in these two programs. However, analyses of the collected data have identified numerous problems. For instance, Huynh, Rupp, and Sears (2002) analyzed data from the 1993 and 1996 SIPP panels that had been matched to SSA administrative records. Among other things, they found underreporting of participation in both programs (especially SSI), confusion between the two programs, and frequent discrepancies in monthly benefit amounts of $100 or more.[11] Coder and Scoon-Rogers (1996) found that the 1990 CPS and SIPP survey estimates of Social Security benefit payments were both lower than National Income and Product Account (NIPA) estimates derived from administrative data, by 8 and 4 percent, respectively, due in part to the fact that these surveys do not cover some segments of the population living in group quarters (She and Stapleton 2009). Similarly, the survey estimates of aggregate SSI income, over all age groups, were 11 percent and 5 percent lower than the NIPA estimates. Several of the surveys, including the ACS, do not distinguish between Social Security disability and retirement benefits. This is primarily problematic for respondents between the age of 62 and the full retirement age (now 66), who can potentially receive either SSDI or early retirement benefits.

SSA conducts sporadic beneficiary surveys, driven by the need for specific information. Currently, Mathematica Policy Research, Inc. is completing SSA's National Beneficiary Survey (NBS) in support of the agency's effort to evaluate Ticket to Work and to obtain better information about the employment efforts of beneficiaries (Table 9.2, bottom panel). The NBS is cross-sectional, but matches to administrative data add longitudinal benefit information to the research file.[12] SSA's last major survey effort, started in 1982, sampled new disabled and aged Social Security beneficiaries (New Beneficiary Survey) and included a 10-year follow-up in 1991 (the New Beneficiary Follow-up).[13]

In summary, extensive information about working-age participants in SSA programs is available in published statistics, including state-level statistics, administrative records, major national surveys, and the agency's own recent survey, the NBS. These statistics and data do have significant limitations, however, which are described later in the chapter.

Center for Medicare and Medicaid Services

CMS is responsible for the Medicare and Medicaid programs. Medicare is a health insurance program for both those who are 65 or over, and those who are under 65 who have been entitled to SSDI benefits for at least 24 months, or who have end-stage renal disease.[14] Like SSDI, Medicare is financed by a payroll tax.[15] The Medicaid program is a federal-state, means-tested health insurance program that provides health coverage to low-income families with children, people with disabilities, and the elderly. Within federal guidelines, Medicaid eligibility and benefits vary substantially across states. A very large majority of SSI recipients are automatically eligible for Medicaid, but in some states the means test for Medicaid is more stringent than that for SSI. The Medicaid Buy-in (MBI) program, now available in most states, offers Medicaid coverage for workers with qualifying physical and mental conditions.[16]

In 2005, an estimated 11.0 million working-age people with disabilities were enrolled in Medicare or Medicaid, including a substantial number enrolled in both (Figure 9.1). The total enrollment in these two programs is equivalent to about 48 percent of the ACS estimate of the total number of people with disabilities in 2005. This number includes the vast majority of the 9.7 million participants in SSDI or SSI, but it also includes a substantial number in neither program—at least 1.3 million, based on the difference between the Medicare and/or Medicaid total and the SSDI and/or SSI total.

Some state-level Medicare statistics by entitlement status (disability or age) are available on the CMS Web site (Table 9.3, top panel), but there is no other state-level information on demographics. Given the federal-state status of Medicaid, many more state-level statistics are available for that program. A CMS chart book has some state-level information on Medicaid enrollment, including dual eligibility for Medicare and Medicaid (CMS 2007b). A second chart book presents 2002 state Medicaid statistics based on data that have been adjusted to address numerous cross-state comparability issues (Wenzlow et al. 2007).

CMS makes Medicare claims and enrollment data available to researchers and others through a system that allows for varying levels of security, administered by a contractor (Table 9.3, second panel).[17] The

Table 9.3 Summary of Sources for Program Statistics and Data on Working-Age Disability Participants in CMS Programs

Published statistics	
Medicare	Summary of statistics available by state
Medicare Enrollment Reports	Number of enrollees by age and entitlement group. http://www.cms.hhs.gov/MedicareEnrpts/
National Health Expenditures Data	Enrolled health expenditures by service type. http://www.cms.hhs.gov/NationalHealthExpendData/05_NationalHealthAccountsStateHealthAccounts.asp
Medicare and Medicaid	
Medicare and Medicaid Statistical Supplement	Benefit payment information. enrollees by type of coverage, entitlement, payments, and service use. http://www.cms.hhs.gov/MedicareMedicaidStatSupp/
Administrative records data available to non-agency researchers	
Medicare	Access
Medicare Research Identifiable Files (RIF) Medicare's eight Standard Analytic Files (for inpatient care, skilled nursing facility care, outpatient care, home health agency care, hospice care, carrier[a] care, and durable medical equipment); Medicare Provider and Analysis Review Files, which have more detailed information on inpatient hospital and skilled nursing facility stays; and several enrollment files, including the Denominator File, which contains substantial demographic and enrollment information on every individual enrolled in Medicare. Longitudinal records can be created.	Available only to those who successfully obtain a Data Use Agreement (DUA) from CMS. Administered by the Research Data Assistance Center (ResDAC). http://www.resdac.umn.edu/Medicare/data_file_descriptions.asp

Medicare Limited Data Set (LDS)	Can be accessed under less stringent conditions than RIF. Public-use file also available. http://www.resdac.umn.edu/Medicare/data_file_descriptions.asp
Version of the RIF without individual identifiers; cannot be used to construct longitudinal records.	
Medicaid	
Medicaid Analytic eXtract (MAX)	Only available to researchers who successfully apply to CMS for a DUA. Information can be found at http://www.cms.hhs.gov/MedicaidDataSourcesGenInfo/07_MAXGeneralInformation.asp
Information about Medicaid enrollment, demographics, hospital stays, outpatient visits, other provider visits, and prescription drugs. Longitudinal records can be constructed.	
Federal surveys that identify Medicare and Medicaid Enrollees in the household population	
Current Population Survey (CPS)	1994–95 NHIS Disability Supplement (NHIS-D)
Health and Retirement Survey (HRS)	Survey of Income and Program Participation (SIPP)
National Health Interview Survey (NHIS)	National Beneficiary Survey (NBS)—SSDI and SSI recipients only
Annual CMS survey of Medicare beneficiaries	
Medicare Current Beneficiary Survey (MCBS)	Ongoing beneficiary survey with a rolling panel design. Contains demographic, socioeconomic, health, and health care utilization information from respondents. Enrollment and expenditure data are added from Medicare administrative data. A public-use file is available to qualified researchers.

NOTE: All URLs accessed September 15, 2007.

[a] Physician and other professional care provided in noninstitutional settings.

Medicare Research Identifiable Files (RIF) are available only to those who successfully obtain a Data Use Agreement (DUA) from CMS. The RIF files are especially important because they include information that allows researchers to build person-specific longitudinal records. The less restricted version of the Medicare data cannot be used in this fashion. CMS has developed a nationwide analytical Medicaid research file, called the Medicaid Analytical eXtract (MAX), which is discussed later in the "Data Initiatives" section.

Most major federal surveys include health insurance questions, and Medicare and Medicaid appear as separate categories in the response options (Table 9.3, third panel). The one major exception is the ACS, but a health insurance question was added to the ACS in 2008. This is an important addition because the ACS is the only major survey large enough to produce annual state-level statistics on working-age Medicare and Medicaid enrollees for all states. The quality of Medicare and Medicaid information in other surveys is limited by the fact that significant numbers of respondents fail to report coverage, or confuse Medicare and Medicaid.[18]

CMS sponsors a continuous, longitudinal survey of Medicare beneficiaries, the Medicare Current Beneficiary Survey (Table 9.3, fourth panel). The survey data are matched to Medicare claims and administrative data, and a public-use file is available to qualified researchers.[19] The sample size is large enough to produce many national statistics for SSDI beneficiaries enrolled in Medicare, but it is not large enough to produce state-level statistics except for the largest states. CMS does not have a survey program for Medicaid enrollees. Many states conduct occasional surveys, but these are irregular and do not follow a common design.

In summary, extensive information about working-age participants in Medicare and Medicaid is available in published statistics (including some state-level statistics), administrative records, major national surveys, and the agency's ongoing, longitudinal survey. The long history of CMS investments in survey data collection, systematic development of analytical files from administrative data, facilitating data access for non-agency researchers in a manner that protects privacy, and improvements in the quality and cross-state comparability of Medicaid data are especially noteworthy. Significant limitations with Medicare and Medicaid statistics for the working-age population with disabilities remain, however, including some that are being addressed by initiatives described later in this chapter.

Rehabilitation Services Administration

The RSA is responsible for federal oversight of state VR agencies. State agencies are responsible for providing employment services to people with disabilities, and they are required to give priority to those with significant disabilities. RSA funds the state services under provisions of the Rehabilitation Act. SSA provides additional funding to pay for services provided to SSDI and SSI clients, provided those clients attain specified earnings levels over a sufficient period. States themselves provide additional funding in varying degrees.

RSA statistics on VR participants differ conceptually from those for the other programs discussed in this chapter, in part because most VR clients participate in the program for two years or less, whereas the typical participant in the other programs is on the rolls for many years. The annual RSA statistics are for "closures," that is, the number of clients exiting the VR program during the year. In 2005, the number of closed VR cases (the standard measure of case activity, see Figure 9.1) was less than 3 per 100 working-age people with disabilities; the number who actually received services during the year was no doubt substantially larger, but data on that number are not routinely published. In 2002, VR expenditures accounted for just 1 percent of federal expenditures for working-age people with disabilities (Goodman and Stapleton 2007). The VR program is the largest federally supported program designed to help people with disabilities work and live independently.

RSA publishes substantial state-level closure statistics for VR clients based on data submitted by state agencies (Table 9.4, first panel). It also produces a public-use version of closure data submitted by the state agencies. These are known as RSA 911 data, and state agencies are required to submit it when a client's case is closed (Table 9.4, second panel). These data include demographic, disability, and program participation information about each client at the time of application and closure; information about service eligibility and receipt; closure status; and employment at closure. These data do not include any information on employment and earnings after closure, however.

Table 9.4 Summary of Sources for Program Statistics and Data on State VR Agency Clients

Published statistics	Summary of statistics available by state
RSA Program Data and Statistics (2005)	Outcomes of cases at the state level, such as employment outcomes, hourly wage at closure, mean age, hours worked per week, services provided, and expenditure. http://www.ed.gov/rschstat/eval/rehab/statistics.html
RSA Management Information System (MIS)	The MIS system includes extensive state-level statistics on applications, eligibility determinations, employment, wages, and SSDI and SSI status, based on state reports. http://rsamis.ed.gov/info_for_new_users.cfm
Administrative records data available to non-agency researchers	**Access**
RSA 911 Data Records on the closed cases of state VR agency clients	RSA makes a public-use version of the data available to researchers. http://www.ed.gov/rschstat/eval/rehab/911-data.html
Federal surveys that identify Medicare and Medicaid enrollees in the household population	
1994–95 NHIS Disability Supplement (NHIS-D)	National Beneficiary Survey (NBS)—SSDI and SSI recipients only.
National survey of VR Clients	
Longitudinal Study of the Vocational Rehabilitation Services Program	Content: Characteristics, service receipt, and employment outcomes on VR participants over a three-year period. http://www.ilr.cornell.edu/edi/lsvrsp/application/index.cfm?cfid=24033099&cftoken=83765168

NOTE: All links accessed September 15, 2007.

Major federal surveys do not include information on receipt of VR services (Table 9.4, third panel). No doubt this reflects the formidable challenges of collecting data for the very small share of the household population that is receiving services at any given time. The one time Disability Supplement to the National Health Interview Survey (NHIS) did collect such information, but those data are now more than 10 years old. The NBS also includes extensive information about beneficiary receipt of many services and identifies those who have received services from a VR agency, but its services cannot be distinguished from those delivered by others.

RSA conducted a longitudinal study of state VR applicants, clients, and recent clients from 1995 through 2000 (Table 9.4, fourth panel). Additional data were extracted from state agency administrative files.[20] A new longitudinal survey of recent VR clients, the Post Vocational Rehabilitation Experiences Study, is in progress.

In summary, RSA makes available extensive statistics and data on participants in state VR programs, including many state-level statistics, based on administrative records. In contrast to those for other programs, VR statistics are based on program exits or closures, rather than current enrollment, reflecting the short-term nature of the program. VR participants and service use are not identified in major ongoing national surveys, but this deficiency has recently been substantially addressed through RSA's own longitudinal participant survey.

Department of Veterans Affairs

The DVA administers a number of programs for veterans. The Veterans' Compensation (VC) program pays income benefits to veterans with service-connected disabilities; the Veterans' Pension (VP) program pays income benefits to low-income veterans with nonservice disabilities; and Veterans' Health Care (VHC) provides health care benefits to all eligible veterans who enroll. VHC eligibility and copays depend on the veteran's priority group assignment. If funding is inadequate, those in the lowest priority groups are ineligible; VC participants are in the highest priority groups (1 to 3), and VP participants are in an intermediate group (5). Several smaller programs offer educational assistance, life insurance, loan guarantees, and vocational rehabilitation.[21]

In 2005, 1.6 million working-age veterans received VC payments (Figure 9.1), or about 65 percent of the estimated 2.7 million working-age veterans with disabilities in the household population (ACS; Appendix 9A). Far fewer working-age veterans received VP payments, only 138,000. We were not able to find a count of the number who received payments from both programs in 2005, nor could we find published statistics for the number of working-age VHC enrollees.

The Veterans Benefit Administration publishes a limited number of VC and VP participation and cost statistics every year (Table 9.5, top panel). More detailed participant characteristics are published at the national level only. County-level statistics are available online for the number of veterans and annual expenditures for each of the three programs (USDVA 2007). DVA does not have a systematic program for making its administrative records available to outside researchers, although DVA has provided restricted access to researchers on some occasions in the past.

All major federal surveys have veteran status questions, often including period of service, and statistics on veterans are often produced from these surveys. Most also include information on VC and VP receipt, although not all surveys distinguish between the two programs (Table 9.5, third panel). Analyses of the CPS and the SIPP for 1990 found that the survey-based estimates of the number of veterans receiving benefits from these two programs combined were 32 percent and 11 percent, respectively, below the number reported by DVA (Coder and Scoon-Rogers 1996). There also appears to be confusion among survey respondents between military retirement benefits and income from veterans' disability programs.

VHC is often included as a health insurance category, although sometimes as part of a larger one that includes TRICARE (formerly CHAMPUS), the health care system for dependents of military employees as well as for civilian employees and their dependents. The DVA conducted the last major survey of veterans in 2001 (Table 9.5, fourth panel).

In summary, published statistics based on DVA administrative data are very limited by comparison to those produced for the other programs we have considered in this chapter, and DVA does not systematically make these research files available to outside researchers. Receipt

Table 9.5 Summary of Sources for Program Statistics and Data on Veterans' Disability Programs

Published statistics	Summary of statistics available by state
Veterans' Compensation (VC)	Participation statistics for broad age groups as well as monthly expenditures.
Annual Benefits Report (2005)	http://www.vba.va.gov/reports/2005_abr.pdf
Veterans' Pensions (VP)	Participation statistics for broad age groups as well as monthly expenditures.
Annual Benefits Report (2005)	http://www.vba.va.gov/reports/2005_abr.pdf
Veterans' Health Care (VHC)	None.
Administrative records data available to non-agency researchers	
No formal program to provide researchers with access to administrative records on individual participants.	
Federal surveys that identify veterans and participants in DVA programs	
American Community Survey (ACS) —VC and VP, combined; not VHA	1994–95 NHIS Disability Supplement (NHIS-D)—VC and VP combined, VHA
Current Population Survey (CPS)—VC, VP, and VHA	Survey of Income and Program Participation (SIPP) —VC, VP, and VHA
Health and Retirement Survey (HRS) —VC and VP combined, VHA	National Beneficiary Survey (NBS)—VC and VP combined, VHA—SSDI and SSI recipients only
National Health Interview Survey (NHIS) —VC and VP combined, VHA	Medicare Current Beneficiary Survey (MCBS)—VC and VP combined, VHA—Medicare beneficiaries only
Annual CMS survey of Medicare beneficiaries	
National Survey of Veterans (NSV) 2001	Contains demographics, financial characteristics, military background, health, and benefit use. http://www1.va.gov/vetdata/page.cfm?pg=5

NOTE: All links accessed June 8, 2008.

of benefits in the major DVA programs is captured in several national surveys, however, and the DVA does periodically collect information about participants through its surveys of all veterans.

Other Programs

Several other government programs that provide benefits for working-age people with disabilities are not covered in the discussion above, primarily because of the lack of federal data on the participants with disabilities. The most notable of these is workers' compensation (WC), a system of programs that provide medical and cash benefits to covered workers for work-related injuries or illnesses. Benefits can be temporary or permanent, and cash payments can be partial or full, depending on the extent and permanence of the injury or illness. A vast majority of workers are covered under WC programs that are designed and administered by state boards. Program administrative and coverage provisions vary widely across states and state laws require employers to obtain insurance or demonstrate the financial ability to self-insure. Employers who are not self-insured pay experience-rated premiums. In addition, federal employees are covered under special federal programs administered by the Department of Labor (DOL), except for active duty military personnel, as the VC program is their WC program.

States and the WC industry collect limited data on coverage and claimants, but the federal government does not make an effort to collect and produce data that are comparable across states. The National Academy of Social Insurance compiles the limited data that are publicly available for all states and produces an annual report on WC,[22] with support from SSA, CMS, DOL, and the WC insurance industry. The most recent National Academy of Social Insurance report (Sengupta, Reno, and Burton 2007) provides state statistics on covered workers and wages, and benefits paid per $100 of covered wages by type of insurer (private, state, self-insured, or medical), type of benefit (medical or cash), per $100 of covered wages.

The CPS, SIPP, and HRS include questions about WC benefit receipt (Table 9.1). Analyses of the CPS and the SIPP for 1990 found that estimates of total WC income based on each of these surveys were 11 percent lower than the total derived from administrative data (Coder and Scoon-Rogers 1996).[23] The ACS has no WC information; hence, there is no reliable information on the characteristics of recipients at the state level other than the limited information from administrative records. The NHIS includes WC benefits among several items in an "other income" category and is included as a separate income item in the NBS.

Numerous other federal and federal-state programs provide services to working-age people with disabilities but serve broader populations. Also, they do not routinely identify this population group in their published state-level statistics. These include Temporary Assistance to Needy Families (TANF), food stamps and other Department of Agriculture programs, unemployment insurance, state workforce development programs under the purview of DOL, the state-administered Section 8 housing programs under the purview of the Department of Housing and Urban Development (HUD), and Department of Transportation programs that provide transportation support for people with disabilities. Five states have short-term disability programs, and many others provide temporary support under variously named general assistance programs. Surveys are the primary source of information on people with disabilities served by these programs, especially the SIPP (Table 9.1), but construction of state-level statistics on participation is problematic for those programs not explicitly included in the ACS, because of small sample sizes. Also, as with the disability income-support programs, income from unemployment insurance, family assistance, and public assistance are underreported in SIPP and the CPS (Coder and Scoon-Rogers 1996).

PROGRAM PARTICIPATION STATISTICS FOR STATES

In this section we present a few state-level statistics on program participation for working-age people with disabilities in 2005. The statistics on participants are all publicly available from agency sources. Our innovation is to compare the number of participants in each state program to an estimate of the size of the state's household population of people with disabilities.

Ideally, we would like to know what percentage of those individuals meeting a program's eligibility criteria in each state are actually in the program (i.e., the state's "participation rate"). Survey-based estimates of such rates are often produced for nondisability programs (e.g., TANF and food stamps), made possible by the fact that surveys collect family demographic and financial information that can be used to approximate eligibility criteria. Participation rates are not available for disability programs, however, because surveys do not collect the detailed medical information needed along with financial information to determine eligibility for disability programs. The difficulties of collecting such information became all too apparent in the 1990s, when SSA's effort to collect such data encountered technical obstacles and escalating costs that eventually led to the termination of the project.[24]

It is possible, however, to produce state statistics on the number of participants relative to the estimated size of the working-age household population with any self-reported disability, hereafter, "participation ratios." The number in the denominator is an estimate of the size of a broader population than those eligible to participate, namely those who would self-report disability based on the ACS questions. The population estimates are from the 2005 ACS (see Weathers 2009). It seems reasonable to assume that variation in participation ratios reflects variation not only in unobserved participation rates but also in the ratio of persons eligible for the program relative to the number of persons with any disability. Although variation in estimated participation ratios across states is almost certainly higher than variation in actual participation rates, it also seems likely that variation in participation rates accounts for a substantial share of variation in the estimated ratios.

The ratios presented below are for SSDI, SSI, Medicare, Medicaid, and state VR services. We also discuss, but do not present state statistics for, VC and VP. These statistics are all derived from data available in administrative and survey sources described in the previous section.[25] The ratios are subject to several limitations, in addition to the fact that the denominator includes many people with disabilities who are not eligible for the program. First, the denominator is a survey-based estimate, which is therefore subject to sampling error. Second, some participants might not be represented in the denominator, either because survey respondents who are participants failed to report their disability or because they do not reside in the household population, and therefore are outside the 2005 ACS sampling frame (She and Stapleton 2009). Third, each statistic is constructed with data from two or more sources, and the sources are usually not fully consistent with respect to the reference date, state (the state recorded in an administrative record might not match actual state of residence), age group categories, or possibly other factors, as detailed in the footnotes to Appendix 9A.

Estimated participation ratios for SSDI and SSI are displayed in Figure 9.2. The ratios are expressed as the number of participants per 100 persons in the household population with self-reported disabilities. The height of each bar is the combined participation ratio for the two programs, the bottom section of the bar (black) is the SSDI-only participation ratio, the middle section (gray) is the concurrent participation ratio, and the top section (white) is the SSI-only participation ratio. The states are ordered by the total participation ratio, and a clear bar for the United States as a whole appears near the middle.

The range of the total SSDI and SSI participation ratio is remarkably wide, from 28 percent or lower in Alaska, Utah, and Wyoming, to 55 percent or higher in West Virginia, Massachusetts, and the District of Columbia. Thus, the highest participation ratios are more than twice as large as the lowest. There is also considerable variation in the distribution of participants across the three program categories.

State-level participation ratios for Medicare and Medicaid are presented in Figure 9.3. The Medicaid figures are especially subject to error because the data are reported in a manner that makes separation of working-age adult enrollees with disabilities from child enrollees with disabilities problematic.[26] "Dual-eligible" participants are those enrolled in both programs. For ease of comparison to Figure 9.1, we have also plotted the SSDI/SSI participation ratio and ordered the states by that variable.

The pattern of Medicare and Medicaid enrollment across states is quite similar to that of SSDI and SSI participation, reflecting the links between these programs. There is, however, substantial variation across states that is not attributable to this variation, reflecting the extent to which Medicaid covers individuals with disabilities who are not SSI participants. In some states, participants in Medicare or Medicaid exceed participants in SSDI or SSI by a substantial margin, most likely

324

Figure 9.2 Ratio of SSDI and SSI Participants to the Working-Age Household Population (Aged 18–64) with Disabilities, by State, 2005

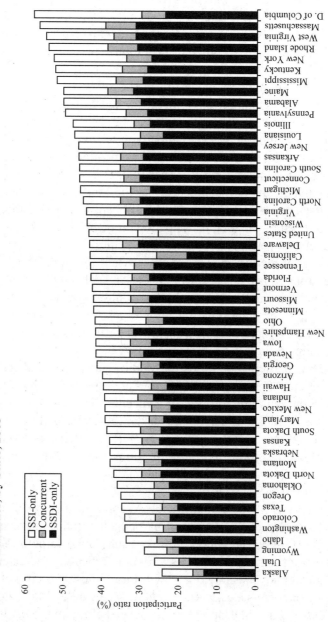

NOTE: The denominator of the participation ratios is the 2005 ACS estimate of the size of the working-age household population with disabilities, many of whom are not eligible for either SSDI or SSI.

SOURCE: Authors' estimates based on the 2005 ACS and SSA published statistics for December 2005. See Appendix 9A for original data, assumptions, and sources.

Figure 9.3 Ratio of Medicare and Medicaid Enrollees to the Working-Age Household Population (Aged 18–64) with Disabilities, by State, 2005

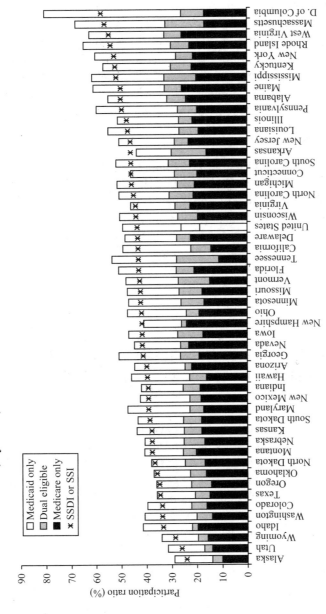

NOTE: The denominator of these participation ratios is the ACS estimate of the size of the working-age household population with disabilities, many of whom are not eligible for either Medicare or Medicaid.

SOURCE: Authors' estimates. See Appendix 9A for original data, assumptions, and sources.

because of enrollment in optional Medicaid categories that vary across states, including medically needed programs, MBI, and programs for which the state agencies have obtained Medicaid waivers. Some states also offer coverage to people with disabilities through state-only Medicaid categories. Variation in participation ratios for these two programs across states is even greater than the variation in participation in SSDI or SSI; only 28.4 percent of Alaskans with disabilities are enrolled in one of these programs, compared to 68 percent in Massachusetts and 80 percent in the District of Columbia. As with the SSA programs, the highest participation ratios are more than twice as large as the lowest ratios.

The numerator of the VR participation ratio is the number of cases closed in 2005 by the state VR agency (Figure 9.4). The VR participation ratio is conceptually different than those for the SSA and CMS programs. VR closures represent the flow of participants through relatively short-term VR programs, whereas participants in the SSA and CMS programs reflect the stocks of participants—that is, the number on the rolls at a point in time—in these agencies' long-term programs.

The VR participation ratio varies from 1.6 in Washington, Tennessee, and Louisiana to 6.8 in Vermont and 6.9 in the District of Columbia. Relative variation in VR participation ratios is even larger than relative variation in ratios for SSA and CMS programs; the largest VR ratios are more than three times as large as the smallest ones.

We attempted to develop state-level participation ratios for VC and VP based on DVA statistics and the ACS estimates of the number of working-age veterans with disabilities in each state (Appendix 9A). We found, however, that our methodology produces VC participation ratios well in excess of 100 percent in three states: Alaska, Hawaii, and Virginia. The apparent reason is that the state VC and VP statistics do not reflect migration of veterans from states where they first received benefits to their current state of residence.

In summary, state-level participation ratios for the major federal and federal-state programs are difficult to construct and have substantial limitations. The constructed statistics show that participation of people with disabilities in these programs varies widely across states, a fact that should be of considerable interest to people concerned about the distribution of resources for these programs and how public policy

Figure 9.4 Ratio of the Number of State VR Cases Closed to the Estimated Working-Age Household Population (Aged 18–64) with Disabilities, by State, Fiscal Year 2005

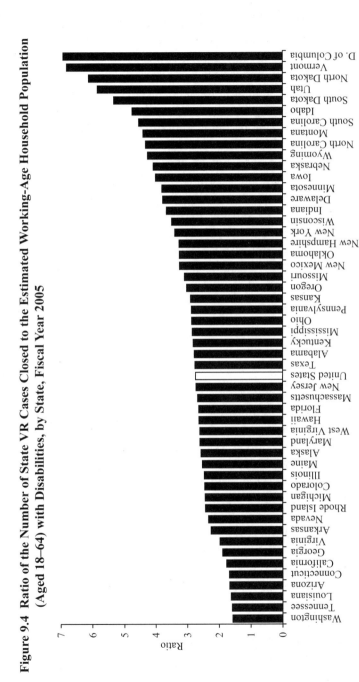

NOTE: The denominator of the VR participation ratio is the ACS estimate of the size of the working-age household population with disabilities. The numerator, VR closures, is the number of cases closed during the fiscal year, as reported to RSA by state VR agencies. The VR closure statistics used to construct these ratios include a small share of closures for clients who are outside the defined working-age range.

SOURCE: Authors' estimates. See Appendix 9A for original data, assumptions, and sources.

and program administration affect participation. At least some of this variation is likely caused by factors other than variation in underlying participation rates, including state demographic, geographic, and cultural factors. But the variation also raises a number of very interesting policy questions. Are substantial numbers of people in low participation ratio states not receiving benefits they are both medically and financially eligible for or is the participation ratio low because many of those who are medically eligible are not financially eligible?[27] If it is the latter, are those medically eligible but not participating financially ineligible because they work and their earnings are too high? Or have they not worked enough in the past to qualify for SSDI and they have income from other sources or assets that make them ineligible for SSI? Is there a very large pool of medically eligible nonparticipants who would likely become participants if their financial circumstances deteriorated? Answers to these and other questions about the causes of variation in participation ratios would likely have important policy implications.

DATA INITIATIVES

In this section we summarize several significant initiatives by federal agencies to make administrative data on program participants with disabilities more useful for research and other purposes. We first describe two recently developed longitudinal research files based on single-agency administrative data. These files are making it possible for researchers to better understand the dynamics of program participation and are supporting the evaluation of several important policy initiatives. We then summarize SSA, CMS, and RSA efforts to match data across agencies. These efforts are providing important opportunities to learn about participants in one program (e.g., VR clients) from the data of other programs (e.g., SSDI and SSI), and how innovations in one program (e.g., the MBI for workers with disabilities) affect the participants in other programs (e.g., SSDI beneficiaries). Finally, we discuss recent efforts to match survey data to administrative data. Such matches expand knowledge about program participants and also provide opportunities to study the dynamics of participation.

Program administrators encounter significant obstacles in the pursuit of efforts like those described here—the absolute need to protect the privacy of individual participants, the challenges of interagency cooperation, technical issues such as ensuring accurate matches, and tight research budgets.[28] The fact that substantial progress is being made on several fronts, despite these obstacles, attests to the value that the agency administrators place on enhancing data on disability program participants.

Research Files Derived from Administrative Data

SSA has supported the development of a longitudinal analytical data file containing an extensive record for each person who has been eligible, as an adult, to receive SSDI or SSI benefits in at least one month from 1996 forward. Each record contains the individual's benefit history from 1994 forward. SSA and Mathematica Policy Research, Inc. staff initially developed the Ticket Research File (TRF) to support the evaluation of the Ticket to Work (TTW) program. The TRF is by far the largest longitudinal file with detailed information about people with severe disabilities ever assembled. A very large share of all working-age people with significant disabilities is represented in the file, as is evident from the fact that the number of working-age SSDI or SSI beneficiaries in December 2005 was equal to 44 percent of the ACS-based estimate of the number of working-age people with disabilities in the household population (Figure 9.2).

The 2006 version of the TRF contains a record for every working-age adult who participated in SSDI or SSI for at least one month from January 1996 through December 2006—more than 19 million beneficiaries. The TRF data are extracted from numerous SSA administrative files. An important feature of the TRF is that data from SSI and SSDI sources are combined into a single TRF record for each beneficiary. The longitudinal variables include monthly benefit payments, program eligibility, use of program work incentives, Employment Network[29] service enrollment, state of residence, and disability diagnosis codes. Other variables include date of birth, sex, race/ethnicity, and mortality. Hildebrand et al. (2007) provide documentation for the most recent version of the TRF. Currently, the TRF can be used only by SSA staff and authorized contractors. Staff can also match the TRF to IRS earnings data.

Many statistics generated from the TRF appear in the TTW evaluation reports (Thornton et al. 2004, 2006, 2007) and in several articles in the *Journal of Vocational Rehabilitation*.[30] In addition, SSA and its contractors are using the file to support other research efforts at SSA, including the Benefit Offset National Demonstration, Youth Transition Demonstrations, Accelerated Benefits Demonstration, and the State Partnership Initiative. The data have also been used to support a HUD assessment of the housing needs of people living with HIV/AIDS. Government Accountability Office (2007) analyzes outcomes for VR clients using TRF data matched to RSA 911 data, and CMS is using it for several projects under a matching agreement with SSA described later in this chapter.

Under a 2003 mandate from Congress, CMS has expanded its effort to make Medicare data available to researchers studying chronic conditions, through the establishment of the Chronic Condition Warehouse.[31] These are longitudinal records for samples of beneficiaries having one of 21 specified conditions. They are based on data extracted from the claim records for a random 5 percent of the beneficiaries from 1999 to 2004, expanded to 100 percent of beneficiaries from 2005 forward. These are research identifiable files; like the Medicare RIF data described earlier, they can only be accessed with permission and in a secure setting.

As mentioned previously, CMS has developed an analytical Medicaid file, called MAX, and made it available to researchers in a controlled manner. MAX data are currently available for all states from 1999 through 2002. Similar State Medicaid Research Files are available for 30 states from 1992 to 1998. As with the Medicare RIF data, the MAX data include information researchers need to construct longitudinal records. The primary source file for MAX is the Medicaid Statistical Information System; MAX incorporates a number of refinements to that data, which improves its utility for researchers and analysts.[32]

Cross-Agency Matches of Administrative Data

One way to address the paucity of data on program interactions is to match administrative data from multiple programs. Many states have been engaged in matching activities for years, but their efforts have largely focused on data for low-income parents and children. The Substance Abuse and Mental Health Treatment Administration, for example, has supported state efforts to match Medicaid data with state mental health agency data.

Three federal agencies, SSA, CMS, and RSA, have recently established two-way agreements for matching data on participants in their respective programs. These efforts are already bearing significant fruit for the disability research of the agencies involved.

SSA and CMS have an interagency agreement to support projects that require matched SSA and CMS administrative data. IRS earnings data held by SSA can be used under this agreement provided that the work is conducted by a qualified SSA employee. The two agencies and their contractors are conducting several disability studies under these agreements. The CMS-funded study of the MBI program is using data from the TRF that is linked to Medicaid and Medicare eligibility and claims data (Liu, Ireys, and Thornton 2008). This study will also link CMS data with SSA's earnings records to study the employment profiles of MBI participants before and after entering this program. Another CMS-funded project has merged extracts from the TRF with Medicare and Medicaid data to study Medicare beneficiaries with behavioral health problems. A third CMS-funded study is analyzing enrollment dynamics in the Medicaid, SSI, and SSDI programs, with special attention to participation patterns of beneficiaries in states where Medicaid enrollment is not automatic for SSI recipients.

These studies are just the tip of the iceberg of research that will take advantage of 1) the existence of well-developed longitudinal analytic extracts for SSA programs (TRF) and CMS programs (Medicare RIF and MAX) and 2) the interagency-sharing agreement. The infrastructure that these two agencies have developed makes it feasible for them to support longitudinal research involving participants in SSDI, SSI, Medicare, and Medicaid.

SSA and RSA have a similar interagency agreement to support projects that require matched SSA and RSA administrative data. SSA's TTW evaluation has used RSA 911 data matched to the TRF to study the extent to which VR agencies are obtaining ticket assignments from their SSDI and SSI clients and to study the impact of TTW on service enrollment.

The GAO used SSA TRF records matched to Social Security earnings records and RSA 911 records to examine the earnings of SSDI and SSI clients of state VR agencies in the year after VR closure (GAO 2007). This appears to be the first published analysis of post-closure VR client earnings based on administrative records. Among other things, the GAO used the data to produce state-level earnings statistics, examine the sensitivity of earnings outcomes to the state's economic environment, and identify VR practices that appear to increase client earnings. The Office of Special Education and Rehabilitative Services in the Department of Education is currently using the data to examine long-term employment and benefit outcomes of transition-age youth receiving VR services. Westat, Inc. is matching these data to survey data from the RSA-sponsored Post Vocational Rehabilitation Experiences Study for data validation purposes.

Matches between Survey and Administrative Data

One important way to address limitations on program participation data in surveys is to match survey data records to administrative records. Such matches can also add important longitudinal information to a cross-sectional survey, potentially including the entire history of participation in a program and, in some cases, earnings. The matched data can also be used to study the reliability of the survey data. Survey–administrative data matches also make it possible to learn much more about the characteristics and activities of program participants that cannot be learned from administrative data alone—because information in the administrative data is essentially limited to that which has an administrative purpose.

Survey–administrative data matches require the consent of the survey respondents as well as common identifiers in the files to be matched. Confidentiality rules also limit researcher access to matched data.

SSA and the Census Bureau have matched numerous years of data from both the CPS and the SIPP to SSA administrative records (including IRS earnings records) and, in some years, to CMS Medicare records.[33] These data have been used extensively to study the characteristics and behavior of people with disabilities, as well as other populations.

A few examples from the substantial disability literature illustrate the value of the matched SIPP and CPS data to disability research. Lahiri et al. (1995) used the matched SIPP data to study how characteristics of program applicants affect outcomes at each stage of SSA's disability determination process. Stapleton et al. (2001–2002) used the matched SIPP data to study the transition of participants in the Aid to Families with Dependent Children program onto SSI in the early 1990s, just prior to welfare reform. Davies et al. (2001–2002) developed a model of financial eligibility for SSI that SSA uses to simulate how changes to the SSI means test would affect program participation and expenditure. Bound, Burkhauser, and Nichols (2003) used the data to track the incomes of working-age SSI and SSDI applicants. Honeycut (2004) used both the matched SIPP data and the matched CPS data to study the participation of SSDI awardees in other public and private support programs prior to the SSDI award.

Researchers must obtain Census Special Sworn Status to use the matched SIPP and SSA data, have their specific project approved by the Census Bureau and the relevant agencies, and access the data through the restricted-access data facilities operated by the Census Bureau. These requirements substantially limit the use of the matched data. To address this limitation, yet continue to meet confidentiality requirements, the Census Bureau has recently developed a "synthetic" SIPP file, which is available to researchers without substantial restriction.[34] The individual records in this file do not correspond to real people. Instead, they were generated in a fashion that makes statistics produced from the file match the statistics that would be produced from the original data. The current file is based on the SIPP panels from 1990 through 1996 and the matched SSA and IRS data.

The SIPP data should continue to be an important source of information on disability in future years, and the Census Bureau is trying to improve their data collection efforts to address concerns regarding attrition, program accuracy, and timeliness. The Census is currently in the field with the 2004 SIPP, which is scheduled to continue through the first quarter of 2008, and is funded to conduct a 2008 SIPP panel, which will extend from February 2008 through January 2012. The data collection methods and content will generally be similar to earlier SIPP panels. The one notable exception, described in more detail below, is that the 2008 SIPP panel will use a different methodology for collecting personal information, which should increase the match rate between the SIPP and SSA administrative records. The Census Bureau is planning to reengineer the SIPP to be a more efficient and cost-effective data collection effort by 2011.[35] The reengineering process should result in better and more timely disability data. The Census Bureau plans to continue to collect the same set of detailed functional limitation information as in earlier panels, and the use of administrative data should enhance its ability to collect more accurate information on disability program outcomes.

The National Center for Health Statistics has an extensive program to match SSA, Medicare, and National Death Index administrative data to the surveys for which it is responsible, including the NHIS, the National Health and Examination Study, the Longitudinal Study on Aging, and the National Nursing Home Survey.[36] This is a relatively new effort, and disability research using these data is just starting to emerge. One example is Riley's (2006) use of the matched NHIS, SSA, and Medicare data to analyze the health insurance and access to care of SSDI beneficiaries during their 24-month waiting period from SSDI entitlement to Medicare entitlement.

HRS data have also been matched to SSA and Medicare administrative data,[37] and they can be used to study working-age people with disabilities over the age of 50, as well as Social Security retirees (Mitchell, Olson, and Steinmeier 2000). SSA has been collaborating with the Census to match SSA records with the ACS data (Obenski and Prevost 2004; Haines and Greenberg 2005). If successful, the match could support the production of a wide array of descriptive statistics on SSDI and SSI beneficiaries for states and metropolitan areas.

Matched survey and administrative data are limited by the accuracy and completeness of the matches. The match rate for the SIPP declined substantially after 1996, primarily because it required respondents to report their SSNs, and a larger and larger share of respondents refused. In 2004, 35 percent of the SIPP respondents refused to cooperate. Similarly, 38 percent of NHIS respondents in 1998 and 23 percent of CPS respondents in 2003 refused to cooperate.[38] Starting in 2006, the Census adopted a methodology that substantially increases the match rate. The interviewer no longer asks for permission to use the respondent's SSN and instead offers the respondent an opt-out postcard that can be mailed in to prevent the match. The match is now made on the basis of name, sex, birth date, and address information. Algorithms are used to identify highly probable matches, and much higher match rates are being achieved. Informed consent requirements prevent the Census Bureau from applying the same methods to the earlier surveys.

CONCLUSION

There is an abundance of administrative and survey data available about working-age people with disabilities who participate in the federal and federal-state programs servicing this population. Despite some significant limitations, these data provide important information about participants in these programs, even at the state level, and have proved to be a rich source for research on the dynamics of disability and program participation. Furthermore, current efforts to improve the quality of these data, primarily through matches between survey and administrative data and between administrative data from different agencies, are already yielding significant dividends. It is very important to maintain the momentum of these efforts.

We are especially encouraged by recent efforts to match administrative data to survey data. It is apparent from historical experience that such matches are the only cost-effective way to obtain high quality participation and benefit information in survey data, as well as extensive socioeconomic information about program participants. The effort to match survey and administrative data has been expanded considerably in recent years, and it is greatly improving the availability of data and statistics on disability program participants. The decline in the match rate after the early 1990s threatened the value of the match effort, but recent efforts by the Census appear to have addressed that threat. We are encouraged by the early Census-SSA effort to match ACS data with SSA records. Among other things, that match would make it possible to generate extensive, reliable information about the characteristics of program participants at the state level.

As discussed in this chapter, state-level program statistics are extremely important for tracking the status of people with disabilities and understanding the consequences of changes in state policy and economic environments. The agencies produce substantial state-level statistics, but we recommend that the agencies consider routine publication of more such statistics, individually or, better, collaboratively—taking advantage of their matched data files. Statistics broken down by characteristics such as age, sex, and impairment would be helpful because the effects of various aspects of the state environment might be quite different for various beneficiary groups. To some extent, program statistics for such subgroups can be matched to subgroup population estimates from the ACS. Thus, for instance, it would be possible to produce state-level participation ratios, like those presented in this chapter, by age and sex. It would be interesting to know the extent to which the reported cross-state variation in participation ratios can be explained by variation in the demographic composition of those who self-report disabilities in the ACS and how much cross-state variation remains within the demographic groups.

Age-specific estimates would be particularly helpful for working-age Medicaid enrollees with disabilities because current statistics include some children. More extensive state-level statistics on employment, earnings, and use of SSA work incentive programs would also be of considerable value, especially for SSDI beneficiaries, because such statistics are already produced for SSI recipients. Statistics on participation in multiple programs could potentially be generated from data that have been matched across agencies.

Existing administrative data would have much greater value for the production of information on people with disabilities if they were more accessible to those who have the resources and capabilities to produce such information outside the agencies. As we have discussed, however, providing access to researchers in a manner that protects individual privacy is a very challenging and costly task, so it should be no surprise that access is more limited than many outside the agencies would like.

The long-term CMS effort to make Medicare data available to researchers is a model that other agencies might do well to follow. The value of the health research that has been conducted with these data is enormous, and the fact that CMS has sustained the program over many years has made it a resource that health researchers have come to rely on. The CMS investment places a considerable direct burden on the agency's budget, but its value to the programs and the people they serve is undoubtedly much greater. Researchers and analysts outside the agency use the data extensively to produce information that helps guide both public health policy and the administration of Medicare, Medicaid, and other programs.

Other agencies would also do well to examine the model that the CMS Medicare Current Beneficiary Survey provides for the collection of data on program participants. The SSA, DVA, and RSA have all invested heavily in special purpose research, but they do not have continuous efforts to survey their programs' participants. A continuous effort would help the agencies and others monitor the well-being of program participants and provide data that can support the design and evaluation of programmatic changes, and it would reduce the need for special-purpose surveys.

Program participation information is critical for monitoring the status of people with disabilities and for supporting the development of better programs and policies. The considerable value of the currently available program participation data and statistics is being significantly increased by current data improvement efforts. Although cost will always be a limiting factor, the value of these data improvement efforts is extremely high, and we would encourage their continuation and expansion.

Appendix 9A

Table 9A.1 Population and Program Data for the Working-Age Population (Aged 18–64) with Disabilities in 2005, by State

State	Working-age population[b]	People with disabilities[c]	SSDI[d]	SSI[e]	SSDI or SSI[f]	Medicare[g]	Medicaid[h]	Medicare or Medicaid[i]	Veterans with disabilities[j]	Veterans' Comp. beneficiaries[k]	Veterans' Pension beneficiaries[k]	VR closures[l]
Total[a]	180,308,000	22,229,000	6,838,148	4,016,727	9,688,845	5,809,035	6,821,880	10,973,000	2,652,413	1,611,699	138,382	609,502
Alabama	2,784,000	490,000	179,203	98,836	245,804	155,136	151,341	270,000	61,403	37,751	2,871	13,628
Alaska	428,000	62,000	10,006	6,683	14,967	8,667	11,738	18,000	8,146	9,568	237	1,592
Arizona	3,508,000	414,000	124,731	55,295	165,051	102,199	93,718	185,000	58,485	36,809	2,435	6,921
Arkansas	1,665,000	308,000	108,717	51,675	142,324	92,293	85,351	135,000	45,266	20,559	2,352	6,946
California	21,876,000	2,297,000	594,961	578,944	993,472	510,432	803,317	1,132,000	220,986	135,053	11,580	40,591
Colorado	2,929,000	290,000	75,221	33,981	98,185	64,393	68,138	115,000	44,919	35,414	1,742	7,117
Connecticut	2,122,000	208,000	71,701	32,748	95,729	59,725	54,912	96,000	20,586	10,135	676	3,496
Delaware	521,000	62,000	21,505	7,947	26,899	17,275	16,116	30,000	7,200	5,048	253	2,341
District of Columbia	327,000	36,000	10,780	12,304	20,880	9,382	22,912	29,000	3,378	2,467	394	2,493
Florida	10,419,000	1,292,000	415,927	197,811	555,720	362,727	387,504	659,000	174,621	121,744	9,301	34,099
Georgia	5,656,000	707,000	210,245	116,203	292,053	187,038	225,074	360,000	89,396	67,011	4,879	13,375
Hawaii	779,000	74,000	20,032	12,293	29,314	16,913	22,040	34,000	7,926	8,884	432	1,949
Idaho	874,000	118,000	30,096	14,191	39,513	25,907	25,718	49,000	18,795	10,326	567	5,607
Illinois	7,730,000	773,000	246,120	155,020	368,999	208,717	229,506	397,000	79,538	36,564	4,674	19,054
Indiana	3,746,000	502,000	153,188	63,861	197,120	127,811	116,936	211,000	69,349	28,904	2,203	18,369
Iowa	1,786,000	200,000	65,071	28,977	83,291	55,111	58,941	94,000	27,585	11,841	1,349	8,009
Kansas	1,658,000	194,000	57,108	25,130	73,528	48,575	49,954	85,000	24,019	15,222	1,390	5,619
Kentucky	2,597,000	496,000	173,362	118,946	259,745	149,750	174,214	283,000	55,993	26,059	2,820	13,973
Louisiana	2,748,000	437,000	131,908	100,522	206,831	117,490	156,994	241,000	45,522	24,054	3,685	7,098
Maine	834,000	126,000	48,817	22,885	63,243	41,118	44,399	77,000	20,303	12,275	1,195	3,182
Maryland	3,451,000	352,000	97,238	53,781	137,802	80,180	106,129	167,000	38,518	32,594	1,727	9,169

Massachusetts	3,952,000	415,000	163,210	104,301	234,641	133,968	213,190	283,000	39,694	25,440	1,790	11,106
Michigan	6,192,000	805,000	263,081	146,604	368,601	221,416	247,762	415,000	100,153	37,828	4,811	19,655
Minnesota	3,179,000	302,000	96,494	44,793	127,624	79,181	90,466	142,000	38,043	25,376	1,623	11,483
Mississippi	1,747,000	318,000	116,304	71,253	165,166	104,190	132,145	196,000	33,194	16,646	1,874	9,042
Missouri	3,530,000	526,000	171,034	76,973	222,604	141,971	156,274	250,000	68,251	31,285	3,431	16,253
Montana	580,000	76,000	21,959	10,224	28,711	19,343	15,570	31,000	12,483	8,513	779	3,344
Nebraska	1,054,000	118,000	35,408	14,864	44,618	29,678	28,032	48,000	14,336	10,301	884	4,811
Nevada	1,490,000	143,000	46,655	17,909	59,494	37,761	30,821	64,000	23,177	16,786	1,548	3,339
New Hampshire	826,000	95,000	33,713	9,502	39,662	24,720	16,139	39,000	12,760	9,002	354	3,095
New Jersey	5,261,000	484,000	167,528	78,665	224,064	138,993	133,589	246,000	41,207	23,555	1,238	13,194
New Mexico	1,170,000	172,000	46,438	29,461	67,367	39,138	41,464	73,000	27,350	16,606	1,360	5,578
New York	11,741,000	1,315,000	444,862	334,873	693,966	369,614	512,907	794,000	112,574	54,019	6,487	44,609
North Carolina	5,268,000	748,000	264,082	110,939	336,720	230,624	220,475	380,000	88,191	67,949	3,738	32,319
North Dakota	393,000	42,000	12,365	5,135	15,437	10,374	8,925	16,000	5,650	4,652	354	2,571
Ohio	6,970,000	941,000	268,629	167,931	394,134	226,908	267,876	447,000	114,099	50,846	8,087	26,947
Oklahoma	2,149,000	361,000	94,842	48,675	129,397	81,762	74,957	134,000	51,120	32,465	3,669	11,727
Oregon	2,271,000	302,000	79,133	38,446	105,422	67,076	65,680	109,000	48,905	24,519	2,919	9,112
Pennsylvania	7,413,000	934,000	317,000	199,599	464,476	256,267	374,221	559,000	121,565	48,031	5,895	26,800
Rhode Island	645,000	80,000	31,016	18,549	43,331	24,112	33,765	52,000	9,440	4,997	399	1,946
South Carolina	2,588,000	396,000	140,239	61,520	182,350	123,278	116,118	206,000	53,706	33,757	2,610	17,967
South Dakota	461,000	53,000	15,801	7,495	20,488	13,427	13,378	23,000	6,728	6,316	572	2,826
Tennessee	3,739,000	617,000	195,240	101,866	265,932	172,349	261,718	331,000	69,930	39,154	3,858	9,814
Texas	13,832,000	1,646,000	397,752	238,539	570,348	341,079	344,751	591,000	192,114	149,377	12,265	45,444
Utah	1,490,000	155,000	30,686	13,999	40,473	26,524	27,305	49,000	16,092	9,327	580	9,065

(continued)

Table 9A.1 (continued)

State	Working-age population[b]	People with disabilities[c]	SSDI[d]	SSI[e]	SSDI or SSI[f]	Medicare[g]	Medicaid[h]	Medicare or Medicaid[i]	Veterans with disabilities[j]	Veterans' Comp. beneficiaries[k]	Veterans' Pension beneficiaries[k]	VR closures[l]
Vermont	400,000	52,000	16,956	8,831	22,155	14,185	17,316	25,000	5,129	3,218	252	3,544
Virginia	4,667,000	518,000	175,800	77,710	229,048	147,725	122,048	239,000	66,865	71,325	2,638	10,239
Washington	3,978,000	537,000	127,988	72,661	181,501	107,990	143,532	219,000	79,722	57,704	2,850	8,444
West Virginia	1,129,000	236,000	87,721	55,304	129,408	77,240	86,804	148,000	31,899	13,538	2,093	6,151
Wisconsin	3,429,000	360,000	120,189	58,128	158,599	98,679	111,639	182,000	46,063	26,780	2,406	12,576
Wyoming	326,000	44,000	10,086	3,945	12,638	8,624	8,064	15,000	7,028	4,105	257	1,873

[a] Total does not include U.S. territories.

[b] Estimates for 2005 are based on the ACS. http://www.disabilitystatistics.org (accessed August 3, 2007).

[c] Estimates for 2005 are based on the ACS, from http://www.disabilitystatistics.org (accessed August 3, 2007).

[d] SSDI estimates for December 2004 from http://www.socialsecurity.gov/policy/docs/statcomps/di_asr/2004/sect01.html#table8 (accessed August 3, 2007).

[e] SSI estimates for December 2004 from http://www.socialsecurity.gov/policy/docs/statcomps/ssi_asr/2004/sect02.html#table9 (accessed August 3, 2007).

[f] Calculated by adding SSDI and SSI, then subtracting concurrent beneficiaries. Concurrent beneficiary data for December 2004 from http://www.socialsecurity.gov/policy/docs/statcomps/ssi_asr/2004/sect04.html#table18 (accessed August 3, 2007).

[g] Medicare enrollees with disabilities (SSDI beneficiaries plus a relatively small number with end stage renal disease). July 2005 estimates from http://www.cms.hhs.gov/MedicareEnRpts/Downloads/05Disabled.pdf (accessed August 8, 2007).

[h] Medicaid enrollees with disabilities, FY 2004. Original source: the State Health Facts Web site. Medicaid Enrollment from http://www.statehealthfacts.org/comparetable.jsp?ind=198&cat=4&typ=27&yr=27&typ=1&sort=a&o=a. Medicaid Distribution by Enrollment Category from http://www.statehealthfacts.org/comparetable.jsp?ind=200&cat=4&yr=27&typ=2. Medicaid enrollment was multiplied by the percent in the disability category to obtain the numbers reported. Some states appear to include some Medicaid enrollees under the age of 18 in this category, but the number of such enrollees is not reported. Both accessed August 8, 2007.

[i] Calculated as the number enrolled in Medicare plus the number enrolled in Medicaid minus the estimated number of Medicaid beneficiaries with dual entitlement to Medicaid. The latter was estimated as the number of working-age people on Medicaid (previous column) times

the percentage of dual eligible beneficiaries in the Medicaid disability category from State Health Facts (see footnote h).

[j] Veterans with disabilities living in the household population in 2005, estimated from the 2005 ACS.

[k] Veterans' Compensation data were only available for veterans under age 75, and pension data were only available for those under age 70. For each, we estimated the number under age 65 by multiplying the value reported by the ratio of veterans under age 65 to veterans in the age range for the reported statistic. Veterans' Compensation and Pension data for FY 2005 from http://www.vba.va.gov/bln/dmo/reports/fy2005/2005_abr.pdf (acessed August 3, 2007). Veterans as of September 30, 2005 are from http://www1.va.gov/vetdata/docs/11.xls (accessed August 3, 2007).

[l] VR closures for FY 2005 from Monitoring Tables—113 and 2—2005, available at http://rsamis.ed.gov/choose.cfm?menu=spreadsheets (accessed January 15, 2008). Closures for the approximately 3 percent of clients under age 18 or over age 64 are included because we have not found published state statistics by age.

Notes

1. In this chapter we define the working-age population as persons aged 18–64. We use a broader age range than in the other chapters because most published administrative statistics for program participants use this range.
2. Goodman and Stapleton (2007) found that federal expenditures to support working-age people with disabilities totaled $226 billion in 2002, or 11.3 percent of all federal outlays, up from 6.1 percent in 1984.
3. SSI also provides income support to children with disabilities and to people age 65 or older in low-income households. See SSA's Annual Statistical Supplement to the Social Security Bulletin for details (SSA 2007a).
4. The SSI employment and earnings statistics appear in the annual report SSI Disabled Recipients Who Work. http://www.ssa.gov/policy/docs/statcomps/ssi_workers/2004/index.html#toc (accessed October 4, 2007). The most recent data are for 2004.
5. Whereas contractors for SSA with appropriate security clearances can access SSA programmatic data, only SSA employees with appropriate clearances can access the IRS earnings data.
6. See SSA's Performance and Accountability Report for FY2006 (SSA 2007b).
7. The statistic for SSI includes both children and working-age adults with disabilities, which are not reported separately; it does not include aged claimants (SSA 2007a).
8. See, for example, Burkhauser, Butler, and Weathers (2002) and Burkhauser, Butler, and Gumus (2004).
9. See Parsons (1991) and Stapleton et al. (1998).
10. See Table 4.B10 in the 2006 Supplement (SSA 2007a).
11. Some benefit discrepancies are caused by benefit adjustments, but most are due to respondent reporting error (Sears and Rupp 2003).
12. A related survey, the Ticket Participant Survey, collects data on participants in Ticket to Work, and subsamples of participant respondents are being followed for two or three years. SSA plans to release public-use files from the NBS in the near future. Statistics from the survey appear in Thornton et al. (2006, 2007) and in several articles in a special issue of the *Journal of Vocational Rehabilitation* 27(2), 2007.
13. The data contain extensive information on demographics, employment, health, income, medical expenditures, and functional capacity. Administrative data have been added to the survey data. SSA makes the data available to researchers through a set of public-use files, the New Beneficiary Data System, available at http://www.socialsecurity.gov/policy/docs/microdata/nbds/index.html (accessed August 1, 2007).
14. The 24-month Medicare waiting period is waived for beneficiaries with amyotrophic lateral sclerosis ("Lou Gehrig's disease").
15. See Centers for Medicare and Medicaid Services (n.d.a)

16. See Centers for Medicare and Medicaid Services (n.d.b). See Gimm et al. (2008) for information on the Medicaid Buy-in program.
17. See Research Data Assistance Center (n.d.c).
18. An informative discussion of the history of survey measurement of health insurance appears in Nelson and Mills (2001).
19. The data are provided by the CMS-funded Research Data Assistance Center. See Research Data Assistance Center (n.d.b).
20. The public-use files are available from Employment and Disabilities Institute (n.d.).
21. The Veterans Benefits Administration is responsible for the administration of all the benefit programs other than health. Descriptions of their programs can be found in Veterans Benefits Administration (2006). The Veterans' Health Administration administers VHC. See Veterans Health Administration (n.d.).
22. See Sengupta, Reno, and Burton (2007) and Sengupta and Reno (2007).
23. These statistics were designed to omit lump-sum payments, although some survey respondents might have misreported them during the survey year as annual income.
24. This project was initially called the Disability Examination Study and then renamed the National Study of Health and Activities. See Wunderlich, Rice, and Amado (2002) for discussion of the plans for this survey.
25. The population and participation counts underlying these statistics are provided in Appendix 9A.
26. The original state enrollment tabulations have four mutually exclusive categories: "children" (under age 19), "adults" (aged 19–64), "elderly" (age 65+), and "disabled" (under age 65). Unfortunately, the "disabled" category includes some children as well as adults. We subtracted the number of SSI children in the state to obtain an estimate for adults only. Also, the "adult" age range in the administrative statistics (aged 19–64) does not exactly coincide with the more conventional age range we have adopted for the "working-age" population (aged 18–64).
27. The medical eligibility criteria for SSDI and SSI are the same among states; the financial criteria differ.
28. These challenges were heightened after the theft of data on more than 25 million veterans from a government analyst's home in 2006. See the testimony of then-Secretary of Veterans Affairs R. James Nicholson before the House Veterans' Affairs Committee, June 29, 2006 (Nicholson 2006).
29. Employment Networks are the provider entities servicing beneficiaries under Ticket to Work; they include state VR agencies as well as many private providers.
30. Vol. 27, No. 2, 2007.
31. See Research Data Assistance Center (n.d.a).
32. Claims and enrollment data in the MAX files reflect final adjustments; claim dates in MAX reflect date of service, rather than date of filing or payment; and Medicare enrollment information for dual eligible beneficiaries has been added from the CMS Medicare enrollment data. See Wenzlow et al. (2007).

33. A history of this effort appears in Haines and Greenberg (2005). SSA data have been matched to March CPS data for 1991, 1994, and 1996 through 2006.
34. See U.S. Census Bureau (n.d.).
35. The four goals of the reengineering effort include 1) a reduction in data collection costs, 2) improved accuracy in collection of data elements, 3) timeliness in file production, and 4) relevance to policy research. To achieve these goals, the Census plans to use an annual data collection to reduce the number of interviews (currently being conducted quarterly), increase its efforts to reduce attrition rates and use administrative data to verify program data elements, improve their internal processing of data collection, and draw samples from the ACS.
36. Details can be found from National Center for Health Statistics (n.d.a).
37. Details can be found at http://hrsonline.isr.umich.edu/rda/ (accessed August 23, 2007).
38. Bates (2005) reported that the refusal rate for the SIPP increased from 12 percent in 1996 to 35 percent in 2004 and that the refusal rate for the CPS increased from 10 percent in 1994 to 23 percent in 2003. The NHIS refusal rate increased from 19 percent in 1994 to 38 percent in 1998. See National Center for Health Statistics (n.d.b).

References

Ballou, Janice, and Jason Markesich. 2009. "Survey Data Collection Methods." In *Counting Working-Age People with Disabilities: What Current Data Tell Us and Options for Improvement*, Andrew J. Houtenville, David C. Stapleton, Robert R. Weathers II, and Richard V. Burkhauser, eds. Kalamazoo, MI: W.E. Upjohn Institute for Employment Research, pp. 265–298.

Bates, Nancy. 2005. "Development and Testing of Informed Consent Questions to Link Survey Data with Administrative Records." Washington, DC: U.S. Census Bureau.

Bound, John, Richard V. Burkhauser, and Austin Nichols. 2003. "Tracking the Household Income of SSDI and SSI Applicants." In *Research in Labor Economics*, vol. 22, Soloman W. Polachek, ed. Amsterdam, London, and New York: Elsevier Science, JAI, pp. 113–158.

Burkhauser, Richard V., J. S. Butler, and Gulcin Gumus. 2004. "A Dynamic Programming Model of Social Security Disability Insurance Application." *Journal of Applied Econometrics* 19(6): 671–685.

Burkhauser, Richard V., J. S. Butler, and Robert R. Weathers II. 2002. "How Policy Variables Influence the Timing of Social Security Disability Insurance Application." *Social Security Bulletin* 64(1): 52–83.

Centers for Medicare and Medicaid Services (CMS). 2005. "Medicare Enrollment Reports." Baltimore, MD: Centers for Medicare and Medicaid

Services. http://www.cms.hhs.gov/MedicareEnrpts/ (accessed August 24, 2007).

―――. 2007a. "Medicare and Medicaid Statistical Supplement." Baltimore, MD: Centers for Medicare and Medicaid Services. http://www.cms.hhs.gov/MedicareMedicaidStatSupp/ (accessed August 24, 2007).

―――. 2007b. "National Health Expenditure Data." Baltimore, MD: Centers for Medicare and Medicaid Services. http://www.cms.hhs.gov/NationalHealthExpendData/ (accessed August 24, 2007).

―――. n.d.a. "Medicare Program—General Information." Baltimore, MD: Centers for Medicare and Medicaid Services. http://www.cms.hhs.gov/MedicareGenInfo (accessed August 1, 2007).

―――. n.d.b. "Medicaid Program—General Information." Baltimore, MD: Centers for Medicare and Medicaid Services. http://www.cms.hhs.gov/MedicaidGenInfo (accessed August 1, 2007).

Coder, John, and Lydia S. Scoon-Rogers. 1996. "Evaluating the Quality of Income Data Collection in the Annual Supplement to the March Current Population Survey and the Survey of Income and Program Participation." SIPP Working Paper no. 9604. Washington, DC: U.S. Census Bureau. http://www.sipp.census.gov/sipp/wp215.pdf (accessed October 10, 2007).

Davies, Paul S., Minh Huynh, Chad Newcomb, Paul O'Leary, Kalman Rupp, and James Sears. 2001–2002. "Modeling SSI Financial Eligibility and Simulating the Effect of Policy Options." *Social Security Bulletin* 64(4): 16–45.

Employment and Disabilities Institute. n.d. "Longitudinal Study of the Vocational Rehabilitation Services Program." Ithica, NY: Cornell University, School of Labor and Industrial Relations. http://www.ilr.cornell.edu/edi/lsvrsp (accessed August 7, 2007).

Gimm, Gilbert, Sarah R. Davis, Kristin L. Andrews, Henry T. Ireys, and Su Liu. 2008. "The Three E's: Enrollment, Employment, and Earnings in the Medicaid Buy-In Program, 2006." Washington, DC: Mathematica Policy Research.

Goodman, Nanette J., and David C. Stapleton. 2007. "Federal Program Expenditures for Working-Age People with Disabilities." *Journal of Disability Policy Studies* 18(2): 66–79.

Government Accountability Office. 2007. "Vocational Rehabilitation: Improved Information and Practices Enhance State Agency Earnings Outcomes for SSA Beneficiaries." Report to Congressional Requesters. GAO-07-521. Washington, DC: Government Accountability Office. http://www.gao.gov/new.items/d07521.pdf (accessed June 19, 2008).

Haines, Dawn E., and Brian V. Greenberg. 2005. "Statistical Uses of Social Security Administrative Data." *Proceedings of the Survey Research Meth-

ods Section, American Statistical Association. Alexandria, VA: American Statistical Association. http://www.amstat.org/sections/srms/Proceedings/y2005/Files/JSM2005-000255.pdf (accessed June 19, 2008).

Hildebrand, Leslie, Miriam Loewenberg, Dawn Phelps, Natalie Justh, and Joel Smith. 2007. "Data Dictionary, TRF.06." Washington, DC: Mathematica Policy Research.

Honneycut, Todd. 2004. "Program and Benefit Paths to the Social Security Disability Insurance Program." *Journal of Vocational Rehabilitation* 21(2): 83–94.

Huynh, Minh, Kalman Rupp, and Jim Sears. 2002. "The Assessment of Survey of Income and Program Participation Benefit Data Using Longitudinal Administrative Records." Survey of Income and Program Participation Report no. 238. Washington, DC: U.S. Census Bureau.

Institute for Social Research. n.d. "The Health and Retirement Study: A Longitudinal Study of Health, Retirement, and Aging Sponsored by the National Institute on Aging." Ann Arbor, MI: University of Michigan, Institute for Social Research. http://hronline.isr.umich.edu/rda (accessed August 23, 2007).

Lahiri, Kajal, Dennis R. Vaughn, and Bernard Wixon. 1995. "Modeling SSA's Sequential Disability Determination Process Using Matched SIPP Data." *Social Security Bulletin* 58(4): 3–42.

Liu, Su, Henry T. Ireys, and Craig Thornton. 2008. Participants in the Medicaid Buy-In Program, 2000–2004: Characteristics, Earnings, and Medical Expenditures. *Journal of Disability Policy Studies* 19(2): 95–102.

Mitchell, Olivia S., Jan Olson, and Thomas Steinmeier. 2000. "Creation of the Earnings and Benefits File for Use with the Health and Retirement Survey." In *Forecasting Retirement Needs and Retirement Wealth,* Olivia S. Mitchell, P. Brett Hammond, and Anna A. Rappaport, eds. Philadelphia: University of Pennsylvania Press, pp. 327–360.

National Center for Health Statistics. n.d.a. "NCHS Data Linkage Activities." Hyattsville, MD: National Center for Health Statistics. http://www.cdc.gov/hchs/red/nchs_datalinkage/data_linkage_activities.htm (accessed August 23, 2007).

———. n.d.b. "NCHS Data Linkage Activities—Tables." Hyattsville, MD: National Center for Health Statistics. http://www.cdc.gov/nchs/data/datalinkage/linkage_rate_tables.pdf (accessed August 23, 2007).

Nelson, Charles T., and Robert J. Mills. 2001. "The March CPS Health Insurance Verification Question and Its Effect on Estimates of the Uninsured." Revised December 7, 2004. Washington, DC: U.S. Census Bureau, Housing and Household Economic Statistics Division. http://www.census.gov/hhes/www/hlthins/verif.html (accessed August 1, 2007).

Nicholson, R. James. 2006. "Testimony to the House Veterans' Affairs Committee, June 29." Washington, DC: U.S. Department of Veterans Affairs. http://www.va.gov/OCA/testimony/hvac/06062900.asp (accessed October 8, 2007).

Obenski, Sally, and Ron Prevost. 2004. "A Policy Application: Using Administrative Records to Supplement Census Bureau Programs." In *Proceedings of the Government Statistics Section of the American Statistical Association.* Alexandria, VA: American Statistical Association.

Olson, Anya. 2005–2006. "Military Veterans and Social Security." *Social Security Bulletin* 66(2): 1–6.

Parsons, Donald O. 1991. "Self-Screening in Targeted Public Transfer Programs." *Journal of Political Economy* 99(4): 859–876.

Research Data Assistance Center. n.d.a. "Chronic Condition Data Warehouse (CCW) Data Available." Minneapolis, MN: University of Minnesota, Research Data Assistance Center. http://www.resdac.umn.edu/CCW/data_available.asp (accessed October 3, 2007).

———. n.d.b. "MCBS Data Available." Minneapolis, MN: University of Minnesota, Research Data Assistance Center. http://www.resdac.umn.edu/MCBS/data_available.asp (accessed August 7, 2007).

———. n.d.c. "Medicare Data Available." Minneapolis, MN: University of Minnesota, Research Data Assistance Center. http://www.resdac.umn.edu/MCBS/data_available.asp (accessed August 7, 2007).

Riley, Gerald. 2006. "Health Insurance and Access to Care Among Social Security Disability Beneficiaries During the Medicare Waiting Period." *Inquiry* 43(3): 222–230.

Rupp, Kalman, Paul S. Davies, and Alexander Strand. 2008. "Disability Benefit Coverage and Program Interactions in the Working-Age Population." *Social Security Bulletin.* 68(1): 1–30.

Sears, James, and Kalman Rupp. 2003. "Exploring Social Security Payment History Matched with the Survey of Income and Program Participation." Paper presented at the Research Conference of the Federal Committee on Statistical Methodology, held in Arlington, VA, November 17–19. http://www.fcsm.gov/03papers/SearsRupp.pdf (accessed October 10, 2007).

Sengupta, Ishita, and Virginia Reno. 2007. "Recent Trends in Workers Compensation." *Social Security Bulletin* 67(1): 17–26.

Sengupta, Ishita, Virginia Reno, and John F. Burton Jr. 2007. "Workers Compensation: Benefits, Coverage and Costs, 2005." Washington, DC: National Academy of Social Insurance. http://www.nasi.org/usr_doc/NASI_Workers_Comp_2005_Full_Report.pdf (accessed June 20, 2008).

She, Peiyun, and David C. Stapleton. 2009. "The Group Quarters Population." In *Counting Working-Age People with Disabilities: What Current Data*

Tell Us and Options for Improvement, Andrew J. Houtenville, David C. Stapleton, Robert R. Weathers II, and Richard V. Burkhauser, eds. Kalamazoo, MI: W.E. Upjohn Institute for Employment Research, pp. 353–380.

Social Security Administration (SSA). 1997. "New Beneficiary Data Systems (NBDS)." Baltimore, MD: Social Security Administration. http://www .socialsecurity.gov/policy/docs/microdata/nbds/index.htm/ (accessed August 1, 2007).

———. 2005. "SSI Disabled Recipients Who Work, 2004." Baltimore, MD: Social Security Administration. http://www.ssa.gov/policy/docs/statcomps/ ssi_workers/2004/index.html#toc (accessed October 4, 2007).

———. 2007a. *Annual Statistical Supplement to the Social Security Bulletin, 2006.* Baltimore, MD: Social Security Administration. http://www .ssa.gov/policy/docs/statcomps/supplement/2006/supplement2006.pdf (accessed June 20, 2008).

———. 2007b. "SSA's Performance and Accountability Report for Fiscal Year (FY) 2007." Baltimore, MD: Social Security Administration. http://www .ssa.gov/finance/ (accessed October 4, 2007).

———. 2008. "Earnings and Employment Data for Workers Covered Under Social Security and Medicare, by State and County." Baltimore, MD: Social Security Administration. http://www.ssa.gov/policy/docs/statcomps/eedata_sc/ (accessed November 3, 2008).

Stapleton, David C., Kevin Coleman, Kimberly Dietrich, and Gina Livermore. 1998. "Empirical Analyses of DI and SSI Application and Award Growth." In *Growth in Disability Benefits: Explanations and Policy Implications*, Kalman Rupp and David C. Stapleton, eds. Kalamazoo, MI: W.E. Upjohn Institute for Employment Research, pp. 31–92.

Stapleton, David C., David C. Wittenburg, Michael E. Fishman, and Gina A. Livermore. 2001–2002. "Transitions from AFDC to SSI Prior to Welfare Reform." *Social Security Bulletin* 64(1): 84 –114.

Thornton, Craig, Thomas Fraker, Gina A. Livermore, David C. Stapleton, Bonnie O'Day, Timothy Silva, Emily S. Martin, John Kregel, and Debra Wright. 2006. "Evaluation of the Ticket to Work Program: Implementation Experience During the Second Two Years of Operations (2003–2004)." Washington, DC: Mathematica Policy Research.

Thornton, Craig, Gina A. Livermore, Thomas Fraker, David C. Stapleton, Bonnie O'Day, David C. Wittenburg, Robert Weathers, Nanette Goodman, Timothy Silva, Emily S. Martin, Jesse Gregory, Debra Wright, and Arif Mamun. 2007. "Evaluation of the Ticket-to-Work Program: Assessment of Post-Rollout Implementation and Early Impacts." Washington, DC: Mathematica Policy Research.

Thornton, Craig, Gina A. Livermore, David C. Stapleton, John Kregel, Bonnie

O'Day, Thomas Fraker, W. Grant Revell, Heather Schroeder, and Meredith Edwards. 2004. "Evaluation of the Ticket to Work Program: Initial Evaluation Report." Washington, DC: Mathematica Policy Research.

U.S. Census Bureau. n.d. "Survey of Income and Program Participation (SIPP)." Washington, DC: U.S. Census Bureau. http://sipp.census.gov/sipp/codebookSIPP_Synthetic_Beta_July92007.doc (accessed August 23, 2007).

U.S. Department of Veterans Affairs (USDVA). 2007. "Geographic Distribution of Expenditures." Washington, DC: U.S. Department of Veterans Affairs. http://www1.va.gov/vetdata/page.cfm?pg=3 (accessed July 24, 2007).

Veterans Benefits Administration. 2006. "Annual Benefits Report, Fiscal Year 2005." Washington, DC: Veterans Benefits Administration.

Veterans Health Administration. n.d. "Health Care—Veterans Health Administration. Washington, DC: U.S. Department of Veterans Affairs. http://www1.va.gov/health/index.asp (accessed August 1, 2007).

Weathers, Robert R. II. 2009. "The Disability Data Landscape." In *Counting Working-Age People with Disabilities: What Current Data Tell Us and Options for Improvement*, Andrew J. Houtenville, David C. Stapleton, Robert R. Weathers II, and Richard V. Burkhauser, eds. Kalamazoo, MI: W.E. Upjohn Institute for Employment Research, pp. 27–67.

Wenzlow, A. T., D. Finkelstein, B. L. Cook, K. Shepperson, C. Yip, and D. Baugh. 2007. *The Medicaid Analytic eXtract Chartbook.* Washington, DC: Centers for Medicare and Medicaid Services.

Wunderlich, Gooloo S., Dorothy P. Rice, and Nicole L. Amado, eds. 2002. *The Dynamics of Disability: Measuring and Monitoring Disability for Social Security Programs.* Washington, DC: National Academies Press.

10

The Group Quarters Population

Peiyun She
Cornell University

David C. Stapleton
Mathematica Policy Research, Inc.

Little is known about the disability status of residents of institutional group quarters (GQ), noninstitutional GQ, and the homeless population as compared to residents of households, especially for those of working age. The National Health Interview Survey (NHIS), the Survey of Income and Program Participation (SIPP), the Current Population Survey (CPS), and recently, the American Community Survey (ACS) are used by researchers and others to produce disability statistics for what is often termed the household population. At the time of writing, none of them included the GQ or homeless population. The ACS added the GQ population in 2006. Instead, research has relied on various surveys of populations in certain institutions such as nursing home residents, the incarcerated, and those obtaining services from homeless shelters. Some surveys, such as the National Long Term Care Survey (NLTCS) and the Medicare Current Beneficiary Survey (MCBS), gather nationally representative data for the elderly population, regardless of where they reside, but no comparable surveys are available for the working-age population or the child population.[1]

As of 2005, the U.S. Decennial Census long form was the only survey to collect disability data for the entire population, with the exception of some who are homeless.[2] Census 2000 was also the first Decennial Census to collect information on major disability types, making it an important source of information for documenting disability status for the population not living in households. These data, however, have not been adequately explored. The 2006 ACS data were not available for this study, but they will soon replace the Decennial Census as the most important data source for studying disability status for the entire population, including the nonhousehold population.

The very limited availability of comparable disability data for the nonhousehold population is problematic for at least three reasons. First, compared to people without disabilities, a much larger share of people with disabilities is in the nonhousehold population. This statement applies to the working-age population as well as the elderly and child populations. Second, variations in how household surveys sample, find, and interview individuals residing in noninstitutional GQ or homeless individuals might be a major source of variation in disability statistics across household surveys. Third, significant trends in the extent to which various groups live in GQ probably affect trends in the prevalence of disability in the household population, as well as the distributions of their demographic and socioeconomic characteristics.

The two most significant, documented trends in residence type are rapid increases in the share of the population, especially young men, residing in correctional facilities, and a slow decline in the share of the population residing in nursing homes (She and Stapleton 2006). These trends might affect statistics (e.g., the employment rate) for people with disabilities in the household population because those people with disabilities on the fringes of the household population might be quite different than those clearly within the household population. The extent of the effect will depend, to some degree, on the extent to which household surveys include people residing in noninstitutional GQ as well as homeless people. This issue is particularly important because of well-documented persistent declines in employment and household income for working-age people with disabilities in the household population (see Weathers and Wittenburg 2009; Burkhauser, Rovba, and Weathers 2009). It is also important because changes in public policy—most notably efforts to help people with disabilities move from institutional settings to community settings and tougher sentencing laws for certain types of crimes—have probably contributed to trends in disability statistics for both the nonhousehold and household populations. Without comparable data for all populations, it is difficult to evaluate how public policy changes such as these affect disability statistics.

In this chapter we describe the gap in knowledge about the disability status of the nonhousehold population and discuss the implications for disability statistics and research. We find that as of 2000, the incarcerated population has become the largest institutional population, surpassing the nursing home population, and that the increase in the institutional population between 1990 and 2000 occurred because incarceration rates for working-age people increased—mostly for young men, especially among those from minority groups. We also find that disability prevalence for the incarcerated population is about two to three times as high as that in the household working-age population.

These findings have important implications for disability research and data collection. They suggest that the prevalence of disability for young men in the household population should have declined relative to that for other groups, perhaps especially for those from minority groups. They also suggest that the change in prevalence might have had an impact on other statistics for young men with disabilities living in the noninstitutional population—including statistics on the nature of their health conditions, disabilities, employment rate, job characteristics, household income, and other characteristics, but given the current data, the direction of the effect is difficult to determine.

We first describe the main data sources available for the working-age institutional population and present estimates derived from these data sources, including the size and distribution of the institutional population; size, proportion, and characteristics of people with disabilities living in institutions; disability prevalence for people living in correctional institutions; and trends in incarceration rates.[3] We also summarize the extent to which existing surveys fill in the gaps left by household surveys with respect to disability statistics. We conclude with a discussion of the implications for data collection and research.

DATA

Census Data

Currently, the only data source on disability for the entire population—with the exception of some homeless people—is the Decennial Census. The 1990 and 2000 Census long-form questionnaires included disability questions. We focus on the 2000 survey because the disability questions are richer and because it gathers more information on social, economic, and housing characteristics of each individual. In the 2000 Census, a nationally representative sample of about one-sixth of the total population participated in the long-form survey. Several special questionnaires for this census were created for the GQ population—questions in the household unit forms were not adequate to capture data for households with substantial numbers of unrelated people. The long-form disability questions, however, are the same for the GQ population as for the household population (U.S. Census Bureau 2005).

The Census 2000 long-form data provide estimates for six domains of disability: sensory, physical, mental, self-care, going-outside-home, and employment.[4] The Census Bureau found evidence of misinterpretation of the questions related to two of these domains—going-outside-home and employment—by those who mailed in the long form (for detailed discussions, see Stern 2003; Stern and Brault 2005; U.S. Census Bureau 2004). The result is that an unknown number of respondents who were able to leave their home without assistance, or who were not limited in their ability to work, were mistakenly identified as having such limitations. For this reason, we do not include these disability domains in the statistics presented later in the chapter.[5]

The disability questions in Census 2000 are significantly different from those in Census 1990; the latter do not cover sensory, physical, and mental disabilities (U.S. Census Bureau 1992, 2001). These changes prevent us from directly measuring how disability prevalence and the characteristics of people with disabilities across the entire population, including the nonhousehold population, changed over the 10-year period.

Surveys for the Incarcerated Population

Disability data for the incarcerated population come from a series of surveys of prison and jail inmates, conducted periodically by the U.S. Census Bureau on behalf of the Bureau of Justice Statistics (BJS). These surveys consist of three separate, but related, surveys: one for jails (the Survey of Inmates of Local Jails, SILJ), a second for state prisons (the Survey of Inmates of State Correctional Facilities, SISCF), and a third for federal prisons (the Survey of Inmates of Federal Correctional Facilities, SIFCF). The jail surveys provide data on persons held in local jails, including those held prior to trial and convicted offenders serving sentences in local jails or awaiting transfer to prison. The two prison surveys provide data on persons held in state and federal prisons. Two-stage, stratified samples were drawn to obtain nationally representative data for each population. The SILJ was conducted in 1989, 1996, and 2002; the SISCF in 1991, 1997, and 2002; and the SIFCF in 1991, 1997, and 2004.

The surveys conducted in the 1996–1997 period were the first to collect detailed disability data, in which inmates were asked a series of questions related to work, sensory, physical, learning, and mental disabilities.[6] This series of questions supports disability prevalence estimates for inmates, although the accuracy of these estimates depends on the ability and willingness of inmates to report such problems. Inmate self-reported data may underestimate the prevalence of some conditions, especially those that require more sophisticated diagnoses or are more personal in nature. Conversely, it is also possible that inmates exaggerate their conditions.

The 2002–2004 jail and prison surveys included comparable questions about learning and sensory disabilities, but they also included new questions about use of a cane, wheelchair, walker, hearing aid, or other aids used for daily activity, as well as about self-perception of having a disability. Moreover, the surveys include a modified structured clinical interview for the symptoms of the *Diagnostic and Statistical Manual of Mental Disorders*, fourth edition (DSM-IV), which captures information on experiences in the past 12 months that would indicate symptoms of major depression, mania, or psychotic disorders. Detailed information and data contained in the 2002–2004 surveys have not yet been fully released for public use, but in the near future, it should be possible to examine the change in disability prevalence for inmates from 1996–1997 to 2002–2004.

RESULTS

The Group Quarters Population

According to the Census Bureau, all people not living in housing units are classified as living in GQ, but not all GQ are considered to be institutions (U.S. Census Bureau 2005). Institutional GQ include correctional institutions, nursing homes, and other institutions, many of which exclusively house people with disabilities (Table 10.1). Only those people living in these institutions under formally authorized, supervised care or custody at the time of the survey are included in the institutional population; staff residing in the same institutions are included in the noninstitutional population. All persons living in other GQ are also in the noninstitutional population (Table 10.1).

We first present estimates of the changes in the size of basic components of the institutional population based on data from the 1990 and 2000 Census (Table 10.2). The institutional population is a small share of the entire population, but it increased from 1.3 percent of the population in 1990 (3.3 million people) to 1.4 percent in 2000 (4.0 million people). The increase was not uniform across institutional types, however. Nursing home residents, the largest institutional population in 1990, decreased from 0.7 percent of the total population to 0.6 percent, while the incarcerated population increased from 0.5 percent to 0.7 percent, surpassing the nursing home population in size. Close to half of the institutional population resided in correctional institutions in 2000, compared to just one-third in 1990. Mirroring this change, nursing home residents dropped from more than half (53 percent) of the institutional population in 1990 to 42 percent in 2000. The population residing in institutions other than nursing homes and correctional institutions is comparatively small, and its size declined both absolutely and relative to the entire population from 1990 (0.2 percent of the population) to 2000 (0.1 percent).

The distribution of the institutional population across major institutional types varies greatly by age group (Table 10.3). In 2000, a large majority of the institutionalized working-age population (86 percent) resided in correctional institutions, and the remaining 14 percent were almost evenly split between nursing homes and other institutions. In contrast, 95 percent of the institutionalized elderly population resided

Table 10.1 Types of GQ, 2000 Census Definition

Type of GQ	Subcategory
Institutional GQ	
Correctional institutions	Prisons, federal detention centers, military disciplinary barracks and jails, local jails and other confinement facilities, halfway houses, and other types of correctional institutions.
Nursing homes	Skilled-nursing facilities, intermediate-care facilities, long-term care rooms in wards or buildings on the grounds of hospitals, or long-term care rooms/nursing wings in congregate housing facilities.
Other institutions	Mental (psychiatric) hospitals; hospitals or wards for people with chronic illnesses; residential schools, hospitals, or wards for people with mental retardation; residential schools, hospitals, or wards for the physically handicapped; hospitals and wards for drug/alcohol abuse treatment; wards in general hospitals for patients who have no usual home elsewhere; and juvenile institutions.
Noninstitutional GQ	
Group homes	Homes for people with mental illness or retardation, or halfway houses for drug/alcohol abuse treatment, and other group homes.
Other GQ	Religious group quarters, college quarters off campus, college dormitories, military quarters, agriculture workers' dormitories, other workers' dormitories, dormitories for nurses and interns in hospitals, and job corps and vocational training facilities.
	Emergency and transitional shelters, shelters for children who are runaways, neglected, or without conventional housing, shelters for abused women, soup kitchens, regularly scheduled mobile food vans, and targeted nonsheltered outdoor locations.
	Crews of maritime vessels, residential facilities providing protective oversight, staff residents of institutions, other nonhousehold living situations, and living quarters for victims of natural disasters.

SOURCE: U.S. Census Bureau (2005).

Table 10.2   Number, Distribution, and Institutionalization Rate by Type of Institution

Measure by year	All institutions	Nursing homes	Correctional institutions	Other institutions
2000 Census				
Number (000s)	4,059	1,721	1,976	363
% of Inst. pop.	100	42.4	48.7	8.9
% of Total pop.	1.4	0.6	0.7	0.1
1990 Census				
Number (000s)	3,334	1,772	1,115	447
% of Inst. pop.	100	53.2	33.4	13.4
% of Total pop.	1.3	0.7	0.5	0.2

SOURCE: Authors' calculations based on detailed tables (P1, P37, and P38) from 2000 Census Summary File 1 (SF 1) 100 Percent data and tables (P001, P015, and P028) from Census 1990 Summary Tape File 1 (STF 1) 100 Percent data.

in nursing homes, and 87 percent of institutionalized persons under age 18 resided in institutions other than nursing homes and correctional institutions.

Working-age people accounted for a much larger proportion of the institutional population in 2000 (56 percent) than in 1990 (46 percent). This change in the age distribution of the institutional population reflects the increase in the share of the incarcerated population and the decline in the share of nursing home residents, as is evident from substantial variation in the age distribution across institution types in 2000. Strikingly, the incarcerated population is predominantly nonelderly adults—98 percent are between the ages of 18 and 64. As expected, the nursing home population is largely elderly persons (90.5 percent are 65 and older); essentially all others (9.5 percent) are of working age. The age distribution for people residing in other institutions (as defined in Table 10.1) is less extreme—38 percent are under the age of 18, 44 percent are between 18 and 64 years old, and 19 percent are 65 and older. Correspondingly, the change in the percentage of the population that is institutionalized from 1990 to 2000 varies greatly by age. The rate of institutionalization increased from 1.0 percent in 1990 to 1.3 percent in 2000 for working-age people, whereas it decreased from 5.4 percent to 4.7 percent for the elderly and was essentially unchanged for those under the age of 18, at 0.2 percent.

Table 10.3 Number, Institutionalization Rate, and Distribution of People by Institutional Type and Age

Age and measure	2000				1990
	All institutions	Nursing homes	Correctional institutions	Other institutions	All institutions
Under 18					
Number (000s)	158	a	21	137	142
% of Inst. pop.	100.0	0.0	13.4	86.6	100.0
% of Age-group pop.	0.2	0.0	0.0	0.2	0.2
% of Pop. in inst. type	3.9	0.0	1.1	37.8	4.3
18–64					
Number (000s)	2,260	163	1,939	158	1,516
% of Inst. pop.	100.0	7.2	85.8	7.0	100.0
% of Age-group pop.	1.3	0.1	1.1	0.1	1.0
% of Pop. in inst. type	55.7	9.5	98.1	43.6	45.5
65 and over					
Number (000s)	1,641	1,558	16	67	1,676
% of Institutional pop.	100.0	94.9	1.0	4.1	100.0
% of Age-group pop.	4.7	4.5	0.1	0.2	5.4
% of Pop. in inst. type	40.4	90.5	0.8	18.6	50.3

a Less than 1,000.

SOURCE: Authors' calculations based on detailed tables (P12 and P38) from 2000 Census Summary File 1 (SF 1) 100 Percent data, and tables (P013 and P041) from 1990 Census Summary Tape File 3 (STF 3).

As described above, substantial changes in residential status occurred from 1990 to 2000, most notably the increased incarceration of working-age people. Because of the nature of these changes, it is very likely that there were substantial changes in both the share and composition of the working-age population with disabilities that resides in institutions, especially for some demographic subgroups. As mentioned earlier, however, the lack of disability data in the 1990 Census makes it impossible to examine such changes. Below we examine disability statistics for the institutional population from the Census 2000 data.

Residence Type and Disability Status

When disability is defined as having self-care, mental, physical, or sensory disabilities, 12 percent of the population have disabilities, including 11 percent of those living in households, 54 percent of those living in institutions, and 22 percent of those living in noninstitutional GQ (2000 Census, Table 10.4). Thus, disability prevalence for the GQ population, especially the institutional population, is much higher than it is for the household population. Even so, the vast majority of people with disabilities live in households; just 6.4 percent (2.2 million out of 34.4 million) live in institutions and 2.3 percent (0.8 million) in noninstitutional GQ.

The distribution of residence type differs markedly by disability status, age, and sex (Table 10.5). With the exception of those aged 18–49, negligible percentages of those without disabilities reside in GQ. For people with disabilities, substantial shares of those aged 18–49 and of those aged 65 and over reside in GQ. For those aged 18–49, the share of males living in institutional GQ is much larger than the share of females (7.7 percent versus 1.7 percent), mostly reflecting the fact that over 9 out of 10 inmates in correctional institutions are male. In contrast, for those age 65 and over, the proportion of females living in institutions, mostly in nursing homes, is larger than that of males (12.8 percent versus 7.3 percent).

Working-age people with disabilities residing in institutions are disproportionately African American—39 percent of those aged 18–49 and 22 percent of those aged 50–64, compared to just 16 percent and 14

Table 10.4 Size and Distribution of the Total Population and the Population with and without Disabilities by Residence Type, 2000 Census

Population (000s)	Total	Households	GQ	
			Institutional	Noninstitutional
Total population[a]	281,422	273,643	4,059	3,719
	(100.0%)	(100.0%)	(100.0%)	(100.0%)
Population with disabilities[b]	34,409	31,409	2,196	804
	(12.2%)	(11.5%)	(54.1%)	(21.6%)
Population without disabilities	247,013	242,234	1,863	2,915
	(87.8%)	(88.5%)	(45.9%)	(78.4%)

NOTE: Population with disabilities consists of persons with self-care, mental, physical, or sensory disabilities.
[a]2000 Census Summary File 1 (SF 1) 100 Percent Data.
[b]2000 Census PUMS data.

percent, respectively, in the household population (Table 10.6). Most are inmates of correctional facilities, as can be inferred from the age distribution by residence type presented earlier. Unfortunately, the Census 2000 Public Use Microdata Samples (PUMS) do not allow us to generate disability statistics by type of GQ. This does not imply, however, that prevalence of disability is higher among aged 18–49 African-American inmates than among inmates of the same age from other races. In fact, the opposite is true, as implied by the fact that the percentage of African-Americans in the institutional population (aged 18–49) without disabilities (44 percent) is higher than that of African-Americans in the institutional population with disabilities (39 percent). Race distributions for residents of noninstitutional GQ by disability status are much more similar to those for the household population.

As a majority of working-age people not residing in households are incarcerated, and 98 percent of the incarcerated population is of working age, we next examine the disability status of the incarcerated population and the change in incarceration rates over time, based on other data sources.

Disability in the Incarcerated Population

Based on studies using data from the 1996 jail survey (Harlow 1998) and the 1997 state and federal prison surveys (Maruschak and Beck 2001), about 37 percent of jail inmates, 31 percent of state prison inmates, and 23 percent of federal prison inmates report a disability of some sort (Table 10.7). About one in five of jail and state prison inmates and one in six of federal prison inmates reported having some condition that limited their ability to work. Mental and learning disabilities are about twice as prevalent in the jail and state prison populations as they are in federal prison. Overall, the prevalence of disability is highest in local jails, second highest in state prisons, and lowest—but still remarkably high—in federal prisons. Disability prevalence for each of the three correctional facility populations appears to be two to three times as high as in the household working-age population.[7] However, exact comparisons based on published data are problematic due to differing definitions of disability and methods of data collection, as well as differences in demographics.

Table 10.5 Population (% of total) by Residence Type, Disability Status, Age, and Sex, 2000 Census

Age and sex	With disabilities residing in			Without disabilities residing in		
	Households	GQ		Housing units	GQ	
		Inst.	Noninst.		Inst.	Noninst.
Males	91.7	5.9	2.4	97.2	1.4	1.4
Age 18–49	87.9	7.7	4.4	95.4	2.2	2.3
Age 50–64	95.0	3.3	1.8	99.2	0.5	0.3
Age 65+	91.3	7.3	1.4	99.2	0.5	0.3
Females	90.9	6.9	2.2	98.6	0.2	1.2
Age 18–49	94.8	1.7	3.5	97.8	0.2	2.0
Age 50–64	97.2	1.8	1.1	99.8	0.1	0.2
Age 65+	84.9	12.8	2.2	98.6	0.9	0.5

NOTE: Population with disabilities consists of persons with self-care, mental, physical, or sensory disabilities. Rows may not total 100 due to rounding.

SOURCE: 2000 Census PUMS data.

Table 10.6 Race and Age of the Working-Age Population (% of total) by Residence Type and Disability Status, 2000 Census

	With disabilities residing in			Without disabilities residing in		
			GQ			GQ
	Households	Institution	Noninst.	Housing units	Institution	Noninst.
Ages 18–49						
Caucasian	71.5	50.8	70.4	74.0	44.5	72.0
African American	15.5	38.6	19.5	11.8	43.7	15.3
Native American	1.7	1.7	1.5	0.8	1.5	0.8
Asian	2.1	0.7	2.4	4.4	0.8	5.4
Other	5.7	5.4	3.3	6.6	7.5	3.9
Multiple races	3.5	2.7	2.9	2.4	1.9	2.6
Ages 50–64						
Caucasian	77.2	71.4	75.4	83.0	59.1	70.4
African American	13.8	22.4	17.8	8.9	33.0	18.7
Native American	1.3	1.0	1.4	0.6	1.3	1.0
Asian	2.0	0.9	1.4	3.6	0.9	3.8
Other	3.2	2.9	2.1	2.6	4.1	4.0
Multiple races	2.4	1.4	1.9	1.4	1.6	2.1
Ages 18–64						
Caucasian	72.7	78.1	77.1	77.3	49.4	71.7
African American	14.0	17.2	15.4	10.7	39.6	15.6
Native American	1.1	0.8	1.2	0.7	1.5	0.9
Asian	3.0	0.7	1.9	4.0	0.9	5.2
Other	6.0	2.1	2.4	5.2	6.8	3.9
Multiple races	3.2	1.1	2.1	2.1	1.9	2.6

NOTE: Population with disabilities consists of persons with self-care, mental, physical, or sensory disabilities. Columns may not total 100 due to rounding.

SOURCE: 2000 Census PUMS data.

Table 10.7 Disability Prevalence (%) for the Incarcerated Population, 1996–1997

| | | Inmates | |
| | | State prison | Federal prison |
Disability category	Jail (1996)	(1997)	(1997)
Any condition	36.5	31.0	23.4
Learning	9.1	9.9	5.1
Speech	3.7	3.7	2.2
Hearing	6.1	5.7	5.6
Vision	9.2	8.3	7.6
Mental	10.4	10.0	4.8
Physical	10.2	11.9	11.1
Condition that limits ability to work	20.7	21.0	17.9

SOURCE: Tabulations from the 1996 SILF as reported by Harlow (1998); tabulations from the 1997 SISCF and SIFCF as reported by Maruschak and Beck (2001).

From 1996 to 2002, overall disability prevalence for jail inmates has been stable (at about 37 percent), according to findings from the SILJ (Harlow 1998; Maruschak 2006). Specifically, speech and hearing disabilities were about the same, vision disability increased from 9 percent to 11 percent, and learning disability rose rapidly from 9 percent to 22 percent. Moreover, based on a single survey question in the 2002 SILJ, 8 percent of jail inmates reported having a mental or emotional condition that kept them from participating fully in school, work, or other activities (Maruschak 2006). When a series of questions about prior diagnoses of mental health problems or symptoms of a mental disorder were used (as specified in the DSM-IV), an estimated 64 percent of jail inmates were found to have a mental health problem (James and Glaze 2006). James and Glaze also reported that 56 percent of state prisoners and 45 percent of federal prisoners had mental health problems. Mental health problems were defined by a recent history or symptoms of a mental health problem, based on clinical diagnosis, treatment, and symptoms specified in the DSM-IV. The 1996–1997 surveys do not have a comparable mental health measure. These findings suggest that mental illness might be substantially underreported when a single self-reported question is used, as in the 1996–1997 surveys.

The incarcerated population more than quadrupled from 1980 to 2003, from a half million to more than two million (Harrison and Beck 2004; U.S. Department of Justice 2000). Although this growth partly reflects population growth, the main reason for growth is increased incarceration rates. From 1989–1991 to 1996–1997, two periods for which we have data by age and sex, the incarceration rate for the working-age population grew by 35 percent (Table 10.8). The change and relative change are greatest among those between the ages of 35 and 44, although the rates are highest among those between the ages of 25 and 34. Further, the change in the incarceration rate is much greater for males than for females, although the relative change is somewhat larger for females.

Table 10.8 Change in Incarceration Rate[a] by Age and Sex, 1989–1991 to 1996–1997

Age & sex	Total		Change	
	1989–91	1996–97	Number	Percent
Age				
18–24	1,113	1,474	361	32.4
25–34	1,262	1,690	428	33.9
35–44	669	1,110	441	65.9
45–54	297	476	179	60.3
55+	66	87	21	31.8
Sex				
Male	926	1,242	316	34.1
Female	66	97	31	47.0
Total	472	638	166	35.2

[a] Incarceration rate is defined as the number of inmates per 100,000 of the total population.

SOURCE: Authors' calculations based on population estimates by age and sex from the Census Bureau (2008) and estimates of inmates by age and sex from the Bureau of Justice Statistics (U.S. Department of Justice n.d.).

SUMMARY OF GAPS IN SURVEY DATA FOR THE NONHOUSEHOLD POPULATION

Gaps in Survey Coverage

The SILJ, SIFCF, and SISCF provide information about the incarcerated population, and the National Nursing Home Survey (NNHS) offers information on nursing home residents. However, we found no surveys covering the population living in institutions other than these except the Decennial Census long-form survey and the 2006 ACS. As shown earlier, this component of the institutional population has declined from 1990 to 2000, but as of 2000, it still represents 8.9 percent of the institutional population as a whole and 7.0 percent of the working-age institutional population. Furthermore, some of these institutions are disability related.

Except for the Decennial Census and the ACS from 2006 forward, major household surveys all exclude the institutional population in their sampling frames and vary in their coverage of persons living in noninstitutional GQ.[8] In addition, it is not always clear what specific types of GQ are included or excluded in these surveys, and users may not be able to identify the types of living quarters through public-use files. Some components of the population for which information is very limited are the homeless and military populations. Most national surveys focus on the civilian population—that is, those in the military, or at least those living in military barracks, are excluded. The homeless population is either not covered at all or covered to an unknown extent in major national surveys including the Census and the ACS. This gap in coverage has a larger impact for the working-age population than for the elderly, as previous research showed that 80 percent of homeless clients of service providers in 1996 were between the ages of 25 and 54 (Burt et al. 1999).[9] Disability prevalence was found to be high among homeless clients; about 45 percent had mental health problems, and almost three-quarters reported an alcohol, drug, or mental health problem in the past year (Burt et al. 1999). There are no reliable data on the number of homeless persons, and there is no way to measure growth in that population.

Infrequent Collection

The one survey to collect data on the entire population, the Decennial Census, is conducted only once per decade, in contrast to the annual collection of data on the household population via major government surveys, including the ACS before 2006. The institutional surveys (e.g., SILJ or SISCF) are conducted less regularly than major household surveys. Surveys for the incarcerated population are available five to six years apart. The nursing home surveys were conducted two years apart from 1995 to 1999, and the most recent one was conducted five years later, in 2004. As shown in Table 10.9, two time periods—1996–1997 and 2000–2004—have more surveys than others, including surveys of the two largest institutional populations, nursing homes and correctional institutions. In addition, no longitudinal data are available for the institutional population.

Table 10.9 Survey Years, 1989–2006

Year	Census	ACS	NNHS	SILJ	SIFCF & SISCF
2006		X			
2005					
2004			X		X
2003					
2002				X	
2001					
2000	X	X			
1999			X		
1998					
1997			X		X
1996				X	
1995			X		
1994					
1993					
1992					
1991					X
1990	X				
1989				X	

Disability Definition

Both the Census and the ACS contain six common subcategories of disability: sensory disabilities, functional limitations, mental disabilities, limitations in activities of daily living (ADL), limitations in instrumental activities of daily living (IADL), and work disabilities. The Census Bureau will change the ACS definition in 2008; unless a careful analysis of the effect of the changes on the number and composition of respondents with disabilities is performed, we will not have reliable information on the changes in the prevalence of disability by residence type from 2000 to 2010—again making comparison of disability statistics across census years problematic, just as they are for 1990 and 2000.

Nursing home surveys have much more detailed disability information, except that work disability is not included; that might reflect an implicit assumption that all respondents either have work disabilities, or that almost all are too old for work to be considered a relevant topic. The surveys on inmates do not ask questions on ADL and IADL disabilities, but they do include questions on learning disabilities that are absent in most household surveys. Although conceptual definitions of disability in these surveys are similar, there are substantial operational differences in the collection of information for each of these definitions.

In sum, coverage for those not in the household population is far less extensive than coverage for those in that population. Data on the military population, people who are homeless, and people residing in institutions other than correctional facilities and nursing homes are especially limited; surveys covering other institutional populations are infrequent and irregular; and disability questions are limited (e.g., no data on ADL and IADL disabilities for inmates). These limitations pose significant problems for research on the entire population of people with disabilities, including those not residing in households.

DISCUSSION

It is apparent from the available data that the size and composition of the institutional population has changed substantially in the last few decades. The changes have been important for the population with disabilities, especially the relatively large number who live in institutions. Growth in incarceration and the high prevalence of disabilities among that population is particularly crucial for understanding trends in disability statistics for the working-age population. In fact, the increase in the size of the institutional population from 1990 to 2000 was caused by the increased incarceration rates for working-age people. The incarcerated population (which is almost all of working age) became the largest institutional population, surpassing the nursing home population (mostly elderly) in size.

As the size of the institutional population is small relative to the size of the household population, the growth in incarceration is not likely to have a substantial effect on the estimates of disability prevalence for the household population as a whole. It could, however, have a substantial impact for the demographic groups that are most likely to be incarcerated: young men, especially from minority populations. To our knowledge, no study has been conducted to examine the impact of incarceration growth on the disability status of young, working-age African-Americans in the household population.

Studies of the effect of higher incarceration on statistics for young black males are suggestive of what studies for young males with disabilities might reveal (Edelman, Holzer, and Offner 2006; Holzer, Raphael, and Stoll 2006). Edelman, Holzer, and Offner reported the proportions of "idleness or disconnection" (i.e., the percentage who are not in school and have been out of work for a substantial period, roughly a year or more) of youth and young adults aged 16–24 by race and ethnicity. Rates are much higher for African-American males than for whites. When including those who are incarcerated, the authors found that the gap in the rates of disconnection between blacks and whites was 5 percentage points larger than when only the noninstitutional population is included—19 percent versus 14 percent.[10]

Although complete trend statistics on disability prevalence for the incarcerated population are not yet available, it is likely that high growth in incarceration has had a significant negative effect on the prevalence of disability among young men in the household population—especially among low-income and some demographic minority groups. More modest declines in the proportion of working-age people living in other types of institutions probably had much smaller effects and for broader demographic groups. Overall, trends in statistics for the working-age household population with disabilities might misrepresent trends in statistics for the entire working-age population with disabilities, especially for some demographic groups. Horvath-Rose, Stapleton, and O'Day (2004) found that the prevalence of work limitations declined for non-institutionalized youth and young adult males from 1988 to 1999, while there was a modest increase for young females and little change for older working-age males. It is possible that growth in the incarceration of young adult males helps to substantially explain the decline in disability prevalence for young males, because the incarceration of young adults with disabilities removes them from noninstitutional survey sampling frames.

Disability information on the entire population is scarce, but the situation is changing. If the Census Bureau follows its current plan, the ACS will continuously and consistently provide annual data for the population living in most GQ, including the major institutional GQ, from 2006 forward.[11]

The Census Bureau released the first disability statistics for the GQ population from the 2006 ACS as this chapter was being completed. Comparisons of these statistics (Table 10.10) to statistics presented earlier are problematic because of differences in disability definitions and the definition of the working-age population (aged 16–64 in the new Census tables). Nonetheless, the statistics confirm a number of key findings from earlier surveys. The share of all persons with disabilities who live in GQ is much higher than the corresponding share for those without disabilities—6.5% of those with disabilities live in GQ whereas only 2.6 percent of those without a disability live there. The percentage of inmates with disabilities is very high (28.8 percent), and inmates constitute the largest single residence group of persons with disabilities outside the household population. Disability prevalence in the wide ar-

Table 10.10 Initial Disability Statistics for All Residence Types from the 2006 ACS, Persons Aged 16–64

| | All | Households | Residence type | | | | |
| | | | | | GQ | | |
			All	Correctional facilities	Nursing homes	Coll./univ. housing	Other
All persons (millions)	197.1	191.0	6.1	2.0	0.2	2.3	1.5
% in residence type	100.0	96.9	3.1	1.0	0.1	1.2	0.8
Any disability (millions)	24.8	23.2	1.6	0.6	0.2	0.1	0.7
% in residence type	100.0	93.5	6.5	2.4	1.0	0.5	2.7
No disability (millions)	172.2	167.8	4.5	1.5	0.0	2.2	0.8
% in residence type	100.0	97.4	2.6	0.8	0.0	1.3	0.5
% with any disability	12.6	12.2	26.7	28.8	97.3	5.1	44.6

SOURCE: American Community Survey, 2006, from the Census Bureau American Factfinder Web site. (See U.S. Census Bureau 2006b.)

ray of "other GQ" combined is also very high (44.6 percent), as is the percentage of all persons with disabilities living in such GQ (2.7 percent). Residents of college/university housing constitute the only GQ group with low disability prevalence (5.1 percent).

Additional disability statistics for the working-age population in all residential groups from the 2006 ACS and later years will be particularly valuable for disability research and statistics given the large gaps in currently available information. For privacy and statistical reasons, research access to the ACS data for the GQ population is more restricted than access to data for the household population; sample sizes by GQ type and state are relatively small. Over time, it will be feasible to increase these sample sizes through pooling of data from multiple years. At some time in the future, the Census Bureau could potentially support research on GQ residents via production of a public-use file with pooled samples.

While the new ACS data on the GQ population are a welcome development, the ACS does not contain the wealth of information that can be found in other surveys of the household population. Hence, enhancements to periodic surveys of the GQ population, especially for those in the "other GQ" group, would substantially improve our knowledge about people with disabilities. Clarification and greater consistency of noninstitutional GQ populations included in the sampling frames of major household surveys would also make a significant contribution to the quality of disability statistics.

Notes

1. The Medicare population includes almost all legal residents aged 65 and over plus those under 65 who receive Social Security Disability Insurance (SSDI) and have completed the 24-month Medicare waiting period or have ALS or have end stage renal disease. The NLTCS and MCBS focus on Medicare enrollees and represent ongoing efforts. The NLTCS consists of a series of nationally representative surveys of Medicare beneficiaries aged 65 or over, with an emphasis on the elderly who are functionally impaired. The NLTCS began in 1982, and follow-up surveys were conducted in 1984, 1989, 1999, and 2004. The MCBS is a continuous survey of a representative national sample of the Medicare population, including enrollees under the age of 65. It began in 1991 as a continuous panel and started using a four-year rotating panel design in 1994. It is the only comprehensive source of

information on the health status, health care use and expenditures, health insurance coverage, and socioeconomic and demographic characteristics of the entire spectrum of Medicare beneficiaries.

2. Census 2000 includes persons without usual residence who use service facilities such as shelters, soup kitchens, and mobile food vans. Only people using the service facility on the interview day were enumerated. In addition, people in targeted nonsheltered outdoor locations and persons without usual residence were also enumerated. The total count, however, does not provide a complete count of the homeless population (U.S. Census Bureau 2005). The long-form survey also samples persons that use service facilities, but it is not a representative sample of the homeless population, and information about sample size is not available.

3. For more information about the nursing home data and the disabilities of residents, see She and Stapleton (2006).

4. The Census 2000 long-form survey includes the following two disability questions: 1) "Does this person have any of the listed long lasting conditions: Blindness, deafness, or a severe vision or hearing impairment; or a condition that substantially limits one or more basic physical activities such as walking, climbing stairs, reaching, lifting, or carrying?" and 2) "Because of a physical, mental, or emotional condition lasting 6 months or more, does this person have any difficulty in doing any of the listed activities: learning, remembering, or concentrating; dressing, bathing, or getting around inside the home; going outside the home alone to shop or visit a doctor's office; or working at a job or business?"

5. These questions were asked only for persons aged 16 and older, so the disability prevalence estimates for working-age and elderly adults are the most affected. Comparison of Census 2000 statistics to the 2003 ACS suggests that the percentage of the noninstitutional population with at least one of the six disabilities, including the domains of going-outside-home and employment, was about 1.5 to 2.0 percentage points higher in 2000 than the prevalence of the four disabilities (based on statistics presented in Erickson and Houtenville 2005 and Weathers 2005).

6. The 1996–1997 jail and prison surveys ask the same disability question: "Do you have: a physical, mental, or other health condition that limits the kind or amount of work you can do; difficulty seeing ordinary newsprint, even when wearing glasses; difficulty hearing a normal conversation, even when wearing a hearing aid; a learning disability, such as dyslexia or attention deficit disorder; a speech disability, such as a lisp or stutter; a physical disability; or a mental or emotional condition?"

7. Based on the 2003 ACS, disability prevalence among all persons aged 25–61 not living in GQ is as follows: 12 percent for any disability, 2.7 percent for sensory disability, 4.0 percent for mental disability, 7.5 percent for physical disability, and 6.9 percent for work disability (Weathers 2005).

8. Concerned about privacy issues, the Census Bureau has not included institution type in the PUMS data.

9. Burt et al. (1999) used data from the National Survey of Homeless Assistance Providers and Clients, which was conducted in 1996 by the Census Bureau and

provides information about the providers of homeless assistance services and the characteristics of homeless clients who use those services.

10. Based on data from the CPS and summary data on youth incarceration rates from the BJS, Edelman, Holzer, and Offner (2006, Table 2.1) reported that, in 1999, among noninstitutional youth aged 16–24, the proportions of disconnection were 8.7 percent for whites and 22.8 percent for blacks; when incarcerated youth were included, the shares increased to 9.6 percent for whites and 28.5 percent for blacks.

11. As of 2006, the ACS excludes the following GQ: domestic violence shelters, soup kitchens, regularly scheduled mobile food vans, targeted nonsheltered locations, natural disaster shelters, transient locations (such as RV campgrounds, marinas, and military hotels), dangerous encampments, and maritime vessels (U.S. Census Bureau 2006a).

References

Ballou, Janice, and Jason Markesich. 2009. "Survey Data Collection Methods." In *Counting Working-Age People with Disabilities: What Current Data Tell Us and Options for Improvement*, Andrew J. Houtenville, David C. Stapleton, Robert R. Weathers II, and Richard V. Burkhauser, eds. Kalamazoo, MI: W.E. Upjohn Institute for Employment Research, pp. 265–298.

Burkhauser, Richard V., Andrew J. Houtenville, and Ludmila Rovba. 2009. "Poverty." In *Counting Working-Age People with Disabilities: What Current Data Tell Us and Options for Improvement*, Andrew J. Houtenville, David C. Stapleton, Robert R. Weathers II, and Richard V. Burkhauser, eds. Kalamazoo, MI: W.E. Upjohn Institute for Employment Research, pp. 193–226.

Burkhauser, Richard V., Ludmila Rovba, and Robert R. Weathers II. 2009. "Household Income." In *Counting Working-Age People with Disabilities: What Current Data Tell Us and Options for Improvement*, Andrew J. Houtenville, David C. Stapleton, Robert R. Weathers II, and Richard V. Burkhauser, eds. Kalamazoo, MI: W.E. Upjohn Institute for Employment Research, pp. 145–192.

Burt, Martha R., Laudan Y. Aron, Toby Douglas, Jesse Valente, Edgar Lee, and Britta Iwen. 1999. "Homelessness: Programs and the People They Serve." Findings of the National Survey of Homeless Assistance Providers and Clients. Technical Report prepared for the Interagency Council on the Homeless. Washington, DC: The Urban Institute.

Edelman, Peter, Harry J. Holzer, and Paul Offner. 2006. *Reconnecting Disadvantaged Young Men.* Washington, DC: The Urban Institute.

Erickson, William A., and Andrew J. Houtenville. 2005. "A Guide to Disability Statistics from the 2000 Decennial Census." Ithaca, NY: Cornell University,

Rehabilitation Research and Training Center on Disability Demographics and Statistics. http://digitalcommons.ilr.cornell.edu/edicollect/187/ (accessed August 18, 2006).

Harlow, Caroline W. 1998. "Profile of Jail Inmates 1996." Washington, DC: U.S. Department of Justice, Bureau of Justice Statistics. http://www.ojp.usdoj.gov/bjs/abstract/pji96.htm (accessed June 20, 2008).

Harrison, Paige M., and Allen J. Beck. 2004. "Prisoners in 2003." Washington, DC: U.S. Department of Justice, Bureau of Justice Statistics. http://www.ojp.usdoj.gov/bjs/abstract/p03.htm (accessed June 20, 2008).

Holzer, Harry J., Steven Raphael, and Michael A. Stoll. 2006. "How Do Employer Perceptions of Crime and Incarceration Affect the Employment Prospects of Less-Educated Young Black Men?" In *Black Males Left Behind*, Ronald B. Mincy, ed. Washington, DC: The Urban Institute, pp. 67–85.

Horvath-Rose, Anne E., David C. Stapleton, and Bonnie O'Day. 2004. "Trends in Outcomes for Young People with Work Disabilities: Are We Making Progress?" *Journal of Vocational Rehabilitation* 21(3): 175–187.

James, Doris J., and Lauren E. Glaze. 2006. "Mental Health Problems of Prison and Jail Inmates." Washington, DC: U.S. Department of Justice, Bureau of Justice Statistics. http://www.ojp.usdoj.gov/bjs/abstract/mhppji.htm (accessed June 20, 2008).

Maruschak, Laura M. 2006. "Medical Problems of Jail Inmates." Washington, DC: U.S. Department of Justice, Bureau of Justice Statistics. http://www.ojp.usdoj.gov/bjs/abstract/mpji.htm (accessed June 20, 2008).

Maruschak, Laura M., and Allen J. Beck. 2001. Medical Problems of Inmates, 1997. Washington, DC: U.S. Department of Justice, Bureau of Justice Statistics. http://www.ojp.usdoj.gov/bjs/abstract/mpi97.htm (accessed June 20, 2008).

She, Peiyun, and David C. Stapleton. 2006. "A Review of Disability Data for the Institutional Population." Ithaca, NY: Cornell University, Rehabilitation Research and Training Center on Disability Demographics and Statistics.

Stapleton, David C., and Richard V. Burkhauser, eds. 2003. *The Decline in Employment of People with Disabilities: A Policy Puzzle*. Kalamazoo, MI: W.E. Upjohn Institute for Employment Research.

Stern, Sharon M. 2003. "Counting People with Disabilities: How Survey Methodology Influences Estimates in Census 2000 and the Census 2000 Supplementary Survey." Census Bureau Staff Research Report. Washington, DC: U.S. Bureau of the Census, Poverty and Health Statistics Branch. http://www.census.gov/acs/www/Downloads/ACS/finalstern.pdf (accessed June 20, 2008).

Stern, Sharon, and Matthew Brault. 2005. "Disability Data from the American Community Survey: A Brief Examination of the Effects of a Question Redesign in 2003." Census Bureau Staff Research Report. Washington, DC: U.S. Bureau of the Census, Housing and Household Economic Statistics Division. http://www.census.gov/hhes/www/disability/ACS_disability.pdf (accessed June 20, 2008).

U.S. Census Bureau. 1992. "Census of Population and Housing, 1990: Summary Tape File 3." Washington, DC: U.S. Census Bureau.

———. 2001. "Major Differences in Subject-matter between the 1990 and 2000 Census Questionnaires." Washington, DC: U.S. Census Bureau, Population Division, Decennial Programs Coordination Branch. http://www.census.gov/population/www/cen2000/90vs00.html (June 20, 2008).

———. 2004. "Meeting 21st Century Demographic Data Needs—Implementing the American Community Survey. Report 9: Comparing Social Characteristics with Census 2000." Washington, DC: U.S. Census Bureau.

———. 2005. "Census 2000 Summary File 1 Technical Documentation." SF1/13 and SF3/15. http://www.census.gov/prod/cen2000/doc/sf1.pdf and http://www.census.gov/prod/cen2000/doc/sf3.pdf (accessed June 20, 2008).

———. 2006a. "2006 ACS Group Quarters Types Codes and Definitions." Washington, DC: U.S. Census Bureau. http://www.census.gov/acs/www/Downloads/2006_ACS_GQ_Definitions.pdf (accessed June 20, 2008).

———. 2006b. "Characteristics of the Group Quarters Population." Washington, DC: U.S. Census Bureau, American FactFinder. http://factfinder.census.gov/servlet/STTable?_bm=y&-geo_id=01000US&-qr_name=ACS_2006_EST_G00_S2601A&-ds_name=ACS_2006_EST_G00_ (accessed May 7, 2008).

———. 2008. "National Population Projections." Washington, DC: U.S. Census Bureau. http://www.census.gov/population/www/projections/natproj.html (accessed November 18, 2008).

U.S. Department of Justice. 2000. "Correctional Populations in the United States, 1997." Washington, DC: U.S. Department of Justice, Bureau of Justice Statistics. http://www.ojp.usdoj.gov/bjs/abstract/cpus97.htm (accessed June 20, 2008).

———. n.d. "Data for Analysis—Crime and Justice Electronic Data Abstracts." Washington, DC: U.S. Department of Justice, Bureau of Justice Statistics. http://www.usdoj.gov/bjs/dtdata.htm (accessed September 29, 2008).

Weathers, Robert R. II. 2005. "A Guide to Disability Statistics from the American Community Survey." Ithaca, NY: Cornell University, Rehabilitation Research and Training Center on Disability Demographics and Statistics. http://digitalcommons.ilr.cornell.edu/edicollect/129 (accessed August 18, 2006).

Weathers, Robert R. II, and David C. Wittenburg. 2009. "Employment." In

Counting Working-Age People with Disabilities: What Current Data Tell Us and Options for Improvement, Andrew J. Houtenville, David C. Stapleton, Robert R. Weathers II, and Richard V. Burkhauser, eds. Kalamazoo, MI: W.E. Upjohn Institute for Employment Research, pp. 101–142.

11

Options for Improving
Disability Data Collection

David C. Stapleton
Gina A. Livermore
Mathematica Policy Research, Inc.

Peiyun She
Cornell University

This book has demonstrated the great value of the extensive federal data on working-age people with disabilities, but it also provides insights on how the value of these data might be enhanced through efforts to coordinate the numerous diverse, and largely independent, federal data collection efforts (Table 11.1).[1] We have used the term national disability data system (NDDS) to informally encapsulate these efforts, but they are not recognized or managed as a system (Livermore and She 2007). The good news is that there are efforts in place to improve coordination, and they are already paying dividends. In this chapter, we summarize the limitations of the NDDS, briefly review how they are being addressed, and present options for further improvement.

The limitations of the NDDS and efforts to address them are described in the next section. We then lay out options that would improve the comparability of disability data across surveys, use linkages across administrative and survey databases to improve statistics on program participants, improve the disability-relevant content in major surveys, and add periodic disability supplements to existing surveys and implement periodic special surveys. We conclude by discussing the priorities of the options presented.

382

Table 11.1 Federal Sources of Data on the Working-Age Population with Disabilities

Major national household surveys
American Community Survey
Current Population Survey
National Health Interview Survey
Survey of Income and Program Participation

National household surveys on specific topics
American Housing Survey
American Time Use Survey
Behavioral Risk Factor Surveillance System
Consumer Expenditure Survey
Medical Expenditure Panel Survey
National Health and Nutrition Examination Survey
Panel Study of Income Dynamics
Survey of Consumer Finances

Surveys of subpopulations
National Longitudinal Survey of Adolescent Health
National Longitudinal Survey of Youth
Health and Retirement Study
National Beneficiary Survey
Medicare Current Beneficiary Survey
National Health Interview Survey—Disability Supplement

Longitudinal Study of the Vocational Rehabilitation
Services Program

Surveys of nonhousehold populations
Nursing Home Minimum Data Set
National Nursing Home Survey
Survey of Inmates of Local Jails
Survey of Inmates of State Correctional Facilities
Survey of Inmates of Federal Correctional Facilities
National Survey of Homeless Assistance Providers and Clients

American Community Survey (includes the
nonhousehold population from 2006 forward)

Administrative data from federal and federal-state programs
Social Security Administration: Social Security Disability Insurance and Supplemental Security Income
Centers for Medicare and Medicaid Services: Medicare and Medicaid Enrollment and Claims
Rehabilitation Services Administration: State Vocational Rehabilitation Service Agency Closure Data

NOTE: The age range for the sampling frame varies from survey to survey; each includes some, if not all, of those age 18 to 65.
SOURCE: Based on Livermore and She (2007).

LIMITATIONS OF THE NATIONAL DISABILITY
DATA SYSTEM

Although extensive information about people with disabilities is collected through national surveys and program administrative data, the information is limited by a variety of factors: the manner in which disability is defined and measured, sample size limitations, exclusion of certain subpopulations or inability to identify them, limitations to disability-relevant survey content, infrequency of data collection, limited availability of longitudinal data, and limitations of data on program participation. In addition, many important topics for people with disabilities are not adequately covered in national surveys. Below, we briefly highlight some key limitations of the existing data on people with disabilities. Livermore and She (2007) offer a more in-depth discussion of these issues as do earlier chapters of this book. We also describe current initiatives to address some of the limitations identified.

Identification of People with Disabilities

The health, functional status, activity limitation, and participation restriction variables that are used to identify people with disabilities vary greatly across survey and administrative data sources. The inconsistencies across the major national surveys—in particular the Decennial Census, the Current Population Survey (CPS), the American Community Survey (ACS), and the National Health Interview Survey (NHIS)—create two important problems when studying persons with disabilities. First, because disability is measured very differently across surveys, these instruments yield very different estimates of the size of the population with disabilities (see Weathers 2009) as well as different characteristics of that population (e.g., demographic characteristics, employment, income, and poverty rates; see Houtenville et al. 2009; Weathers and Wittenburg 2009; Burkhauser, Rovba, and Weathers 2009; and Burkhauser, Houtenville, and Rovba 2009). Although the sometimes widely different estimates can be explained by technical differences in questionnaires, survey methods, and instruments, inconsistencies of the estimates can undermine their perceived credibility among nontechnical audiences. This can negatively affect their usefulness in supporting arguments for change. Second, the lack of consistent indicators across data sources prohibits researchers and policymakers from identifying a common target population for which information from multiple data sources can be generated and thereby providing much richer information about people with disabilities than can be obtained from a single data source.

In addition, some national surveys, in essence or in fact, do not have questions to identify people with disabilities; hence, statistics on the topics of these surveys cannot be generated for any population with disabilities. The indicators available in most surveys perform particularly poorly in identifying people with psychiatric, cognitive, and intellectual disabilities.

Since we began work on this book, the government has undertaken an extremely important step toward addressing this issue. As of 2008, the ACS and the CPS will adopt a common set of questions for the identification of respondents with disabilities (Table 11.2), and the NHIS will soon adopt the same questions.[2] The Bureau of Labor Statistics (BLS) announced their decision to adopt the new ACS questions for the CPS after parallel efforts by the BLS and the Census Bureau to develop better disability questions for these surveys led to two sets of questions that were conceptually quite similar (McMenamin et al. 2005).[3] As a consequence of the adoption of the ACS questions by the CPS, another important survey—the American Time Use Survey (ATUS)—that uses the CPS as its sampling frame will implicitly use the same questions to identify respondents with disabilities.

The questions that will be adopted by the ACS, CPS, and NHIS were developed by the Disability Subcommittee of the ACS Interagency Committee, under the auspices of the Office of Management and Budget (OMB), and chaired by the National Center for Health Statistics (NCHS). The committee took the data needs of its many member agencies into consideration, using the Classification of Functioning, Disability and Health (ICF) model of disability (see Weathers 2009) as a conceptual framework. The questions were designed to identify people who are "at risk" for disability, specifically people who, without accommodation, are likely to experience restrictions in participation because of a functional limitation, as well as the population needing assistance to maintain independence. The questions cover three con-

Table 11.2 New Disability Questions for the ACS and the CPS, 2008

1. a. Is this person deaf or does he/she have serious difficulty hearing?
    b. Is this person blind or does he/she have serious difficulty seeing even when wearing glasses?

For persons aged 5 years or over:

2. a. Because of a physical, mental, or emotional condition, does this person have serious difficulty concentrating, remembering, or making decisions?
    b. Does this person have serious difficulty walking or climbing stairs?
    c. Does this person have difficulty dressing or bathing?

For persons aged 15 years or over:

3. Because of a physical, mental, or emotional condition, does this person have difficulty doing errands alone such as visiting a doctor's office or shopping?

SOURCE: U.S. Census Bureau (2006b).

ceptual domains: functional limitations (vision, hearing, mobility, and cognitive), activities necessary to support independent living (self-care and mobility in the community), and one major participation restriction (work limitations).

The new questions for the ACS, CPS, and NHIS are also quite similar to the set of questions developed and recommended by the United Nations affiliated Washington City Group (WCG) on Disability Statistics.[4] The WCG questions were designed to identify people (in any country) at risk of not being able to perform activities of daily living (ADL) or participate in major life activities because of significant functional limitations. The four core WCG questions cover the same types of functional limitations as the Census questions, although the wording differs. Two additional questions ask about specific activity limitations: difficulty with self-care and difficulty with communication. Hence, statistics from the ACS and the CPS will not be comparable to those from countries that adopt the WCG questions. Nonetheless, it seems likely that the ACS and, especially, the CPS disability statistics will be more comparable to those from other countries than they have been in the past.

Small Sample Sizes

Although people with disabilities represent a sizeable share of the working-age population, they are in a minority. Hence, the samples of most surveys limit the ability to analyze specific subgroups of people with disabilities. Subgroups of interest often include people of certain age ranges (e.g., transition-age youth or working-age individuals), people with specific health conditions or types of disabilities, residents of particular states and smaller geographic regions, users of specific programs or services, and people categorized by length of disability duration. The national surveys with the largest sample sizes (Decennial Census, the ACS, and the CPS) generally have the most limited amount of information about disability. These surveys can allow some analyses of people with disabilities as a group at the state and substate level, but they cannot provide much information about specific health conditions causing disability. The Behavioral Risk Factor Surveillance System (BRFSS) and NHIS can provide more detail about some specific health conditions, but they are narrower in terms of addressing the breadth of disability-related issues.

The major national surveys generally do not have sample sizes large enough to permit in-depth analyses of people with disabilities who use particular programs or services. In some instances, pooling data across survey years and linking survey data to administrative data can provide large enough samples to study program participants, but these approaches are challenging.

Exclusion of People with Disabilities from Survey Samples

The major surveys that provide disability data exclude most individuals residing in most group quarters (GQ), many of whom have disabilities. Data on people residing in GQ other than correctional facilities and nursing homes are especially limited (e.g., long-term psychiatric facilities and noninstitutional group homes). Until very recently the Decennial Census long-form survey was the only one to collect disability data on the entire population, regardless of residence type. Starting in 2006, the ACS has been expanded to do so every year. This represents a major improvement in the NDDS and one that is already starting to yield important new disability information. Nonetheless, the extensive information that is available about people living in the household population from other surveys will remain unavailable or limited for those living in institutions and other GQ.

Disability prevalence is also high among homeless people (see She and Stapleton 2009), and they too are unlikely to be captured in any survey sample. In addition, individuals with disabilities captured in the sample frames for household surveys can be excluded from the survey sample because of access issues related to location and interview methodologies.

Subject Areas Poorly Addressed

A number of important topic areas are inadequately addressed for people with disabilities in national surveys, for at least one of three reasons: 1) surveys that address the topic area do not include adequate disability measures; 2) surveys that address the topic area are conducted very infrequently or cover only very specific subpopulations of people with disabilities; or 3) the topic area, as relevant to people with disabilities, is simply not addressed in any survey. Examples of subject areas that are poorly addressed for people with disabilities include time use and allocation of expenditures, transportation issues, program participation and benefits, employment services and supports, community participation, living arrangements, and the characteristics of disability onset and progression.

The inclusion of new disability questions in the CPS, discussed previously, will expand knowledge about the household population with disabilities in the subject areas covered by the CPS because this information was previously only available for the "work-limited" disability population captured by the pre-2008 CPS question. It will also allow researchers to produce statistics on time use for people with disabilities from the ATUS, which uses the CPS as its sampling frame.[5]

Untimely or Outdated Data

The surveys that provide the most in-depth information about people with disabilities are those that are conducted very infrequently or have only been conducted once. The NHIS Disability Supplement

(NHIS-D) represents the most ambitious effort to date to collect a wide range of disability-relevant information from a large, nationally representative sample of people with disabilities of all ages. The survey was conducted in two phases in 1994 and 1995. The data are now more than a decade old, and the survey has not been repeated. Similarly, the major programs serving people with disabilities only survey their populations very infrequently. The Social Security Administration (SSA) has conducted five large-scale survey efforts over the last three decades, covering various subgroups of its disability beneficiary population. All were special-purpose surveys, spaced many years apart, and not part of a systematic survey program that generates comparable information over a long period. Only one survey of state/federal vocational rehabilitation (VR) service users has ever been conducted, and that was in the mid 1990s. Although data from the large national surveys (e.g., the ACS and the CPS) are generally released fairly quickly, the public-use files for surveys that provide the most in-depth information about people with disabilities (e.g., the Survey of Income and Program Participation [SIPP] and the NHIS) are generally not released for two or more years after they are fielded.

Limited Longitudinal Information

Longitudinal survey data are more difficult and costly to collect than cross-sectional data. As most survey data are cross-sectional in nature, they do not permit analyses of the progression of disability and disability-related consequences over long periods. The most significant longitudinal national survey of the general household population, the Panel Study of Income Dynamics (PSID), included only very limited measures of disability until recently. The SIPP provides a limited longitudinal perspective (two and a half or four years, depending on the panel), but the sample sizes of people with disabilities are too small to conduct anything more than very high-level descriptive analyses of disability onset and progression unless data are pooled from multiple years. The data sources that provide the most in-depth longitudinal information focus on very specific subpopulations, such as older adults (e.g., the Health and Retirement Study) and youth (e.g., the National Longitudinal Survey of Youth).

Efforts to match data from the SIPP, CPS, NHIS, and several other surveys to administrative data from the SSA and, for some, the Centers for Medicare and Medicaid Services (CMS) have added important longitudinal information to major surveys (see Stapleton, Wittenburg, and Thornton 2009). The matches do not, however, add longitudinal information in content domains covered only by the surveys, and access to the data is restricted because of privacy issues. Incomplete matches are also a significant problem for some years.

Inadequate Program Participation Data

As discussed in Stapleton, Wittenburg, and Thornton (2009), there are numerous limitations associated with data on the program participation of people with disabilities. Administrative data from each major program are rich in many respects, but quality information is largely limited to items that are important for administrative purposes, and privacy issues create significant barriers to researcher access. Although many agencies produce public-use files that contain administrative data from the programs they oversee, the data in such files are necessarily limited to protect privacy. Further, each agency's data contain little or no information about participation in programs administered by other agencies. This limitation is important because many people with disabilities participate in multiple programs. Matches across multiple program administrative databases can help address this issue, but privacy issues and the challenges of interagency cooperation have limited the number and utility of such efforts to date.

In general, it is extremely difficult, if not impossible, for individual researchers or state governments to obtain access to federal program administrative data with identifiers that would support matches to data from other sources. It can also be very difficult for federal agencies to obtain data from other federal agencies unless specifically needed for purposes of administering their programs. Interagency agreements to match data can take years to develop, and once in place, the actual matching process, development of analytic files and documentation, and establishment of protocols to allow secure access to the matched data can be very time consuming and costly. Fairly recent bilateral agreements between SSA and CMS and the Rehabilitation Services Administration (RSA) are supporting the production of statistics on participation in multiple programs that have previously been unavailable.

In addition, survey data on program participation is generally poor. Participants living in institutions and some group homes are excluded from the sampling frame. Questions about participation in some programs are not included, or they are lumped in with other programs. Respondents often fail to report participation when they are asked, or confuse similar programs (most notably Social Security Disability Insurance [SSDI] with Supplemental Security Income [SSI], and Medicare with Medicaid).

The limitations of administrative and survey data are being partially addressed by the previously mentioned efforts to match administrative records to survey records. Despite the limitations of these efforts, they have added considerably to our knowledge about program participants, as well as to our understanding of the quality of survey data.

IDENTIFICATION AND INCLUSION OF PEOPLE WITH DISABILITIES IN FEDERAL SURVEYS

In this section we describe six options to improve the identification and inclusion of people with disabilities in federal surveys. The first three options pertain to the identification of people with disabilities in survey questionnaires; the next two apply to the definition of the sampling frames from which federal survey samples are drawn; and the last concerns the methods used to locate and interview survey respondents.

Defining Disability in Federally Funded Surveys

The government's decision to adopt a common set of questions for the ACS, CPS, and NHIS is a major step toward the establishment in all federal surveys of a definition of the population "at risk" for disability. Our recommendation goes further—deploy, and eventually require, the inclusion of the new ACS disability questions in all federally funded surveys. In a similar vein, the National Council on Disability recently included promotion of a standard set of disability questions in national surveys among its recommendations for the Government Accountability Office's Key National Indicator Initiative.[6]

It would be enormously helpful to researchers, policymakers, advocates, administrators, and others to have a common understanding of how the population at risk for disability is defined in federal surveys. There would no longer be competing statistics about people with disabilities that vary solely because of differences in the questions used to identify this population. Statistics on prevalence, demographic characteristics, income, employment, and participation in other activities would continue to vary across surveys, but the variation would presumably be much narrower, and the plausible causes of variability would be narrowed in a very important way. With a standard definition in place, researchers and others could draw on disparate surveys to describe this population, with less concern about whether the disability statistics from different surveys are representative of the same populations. A standard definition would also help in developing a more comprehensive and coherent indicator system for the status of people with disabilities than is currently available—comparable statistics on various aspects of the status of this population could be drawn from multiple survey sources.

It must be acknowledged that these disability questions will not meet the needs of all researchers, administrators, policymakers, and advocates. Some people who are truly at high risk of disability will not be captured by these questions, and others at little or no risk will be. These questions will also fail to identify important subgroups of people at risk for disability. No short set of questions can adequately define this population for specific purposes, but specific surveys can add additional disability questions consistent with the survey's objectives. Such questions will also be instructive about those who are at risk but who are not captured by the common questions and those at low risk who are. Such research would likely lead to modifications of these questions in the future. One particular concern is that the ACS might fail to identify many people with significant psychiatric conditions.

It seems especially important to include the common questions in the SIPP, which provides a great deal of information about health conditions, functional limitations, disability, employment, income, and program participation not found in other surveys. The longitudinal nature of SIPP would also provide the opportunity to better understand the dynamics of self-identification of disability under the common questions.[7]

More broadly, it would be extremely valuable to include the ACS questions in all federal surveys, including those that currently have very poor or no disability questions (e.g., the Consumer Expenditure Survey, American Housing Survey, and Survey of Consumer Finances). The inclusion of these questions in all federal surveys would greatly expand the extent of information that we have about the population at risk for disability.

In 1977, the OMB mandated the use of a standardized set of questions on race and ethnicity in all federal data collection.[8] A similar mandate for those at risk for disability now seems justified and would be welcomed by many users of disability data and statistics.

Maintain Old Disability Questions for a Transition Period

In order to monitor the status of people with disabilities and identify trends, it is necessary to have data for comparable groups over long periods. Statistics for people with disabilities are very sensitive to seemingly small changes in the definition of disability. Hence, as survey measures are improved, the risk of losing historical continuity becomes a factor. Every change can create a "seam" in the data; trends can be observed before and after the seam but not across the seam. This gap can be bridged by continuing to ask the old questions for some period of time, perhaps to just a random sample of survey respondents. This would allow researchers to examine how statistics for the newly defined population relate to those of the previous one. Continuation for a single survey period would permit simple adjustments to the level of historical statistics. A longer continuation period would permit examination of differences in the trends of statistics under the new and old populations.

There is also great concern about the possible loss of continuity in statistics for people with work limitations. Currently, work-limitation questions are the only disability questions in the CPS, but they also appear in the ACS, NHIS, SIPP, and others. Conceptually at least, these questions are the standard across these important surveys, although the questions themselves are not identical. Work-limitation questions have been heavily criticized (Hale 2001). The National Council on Disability (NCD) has even recommended that the federal government cease funding and reporting research on people with disabilities that uses "unreliable databases" such as the CPS (National Council on Disability 2001). Although we think many of the criticisms of the work-limitation question are justified, this question also has the significant merit of being used in multiple surveys over a long period of time. Further, research based on the NHIS and SIPP, both of which include other disability questions, has shown that long-term trends in employment and income for people with work limitations, after controlling for the business cycle, are similar to those for disability populations defined by broader functional and activity limitation measures less sensitive to the economic environment (Burkhauser et al. 2002; Weathers and Wittenburg 2009; Burkhauser, Rovba, and Weathers 2009). As experience is gained with a standard set of functional limitation questions in all these surveys, the value of work-limitation questions will likely decline, and perhaps they could eventually be dropped from some, or even all, surveys without loss of significant information.

Comprehensive Sampling Frame for the ACS

Disability statistics can be affected in substantial ways because people with disabilities are not uniformly distributed throughout the population. How the Census Bureau determines who is in a population, how it classifies residence status, and how it and other agencies draw samples for various surveys supported by the Census sampling frame can all impact these statistics. Disproportionately large numbers of people with disabilities live in nonconventional housing, including institutional GQ such as nursing homes, prisons, and long-term psychiatric facilities, and noninstitutional GQ such as various group homes for people with disabilities (She and Stapleton 2009). Changes in policies and the economic environment can affect where people with disabilities live. With the exception of the ACS and surveys of specific institutional populations, all federal surveys exclude people living in some or all types of GQ. Hence, changes in the policy and economic environment can affect disability statistics by changing the number and characteristics of the disability population in a survey's sampling frame.

Over the past two decades, increased levels of incarceration and efforts to move people with disabilities out of nursing homes and other institutions have likely had substantial effects on statistics for some groups of people with disabilities in the household population, but these effects are hard to identify because of inadequate data on the nonhousehold population. This illustrates the importance of including all living quarters, especially GQ, in the ACS sampling frame. The ACS is by far the survey with the most extensive coverage of the entire population, and it should continue to adopt and maintain a comprehensive sampling frame.

The Census Bureau maintains the national Master Address File (MAF), which is the official inventory of known living quarters (housing units and GQ) and selected nonresidential units (public, private, and commercial; U.S. Census Bureau 2006c). The MAF is used as the source of addresses for the ACS, the decennial census, and other demographic surveys supported by the Census Bureau, including the SIPP, CPS, and NHIS.

Only people living in housing units were included in the ACS before 2006. After that, the ACS started to include GQ. The new ACS sampling frame covers most institutional and noninstitutional GQ populations, but it does not provide 100 percent coverage of the entire population.[9] Locations that were classified in the 2000 Census as specific GQ types but excluded from the ACS sample frame include domestic violence shelters, soup kitchens, regularly scheduled mobile food vans, targeted nonsheltered outdoor locations, crews of commercial maritime vessels, natural disaster shelters, and dangerous encampments (U.S. Census Bureau 2006a, 2006c). The reasons for their exclusion include concerns about privacy and the operational feasibility of repeated interviewing for a continuing survey.

As the ACS has now replaced the Decennial Census long-form survey, it has become the only survey that has nearly complete coverage of the entire U.S. population. Thus, it is very important for the ACS to continuously and consistently provide annual data for the population living in housing units and most GQ.[10] This information will be particularly valuable for disability research and statistics, especially for the working-age and child populations, given the large gaps in currently available information.[11] Additionally, the Census Bureau should continue to explore ways to include the GQ types that are currently out of the scope of the ACS. Although the GQ excluded represent a very tiny share of the entire population, we suspect that a disproportionately large number of residents have disabilities. The ultimate goal is to gather data that are representative of the entire population, and the ACS is the only survey that comes close.

Consistency in Other Federal Surveys

Other federal surveys need to clearly define the residence types in their sampling frames, use well-developed frames, and sample in a clear and consistent manner. Sampling frames for other surveys will not be as comprehensive as the ACS sampling frame, in part because of cost, and in part because the surveys focus on collection of information that is only germane for the household population. Because many people with disabilities live in residential settings that are at the margins of the sampling frames used in household surveys (i.e., noninstitutional GQ), some disability statistics may be very sensitive to how the sampling frame is defined and the sample drawn. The Census Bureau coordinates sampling for many federal surveys (U.S. Census Bureau 2006d), but survey rules and procedures might result in coverage differences that are important for people with disabilities, even if they are immaterial for those without disabilities.

We are particularly concerned that the household populations captured in the ACS, CPS, SIPP, and NHIS are not identical. It is possible that the differences in the disability prevalence estimates from these surveys (see Weathers 2009) reflect differences in sampling, although there are many other possible causes. The sample frame for the NHIS, unlike those for the ACS, CPS, and SIPP, cannot use the address file that the Census Bureau develops from the most recent Decennial Census; instead, it must rely on other sources of address information. One result is that the collection of data for the NHIS must rely on field interviewers to identify GQ and make a decision about whether each unit identified meets the survey's inclusion criteria (Botman et al. 2000).[12] It is unknown at this time how important this difference between surveys is for disability statistics.

Federal surveys that use a sampling frame not maintained by the Census Bureau are of greater concern. The triennial Survey of Consumer Finances provides an example. Sponsored by the Federal Reserve System, the survey uses a dual sample frame (Kennickell and McManus 1993). One frame is described as an area probability design and the other is a list sample, drawn from tax records and weighted in a manner to ensure adequate representation of households with relatively high income and wealth, reflecting the survey's purpose. We have found no information on the extent to which the sampling methodology includes those living in GQ of any kind.

As a first step in pursuit of this option, it would be worthwhile to conduct a review of sampling methodologies for all federal household surveys and assess what is known about the inclusion of subjects residing in GQ.

Survey Methodology

Ballou and Markesich (2009) describe how people with disabilities can be excluded at every stage in the survey data collection process. Every federal survey would likely benefit from a review by experts, including experts with disabilities, in the collection of data from and about people with disabilities. Such a review could lead to modest changes in locating methods, respondent selection, interview mode and accommodations, use of proxy respondents, interviewer training, item and response wording, and possibly other aspects of a survey's methodology that would increase the inclusion of people with disabilities and improve the quality of disability data. Although we do not know enough about how various aspects of survey methodologies affect disability data quality, a body of knowledge is emerging. The long-term goal would be to establish standards for all federal surveys.

LONGITUDINAL AND ADMINISTRATIVE
DATA ENHANCEMENTS

Longitudinal survey data on people with disabilities are important because of the dynamics of disability and related events, but they are also very limited. Administrative data, however, can help address these limitations because they can often be used to create longitudinal administrative files. In addition, administrative data are the best source of information on the participation of people with disabilities in public programs. As discussed by Stapleton, Wittenburg, and Thornton (2009), there have been numerous efforts to make use of administrative data, often matched to survey data. These efforts have resulted in substantial, fruitful research, especially that which requires both longitudinal and program data. A great advantage of such efforts to use administrative data is that they do not impose additional burden on respondents and program participants; instead, they make better use of the data already being collected. We offer five options for strengthening longitudinal and administrative data in ways that would improve disability statistics.

Maintain and Strengthen the Federal Government's Longitudinal Survey Efforts

Recently, budgetary pressures and an array of data collection problems have threatened the continuation of the SIPP. This would be a great loss for disability statistics because it is the primary source of longitudinal survey data on disability, employment, income, and program participation. At this writing, it appears that SIPP will continue for at least the near future, but with a diminished sample size. The Census Bureau has been developing a replacement longitudinal data collection system, called the Dynamics of Economic Well-being System (DEWS). In principle, DEWS would address some of the limitations of SIPP, at least in part by relying more heavily on administrative records and reducing the burden of data collection on both respondents and the federal government. True improvements to the collection of longitudinal data focused on SIPP topic areas, especially those with significant disability content, would be of great value to disability researchers, policymakers, and the disability community, but replacement of SIPP with a system of lesser quality for the sole purpose of reducing data collection costs would undermine this very valuable component of the NDDS.

Maintain and Strengthen Efforts to Match Survey Data to Administrative Records

Past efforts to match survey data to administrative records have proven very effective as a means to learn more about characteristics of program participants and how they compare to nonparticipants, factors that affect participation, and the experiences of participants before, during, and after program entry. SSA and Internal Revenue Service (IRS) administrative records have been matched to survey data from many of the SIPP panels, and continuation of that effort through SIPP or its successor is critical. Recent matches between the NHIS and both SSA and Medicare records are likely to be the source of many statistics on people with disabilities in the near future.

One other survey-administrative data matching effort deserves attention. As described by Stapleton, Wittenburg, and Thornton (2009), the SSA and the Census Bureau have pursued a pilot effort to match records from the ACS to SSA administrative data. The success of this effort has not been reported, and it appears that the effort is languishing because of other agency priorities. However, this data matching effort would have enormous value for policy research and development. It would, for the first time, provide substantial socioeconomic information about participants in major programs at the state level on an annual basis. It would also introduce a longitudinal dimension to the ACS that, among other things, would allow production of state-level statistics on individuals who participate in a program (e.g., SSDI) before, during, and after entry. Matches of the SIPP, NHIS, and CPS to SSA data have been used to produce such statistics at the national level, but these surveys are not large enough to support state-level participation statistics on an annual basis. At the state level, such statistics would be a valuable tool for monitoring the status of people with disabilities as the economy and disability policies change.

Finally, we encourage the continuation of recent efforts by the Census Bureau to improve match rates for federal surveys, as described in Stapleton, Wittenburg, and Thornton (2009). The considerable increase in the match rate reported for the 2006 SIPP data, reversing a long decline, is a welcome development.

Maintain and Strengthen Efforts to Match Administrative Data Across Agencies

As described in more detail in Stapleton, Wittenburg, and Thornton (2009), fairly recent bilateral agreements between the SSA, CMS, and RSA have allowed these agencies to match their records for research and administrative purposes. Such matches help address the very limited nature of other data on participation in multiple programs and support analysis of how various programs interact. For example, Medicare and Medicaid records from CMS provide extensive information about the insurance coverage, medical diagnoses, and service utilization of SSDI and SSI beneficiaries, and SSA records provide longitudinal information on the SSDI and SSI participation of state VR agency clients. Although use of these recent agreements has been limited to date, they have great potential to enhance the value of the NDDS. Efforts to build matched analytic files under these agreements, especially longitudinal files, could be quite valuable.

Allow the Matching of Unemployment Insurance Records to Administrative Records

State unemployment insurance (UI) programs must submit their records to SSA for two administrative purposes, as specified by law: to support the efforts by the Office of Child Support Enforcement to enforce child support orders and to support the administration of SSI (see Stapleton, Wittenburg, and Thornton 2009). These records contain quarterly wage data for most people who are not self-employed, as well as information about new hires and UI benefits. SSA and other federal agencies are not allowed to use these data for purposes other than those indicated above, including research.

Many states have successfully used matches between UI data and other state administrative data to support welfare and, to some extent, disability research. The UI wage data are complementary to the IRS earnings data. Most importantly, the wage data are quarterly, not just annual, which can be critical for observing the timing of changes in employment and earnings when a policy or program is changed. Although the UI data for individual states can sometimes be accessed for research purposes, it can be very cumbersome to do so, and single-state data have the distinct disadvantage of not including records for residents who are employed in other states.

Improve Researcher Access to Administrative and Matched Records

Agencies must necessarily protect the privacy of their administrative data, and this means imposing substantial restrictions on access. In general, these data are accessible to qualified employees of the agency and qualified staff of contractors conducting work on an agency's behalf; in the latter case, usage is limited to the scope of work of the contract. The IRS earnings data are an important exception; only qualified federal employees are allowed to access these data.

Researchers conducting independent projects have much more limited access to data derived from administrative records, and it seems very likely that numerous disability-related research efforts have been thwarted or never pursued because of these barriers. There are important exceptions, however (see Stapleton, Wittenburg, and Thornton 2009). CMS has a long-standing and extensive system for providing independent researchers with access to Medicare and Medicaid administrative data, including Medicare Current Beneficiary Survey records that are matched to Medicare enrollment and claims data. The National Institute on Aging and SSA have established an application process through which independent researchers can obtain access, under restrictive conditions, to the Health and Retirement Survey data that have been matched to SSA data. The Census Bureau, under an agreement with the SSA and IRS, also has a process to provide restricted access to SIPP data matched to SSA and IRS data, but the research project must support the legislated goals of the Census. Very recently, the Census Bureau developed synthetic matched SIPP files. These files will provide researchers with access to data that are designed to have all the characteristics of the real matched files, but they are not data for real respondents.

None of these efforts are designed for the specific purpose of supporting disability research and statistics. Yet their value for disability research and statistics is considerable, in part because such a large share of the population with disabilities receives a benefit from at least one federal or federal-state program (see Stapleton, Wittenburg, and Thornton 2009). Improvements in researcher access to matched data, in ways that protect privacy, will substantially increase the value of data that are already being collected.

ENHANCING THE DISABILITY CONTENT OF EXISTING SURVEYS

Adding disability measures to surveys with poor or nonexistent measures is the most important way that disability-relevant content in existing national surveys can be improved. The addition of questions to the PSID in 2003 and the planned addition of disability questions to future rounds of the CPS (and, by extension, ATUS) will make the data from these surveys much more valuable for studying and understanding disability issues.

Aside from improving the identification of people with disabilities in surveys, there are at least two low-cost ways of improving disability-relevant content.

Modify Existing Questions, Probes, or Response Options

A careful review of the instruments for each major federal survey from the perspective of individuals with a wide range of disabilities would likely identify numerous small changes to the questions, probes, and response options that would improve disability content. For example, take disability services, resources, and concepts out of the "other" response option category. When soliciting information about service programs, response options and probes should explicitly include programs like state VR and independent living centers. Questions about employment services should include probes for services such as job coaching and assistance with accommodations. Another change would be to add disability-relevant education categories as response options. For example, some individuals in special education complete high school but receive a special certificate that is not equivalent to a high school diploma. Finally, survey developers should refrain from using responses to work- or activity-limitation questions as the only means for skip patterns into questions about disability-related topics. Many individuals with sensory, intellectual, and other types of disabilities do not view their activities as limited by their conditions.

Of course, it only pays to make the survey questions more disability sensitive if the surveys include an adequate set of questions to identify respondents with disabilities and the sample sizes are large enough to conduct analyses of their responses. For large surveys with disability identifiers, however, very small changes can be enough to significantly improve disability content.

Add a Few Disability-Related Questions in Selected Surveys

In some cases, a few additional questions might substantially improve the usefulness of the survey data for purposes of studying issues related to disability. For example, questions about specific barriers to employment, reasons for not working, employer accommodations, and job demands could be included in the CPS. Questions related to transportation and community accessibility could be added to the ACS.

It is not easy to add even a small number of new questions to an existing survey. Aside from potential cost and logistical issues, changes and added questions can affect other items in the survey and comparisons with statistics derived from past surveys. Convincing the responsible agency that such changes are good investments is likely to require substantial effort. We think, however, that there is a compelling argument to review major federal surveys with respect to the potential of adding significant content through just a few additional questions in each survey.

PERIODIC DISABILITY SUPPLEMENTS
AND SPECIAL SURVEYS

As noted previously and described in more detail in Livermore and She (2007), there are many disability-related topics for which little or no information is routinely collected. We discuss three approaches to addressing limitations of this sort: supplements to existing surveys, periodic surveys of specific subpopulations of people with disabilities, and a stand-alone national disability survey.

Develop Periodic Disability Supplements to Existing Surveys

Adding a topical supplement to an existing national survey would seem to be a useful approach when a large amount of new information is required (e.g., extensive information about environmental factors that might contribute to, or reduce, disability),[13] or when there is a need to study a specific subpopulation that cannot be easily identified with existing information. In either case, an existing, large national survey would act as the screener, as well as provide additional information that enhances the supplement in ways that make this addition to an existing survey more efficient than conducting a stand-alone survey. If this is done, the national survey would have to include disability identifiers; the use of a standard set of identifiers in all federal surveys would increase the utility of this approach.

We have identified three models for supplements to existing surveys. "Topical modules" are supplementary questionnaires administered during one of many interviews. SIPP exemplifies this model because it is built around a core of labor force, program participation, and income questions designed to measure the economic situation of people in the United States. Because SIPP is a longitudinal survey, these core questions are repeated at each wave of interviewing, to capture the dynamics of income and program participation. In addition, the survey was designed to provide a broader context for the analysis of income and program participation dynamics by adding questions on a variety of topics not covered in the core survey. These questions are part of what is termed topical modules and are only administered at particular interviewing waves of the survey. Topics covered by the modules span a variety of subjects, including personal history, child care, wealth, program eligibility, child support, health care, school enrollment, taxes, income sources, and disability. SIPP sample sizes substantially limit the value of SIPP supplements for studying subpopulations of people with disabilities. Uncertainty about the future of the survey and the planned replacement (DEWS) means that we do not know whether the disability information collected via the SIPP disability module will be available at any time in the future, let alone whether the disability supplements could be improved.

SIPP's longitudinal design makes it possible to spread the burden of asking questions in topical modules over multiple interviews. Supplementary questions to those with disabilities identified during an interview for a cross-sectional survey would presumably be asked during the same interview. This would add to the length of the interview and potentially impose an unacceptably large burden on the respondents. The CPS is fielded monthly and has a rotating panel design, under which each subject is interviewed eight times. Similar to SIPP, the CPS already takes advantage of this design by routinely including supplementary questionnaires.

The second supplementary survey model is a "topical survey." This is a survey that appears to be a stand-alone survey but derives its sample from a parent survey, and in essence, it is an extensive topical module of the parent survey. For example, the ATUS derives its sample from the CPS sample, and the Medical Expenditure Panel Survey sample is derived from the NHIS sample. In each case, supplemental interviews are conducted separately from the original interviews, but the data from the original survey can be combined and used with the topical survey data. The NHIS-D also falls in this category, although unlike the other examples of topical surveys, the NHIS-D was designed to be a one-time survey. We return to the NHIS-D in our later discussion of a national disability survey.

The third supplementary survey model is a "topical question battery" that can be added to a core survey questionnaire, perhaps only to respondents identified by a short screen. This model is exemplified by the BRFSS, the Centers for Disease Control (CDC) survey under which topical supplements can be used in concert with a core national survey and administered in a single interview. Under cooperative agreements with the CDC, each state administers the core BRFSS questionnaire every year. The survey's platform provides flexibility to meet the information needs of states, and at the same time, support national and state-level estimates of a core set of items. In addition, each year the CDC offers a variety of approved topical modules that can be used by the state at its discretion and cost. States can also add their own sets of questions, subject to certain procedures and requirements, at their own expense.

Given the inadequacies of disability content in existing surveys, it seems highly desirable to add disability supplements to existing surveys, following one or more of the above models. A single topical module added to a single survey, fielded periodically, could add considerable information to existing data. A program of multiple supplements to multiple surveys, strategically designed to address gaps in current disability data, would be very powerful—especially if all surveys had a standard set of disability questions.

Adding a periodic disability supplement to the ACS is an extremely attractive idea because of the survey's size and ability to produce state and even smaller area estimates. The ACS is already a critical tool for measuring the status of people with disabilities at the state and local level. Adding questions would provide the opportunity to find out about aspects of status that are specific to people with disabilities, such as access to public places, transportation options, and use and availability of assistive devices. From a technical perspective, it seems feasible to develop an infrastructure and process for prioritizing the implementation of relatively brief topical modules attached to the ACS.

As noted previously, the means to add supplemental questionnaires already exists in the CPS. With the adoption of the new ACS disability questions, the CPS has the potential to become a very useful avenue for topical supplements on disability issues, particularly those related to employment.

We do not wish to minimize the challenges of adding disability modules to existing surveys. Resources and support for any supplement must be obtained and, in many cases, might require the cooperation of two or more agencies, including the agency that sponsors the parent survey. There are likely to be numerous technical issues to resolve regarding how the module will be administered. Ideally, administration will maximize efficiency and quality but not alter the nature of the other data that are collected by the parent survey; there can, however, be significant trade-offs between these two objectives. The value of the data collected through some new supplements, however, might greatly exceed the cost of meeting such challenges.

Periodic Surveys of Specific Subpopulations

Periodic surveys of specific subpopulations of people with disabilities would add significant value to the NDDS. We discuss two types of populations of particular interest: 1) the nonhousehold population (including those without disabilities) and 2) participants in major disability programs.

The household population has been surveyed on a regular basis, but the nonhousehold population has been surveyed irregularly, component by component. The two examples of fairly systematic data collection for the nonhousehold population are surveys of nursing home residents and the incarcerated population. We do not have periodic surveys of groups that live in other types of GQ, many of which are intended to house people with disabilities. These include group homes, long-term psychiatric facilities, and residential care facilities. The ACS added these populations in 2006, and they are also included in the Decennial Census, but these data are limited. Periodic surveys that provide more detail about the residents of all GQ seem critical if we are to adequately track the status of people with disabilities.

We also need periodic surveys of homeless people. This population is either not covered at all or covered to an unknown extent in all national surveys, including the Decennial Census and the ACS. One past survey—the 1996 National Survey of Homeless Assistance Providers and Clients—collected information on homeless persons who used homeless assistance programs. There are no more recent data about the homeless population and no data about those who are homeless but do not use homeless services. A national effort led by the Department of Housing and Urban Development (HUD) is implementing the Homeless Management Information Systems (HMIS) in communities across the country, partly to support the collection of national data without having to mount a national survey of this population. Objectives include production of unduplicated counts of homeless individuals and the identification of disabling conditions.[14] In 2007, HUD reported to Congress that local communities have made great progress toward HMIS implementation, and HUD will continue to build local and national capacity to collect, report, and analyze data on the homeless population (U.S. Department of Housing and Urban Development 2007). Successful national implementation of HMIS will add substantially to the NDDS and might also pave the way for special surveys that target the homeless population.

It would also be very useful to periodically survey participants in major programs designed to serve people with disabilities, such as SSDI, SSI, Medicare, Medicaid, and state VR programs. As detailed by Stapleton, Wittenburg, and Thornton (2009), the agencies that run these programs do conduct surveys of the participants, but only the Medicare program has a continuous, systematic survey program, the Medicare Current Beneficiary Survey, which is in its 15th year. RSA has conducted one major survey of VR clients. There is no systematic, ongoing survey program for Medicaid enrollees, SSDI beneficiaries, or SSI recipients. SSA's recent National Beneficiary Survey, conducted to support the Ticket to Work evaluation, was designed as a one-time effort. The last previous SSA survey of adult beneficiaries, the New Beneficiary Survey, was initially fielded in 1982, with a 10-year follow-up in 1991. The population for this survey was limited to new SSDI enrollees and new recipients of Social Security retirement benefits; existing beneficiaries and SSI-only entrants were not included. SSA conducted a survey of SSI children in 2001. States occasionally survey their Medicaid enrollees, but there is no national survey of this population.

Periodic National Disability Surveys

A final approach to improving the NDDS is to conduct periodic national surveys. We think this is the least preferred option for feasibility reasons. It seems to us that the options described above, which improve existing data collection efforts with respect to their disability content, are more feasible, less expensive, and more likely to provide higher quality data for almost all purposes. It seems that the only reason to implement a periodic national survey is the inability to take sufficient advantage of the other options. In principle, a periodic, national disability survey could address many of the limitations of existing disability data: inadequate sample sizes, limited disability measures, limited longitudinal information, limited disability-relevant content, and others. But these and other limitations could, in principle, be addressed by the other options discussed in this chapter, and the return on investment, measured in terms of the extent to which they would address existing data limitations relative to their cost, is higher than that in a periodic national disability survey. The other options generally allow direct comparisons of respondents with disabilities to those without disabilities on the many items that are relevant to both groups (e.g., household structure, living conditions, education, employment, participation in other social activities, consumer expenditure, time use, etc.).

The NHIS-D represents the only large-scale national disability survey ever undertaken in the general population. As mentioned earlier, it is an extensive topical module of a major survey, not a stand-alone survey. For that reason, comparable data on many items were available for respondents without disabilities. The NHIS-D was implemented in two phases. The first phase was conducted along with the NHIS core, and the second was administered approximately one year later to a subset of respondents selected, in part, on the basis of first phase questions.

The NHIS-D differs from the other examples of disability topical modules noted above in two important respects. First, the supplement was designed to be a one-time survey, although many of its developers probably hoped it would be repeated periodically in the future.

Second, a significant number of questions were added to the parent survey interview for the purpose of screening respondents for inclusion in the later topical module, as well as to support the design of the module's response categories and skip patterns. The addition of screening questions to a parent survey can greatly increase the cost and complexity of the design relative to a design that relies solely on responses to existing parent-survey questions. Adding questions to the parent survey can also create some risk that answers to other questions in the survey will systematically differ from those in earlier or later rounds because of changes in the context of those questions.

The NHIS-D was very large, costly, and complex. It involved funding from and coordination across 10 or more federal agencies. Some experts believe that the many compromises necessary to obtain agreement from multiple stakeholders may have created unnecessary complexity, reduced its usefulness, and lowered its chances of ever being replicated in the future. Questions regarding who is responsible for funding and development, what topics to include, how large the samples should be, how they should be derived, and how the survey will be administered all had to be addressed.

At the same time, however, the NHIS-D produced valuable disability information that had not previously been collected (e.g., on accommodations, assistive devices, and personal assistance services), and it has been used extensively to study a wide variety of disability issues (Hendershot 2005). Further, the valuable lessons and experiences from the development and use of the NHIS-D could inform the development of periodic national disability surveys and help make them more useful and efficient. It appears to us, however, that the bulk of needs to be met by a national survey could be met by a less expensive, and less logistically challenging, effort to improve the disability content of other surveys. The fact that the NHIS-D is really an extremely large topical module of the NHIS reinforces this point; much less ambitious topical modules attached to a variety of surveys could address the same needs as a national disability survey.

There are two important, but implicit, features of the NHIS-D that could not be replicated through a series of supplements to existing surveys unless there are other important changes to those surveys. All of the NHIS-D disability statistics are based on a single set of disability identifiers, and they are obtained from data that were collected via a single set of methodologies (i.e., the sampling methodology, the methods for finding and interviewing respondents, and the methods for addressing nonresponse and missing data). These implicit features of the NHIS-D serve to emphasize the importance of including a standard set of disability questions in all major surveys, and using consistent, well-defined data collection methods. Without improvements in these areas, researchers cannot expect to collect information on comparable disability populations from a system of disability topical modules attached to diverse surveys. In the absence of such improvements, a periodic national survey might be the only feasible way to obtain this important information.

PRIORITIES

In this chapter we have described options that would greatly enhance the quality and value of the data collected by the NDDS. Most of these are of relatively low cost because they require collection of little or no new data. Instead, they focus on better use of already collected data, or on relatively small, but important improvements to collection efforts that are already in place. Institutional constraints are likely to be the greatest obstacle to implementation, not costs. The limitations of the NDDS can be attributed in part to the fact that the government has not viewed, developed, and managed its components as a system, formal or informal, reflecting the diverse interests and constraints of the various agencies involved.

A list of the options, organized by section, appears in Table 11.3.[15] The columns identify specific limitations of the NDDS (see Section 2), double check marks indicate the limitations that would be addressed by each of the options, and single check marks indicate limitations that might be addressed by the option, depending on how it is implemented.

In general, we think the greatest gains can be achieved by deploying the new ACS questions in all federal surveys (first section of Table 11.3), building on the significant gains that will already be achieved by using common, carefully designed questions in the ACS, CPS, and NHIS. As noted earlier, these questions will apply to ATUS, too, because those surveys use the CPS as their sampling frame. The second option, continuation of old disability questions during a transition period, is important to maintain the historical continuity of disability statistics as the new ACS questions are deployed.

We also think that options to strengthen longitudinal and administrative data should receive high priority (second section of Table 11.3), in part because they do not call for extensive collection of new data. The first of the five options in this area calls for the continuation and strengthening of existing longitudinal data collection efforts, most importantly the SIPP, and the rest call for making better use of data that are already collected. Attending to the first option is particularly urgent and needs to be given very high priority; we do not have strong views about priorities of the remaining four.

We give lower priority to options for collecting additional disability content (last section of Table 11.3) than to those that would improve the identification and inclusion of people with disabilities, and options to improve longitudinal and administrative data. Pursuit of the options in these first two areas will greatly increase disability content without requiring additional data collection.

We place a periodic national disability survey at the end of the options list. As discussed previously, a very large share of the informational gain that could be obtained from a national survey would be gained by implementation of other, more practical improvements. A national disability survey is a very expensive undertaking and requires the extensive cooperation of many interested agencies. In contrast, many of the other options require no new data collection and less interagency cooperation, if any.

Perhaps we are too optimistic about the implementation of what we think are much more practical options for improving the implicit NDDS. Recent developments feed our optimism, however, most notably the adoption of common disability questions in the ACS and CPS, progress toward increasing the completeness of matches between SIPP and SSA administrative data, and establishment and productive use of interagency matching agreements. Furthermore, the Department of Labor has now announced that it will start to routinely produce and publish CPS-based statistics on the population with disabilities.[16] People with disabilities will finally be counted.

Table 11.3 Summary of Options to Address Limitations of the National Disability Data System

Options	Limitations of the national disability data system										Limitations of disability program data				
	Limitations on identification of people with disabilities			Small samples of people with disabilities	Limitations of data on subpopulations of people with disabilities			Subject areas poorly addressed[a]	Untimely and outdated information	Limited longitudinal data	Research access	Survey data	Admin. data	Multiple programs	Match limitations
	Compara-bility	Poor/no measures	Mental disabili-ties		GQ residents	Homeless people	Collection methods								
Identification and inclusion of people with disabilities in federal surveys															
Deploy new ACS disability questions in all federal surveys	√√	√√						√√							
Continue old disability questions for a transitional period	√√								√√						
Maintain a comprehensive sampling frame for the ACS				√√	√√	√√									
Improve sampling methodologies					√√	√									
Address methods that exclude people with disabilities							√√								
Longitudinal and administrative data															
Strengthen the collection of longitudinal survey data				√√				√√	√√	√√	√√	√√	√√	√√	
Strengthen efforts to match survey and administrative records										√√	√√	√√	√√	√√	√√

Strengthen efforts to match data across agencies

Allow the matching of unemployment insurance records

Improve research access to administrative and matched data

Disability content

Modify existing questions, probes, and response options

Add a few disability-related questions in selected surveys

Add periodic disability supplements to existing surveys

Conduct periodic surveys of specific subpopulations

Conduct periodic national disability surveys

NOTE: √ = Some variants of option would address the limitation; √√ = option would be designed to address limitation.

[a]These include time use, consumer expenditures, transportation, employment supports, community participation, living arrangements, and disability onset and progression.

Notes

1. See Stapleton et al. (2009) for additional details.
2. The planned use of these questions in the NHIS is documented in a letter from Jim Nussle, Director of the Office of Management and Budget, to Congressman William Lacy, Chairman of the Information, Policy, Census, and National Archives Subcommittee of the Committee on Oversight and Government Reform, U.S. House of Representatives, July 24, 2008.
3. See Washington Group on Disability Statistics (2008).
4. Terence McMenamin announced the decision at a public meeting of the Interagency Subcommittee on Disability Statistics in January 2007. The introduction to the BLS questions will differ somewhat from that in the ACS because of contextual differences in the two surveys, and the questions will be converted to a household format, rather than the individual format used by the ACS.
5. The ATUS sample is much smaller than the CPS sample, so production of time-use statistics for persons with disabilities from ATUS will probably require pooling of ATUS data over several years.
6. See U.S. Government Accountability Office (n.d.).
7. This assumes continuation of SIPP. As discussed later, this is doubtful, and it is not clear that any successor to SIPP will collect extensive disability information.
8. See OMB's Statistical Policy Directive 15 adopted in 1977 and most recently revised in 1997 at Office of Management and Budget (1997).
9. Nevertheless, ACS estimates of the total population are controlled to be consistent with the intercensal population estimates (U.S. Census Bureau 2006c). The exclusion of certain GQ types may result in a small bias in some ACS estimates.
10. Due to differences in the sampling method or the sampling frame, statistics based on the 2005 ACS would not be comparable with those of the 2004 ACS.
11. Medicare statistics for those aged 65 and over can be considered very close to statistics for the entire population aged 65 and over.
12. The NHIS excludes only institutional and military GQ.
13. The Craig Hospital Inventory of Environmental Factors includes 25 such factors (Harrison-Felix 2001).
14. See U.S. Department of Housing and Urban Development (2004).
15. These options and their ordering benefited substantially from input received during and as follow-up to the October 2006 conference organized by the Rehabilitation Research and Training Center on Disability Statistics and Demographics, "The Future of Disability Statistics: What We Know and Need to Know," held in Washington, DC, and sponsored by the National Institute for Disability and Rehabilitation Research.
16. This policy was announced by Neil Romano, Assistant Secretary for the Office of Disability Employment Policy, at "A Summit on Disability Employment Policy," Gallaudet University, June 3, 2008.

References

Ballou, Janice, and Jason Markesich. 2009. "Survey Data Collection Methods." In *Counting Working-Age People with Disabilities: What Current Data Tell Us and Options for Improvement*, Andrew J. Houtenville, David C. Stapleton, Robert R. Weathers II, and Richard V. Burkhauser, eds. Kalamazoo, MI: W.E. Upjohn Institute for Employment Research, pp. 265–298.

Botman, Steven L., Thomas F. Moore, Christopher L. Moriarity, and Van L. Parsons. 2000. "Design and Estimation for the National Health Interview Survey, 1995–2004." Hyattsville, MD: National Center for Health Statistics. *Vital and Health Statistics* 2(130). http://www.cdc.gov/nchs/data/series/sr_02/sr02_130.pdf (accessed June 20, 2008).

Burkhauser, Richard V., Mary C. Daly, Andrew J. Houtenville, and Nigar Nargis. 2002. "Self-Reported Work Limitation Data: What They Can and Cannot Tell Us." *Demography* 39(3): 541–555.

Burkhauser, Richard V., Andrew J. Houtenville, and Ludmila Rovba. 2009. "Poverty." In *Counting Working-Age People with Disabilities: What Current Data Tell Us and Options for Improvement*, Andrew J. Houtenville, David C. Stapleton, Robert R. Weathers II, and Richard V. Burkhauser, eds. Kalamazoo, MI: W.E. Upjohn Institute for Unemployment Research, pp. 193–226.

Burkhauser, Richard V., Ludmila Rovba, and Robert R. Weathers II. 2009. "Household Income." In *Counting Working-Age People with Disabilities: What Current Data Tell Us and Options for Improvement*, Andrew J. Houtenville, David C. Stapleton, Robert R. Weathers II, and Richard V. Burkhauser, eds. Kalamazoo, MI: W.E. Upjohn Institute for Unemployment Research, pp. 143–190.

Hale, Thomas. 2001. "The Lack of a Disability Measure in Today's Current Population Survey." *Monthly Labor Review* 125(6): 38–40.

Harrison-Felix, Cindy. 2001. "The Craig Hospital Inventory of Environmental Factors." Denver, CO: Craig Hospital, The Center for Outcome Measurement in Brain Injury. http://www.tbims.org/combi/chief (accessed September 7, 2007).

Hendershot, Gerry E. 2005. "Statistical Analyses Based on the National Health Interview Survey on Disability: A Bibliography and Summary of Findings." Minneapolis, MN: University of Minnesota, College of Education and Human Development, Research and Training Center on Community Living and the Institute on Community Integration. http://rtc.umn.edu/docs/NHIS-DBibliography.pdf (accessed June 20, 2008).

Houtenville, Andrew J., Elizabeth Potamites, William A. Erickson, and S.

Antonio Ruiz-Quintanilla. 2009. "Disability Prevalence and Demographics." In *Counting Working-Age People with Disabilities: What Current Data Tell Us and Options for Improvement*, Andrew J. Houtenville, David C. Stapleton, Robert R. Weathers II, and Richard V. Burkhauser, eds. Kalamazoo, MI: W.E. Upjohn Institute for Unemployment Research, pp. 69–99.

Kennickell, Arthur B., and Douglas A. McManus. 1993. "Sampling for Household Financial Characteristics Using Frame Information on Past Income." Washington, DC: Board of Governors of the Federal Reserve. http://www.federalreserve.gov/pubs/oss/oss2/papers/asa93.pdf (accessed June 20, 2008).

Livermore, Gina A., and Peiyun She. 2007. "Limitations of the National Disability Data System." Ithaca, NY: Cornell University, Rehabilitation Research and Training Center on Disability Demographics and Statistics.

McMenamin, Terence M., Thomas W. Hale, Douglas Kruse, and Haejin Kim. 2005. "Designing Questions to Identify People with Disabilities in Labor Force Surveys: The Effort to Measure the Employment Level of Adults with Disabilities in the CPS." Washington, DC: Bureau of Labor Statistics. http://www.bls.gov/osmr/pdf/st050190.pdf (accessed September 29, 2008).

National Council on Disability. 2001. "National Disability Policy: A Progress Report, November 1999–November 2000." Washington, DC: National Council on Disability.

———. 2007. "Keeping Track: National Disability Status and Program Performance Indicators." Washington, DC: National Council on Disability.

Office of Management and Budget. 1997. "Revisions to the Standards for the Classification of Federal Data on Race and Ethnicity." Washington, DC: Office of Management and Budget. http://www.whitehouse.gov/omb/fedreg/1997standards.html (accessed May 30, 2008).

She, Peiyun, and David C. Stapleton. 2009. "The Group Quarters Population." In *Counting Working-Age People with Disabilities: What Current Data Tell Us and Options for Improvement*, Andrew J. Houtenville, David C. Stapleton, Robert R. Weathers II, and Richard V. Burkhauser, eds. Kalamazoo, MI: W.E. Upjohn Institute for Unemployment Research, pp. 353–380.

Stapleton, David C., Andrew J. Houtenville, Robert R. Weathers II, and Richard V. Burkhauser. "Purpose, Overview, and Key Conclusions." In *Counting Working-Age People with Disabilities: What Current Data Tell Us and Options for Improvement*, Andrew J. Houtenville, David C. Stapleton, Robert R. Weathers II, and Richard V. Burkhauser, eds. Kalamazoo, MI: W.E. Upjohn Institute for Unemployment Research, pp. 1–26.

Stapleton, David C., David C. Wittenburg, and Craig Thornton. 2009. "Program Participants." In *Counting Working-Age People with Disabilities: What Current Data Tell Us and Options for Improvement*, Andrew J. Houtenville,

David C. Stapleton, Robert R. Weathers II, and Richard V. Burkhauser, eds. Kalamazoo, MI: W.E. Upjohn Institute for Unemployment Research, pp. 299–352.

U.S. Census Bureau. 2006a. "2006 ACS Group Quarters Types Codes and Definitions." Washington, DC: U.S. Census Bureau. http://www.census.gov/acs/www/Downloads/2006_ACS_GQ_Definitions.pdf (accessed June 20, 2008).

———. 2006b. "American Community Survey: 2006 Subject Definitions." Washington, DC: U.S. Census Bureau. http://www.census.gov/acs/www/Downloads/2006/usedata/Subject_Definitions.pdf (accessed January 30, 2008).

———. 2006c. "Design and Methodology, American Community Survey." Technical Paper no. 67. Washington, DC: U.S. Government Printing Office. http://www.census.gov/acs/ www/Downloads/tp67.pdf (accessed June 6, 2008).

———. 2006d. "Design and Methodology, Current Population Survey." Technical Paper no. 63RV. Washington, DC: U.S. Census Bureau. http://www.census.gov/prod/2002pubs/tp63rv.pdf (accessed June 20, 2008).

U.S. Department of Housing and Urban Development. 2004. "HMIS Data and Technical Standards." Washington, DC: U.S. Department of Housing and Urban Development. http://www.hud.gov/offices/cpd/homeless/library/webcast101804/presentation.pdf (accessed September 8, 2007).

———. 2007. "Report to Congress: Sixth Progress Report on HUD's Strategy for Improving Homeless Data Collection, Reporting and Analysis." Washington, DC: U.S. Department of Housing and Urban Development. http://www.hud.gov/offices/cpd/homeless/library/improvingDataCollection.pdf (accessed June 20, 2008).

U.S. Government Accountability Office. n.d. "Key National Indicators." Washington, DC: U.S. Government Accountability Office. http://www.gao/gov/cghome/2005/ngfipi05182005/img24.html (accessed September 8, 2007).

Washington Group on Disability Statistics. 2008. "W.G. Short Set of Questions on Disability." Hyattsville, MD: National Center for Health Statistics. http://www.cdc.gov/nchs/about/otheract/citygroup/shortsetquestions.htm (accessed September 6, 2008).

Weathers, Robert R. II. 2009. "The Disability Data Landscape." In *Counting Working-Age People with Disabilities: What Current Data Tell Us and Options for Improvement*, Andrew J. Houtenville, David C. Stapleton, Robert R. Weathers II, and Richard V. Burkhauser, eds. Kalamazoo, MI: W.E. Upjohn Institute for Unemployment Research, pp. 27–68.

Weathers, Robert R. II, and David C. Wittenburg. 2009. "Employment." In *Counting Working-Age People with Disabilities: What Current Data Tell*

Us and Options for Improvement, Andrew J. Houtenville, David C. Stapleton, Robert R. Weathers II, and Richard V. Burkhauser, eds. Kalamazoo, MI: W.E. Upjohn Institute for Unemployment Research, pp. 101–144.

The Authors

Janice Ballou is a senior fellow at Mathematica Policy Research. She has more than thirty years of survey research experience and has worked on a range of research projects and methodological issues related to people with disabilities. Ballou earned an MA in political science from Rutgers University.

Richard V. Burkhauser is the Sarah Gibson Blanding Professor of Public Policy in the Department of Policy Analysis and Management and professor of economics, Cornell University. He has published widely on how public policies affect the economic behavior and well-being of vulnerable populations, including working-age people with disabilities. He received his PhD in economics from the University of Chicago.

William A. Erickson, MS, is a research specialist at Cornell University's Employment and Disability Institute. Mr. Erickson is a member of Cornell's Disability Statistics RRTC and works with disability data from several federal data sets including Census 2000, the American Community Survey, and the CDC's Behavioral Risk Factor Surveillance Survey.

Benjamin H. Harris is a senior research associate with the Brookings Institution. His current research interests include tax policy, retirement saving, and labor force participation.

Gerry E. Hendershot is a consultant on disability and health statistics. For 25 years, he was a health statistician in the federal statistical system, and before that was on the sociology faculties of several colleges and universities. He is the author of more than 60 journal articles, book chapters, and government reports on disability and health statistics.

Andrew J. Houtenville is a senior research associate at New Editions Consulting, Inc. and co-principal investigator of the Hunter College Rehabilitation Research and Training Center on Disability Statistics and Demographics. He received his PhD in economics from the University of New Hampshire.

Gina A. Livermore, PhD, a senior researcher at Mathematica Policy Research, is an expert in health insurance and employment policy issues for people with disabilities. Her research focuses on the effects of health and disability on economic well-being, the impact of public programs and policies on low-income populations, and improving the quality of national disability data.

Jason Markesich is the director of survey operations at Mathematica Policy Research. He has designed and directed many surveys conducted in the fields of disability and health that have included populations with multiple disabling conditions and age-associated vulnerabilities. Markesich earned an MA in public policy from Rutgers University.

Elizabeth Potamites received her PhD in labor economics from New York University. She is a researcher at Mathematica Policy Research in Washington, DC.

Ludmila Rovba is an economist with The Analysis Group, Inc. in Montreal, Quebec. She received her PhD in economics from Cornell University.

S. Antonio Ruiz-Quintanilla is the director of the Disability and Business Technical Assistance Center for the Northeast Region (DBTAC-Northeast). He is also a senior research associate in the Employment and Disability Institute at the ILR School of Cornell University. His current research interests include workforce diversity, organizational climate, and human resource issues as they relate to the employment of persons with disabilities.

Peiyun She received her PhD in demography from the University of California, Berkeley in 2004. Her research was in disability and poverty, and disability statistics. She's contribution to this book was completed while she was a research associate at Cornell University's Institute for Policy Research.

David C. Stapleton is the director of the Center for Studying Disability Policy at Mathematica Policy Research and co-principal investigator for the Rehabilitation Research and Training Center on Disability Demographics and Statistics. He received his PhD in economics from the University of Wisconsin.

Craig Thornton has conducted research into disability policy issues for more than 25 years. His most recent work examines efforts to help people receiving Social Security disability benefits find meaningful and sustaining employment. He received a PhD in economics from the Johns Hopkins University and is currently the managing director of health research at Mathematica Policy Research.

Robert R. Weathers II is an economist with the Social Security Administration in Baltimore, Maryland. He earned an MA and PhD in economics from Syracuse University.

David C. Wittenburg is a senior researcher in the Center for Studying Disability Policy at Mathematica Policy Research. He received his PhD in economics from Syracuse University.

Index

The italic letters *f, n,* and *t* following a page number indicate that the subject information of the heading is within a figure, note, or table, respectively, on that page. Double italics indicate multiple but consecutive elements.

AAOPR (American Association for Public Opinion Research)
method of describing survey disposition categories, 273
"Standard Definitions," 267*t*
ACS (American Community Survey). *See also* CPS-ASEC (Current Population Survey Annual Social and Economic Supplement); Decennial Census data; NHIS (National Health Interview Survey); SIPP (Survey of Income and Program Participation)
for 2006, 6, 10, 13, 15, 21, 22, 27
addition of periodic disability supplement, 405
advantages and limitations, 33, 58, 59, 117–118, 125, 128
best concept to use for employment rate data, 128
comprehensive sampling frame, 393–395
data on GQ and homeless populations, 353–354
data on residence types and disability status, 370, 373*t*, 374
definition of disabilities, 55, 57
disability and household income definitions compared with March CPS, 186*t* –189*t*
disability question, 32–33
disability question standardization with CPS and NHIS, 384–385
employment and disability conceptualizations, 106, 107*t*
employment definitions, 131*t* –132*t*
employment disability compared with CPS work limitations, 81

employment rate estimates compared with other household surveys, 111, 113, 114*t*, 117
estimating poverty rates for population with disabilities from, 195, 200
health insurance question, 314
household income analysis from, 172–183, 173*t*,176*t* –177*t*, 178*t* –180*t*, 181*f*
matches with administrative records data, 334, 336
new questions considered for, 61–62
prevalence rates for six disability categories, 43*t*, 45
questions used to identify ADLs, 51, 52*t*
questions used to identify IADLs, 53, 54*t*
questions used to identify mental impairments, 49*t*, 50
questions used to identify physical impairments, 46*t* –47*t*
questions used to identify sensory impairments, 42, 44, 45
questions used to identify work limitations, 55, 56*t*
state- and local-level employment rate analysis from, 118–123, 119*t*, 120*t* –122*t*
summary of program participation information in, 303*t*
types of group quarters (GQ) non included as of 2006, 376*n*11
use for program participation ratios, 322–323
usefulness for economic well-being data, 146
workers' comp benefits estimates, 321

Activity limitation, 27, 29, 30. *See also* ADL (activity of daily living) limitations; Participation restriction
  causes and risks associated with different conditions, 238
  as composite measure of functioning and disability, 236–237, 238–240, 239*t*
  NHIS definition, 260*n*4
  relationship with ADL/IADL and participation restrictions, 241
ADA (Americans with Disabilities Act of 1990), 7, 8, 10, 11, 95
  definition of disability, 29–30, 55
ADL (activity of daily living) limitations, 27, 29. *See also* IADL (instrumental activity of daily living); Self-care impairments
  definitions, 96*n*2, 187*t*
  differences in employment rates for adults with, 109*f*, 110
  and disability prevalence, 72–73
  and the elderly, 72
  employment rate estimates in four major household surveys, 113, 114*t*, 118
  household income estimates, 173*t*
  household income estimates by state, 176*t* –177*t*, 178*t* –180*t*
  of incarcerated population, 370
  measures used for testing functional status, 235
  in NHIS surveys, 38
  and poverty rates, 203
  prevalence, 243*t*
  prevalence rate by survey, 43*t*
  questions on major national surveys about, 50–51, 52*t*
  relationship with self-reported health status, 244–251, 245*t*, 247*t*, 250*t*, 252*t*, 258*t* –259*t*
Administrative records data, 13, 15, 299–300. *See also* Data on program participants; National disability data system (NDDS)

cautions about using linked data from, 140*n*10
  enhancements needed, 397–401
  estimates on workers' compensation from, 320–321
  gaining access, 329, 336–337
  improving researcher access, 400–401
  limitations for studying program participants, 302
  limitations for use in national disability data system (NDDS), 389
  longitudinal, 12
  longitudinal analysis of SSI and SSDI, 329–330
  matching with survey data, 328, 332–335
  national household surveys that link, 125–127, 126*t*
  and sample designs, 271–272
  and SIPP surveys, 41
  SSDI, OASDI, SSI, and other SSA programs, 306*t* –307*t*
AFDC (Aid to Families with Dependent Children), 333
African Americans
  disability prevalence rates, 80*t*, 81
  future research needed, 94
  and prevalence of work limitations, 1981–2007, 91*t*, 92, 92*f*
  who reside in institutions, 362–363, 362*t*, 365*t*
Age and aging
  age categories, 97*n*12
  age distribution across education groups, 1981–2007, 93
  and composition of institutional group quarters (GQ) population, 360– 361, 360*t*, 361*t*, 364*t*, 365*t*
  and disability prevalence, 70, 79, 79*f*, 80*t*, 84–89, 87*t*, 88*t*
  elderly populations and disability prevalence, 72
  gender and age-adjusted prevalence of work limitations, 89, 90*t* –91*t*
  suggestions for improving program data for research, 336

Agencies. *See* Federal funding of
    programs; Program participants;
    State- and local-level data on
    working-age people
AHRQ (Agency for Heatlhcare Research
    and Quality), 240
Aid to Families with Dependent
    Children. *See* AFDC (Aid to
    Families with Dependent
    Children)
American Association for Public Opinion
    Research. *See* AAOPR (American
    Association for Public Opinion
    Research)
American Community Survey. *See* ACS
    (American Community Survey)
Americans with Disabilities Act. *See*
    ADA (Americans with Disabilities
    Act of 1990)
American Time Use Survey. *See* ATUS
    (American Time Use Survey)
*Annual Report on Income, Poverty and
    Health Insurance Coverage in the
    United States* (U.S. Census
    Bureau), 1–2
"Any disability" definition in NHIS, 239*t*
Arthritis and disability, 251, 260*n*8
Asian Americans disability prevalence
    rates, 2006, 80*t*, 81
"Ask Me!" project (Maryland), 289
At-risk population groups
    operational definitions, 7
    statistics, 1–2, 6
ATUS (American Time Use Survey),
    384, 387, 401, 404

Back/neck problems and disability, 251
Behavioral Risk Factor Surveillance
    System. *See* BRFSS (Behavioral
    Risk Factor Surveillance System)
BJS. *See* Bureau of Justice Statistics
    (BJS)
BLS. *See* Bureau of Labor Statistics
    (BLS)
BMI categories and disability, 249, 250*t*
BMI calculation, 260*n*6

BRFSS (Behavioral Risk Factor
    Surveillance System), 14, 61, 240,
    254–255, 386, 404–405
Bureau of Justice Statistics (BJS), 356
Bureau of Labor Statistics (BLS), 34, 61,
    102–103, 384
    employment measures based on levels
        of attachment to the labor force,
        105–106
    statistical sources for income, 147,
        148
Business cycles
    and age-adjusted disability prevalence
        rates, 89
    defined, 190*n*4, 193
    and disability prevalence rates, 84–85
    and economic well-being of people
        with and without work limitations,
        198
    employment rate estimates for
        working-aged people with
        disabilities and, 117
    household income analyses and,
        148–152, 148*f*, 150*t*–151*t*
    poverty rates decomposed by
        demographic categories over,
        213–219, 216*t*–217*t*, 218*t*, 219*f*
    self-reported work limitations and,
        242
    trends in poverty rates over, 208–213,
        210*t*–211*t*, 212*t*, 220
    troughs *vs.* peaks, 97*n*10

Canadian Community Health Survey
    (Statistics Canada), 279, 280, 282*t*
Canadian Participation and Activity
    Limitation Survey, 275, 276*f*
CART (Communications Access
    Realtime Translation), 285,
    293*n*11
CDC (Centers for Disease Control),
    61, 404–405. *See also* BRFSS
    (Behavioral Risk Factor
    Surveillance System); NCHS
    (National Center for Health
    Statistics)

Census 2000 Supplementary Survey
(C2SS), 280, 282, 353, 354–355
Centers for Medicare and Medicaid
Services. *See* CMS (Centers for
Medicare and Medicaid Services)
Child data, 37
Chronic Condition Warehouse at the
CMS, 330
CMS (Centers for Medicare and
Medicaid Services), 299, 311–315,
312*t*–313*t*, 330
data agreements with other agencies,
331–332, 389–390
data matches with national household
surveys, 333–334
researcher access to data, 400
researcher access to Medicare data,
337
Cognitive impairments and survey data
collection modes, 284, 285
Collection mode impact on surveys, 271,
273
College and university student
populations, 374
Committee to Review the Social Security
Administration's Disability
Decision Process Research, 292*n*4
Communications Access Realtime
Translation. *See* CART
(Communications Access
Realtime Translation)
Comorbidity, 241
Condition approach to analyzing health
and disability, 237, 238, 249,
253–254
conditions in current NHIS (National
Health Interview Survey), 260*n*3
Consumer Price Index. *See* Urban
Consumer Price Index (CPI-U)
Correctional facilities. *See* Incarcerated
population
*Counting Working-Age People with
Disabilities,* 2–3, 15–19
CPI-U. *See* Urban Consumer Price Index
(CPI-U)

CPS. *See* Current Population Survey
(CPS)
CPS-ASEC (Current Population Survey
Annual Social and Economic
Supplement), 27, 34–36. *See also*
ACS (American Community
Survey); Current Population
Survey (CPS); Decennial Census
data; March CPS; NHIS (National
Health Interview Survey); SIPP
(Survey of Income and Program
Participation)
advantages and limitations, 59–60,
104–105, 125, 128, 129
annual employment rates of men
using alternative disability
concepts, 135*t*–136*t*, 137*t*–139*t*
best concept to use for employment
rate data, 128
Bureau of Labor Statistics use of,
102–103, 104
definition of disabilities, 55, 57
disability questions, 104
employment and disability
conceptualizations, 106, 107*t*
employment definitions, 131*t*–132*t*
employment rate estimates compared
with other household surveys, 111,
111*f*, 114*t*, 115–117, 116*f*
new questions considered for, 61
prevalence rates for six disability
categories, 43*t*
questions used to identify ADLs, 52*t*
questions used to identify IADLs, 54*t*
questions used to identify mental
impairments, 49*t*
questions used to identify physical
impairments, 46*t*–47*t*
questions used to identify sensory
impairments, 44*t*
questions used to identify work
limitations, 54*t*, 55, 58
using for state- local-level
employment rate estimates, 118
Cross-agency matches of administrative
records data, 331–336, 389–390

Cross-sectional surveys
    compared with SIPP and other panel
        data sets, 41, 220
    use for long-term trend analyses,
        113–117, 114*t*, 116*f*
Current Population Survey (CPS), 8,
        13. *See also* CPS-ASEC (Current
        Population Survey Annual Social
        and Economic Supplement);
        March CPS
    addition of disability questions, 401,
        402
    addition of periodic disability
        supplement, 405
    data on participants in state programs,
        321
    estimates of Social Security benefit
        payments, 310
    estimates of veterans benefits
        payments, 318
    household income statistics, 145–146
    major limitation, 146
    matches with administrative records
        data, 333–334
    new disability questions, 387
    omission of GQ and homeless
        populations, 353
    summary of program participation
        information in, 303*t*
    workers' comp benefits estimates,
        320–321

Data collection using surveys, 269*t*. *See
        also* National disability data
        system (NDDS); Surveys
    about, 265
    best practices guidelines, 268–289,
        269*t*, 287*t*, 290
    documenting information about,
        266–267, 291
    identifying priorities for disability
        research, 267–268
    interviewers, 275, 286–289, 287*f*, 290
    offering respondents choices among
        data collection modes, 284
    overview, 269*t*

    of program participants, 300
    proxy respondents, 274–277, 276*f*,
        293*n*8
    qualitative modes, 284–286
    quantitative modes, 283–284
    questionnaire design, 277–282, 280*f*,
        281*f*
    recommended best practices, 290–291
    research design, 270
    respondent selection, 272–274
    sample design, 270–271
    sampling frame, 271–272, 283
    summary, 289
Data on program participants. *See also*
        Administrative records data
    about, 299–301
    agencies and other organizations that
        provide, 301, 320–321
    conclusions about, 335–337
    cross-agency matches from
        administrative records, 328, 331–
        335
    discrepancies among different data
        sources, 310
    estimates of number of participants,
        305*f*
    inadequate, 389–390
    longitudinal, 328–330
    Medicare, Medicaid and other CMS
        programs, 312*t*–313*t*, 374*n*1
    in national household surveys, 303*t*
    need for periodic disability surveys,
        407
    SSI, SSDI, and other SSA programs,
        304–310, 305*f*, 306*t*–307*t*
    state-level data, 311, 314, 321–328,
        324*f*, 325*f*, 327*f*
    survey refusal rates when Social
        Security number used, 335
    uses for, 302
    in veterans' programs, 317–321, 319*t*
    in vocational rehabilitation (VR)
        programs, 314–317, 316*t*
    and working-age population and
        disability programs by state, 340*t*–
        343*t*

Data on working-age people with
    disabilities. *See also*
    Administrative records data;
    Demographic data; Longitudinal
    studies of working-age people
    with disabilities; State- and local-
    level data on working-age people
    with disabilities; Surveys
  dearth of, 1–2, 6
  evaluating quality, 266–267, 267*t*
  federal government agency uses, 3–5
  group quarters (GQ) and homeless
    populations, 353–357, 386–387,
    393–396
  group quarters (GQ) population and
    homeless populations, 368–370
  improving quality in collection of,
    267–268
  information about physical and social
    barriers, 12
  most comprehensive geographic
    detailed trend data, 33
  most cost-effective method of using, 3
  "public good" aspect, 4
  reasons for dearth of, 7–13
  summary of emerging landscape,
    60–62
Decennial Census data, 15, 145. *See also*
    ACS (American Community
    Survey); CPS-ASEC (Current
    Population Survey Annual Social
    and Economic Supplement); NHIS
    (National Health Interview
    Survey); SIPP (Survey of Income
    and Program Participation); 2000
    Decennial Census
  group institutional quarters (GQ)
    population, 358–367, 359*t*, 360*t*,
    361*t*, 362*t*, 364*t*–365*t*, 366*t*, 367*t*
  uniqueness as source for GQ
    population data, 353, 355, 394
  2000 version compared to 1990
    version, 356
  2000 version compared with Census
    2000 Supplementary Survey, 280,
    282

Delphi Method, 292*n*3
Demographic data
  ACS, 32
  annual employment rates of men
    using alternative disability
    concepts from CPS and NHIS,
    135*t*–136*t*, 137*t*–139*t*
  CPS-ASEC, 34
  differences in employment rates
    between men and women, 140*n*8
  disability prevalence, 74, 79–81, 79*f*,
    80*t*
  disability prevalence rates, 93–94
  employment rates, 120*t*–122*t*
  gender self-reports on height and
    weight, 248
  geographic distribution of
    employment, 119*f*
  on health and activity limitations,
    239, 239*t*
  household income by sex, race,
    education and state, 174–175
  household income for working-age
    men, 146–148
  household income of working-age
    women, 190n1
  incarcerated population, 360–361,
    360*t*, 361*t*
  on incarcerated population, 367, 367*t*
  median income statistics, 195, 196*t*–
    197*t*
  NHIS, 37–38
  nursing home population, 360–361,
    360*t*, 361*t*
  patterns in prevalence of disability in
    data from national household
    surveys, 69–70
  from poverty rate estimations in this
    book, 200–201
  poverty rate growth broken down by
    categories, 209–213, 210*t*–211*t*,
    212*t*
  poverty rates over long-term
    decomposed by categories, 213–
    219, 216*t*–217*t*, 218*t*, 219*f*

Demographic data, *cont.*
  by residence type and disability
    status, 361–363, 362*t*, 364*t*, 365*t*
  by residence type and disability status
    from 2006 ACS, 373*t*
  SIPP, 40
  state-level, from Medicare and
    Medicaid, 311
Department of Agriculture programs, 321
Department of Education (ED), 4
  Office of Special Education and
    Rehabilitative Services, 332
Department of Health and Human
  Services (HHS), 4
Department of Housing and Urban
  Development (HUD), 321, 330,
  406–407
Department of Labor (DOL), 320
Department of Transportation programs,
  321
Department of Veterans Affairs (DVA),
  4, 299, 317–320, 319*t*, 321
  limitations of data collection, 337
Depression or anxiety and disability, 251
Developmental disabilities. *See* IDD
  (Intellectual and developmental
  disabilities)
DEWS (Dynamics of Economic Well-
  being System), 397–398, 404
*Diagnostic and Statistical Manual of
  Mental Disorders. See* DSM-IV
Disability. *See also* Disability measures;
  Trends; Working-age people with
  disabilities
  and access to technology, 284
  categories, 240–241
  caution about attributing causation to
    underlying conditions, 251
  changes in reporting of, 73
  composite measure of functioning
    and, 236
  conditions underlying, 249, 251, 252*t*,
    253–254, 258*t*–259*t*
  as dynamic concept, 103–104
  identification of people with, 383–
    386, 385*t*

in larger context of environment,
    personal characteristics, and
    health, 228–229
  and obesity, 248–249, 250*t*, 251
  person and condition approach to
    analyzing health and, 237–238
  persons reporting more than one type,
    242, 244
  population with at least one of six
    types, 242
  relation to health, 228–229, 238–240,
    239*t*
  relation to self-reported health status,
    244–251, 245*t*, 247*t*, 250*t*, 252*t*,
    257*t*–259*t*
Disability classifications, 27–28. *See also*
  ICF (International Classification
  of Functioning, Disability and
  Health)
Disability definitions, 28–30, 55–57, 56*t*,
  186*t*–189*t*
  CPS data use of "work limitations" in
    place of, 128, 146, 147
  and data on those not in household
    population, 370
  and definitions of employment in
    major national household surveys,
    107*t*
  differences in employment rates
    based on, 109–110, 110*f*, 113–117,
    114*t*, 116*t*
  from federally funded surveys, 390–
    392
  from the ICF, 228
  impact on employment rate estimates,
    101–102, 118
  and long-term disability prevalence
    trends, 81
  need for official national definition,
    128
Disability insurance. *See* SSDI (Social
  Security Disability Insurance)
Disability measures
  on Census 2000 long-form and 1990
    Census, 356
  and disability prevalence trends, 94

Disability measures, *cont.*
  duration of work limitations and
    poverty rates, 220
  for group quarters (GQ) and homeless
    populations, 370
  impacts of national household surveys
    use of differing, 383
  and poverty rates by state for
    working-age persons, 204*t*–206*t*
  and poverty rates in national
    household surveys, 202, 203
  two-period, 148, 186*t*
  used for long-term prevalence rates
    estimates, 81–82, 82*f*
Disability prevalence
  about, 69–71
  and aging of baby boom cohort,
    85–89, 87*t*, 88*t*
  difficulty of generalizing from data,
    71–74
  estimated increase by age, 1984–
    1996, 73*t*
  long-term trends, 81–85, 82*f*, 83*t*, 85*f*
  statistics for states and demographic
    groups, 74–81, 75*f*, 76*t*–78*t*, 79*f*,
    80*t*
  of work limitations across
    demographic groups and over
    time, 93–95
Disability prevalence rates. *See also*
    Trends
  among incarcerated population, 355,
    363, 366, 366*t*
  data sources, 241
  and disability status among homeless,
    368
  estimates from inconsistent survey
    data, 395
  for IDD, 255–256
  by six categories, 43*t*, 45, 242–244,
    243*t*
  by type of residence, 361–363, 362*t*,
    364*t*, 365*t*
Disability questions. *See also* ADL
    (activity of daily living)
    limitations; IADL (instrumental

activity of daily living); Mental
    impairments; National household
    surveys; Physical impairments;
    Questionnaire design; Screening
    questions; Sensory impairments;
    Work limitations
  Census 2000 long-form, 375*n*4
  common set for identifying
    respondents on national household
    surveys, 384–385, 390–392
  differences among national household
    surveys, 104
  income questions, 34–35
  maintaining continuity in survey
    statistics over long-run, 392–393
  modification of existing, 401–402
  structured questions, 285
  subject areas poorly addressed, 387
  taxonomy, 27–28, 60–61
  translating into six concepts based on
    ICF, 41–42
  used by United Nations, 385
  wording and response choices, 278–
    282, 280*f*, 281*f*, 282*t*
Disability Status Report, 2006
    (Rehabilitation Research and
    Training Center on Disability
    Demographics and Statistics), 71
Disability subpopulations, 388, 403
  periodic surveys, 406–407
Diseases. *See* Condition approach to
    analyzing health and disability
Disposition codes in surveys, 273
DOL. *See* Department of Labor (DOL)
*DSM-IV (Diagnostic and Statistical
    Manual of Mental Disorders)*, 357,
    366
DVA. *See* Department of Veterans Affairs
    (DVA)
Dynamics of Economic Well-being
    System. *See* DEWS (Dynamics of
    Economic Well-being System)

Earnings. *See also* Household income of
    working-age men; Income data
  data sources, 331, 333

Earnings, *cont.*
  labor earnings of households of men
    with work-limitations, 1980–2005,
    161–165, 171
  and SSA program participation rates,
    127
Economic Report of the President, 193
Economic well-being data, 33, 70–71
  need for federal tracking of people
    with disabilities in, 223
Economic well-being of working-
    age people with and without work
    limitations through business
    cycles, 198–199
ED. *See* Department of Education (ED)
Education levels
  as a demographic characteristic, 96n5
  and disability prevalence rates, 80t,
    81
  prevalence of work limitations and,
    90t–91t, 92, 92f, 93
  questions in March CPS, 201
Employment as dynamic concept,
    103–104
Employment data, 33, 34, 117. *See also*
    Earnings
Employment disability
  Census 2000 long-form data, 356
  compared with work limitations, 81
  prevalence by demographic groups,
    80t
Employment exit and re-entry rates, 127
Employment measures. *See also*
    Disability measures
  based on levels of attachment to labor
    force, 105–106, 115–116, 118
  in major national household surveys,
    102–104, 131t–133t
Employment rate estimates for working-
    aged people with disabilities,
    101–102
  analysis of various aspects, 113–127,
    114t, 116f, 119f, 120t–122t, 124t,
    126t
  and business cycles, 117
  estimation methods, 104–106, 107t

reason for differences in, 108–112
  use of national household surveys for,
    102–104
Employment rates, 127–129
  annual rates of men using alternative
    disability concepts from CPS and
    NHIS, 135t–136t, 137t–139t
  best concepts to use in national
    surveys to find, 128
  longitudinal analysis with SIPP, 123–
    125, 124t
  from SIPP using alternative disability
    concepts and reference periods,
    134t
  SSA linked data for, 125–127, 126t
Employment rates of working-age people
    with disabilities, 70
  advantages of using SIPP for current
    estimates, 117–118
  comparisons across data sources,
    113–127, 114t, 116f, 124t, 126t
  declining trend in, 7–8, 10, 116–117,
    354
  differences across disability concepts,
    109–112, 110f, 116–117
  differences for adults with work
    limitations, 108, 109f, 115, 116,
    116f
  need for official disability
    employment measures, 103
  rates by demographic groups, 120t–
    122t
  relative reference period rates by
    state, 118, 119t, 123

Federal funding of programs, 70. *See
    also* Data on program participants;
    Program participants
Federal household surveys. *See* National
    household surveys
Federal surveys. *See* Surveys
Focus groups of people with disabilities,
    270, 284–285
Food stamps, 303t
Foreign visitor data, 40

Functioning. *See also* Health and
functional status
contexts for evaluating, 228
defined, 228
four levels used by NHIS, 237
objective tests, 231
relationship between objective and
subjective measures, 234–235
statistical relationship between health
and function, 237–240, 239*t*

(GAO) General Accounting Office, 332
Gender
and disability prevalence rates, 2006,
80*t*
and prevalence of work limitations,
1981–2007, 89, 90*t*–91*t*
General Accounting Office. *See* GAO
(General Accounting Office)
General self-rated health. *See* GSRH
(General self-rated health)
Go-outside-home limitations, 96*n*6. *See
also* IADL (instrumental activity
of daily living) limitations
Census 2000 long-form data, 356
disability prevalence by demographic
groups, 80*t*
reason for different results in surveys,
280, 282
GQ (group quarters) population, 28–30.
See also Homeless population;
Institutional GQ (group quarters)
population; Noninstitutional group
quarters (GQ) population
about, 371–372, 373*t*
data, 40, 255
defined, 358, 359*t*
exclusion/inclusion in ACS, 32
impact on survey-based estimates, 310
national survey coverage, 57, 386–
387, 396
national survey data sources, 353
periodic surveys, 406
size of basic components within,
358–367, 360*t*, 361*t*, 362*t*, 364*t*,
365*t*, 366*t*

those classified as living in
institutions, 62*n*10
Group homes, 359*t*, 406
Group quarters (GQ) population. *See* GQ
(group quarters) population
GSRH (General self-rated health), 236
related to NHIS activity limitation
measure, 239–240
*Guide to Disability Statistics from the
National Health Interview Survey,*
240, 241, 242, 248, 249, 251

Health, United States (NCHS, 2006), 238
Health and functional status. *See also*
Functioning
about, 227
advantages and disadvantage of NHIS
data for research, 251, 253–256
approaches to measuring, 229–230
composite or global measures of
disability and health, 238–240
composite or global measures of
subjective health and function,
235–237
definitions, 227–229
NHIS descriptive statistics, 240–251,
243*t*, 245*t*, 247*t*, 250*t*, 252*t*, 258*t*–
259*t*
objective measures, 230–232
ongoing and recent federal surveys,
240
related to activity limitations, 238–239
relationship between NHIS objective
and subjective measures, 233–235
single measures, 235
statistical relationship between health
and function, 237–240, 239*t*
subjective measures, 232–233, 235–
237
Health and Retirement Study. *See* HRS
(Health and Retirement Study)
Health care access, 95
Health data, 22
ACS, 33
longitudinal analysis using SIPP,
123–125, 124*t*

Health data, *cont.*
  NHIS, 37–38
  SIPP, 40–41
Health insurance questions on surveys,
  314, 318
Hearing impairment
  definitions, 42
  devices, 293*n*9
  survey data collection modes, 284,
  285
HHS. *See* Department of Health and
  Human Services (HHS)
Hispanics and prevalence of work
  limitations, 1981–2007, 90*t*–91*t*,
  92
HIV/AIDS data, 330
Homeless Management Information
  Systems (HMIS), 406–407
Homeless population. *See also* GQ
  (group quarters) population
  data sources, 375*n*2
  disability-related data, 14, 15, 387
  national survey data, 353
  periodic surveys, 406–407
  survey data gaps, 368
Household income of working-age men.
  See also Earnings
  data sources for analysis, 145–148,
  186*t*–189*t*
  income during business cycles, 1980-
  2005, 148–153, 149*f*, 150*t*–151*t*
  sources of income during business
  cycles, 1980–2005, 153–171,
  154*t*–155*t*, 156*t*–157*t*, 158*t*–159*t*,
  166*t*–167*t*, 168*t*–169*t*, 170*t*
Household population. *See also*
  GQ (group quarters) population;
  Homeless population; National
  household surveys
  disability prevalence by state, 76*t*–
  78*t*, 79*f*
  income of working-age persons,
  172–180, 173*t*, 176*t*–177*t*, 178*t*–
  180*t*, 354
  income of working-age persons in,
  85*f*

Household surveys. *See* National
  household surveys
Housing data in ACS, 32
HRS (Health and Retirement Study), 14
  matches with administrative records
  data, 334
  question on workers' comp benefits,
  320
  summary of program participation
  information in, 303*t*
HUD. *See* Department of Housing and
  Urban Development (HUD)

IADL (instrumental activity of daily
  living) limitations, 27, 29. *See
  also* ADL (activity of daily
  living) limitations; Go-outside-
  home limitations
  age-adjusted disability prevalence,
  1997–2006, 88*t*
  definition, 96*n*2
  differences in employment rates for
  adults with, 109, 110*f*
  and disability prevalence, 72–73, 73*t*
  and the elderly, 72
  employment rate estimates in four
  major household surveys, 113,
  114*t*, 118
  household income estimates, 173*t*
  household income estimates by state,
  176*t*–177*t*, 178*t*–180*t*
  of incarcerated population, 370
  measures used for testing functional
  status, 235
  in NHIS surveys, 38
  and poverty rates, 203
  prevalence, 243*t*
  prevalence rate by survey, 43*t*
  relationship with self-reported health
  status, 244–251, 245*t*, 247*t*, 250*t*,
  252, 258*t*–259*t*
  survey questions on major national
  surveys about, 51, 53, 54*t*
ICD (International Classification of
  Diseases), 228–229

ICDR (Interagency Committee on
    Disability Research), 28, 292n4
ICF (International Classification of
    Functioning, Disability and
    Health), 27, 28–29, 30, 31f, 292n4,
    384
  participation restriction, 236
  six operational concepts derived from,
    27, 41–42
  use for disability research, 268
  use for employment rate estimates,
    104–105
  using for analyses of health and
    functional status, 228–229
IDD (Intellectual and developmental
    disabilities), 255–256
  and sample design, 272
Illness in relation to disability, 229. *See
    also* Health and functional status
Impairment, 27, 29–30
  length of time and other qualifiers, 42
Incarcerated population
  correctional institutions, 359t
  demographic data on disability status
    within, 363, 366
  demographics, 360–361, 361t
  impact of increase in, 354, 355, 371
  size, 358
  survey frequency, 369t
  survey gaps, 370
  surveys, 14, 20–21, 94, 356–357
Income data. *See also* Earnings;
    Household income of working-age
    men; Median income in U.S.
  CPS-ASEC, 34
  NHIS, 38 39
  SIPP, 39–41
Individuals with Disabilities Education
    Act, 11
Inflation adjustments to income, 148
Inmates. *See* Incarcerated population
Institute of Medicine, 73–74, 231, 292n4
Institutional GQ (group quarters)
    population. *See also* GQ (group
    quarters) population; Incarcerated
    population; Nursing home

population; Working-age
    institutional population
  data sources, 355–357, 359t
  demographic composition, 359–361,
    359t, 360t, 361t
  distribution across type of institution,
    358, 359t
  exclusion from surveys, 271–272
  GQ population classified as, 62n10
  health information about, 255
  impact of incarcerated population on,
    355
  national household survey exclusion/
    inclusion, 13
  residence type and disability status,
    361–362, 361t, 364t, 365t
Instrumental activity of daily living. *See*
    IADL (instrumental activity of
    daily living)
Intellectual and developmental
    disabilities. *See* IDD (Intellectual
    and developmental disabilities)
Interagency Committee on Disability
    Research. *See* ICDR (Interagency
    Committee on Disability
    Research)
International Classification of Diseases.
    See ICD (International
    Classification of Diseases)
International Classification of
    Functioning, Disability and
    Health. *See* ICF (International
    Classification of Functioning,
    Disability and Health)
Interviewer training, 286–289, 287t, 290
  about use of proxy respondents, 275
Interview methodologies. *See also*
    Questionnaire design
  changes, 96–97n9
  March CPS rotating panel for
    interviews, 81
IRS earnings data, 308

Journal of Vocational Rehabilitation, 330

Kessler Index, 50

Lifestyle factors and disability
    prevalence, 95–96
Longevity and disability prevalence, 71,
    95–96
Longitudinal data on working-age people
    with disabilities, 12, 33, 39,
    40–41. *See also* MCBS (Medicare
    Current Beneficiary Survey);
    SIPP (Survey of Income and
    Program Participation)
    enhancements needed, 397–401
    limitations, 388–389
    Medicare Research Identifiable Files
        (RIF), 314
    state VR applicants and clients, 316*t*,
        317
    survey data, 60
Longitudinal studies of working-age
    people with disabilities, 5, 8–9
    vs. cross-sectional surveys for trend
        estimates, 41
Longitudinal Study of the Vocational
    Rehabilitation Services Program,
    14
Longitudinal Study on Aging, 334

MAF. *See* Master Address File (MAF)
March CPS, 146. *See also* CPS-ASEC
    (Current Population Survey
    Annual Social and Economic
    Supplement)
    advantages and limitations, 199, 208
    analysis of economic well-being
        of working age men, 1967–2005,
        148–170, 150*t*–151*t*, 150*t*–151*t*,
        154*t*–155*t*, 156*t*–157*t*, 158*t*–159*t*,
        166*t*–167*t*, 168*t*–169*t*, 170*t*
    capturing population with disabilities
        with, 147–148
    compared with ACS for household
        income analysis, 172–180, 173*t*
    disability and household income
        definitions compared with ACS,
        186*t*–189*t*
    education questions, 201
    estimating poverty rates for

population with disabilities from,
    195, 196*t*–197*t*, 198–199, 200–201
    median income statistics, 193, 194*f*
    poverty rates compared with other
        national surveys, 201–208, 202*t*
    rotating panel for interviews, 81
    work limitations, 81, 83*t*
    work limitations, compared with ACS
        employment disability, 81
Maryland "Ask Me!" project, 289
Master Address File (MAF), 394
Matches of administrative records data
    among agencies, 331–336, 389–
    390
Matches of survey with administrative
    records data, 333–334, 398–399
    improving researcher access, 400–401
    limitations for longitudinal research,
        389
Mathematica Policy Research, Inc., 310,
    329
MAX. *See* Medicaid Analytical eXtract
    (MAX) research file
MBI program, 326, 328, 331
MCBS (Medicare Current Beneficiary
    Survey), 14, 70, 313*t*, 314, 337,
    353, 374–375*n*1
    summary of program participation
        information in, 303*t*
MEC (Mobile Examination Centers),
    230–231
Median income in U.S., 193, 194*f. See
    also* Poverty rates
Medicaid
    enrollment by state, 340*t*–343*t*
    matching data on program
        participants, 331
Medicaid Analytical eXtract (MAX)
    research file, 314, 330
Medicaid programs, 9. *See also* CMS
    (Centers for Medicare and
    Medicaid Services)
    about, 311
    data, 22, 303*t*, 311–315, 312*t*–313*t*
    participation ratios, 322, 323, 325*f*,
        326

Medicaid Statistical Information System, 330
Medical advances and disability prevalence, 71
Medical conditions. *See* Condition approach to analyzing health and disability
Medical Expenditure Panel Survey, 14, 240, 404
Medicare. *See also* CMS (Centers for Medicare and Medicaid Services); MCBS (Medicare Current Beneficiary Survey)
  about, 311
  beneficiary population defined, 374–375n1
  data, 22, 303t, 311–315, 312t,–313t
  and disability prevalence, 70
  enrollment by state, 340–343
  matching data on program participants, 331, 334
  participation ratios, 322, 323, 325f, 326
  SSA information about program participants, 304, 308
Medicare Current Beneficiary Survey. *See* MCBS (Medicare Current Beneficiary Survey)
Mental impairments, 48–50, 49t. *See also* Psychological distress measures
  age-adjusted disability prevalence, 1997–2006, 88t
  comorbidity with other impairments, 244
  definitions, 187
  differences in employment rates for adults with, 109, 110
  disability prevalence by demographic groups, 80
  employment rate estimates in major household surveys, 113, 114t, 118
  household income estimates, 173, 174t
  household income estimates by state, 176t–177t, 178t–180t
  and income from SSI and SSDI, 161
  number of persons with, 242

  and poverty rates, 203
  prevalence, 243t
  prevalence rate by survey, 43t
  relationship with self-reported health status, 244–251, 245t, 247t, 250t, 252t, 258t–259t
  SAMHSA surveys with data, 240
  survey questions on major national surveys about, 49t
  underlying conditions, 251
Mental retardation, 255–256
  and sample design, 272
  and survey data collection modes, 285
Military personnel, 34, 40
  gaps in data, 368
Mobile Examination Centers. *See* MEC (Mobile Examination Centers)
Mobility testing, 234–235
Mortality predictors, 236. *See also* Longevity and disability prevalence

Nagi, Saad, 28
National Academy of Social Insurance, 320
National Beneficiary Survey. *See* NBS (National Beneficiary Survey)
National Bureau of Economic Research Shared Capitalism Research Project, 277
National Center for Health Statistics. *See* NCHS (National Center for Health Statistics)
National Comorbidity Survey (NCS) Replication Survey, 240
National Council on Disability. *See* (NCD) National Council on Disability
National Death Index administrative data, 334
National disability data system (NDDS), 3, 12–15, 22–24
  about, 381
  federal sources of data on working-age population with disabilities, 382t

National disability data system, *cont.*
limitations, 20–21, 383–390
need for federal tracking of economic
well-being of people with
disabilities, 223
official disability employment
measure, 103
priorities, 410–411, 412*t*–413*t*
standard set of questionnaire items for
national surveys, 277
National Health and Nutrition
Examination Survey. *See*
NHANES (National Health and
Nutrition Examination Survey)
National Health Interview Survey. *See*
NHIS (National Health Interview
Survey)
National Health Interview Survey on
Disabilities. *See* NHIS-D
(National Health Interview Survey
on Disabilities)
National Health Survey Act of 1956, 37
National household surveys, 13–14. *See*
also ACS (American Community
Survey); CPS-ASEC (Current
Population Survey Annual Social
and Economic Supplement);
Current Population Survey (CPS);
Data collection using surveys;
Decennial Census data; NHIS
(National Health Interview
Survey); SIPP (Survey of Income
and Program Participation)
common set of disability questions
for, 23
common set of questions for
identifying disability status of
respondents, 390–392
comparing poverty rates with data
and concepts from, 201–208, 202*t*,
204*t*–206*t*, 207*f*
data about group quarters (GQ) and
homeless populations, 353–354
data matches with administrative
records data, 332

definitions of employment from,
131*t*–133*t*
discrepancies among, concerning
employment rates, 127–129
discrepancies among, concerning SSA
benefits, 310
discrepancies among, concerning
state disability programs, 321
discrepancies among, concerning
veterans benefits, 318
employment measures in, 102–104
enhancing the disability content of
existing, 401–402
exclusion of people with disabilities
from, 386–387
identification and inclusion of people
with disabilities, 390–396
inconsistencies among, 383–384
methodologies used in, 265–268, 396
need for noninstitutional GQ
population inclusion, 374
periodic disability supplements,
403–409
questions about health insurance, 314
recommendations for improving,
289–291
small sample sizes for disability
population analysis, 386
strengths and limitations major, 57–59
subject areas poorly addressed, 387
summary of program participation
information in, 303*t*
untimely or outdated data, 387–388
National Income and Product Account
(NIPA), 310
National Institute for Disability and
Rehabilitation Research, 414*n*15
National Institute on Aging, 72
researcher access to data, 400
National Long Term Care Survey. *See*
NLTCS (National Long Term Care
Survey)
National Nursing Home Survey. *See*
NNHS (National Nursing Home
Survey)
National Research Council, 292*n*4

National Science Foundation (NSF)
disability questions, 279, 280*f*, 281*f*
National Study of Health and Activity.
See NSHA (National Study of
Health and Activity)
National Survey of Homeless Assistance
Providers and Clients, 406
Native Americans disability prevalence
rates, 2006, 80*t*, 81
NBS (National Beneficiary Survey), 14,
270, 310, 344*n*12, 407
summary of program participation
information in, 303*t*
NCD (National Council on Disability),
390, 392
NCHS (National Center for Health
Statistics), 27, 230, 232, 292*n*4,
384
data matching with national health
survey and other agency data, 334
data sources for analyzing statistical
relationship between health and
function, 237
Health, United States, 2006, 238
NCS. *See* National Comorbidity Survey
(NCS) Replication Survey
NDDS. *See* National disability data
system (NDDS)
New Beneficiary Survey and New
Beneficiary Follow-up, 310, 407
New Jersey Commission for the Blind
and Visually Impaired, 284
NHANES (National Health and Nutrition
Examination Survey), 334
advantages and limitations, 253–254
objective measures of health and
function, 230–231
subjective measures of health and
function, 232
NHIS-D (National Health Interview
Survey on Disabilities), 255–256,
387–388, 404, 408–409
summary of program participation
information in, 303*t*
NHIS (National Health Interview
Survey), 13, 27, 37–39, 233. *See*

also ACS (American Community
Survey); CPS-ASEC (Current
Population Survey Annual
Social and Economic
Supplement); Decennial Census
data; NHIS-D (National Health
Interview Survey on Disabilities);
SIPP (Survey of Income and
Program Participation)
ADL/IALD measure, 81–82, 82*f*, 83*t*
advantages and limitations, 58, 59,
105, 128–129
advantages and limitations for health
and function research, 253–256
age-adjusted results, 1997–2006, 86,
88*t*
annual employment rates of men
using alternative disability
concepts, 135*t*–136*t*, 137*t*–139*t*
approaches used by researchers
analyzing health and disability,
237–238
approaches used in family and adult
questionnaires about health and
function, 233–235
changes in some annual versions, 82
composite or global measures of
subjective health and functioning,
236–237
conditions in current survey, 260*n*3
definition of disabilities, 57
disability questions, 104
disability question standardization
with ACS and CPS, 384–385, 385*t*
disadvantages for disability analysis,
386
employment and disability
conceptualizations, 106, 107*t*
employment definitions, 131*t*–133*t*
employment rate estimates compared
with other household surveys,
111*f*, 113–117, 114*t*, 116*f*
estimating poverty rates for
population with disabilities from,
200
intra-year inconsistencies, 140*n*1

NHIS, *cont.*
matches with administrative records data, 334, 335
measures of health and function, 232–235
omission of GQ and homeless populations, 353
prevalence rates for six disability categories, 43, 45, 243
questions on disability, 234
questions on health status, 244, 246
questions on impairments and work restrictions, 242–244, 243*t*
questions used to identify ADLs, 51, 52*t*
questions used to identify IADLs, 53, 54*t*
questions used to identify mental impairments, 49*t*, 50
questions used to identify physical impairments, 45, 46*t*–47*t*, 48
questions used to identify sensory impairments, 44*t*, 45
questions used to identify work limitations, 55, 56*t*
self-reported health status statistics, 244–251, 245*t*, 247*t*, 250*t*
as source for descriptive statistics on disability prevalence, 240–241
summary of program participation information in, 303*t*
2002 and 2006 version differences, 241
workers' comp benefits estimates, 321
work-limitation question, using for trend description, 74
work limitations data, 81–82, 82*f*, 83*t*
NHIS (National Household Income Survey)
coordination with other surveys, 22, 23
1994–1995 Disability Supplement, 15, 24
NIPA. *See* National Income and Product Account (NIPA)

NLTCS (National Long Term Care Survey), 353, 374–375*n*1
NNHS (National Nursing Home Survey), 334, 368
Nonhousehold units excluded from surveys, 272, 394, 406–407
limitations of data, 368–370
Noninstitutional group quarters (GQ) population, 359*t*, 368. *See also* GQ (group quarters) population; Homeless population
need for consistent data, 395–396
NSF. *See* National Science Foundation (NSF)
NSHA (National Study of Health and Activity), 231–232, 345*n*25
Nursing home population, 334, 354. *See also* Working-age institutional population
demographic data, 360*t*–361*t*
institutions, 359*t*
size, 358
survey frequency, 369*t*
survey gaps, 370
surveys, 255

OASDI (Old Age, Survivor, and Disability Insurance) program, 304, 308
sources for program statistics, 306*t*, 309
Obesity and disability, 248–251, 250*t*
Office of Disability Employment Policy, "A Summit on Disability Employment Policy," 414*n*16
Office of Management and Budget, 384
poverty level determination method, 190*n*3
poverty thresholds, 199–200
Questions and Answers When Designing Surveys for Information Collections, 266
Old Age, Survivor, and Disability Insurance. *See* OASDI (Old Age, Survivor, and Disability Insurance) program

OMB. *See* Office of Management and
    Budget
Operational disability definitions, 7–8
    lack of agreement on, 6

Panel Study of Income Dynamics
    (PSID), 220, 388
    addition of new disability questions,
    401
PAR. *See* Participatory action research
    (PAR)
Participant selection. *See* Respondent
    selection approaches for surveys
Participation and Activity Limitation
    Survey (Statistics Canada), 279,
    280, 282*f*
Participation rates in programs. *See also*
    Participation ratios
    for disability programs within
        individual states, 322
    estimating, from self-reported
        disabilities, 301
    of people eligible for, but not
        receiving disability services, 300,
        309, 322
Participation ratios, 322–328, 324*f*, 325*f*,
    327*f*
    defined, 322
    programs studied, 322
    public policy issues, 327*f*, 328
Participation restriction, 27, 29, 30, 236.
    See also Work restrictions
    employment category, 241
Participatory action research (PAR), 270,
    283, 286, 288–289, 290
Person approach to analyzing health and
    disability, 237–238, 249
Physical impairments, 45–48, 46*t*–47*t*
    age-adjusted disability prevalence,
        1997–2006, 88*t*
    comorbidity with other impairments,
        244
    definitions, 187*t*
    differences in employment rates for
        adults with, 109*f*, 110*f*

disability prevalence by demographic
    groups, 2006, 80*t*
employment rate estimates in four
    major household surveys, 113,
    114*t*, 118
household income estimates, 173*t*
household income estimates by state,
    176*t*–177*t*, 178*t*–180*t*
number of persons with, 242
and poverty rates, 203
prevalence, 243*t*
prevalence rate by survey, 43*t*
relationship with self-reported health
    status, 244–251, 245*t*, 247*t*, 250*t*,
    252*t*, 258*t*–259*t*
relationship with work limitations and
    poverty rates, 203, 208
survey questions on major national
    surveys about, 46*t*–47*t*
Populations. *See also* GQ (group
    quarters) population; Homeless
    population; Household population
    captured by major national surveys,
        43*t*, 45, 57
    capturing alternative, 58
    changes in underlying health of, 73
Post Vocational Rehabilitation
    Experiences Study, 332
Poverty, definitions, 199–200
Poverty rates, 194–198, 194*f*, 196*t*–197*t*
    about, 221–223
    data used to estimate, 198–201
    and duration of work limitations, 220
    over the last two business cycles,
        208–219, 210*t*–211*t*, 212*t*, 216*t*–
        217*t*, 218*t*, 219*f*
    for people with *vs.* without work
        limitations, 201, 202, 203–213,
        204*t*–206*t*, 207*f*, 210*t*–211*t*, 212*t*,
        218*t*, 219, 219*f*
Prevalence. *See* Disability prevalence
Program participants. *See also*
    Administrative records data;
    Participation rates in programs
    Center for Medicare and Medicaid
        Services, 299, 311–315, 312*t*–313*t*

Program participants, *cont.*
conclusions about research results, 335–337
Department of Veterans Affairs, 299, 317–321, 319*t*
existing data, 299–304, 303*t*
miscellaneous programs, 320–321
new data initiatives to learn about, 328–335
periodic surveys, 406–407
Rehabilitation Services Administration, 299, 315–317, 316*t*
Social Security Administration, 299, 304–310, 306*t*–307*t*
state-level data, 311, 314, 321–328, 324*f*, 325*f*, 327*f*
surveys about, 390
Temporary Assistance to Needy Families (TANF), 321
workers' compensation, 303t, 320, 322
Proxy respondents, 274–277
alternative to, 293*n*8
PSID. *See* Panel Study of Income Dynamics (PSID)
Psychological distress measures, 38. *See also* Mental Impairments
Public policy
need for common dialogue, 23
participation ratios issues, 327*f*, 328
responses to working-age people with disabilities, 5–6
state implementation of federal, 9
for working-age people with disabilities, 11
PUMS (Public Use Microdata Sample), 117, 363, 375*n*8

Qualitative data collection modes, 284–286
Quantitative data collection modes, 283–284
Questionnaire design, 277–282. *See also* Disability questions; Interview methodologies

Questions and Answers When Designing Surveys for Information Collections (Office of Management and Budget), 266

Race/ethnicity disability prevalence rates, 79–81, 80*t*, 93, 94
work limitations, 1981–2007, 90–92, 90*t*–91*t*
Random Digit Dial (RDD) surveys, 273
Rehabilitation Act, 11, 315. *See also* Vocational rehabilitation services
Rehabilitation Research and Training Center on Disability Demographics and Statistics (StatsRRTC), 223*n*3
2006 Disability Status Report, 71
"The Future of Disability Statistics," 414*n*15
Rehabilitation Services Administration (RSA), 299, 315–317, 316*t*
agreements with other agencies to match data on participants in programs, 331–332
data agreements with other agencies, 389–390
disability survey, 407
limitations of data collection, 337
RSA 911 data, 315, 316*t*
Research design that includes people with disabilities. *See also* Interview methodologies; Questionnaire design
meta-analysis of current research, 291
methodological and experimental research needed, 291
for national household surveys, 269*t*, 270
for national household survey supplements and special surveys, 269*t*, 270, 403–409
Respondent selection approaches for surveys, 272–274. *See also* Participatory action research (PAR)
use of proxy respondents, 274–277

RIF files (Medicare Research Identifiable
    Files), 314, 330
RSA. *See* Rehabilitation Services
    Administration (RSA)

SAMHSA (Substance Abuse and Mental
    Health Services Administration),
    240, 331
Sample design decisions that include
    people with disabilities, 269*t*,
    270–271
Sampling frame issues, 271–272, 283
    for the ACS, 393–395
    for other federal surveys, 395–396
Screening questions, 272–273
Section 8 housing, 321
Self-care impairments. *See also* ADL
    (activity of daily living)
    limitations
    age-adjusted prevalence, 1997–2006,
        88*t*
    prevalence by demographic groups, 80*t*
Self-reported health status, 244–246,
    245*t*, 248, 253–254
Self-reports in surveys, 275, 277
    use for program participation ratios,
        322
Sensitivity training, 286–287
Sensory impairments, 38, 42–45, 43*t*, 44*t*
    age-adjusted disability prevalence,
        1997–2006, 88*t*
    comorbidity with activity limitations
        and work restrictions, 244
    definitions, 187*t*
    differences in employment rates for
        adults with, 109*f*, 110*f*, 112
    disability prevalence by demographic
        groups, 80*t*
    employment rate estimates in major
        household surveys, 113, 114*t*, 118
    household income estimates, 173*t*
    household income estimates by state,
        176*t*–177*t*, 178*t*–180*t*
    number of persons with, 242
    objective tests, 231
    and poverty rates, 203

prevalence, 243*t*
relationship with self-reported health
    status, 244–251, 245*t*, 247*t*, 250*t*,
    252*t*, 258*t*–259*t*
survey questions on major national
    surveys about, 44*t*
SES. *See* Socioeconomic status (SES)
    and life expectancy
SIFCF (Survey of Inmates of Federal
    Corrections Facilities), 357, 368,
    369, 369*f*
SILJ (Survey of Inmates of Local Jails),
    356, 357, 366, 368, 369, 369*f*
SIPP (Survey of Income and Program
    Participation), 21–22, 27, 39–41.
    See also ACS (American
    Community Survey); CPS-ASEC
    (Current Population Survey
    Annual Social and Economic
    Supplement); Decennial Census
    data; NHIS (National Health
    Interview Survey)
    advantages and limitations, 58, 60,
        123, 129
    data on participants in state programs,
        321
    definition of disabilities, 57
    employment and disability
        conceptualizations, 106, 107*t*
    employment definitions, 131*t*–133*t*
    employment rate estimates compared
        with other household surveys,
        108–112, 111*f*, 113, 114*t*, 117
    employment rates from SIPP using
        alternative disability concepts and
        reference periods, 134*t*
    estimates of veterans benefits
        payments, 318
    estimating poverty rates for
        population with longer term
        disabilities from, 198, 220
    impact of recent changes, 397–398
    intra-year differences, 112
    linked data from SSA program
        records, 125–127, 126*t*
    longitudinal data, 388

SIPP, *cont.*
    longitudinal employment rate analysis with, 123–125, 124*t*
    matches with administrative records data, 333–334, 334–335
    need for common set of questions with other surveys, 391–392
    omission of GQ and homeless populations, 353
    prevalence rates for six disability categories, 43*t*, 45
    questions used to identify ADLs, 51, 52*t*
    questions used to identify IADLs, 53, 54*t*
    questions used to identify mental impairments, 49*t*, 50
    questions used to identify physical impairments, 47*t*, 48
    questions used to identify sensory impairments, 44*t*, 45
    questions used to identify work limitations, 55, 56*t*
    summary of program participation information in, 303*t*
    supplementary questionnaires, 403–404
    use in revealing limitations of SSA data, 310
    workers' comp benefits estimates, 320–321
SISCF (Survey of Inmates of State Correctional Facilities), 356, 357, 368, 369*f*
Smoking, 95
Social environment and poverty rate changes, 222–223
Social problem analysis, 4–5
Social Security Administration. *See* SSA (Social Security Administration)
Social Security Disability Insurance. *See* SSDI (Social Security Disability Insurance)
Social security numbers, 335
Socioeconomic status (SES) and life expectancy, 95–96

Spell analysis alternative, 220
SSA (Social Security Administration), 4. *See also* NBS (National Beneficiary Survey); SSDI (Social Security Disability Insurance); SSI (Supplemental Security Income); Ticket to Work program
    administrative data links to major household surveys, 41, 107*t*
    data about program participants, 304–310, 305*f*, 306*t*–307*t*
    data about working age people with disabilities in SSA programs, 22
    data agreements with other agencies, 331–332, 389–390
    data matches with national household surveys, 333, 336
    eligibility criteria changes, 73
    health and functional status survey, 231
    limitations of data collection, 337
    miscellaneous programs for research data, 330
    programs, 299
    researcher access to data, 400
    SIPP use of linked data from, 125–127, 126*t*
    special-purpose surveys, 388
SSDI (Social Security Disability Insurance), 5, 9, 35, 53, 55, 70
    about, 304
    data matches with national household surveys, 333, 334
    and disability prevalence, 70
    eligibility criteria changes, 73, 95
    enrollment by state, 340*t*–343*t*
    longitudinal study from data, 329–330
    matching data on program participants, 331
    number of program participants, 2005, 305*f*
    participation ratios, 322, 323, 324*f*
    SIPP links with SSA data, 126*t*, 127
    sources of statistics on program participants, 303*t*, 306*t*–307*t*, 308–310

SSDI, *cont.*
    SSA health and functional status
        survey and, 231
    working-age male population shifts
        to, 146, 161–165, 171
SSI (Supplemental Security Income), 9,
    35
    about, 304
    data matches with national household
        surveys, 333
    enrollment by state, 340*t*–343*t*
    longitudinal study, 329–330
    matching data on program
        participants, 331
    means test simulation study, 333
    number of program participants,
        2005, 304, 305*f*
    participation ratios, 322, 323, 324*f*
    SIPP links with SSA data, 126*t*, 127
    sources of statistics on program
        participants, 303*t*, 306*t*–307*t*,
        308–310
    SSA health and functional status
        survey and, 231
    working-age male population shifts
        to, 146, 161–165, 171
Standardized medical tests, 230–232
State- and local-level data on working-
        age people
    county level data on veterans, 318
    disability prevalence, 74–79, 75*f*,
        76*t*–78*t*, 79*f*
    employment rate estimates from ACS,
        118–123, 119*f*, 120*t*–122*t*
    health insurance questions in national
        surveys, 314
    from Medicare and Medicaid, 311, 314
    National Academy of Social
        Insurance statistics, 320
    recommendations for improving
        program data for research, 336
    short-term disability programs, 321
    State Medicaid Research Files, 330
    by total population, disability
        population and disability programs by
        state, 340*t*–343*t*

State- and local-level data on working-
        age people with disabilities, 6,
        9–11, 32, 39, 58–59
    employment information sources, 107*t*
    implications for federal and state
        programs, 70
    program data, 300–301, 311, 314,
        321–328, 324*f*, 325*f*, 327*f*
    variations across states, 94, 301
State Children's Health Insurance
        Program, 34
State-level data
    on health and functional status, 254–
        255
    household income by sex, race,
        education, disability definition,
        and state, 174–175, 176*t*–177*t*,
        178*t*–180*t*, 181*f*
    poverty rates, 203–208, 204*t*–206*t*,
        207*f*
    on preventative health practices and
        risk behaviors of adults, 240
State-level public sources of household
        income, 165
State vocational rehabilitation (VR)
        services, 299, 315–317, 316*t*
    matching data studies, 332
    number of program participants,
        2005, 305*f*
    participation ratios, 322, 326, 327*f*
    by state, 340*t*–343*t*
    survey, 388
Statistics. *See* data on working-age
        people with disabilities
Statistics Canada, 279, 280, 282*f*
StatsRRTC. *See* Rehabilitation Research
        and Training Center on Disability
        Demographics and Statistics
        (StatsRRTC)
Substance Abuse and Mental Health
        Services Administration. *See*
        SAMHSA (Substance Abuse
        and Mental Health Services
        Administration)
Supplemental Security Income. *See* SSI
        (Supplemental Security Income)

Surveying Persons with Disabilities: A Source Guide (Markesich, Cashion, and Bleeker), 266, 290
Surveying Persons with Disabilities (Markesich, Cashion, and Bleeker), 266
Survey of Consumer Finances, 396
Survey of Income and Program Participation. *See* SIPP (Survey of Income and Program Participation)
Survey of Inmates of Federal Corrections Facilities. *See* SIFCF (Survey of Inmates of Federal Corrections Facilities)
Survey of Inmates of Local Jails. *See* SILJ (Survey of Inmates of Local Jails)
Survey of Inmates of State Correctional Facilities. *See* SISCF (Survey of Inmates of State Correctional Facilities)
Surveys. *See also* Data collection using surveys; Disability questions; Interviewer training; National disability data system (NDDS); National household surveys; Questionnaire design; Research design that includes people with disabilities
best practices guidelines, 268–289, 269*t*
best practices recommendations, 289–291
cross-sectional survey advantages over SIPP, 41
data collection methods and priorities for disability research, 267–268
deficiencies, 11–12
designing or evaluating, 266, 267*f*, 278–282
of health and functional status, 230–233
inclusion of persons with disabilities, 268
infrequent collection of data on

group quarters (GQ) and homeless populations, 369
with larger amount of questions, 57
limitations for studying program participants, 302, 304
limitations for the national disability data system, 383–390
matching with administrative data, 328, 332–335
periodic national surveys *vs.* supplements to existing surveys, 407–409
reason for biased reports, 292–293*n*7
recommendations for additional, 256
special purpose, 13–15, 403–409
SSA special purpose, 388
that utilize self-reports, 260*n*2
underreporting of chronic health conditions in, 233–234
use for estimating long-term time trends, 59
use for identification of working-age people with disabilities, 7

(TANF) Temporary Assistance to Needy Families, 9, 303*t*, 321
Target populations of federal agencies, 4
Taxonomy for disability questions, 27–28, 60–61
Technological advances and disability rates, 96*n*1
Telephone surveys, 286, 287–288
for hearing impaired, 293*n*9
Temporary Assistance to Needy Families *See* (TANF) Temporary Assistance to Needy Families
Ticket Participant Survey, 344*n*12
Ticket to Work and Work Incentives Improvement Act, 11
Ticket to Work program, 310, 407
Ticket Research File (TRF), 329–330, 331, 332
Topical modules, 403–404
Topical question battery, 404–405
Topical surveys, 404

Trends. *See also* Business cycles;
    Disability prevalence rates;
    Longitudinal data on working-age
    people with disabilities
  age-adjusted work limitations, 86–89,
    87*t*, 88*t*
  changes in health during past year,
    246–249, 247*t*
  declining employment rates of
    working-age people with
    disabilities, 7–8, 10, 116–117
  disability prevalence, 69–71, 73–74,
    73*t*, 81–85, 82*f*, 83*t*, 85*f*
  in earnings and sources of income
    of households of men with work-
    limitations, 1980–2005, 163–165,
    171
  in health and functional status, 254
  less than perfect analyses, 223
  in life expectancy, 94
  need for study of aging and health of
    disability population, 246
  number of persons with disabilities,
    2002 and 2006, 242
  obesity and disability between 2002
    and 2006, 249
  in poverty rates over the last two
    business cycles, 208–220, 210*t*–
    211*t*, 212*t*, 216*t*–217*t*, 218*t*, 219*f*
  relative decline in household income
    for working-age men with work
    limitations, 1980–2004, 153
  survey data for long-term studies, 59
  use of ACS for trend analysis, 107*t*
  using cross-sectional data for long-
    term studies, 113, 115–117
  TTW and TTR. *See* Ticket to Work
    program
2000 Decennial Census, 27, 36–37. *See
    also* Census 2000 Supplementary
    Survey (C2SS); PUMS (Public
    Use Microdata Sample)
  decennial census data, 10, 15
  definition of disabilities, 57
  disability questions, 32

  prevalence rates for six disability
    categories, 43*t*, 45
  questions used to identify ALDs, 51,
    52*t*
  questions used to identify IADLs, 53,
    54*t*
  questions used to identify mental
    impairments, 49*t*, 50
  questions used to identify physical
    impairments, 45, 46*t*, 48
  questions used to identify sensory
    impairments, 42, 44*t*, 45
  questions used to identify work
    limitations, 55, 56*t*
  special usefulness, 58

Unemployment insurance, 303*t*
Unemployment rate for working-age
    people with disabilities, 105–106
United States government data
    collection, 3–6
Urban Consumer Price Index (CPI-U),
    148, 199
U.S. Census Bureau, 384. *See also*
    Census 2000 Supplementary
    Survey (C2SS); Master Address
    File (MAF); SIPP (Survey of
    Income and Program
    Participation); 2000 Decennial
    Census
  *Annual Report on Income, Poverty
    and Health Insurance Coverage in
    the United States,* 1–2
  changes considered for ACS, 61–62
  coordination of sampling for federal
    surveys, 395
  data matches with national household
    surveys, 333–334
  definition of disabled persons, 33, 55
  four major data sets, 27
  long form changes in 2000, 21
  poverty thresholds, 199–200
  PUMS (Public Use Microdata
    Sample), 117, 363, 375*n*8
  researcher access to data, 400

U.S. Congressional Budget Office, 95–96
U.S. Department of Labor. *See* Bureau of
    Labor Statistics (BLS)
U.S. Government Accountability Office,
    330
    Key National Indicator Initiative, 391
U.S. Surgeon General on disability (2005
    report), 229

Van service for disabled people, 96*n*1
VC (Veterans' Compensation), 303*t*, 317,
    318, 319, 340*t*–343*t*
    participation ratios, 322, 326
Veterans Benefits Administration,
    345*n*21
Veterans benefits programs,
    299, 317–320, 319*t*. *See also*
    Department of Veterans Affairs
    (DVA); Rehabilitation Services
    Administration (RSA)
    data sources, 303*t*
    enrollment by state, 340*t*–343*t*
    number of program participants, 305*f*
Veterans' Health Administration, 345*n*21
VHC (Veterans' Health Care), 303*t*,
    317–318, 319*t*
Vocational rehabilitation services, 55.
    See also State vocational
    rehabilitation (VR) services
    data sources, 303*t*, 330
    GAO study on, 332
VP (Veterans' Pension), 303*t*, 317, 318,
    319*t*, 340*t*–343*t*
    participation ratios, 322, 326

Walking tests, 234–235
Washington City Group (WCG), 292*n*4
    on Disability Statistics, 385
Well being and disability prevalence, 70.
    See also Economic well-being
    data; Health and functional status
Westat, Inc., 332
WHO. *See* World Health Organization
    (WHO)
Workers' compensation, 9, 303*t*, 320, 322
Workforce Investment Act, 11

Working-age institutional population
    with disabilities, 6
    lack of data about, 255
    limitations of knowledge about, 20–21
    proportions with disabilities, 1990
        and 2000, 360–361, 361*f*
    surveys, 14–15
Working-age people with disabilities. *See
    also* Data on working-age people
    with disabilities; Longitudinal
    studies of working-age people
    with disabilities; Operational
    disability definitions
    estimated number, 6
    federal expenditures to support, 70
    numbers of, compared with number
        of disability program participants,
        2005, 305*f*
    program data about, 300–301
    what is currently known, 15–18, 20
    what isn't known, 18–19, 20–21
    what needs to be improved to know
        more about, 21–24
Working-age population definitions,
    24*n*3, 344*n*1
Work limitations. *See also* Work
    restrictions
    age-adjusted, 86
    age-adjusted disability prevalence,
        1997–2006, 88*t*
    compared with employment
        disability, 81
    CPS use of term in place of
        "disabilities," 128, 146, 147
    defined for two groups, 199
    differences in employment rates for
        adults with, 108, 109*f*, 110*f*, 111–
        112, 111*f*
    disability prevalence by demographic
        groups, 80*t*, 81
    and education levels, 92*f*
    employment rate estimates in four
        major household surveys, 113,
        114*t*, 118
    household income estimates, 172–
        175, 173*t*

Work limitations, *cont.*
    household income estimates by state,
        176*t*–177*t*, 178*t*–180*t*, 181*f*
    long-term-trend employment rate
        estimates for men with and
        without disabilities, 115–117
    maintaining continuity in survey
        statistics over long-run, 392
    measures used for long-term
        prevalence rate estimates, 81–87,
        82*f*, 83*f*, 85*f*, 87*t*, 88*t*
    national data set for trend estimation,
        35
    in NHIS surveys, 38
    of nursing home population, 370
    one-period *vs.* two-period trend rates,
        83*t*, 84
    and participation restriction, 29
    poverty rates decomposed by
        demographic categories over
        1980s and 1990s, 213–219, 216*t*–
        217*t*, 218*t*
    poverty rates for those with and
        without, 208–213, 210*t*–211*t*,
        212*t*, 218*t*, 219, 219*f*
    poverty rates for those with longer-
        term, 220
    prevalence rates by survey, 43*t*
    pros and cons of use as proxy for
        disability, 393
    relationship with physical limitations
        and poverty rates, 203, 208
    short-term *vs.* long-term, 8
    SIPP survey question, 40–41
    SIPP usefulness for study, 123–125
    survey questions on major national
        surveys about, 53–55, 54*t*
Work restrictions
    number of persons with, 242
    and other impairments, 242–244, 243*t*
    prevalence, 243*t*
    relationship with self-reported health
        status, 244–251, 245*t*, 247*t*, 250*t*,
        252*t*, 258*t*–259*t*
    and sensory impairments, 244

World Health Organization (WHO),
    27. *See also* ICF (International
    Classification of Functioning,
    Disability and Health)
    definition of health, 229

About the Institute

The W.E. Upjohn Institute for Employment Research is a nonprofit research organization devoted to finding and promoting solutions to employment-related problems at the national, state, and local levels. It is an activity of the W.E. Upjohn Unemployment Trustee Corporation, which was established in 1932 to administer a fund set aside by Dr. W.E. Upjohn, founder of The Upjohn Company, to seek ways to counteract the loss of employment income during economic downturns.

The Institute is funded largely by income from the W.E. Upjohn Unemployment Trust, supplemented by outside grants, contracts, and sales of publications. Activities of the Institute comprise the following elements: 1) a research program conducted by a resident staff of professional social scientists; 2) a competitive grant program, which expands and complements the internal research program by providing financial support to researchers outside the Institute; 3) a publications program, which provides the major vehicle for disseminating the research of staff and grantees, as well as other selected works in the field; and 4) an Employment Management Services division, which manages most of the publicly funded employment and training programs in the local area.

The broad objectives of the Institute's research, grant, and publication programs are to 1) promote scholarship and experimentation on issues of public and private employment and unemployment policy, and 2) make knowledge and scholarship relevant and useful to policymakers in their pursuit of solutions to employment and unemployment problems.

Current areas of concentration for these programs include causes, consequences, and measures to alleviate unemployment; social insurance and income maintenance programs; compensation; workforce quality; work arrangements; family labor issues; labor-management relations; and regional economic development and local labor markets.